AGENTS OF REFORM

Princeton Studies in Global and Comparative Sociology

Andreas Wimmer, Series Editor

Agents of Reform

Child Labor and
the Origins of the
Welfare State

Elisabeth Anderson

PRINCETON UNIVERSITY PRESS
PRINCETON AND OXFORD

Published by Princeton University Press
41 William Street, Princeton, New Jersey 08540
6 Oxford Street, Woodstock, Oxfordshire OX20 1TR

press.princeton.edu

All Rights Reserved

Library of Congress Control Number 2021911587
ISBN 978-0-691-22090-1
ISBN (pbk.) 978-0-691-22089-5
ISBN (e-book) 978-0-691-22091-8

British Library Cataloging-in-Publication Data is available

Editorial: Meagan Levinson and Jacqueline Delaney
Production Editorial: Jill Harris
Cover Design: Layla Mac Rory
Production: Erin Suydam
Publicity: Kate Hensley and Kathryn Stevens
Copyeditor: Cindy Milstein

Cover image: Edward Gooch Collection / Stringer

This book has been composed in Adobe Text and Gotham

10 9 8 7 6 5 4 3 2 1

For Andy

Insofar as the age at which children are hired [in cotton and woolen mills], the claim is that they begin at age 7 or 8 years, but in the Geldern district it is age four. The [Düsseldorf] government believes, however, that in most factories, children are employed already at the age of 6 years. The number of working hours is 10, 11, 12 and also in some places 15 and 16 hours. The government believes, that greed for money goes a long way in explaining this situation; such that, when a product is in high demand on the market, the manufacturer requires the children to work beyond the normal daily hours, so long as no legal provisions restrain him.

The number of night workers is now normally 125, but in the Duisburg district, 80 to 100 children work at night in exceptional circumstances. . . .

The most credible persons report that the factory children have unmistakably inferior strength and health compared to those who do not work in factories; that this is evident in their pale faces, dull eyes, their bloated bodies and cheeks, swollen lips and nostrils and swollen glands, and in their posture; that infected eyes, bad skin afflictions and asthmatic episodes are not uncommon among these children. The cause of these evils in the woolen and cotton mills is the fine wool particles that impregnate the air [and] . . . also in the long duration of the working hours and the bad food, or more accurately the unnatural way in which it is consumed. With regard to the latter, it is reported that the children bring their food, which as a rule consists only of cold potatoes, from home and then eat it cold, which must have a negative effect on the condition of their health. . . .

In the districts of Düsseldorf, Elderfeld, Lennep, Solingen and Kempen many of the children do not receive any schooling; others get it only in the evenings, and in the Solingen district, only when the work is not pressing. In the district of Grevenbroich, no provision at all is made for their education. . . .

However [the government] notes also, that the employment of children in the factories is necessary if the manufacturers are not to be rendered incapable of withstanding foreign competition.

—REPORT OF THE DÜSSELDORF DISTRICT GOVERNMENT, 1824

CONTENTS

ILLUSTRATIONS

TABLES

ACKNOWLEDGMENTS

Research can be lonely work, but no researcher can do it alone. I am grateful to many people who helped me on the long road to completing this book. It began as a PhD thesis in sociology at Northwestern University, where my dissertation committee—Bruce Carruthers, Ann Orloff, Chas Camic, and Nicki Beisel—mentored and supported me, molded me into a social scientist (more or less), and never told me I was taking too long to figure out what I was doing. I'm thankful for how they guided me while allowing me to carve my own path. Jim Mahoney and Monica Prasad were not on my committee, but still took the time to help me think through my methodology and sharpen my arguments. Kieran Bezila, Marina Zaloznaya, Liz Onasch, Gabrielle Ferrales, and Heather Schoenfeld motivated me intellectually while seeing to it that work was leavened with fun. Financial support for my dissertation research came from Northwestern, the National Science Foundation, and the Deutsche Akademische Austauschdiest (DAAD).

Since joining New York University Abu Dhabi (NYUAD), I've deeply appreciated the friendship and intellectual camaraderie of my wonderful colleagues. Eman Abdelhadi, Swethaa Ballakrishnen, David Cook-Martin, Paula England, Maria Grigoryevna, Danny Karell, Elena Korchmina, Kinga Makovi, John O'Brien, Blaine Robbins, and Rana Tomaira all provided valuable feedback on various chapter drafts. Zeynep Ozgen gave me the benefit of her keen intelligence and warm encouragement on many occasions. Sabino Kornrich scrutinized my introductory chapter and excised every unnecessary word. Melina Platas and Fiona Kidd helped keep me on track, and Christina Zenker, Jeff Jensen, Maya Allison, and Mark Swizlocki kept me laughing. I also learned much from visitors to NYUAD who took the time to read drafts and offer comments. These included Miguel Centeno, Alejandro Portes, Mustafa Emirbayer, and especially Kimberly Morgan and Cybelle Fox, who both shared thoughtful suggestions and their deep knowledge of the welfare state to push me in fruitful new directions.

As the book was nearing completion, Richard Lachmann, Edgar Kiser, and Monica Prasad generously read the whole manuscript, and provided extensive and incisive feedback. In August 2019, I was fortunate to have David Cook-Martin, Ivan Ermakoff, Sonya Michel, Stephanie Mudge, and Adam Sheingate participate in a book workshop. Even though I've been unable to meet every one of their expectations, their critiques and suggestions improved the manuscript immeasurably. The workshop was hosted by the NYUAD Institute in New York; I offer my thanks to Ralph Raymond and Sharon Bergman for organizing it.

My warmest thanks to Kyle Michiels, research assistant extraordinaire; chapter 3 could not have been written without him. That chapter also owes much to Eriks Uskalis, who translated hundreds of pages of source material from French into elegant, clear English. Chapter 2 benefited from Karin Lackner's excellent transcriptions of those handwritten German documents that exceeded my decoding capabilities. NYUAD undergraduates Erik Olson, Sharif Hassan, and Sara Booth also provided valuable research assistance. Helen Glenn Court applied her editorial acumen to reduce the manuscript by many thousand words.

I am immensely grateful to all the wonderfully dedicated, competent, responsive librarians and archivists who have helped me over the years. In particular, Caitlin Jones of the Massachusetts Archives patiently answered an inordinate number of emails, and Thomas Breitfeld of the Landeshauptarchiv in Koblenz generously assisted with an especially tricky transcription. Ron Guilmette of the Massachusetts State Police Museum and Learning Center made an extra effort to dig up a fine portrait of Rufus Wade.

A book needs a publisher, and I found mine thanks to Andreas Wimmer, who took the chance on including *Agents of Reform* in his Global and Comparative Sociology series at Princeton University Press, and provided smart, constructive feedback at multiple critical moments. Meagan Levinson and Jill Harris skillfully shepherded the manuscript through the publishing process. Three anonymous reviewers helped shape the manuscript into its final form, and Cindy Milstein meticulously edited the final draft.

Finally, my family has given me all the love and support I needed to see this journey through to the end. My parents, Barbara and Lanny Anderson, taught me to value the life of the mind; this book is a product of all they invested in me. My husband, Andy Tillotson, has been the very soul of forbearance and helped with everything from formatting graphs to getting past those academia-induced moments of despair. Our daughter, Ellie, grew up with this book—and still managed to turn out very well indeed. I'm grateful for her spunky wit and cheerful outlook on life. Whenever my obsessions got out of hand, these two brought me back to a more grounded place and put it all into a healthier perspective.

AGENTS OF REFORM

1

Introduction

The early modern economy was replete with regulation. Guilds imposed rules specifying the rights and mutual obligations of masters, journeymen, and apprentices, and even in the "free" labor market, governments sometimes intervened by fixing wages or prohibiting arbitrary dismissals.[1] But toward the end of the eighteenth century, as laissez-faire ideologies took hold and the new industrial bourgeoisie began its ascendance, most of these rules were swept away.[2] Workers and employers now encountered one another as formally equal parties, at liberty to make contracts unfettered by the restraining hand of the state or moderating influence of the guilds. Unprotected by law or custom, the new industrial proletariat was exposed to intense exploitation. Almost as soon as economic liberalization reached its apex, however, a countermovement emerged (Polanyi 2001). Tentatively and gradually, states reversed their retreat from the market to stem its most extreme abuses.

Laws regulating child labor in factories were at the forefront of this countermovement.[3] Before the standardized working day, the minimum wage, special protections for working women, or workplace safety and sanitation rules, European and US governments intervened in the relationship between the manufacturing bourgeoisie and the child labor it employed. Governments protected (and controlled) working children in part because they seemed clearly incapable of defending their interests in the harsh early industrial labor market. Vulnerable young people—grinding away at mindless repetitive tasks, their health imperiled by bad air and physical strain, deprived of opportunity to learn and play—aroused pity in humanitarian lawmakers. But child labor regulation was not simply a matter of compassion. Most fundamentally, it was part of a broader state-building project carried over from previous centuries that aimed to create a new and improved working-class citizenry—one that was healthy, intelligent, and most important, morally self-disciplined (Gorski 2003). It reflected elites' fears about the dangers posed by the nascent industrial working class as well as elites' hopes for a harmonious and prosperous nation.

Earlier generations of scholars recognized that states' first attempts to protect workers against the abuses of industrial capitalism came in the area of employment regulation. Karl Marx (2011, 310–11) considered the 1847 Ten Hours Act to be the British labor movement's first major legislative victory. Karl Polanyi (2001, 152, 174–75) pointed to this and other regulatory measures as important initial steps in the countermovement against economic liberalism. Today, though, the welfare state and regulatory state are often treated as distinct (see, for example, Majone 1994, 1997; for a similar point, see Levi-Faur 2014). Welfare state scholars pay little attention to worker protection, focusing instead on social provisions such as pensions and insurance. Similarly, historical accounts tend to date the modern welfare state to the 1880s, the decade when the Bismarckian health, accident, and old age insurance programs were passed (see, e.g., Pierson 2007, 110–11). Likewise, with few exceptions, analyses of contemporary welfare policy tend to leave worker protection out. In his influential classification of the three worlds of welfare capitalism, for instance, sociologist Gøsta Esping-Anderson (1990) does not take regulatory labor laws into consideration. The *Oxford Handbook of the Welfare State* (Castles et al. 2010) includes chapters on pensions, health insurance and services, accident and sickness benefits, social assistance, and the like, but no chapter on employment protections.[4]

This book refocuses attention on the modern regulatory welfare state. Doing so necessarily pushes the welfare state's origin back about fifty years, from the 1880s to the 1830s. I define regulatory welfare as the web of policies that protect or empower workers by limiting employers' arbitrary power over them. These policies include child labor laws as well as the standard working day, overtime pay requirements, protections against arbitrary dismissal, workplace safety and hygiene standards, family leave laws, the minimum wage, and workers' legal right to organize and engage in collective bargaining. The regulatory welfare state also includes the administrative apparatuses used to carry out and enforce these protections.[5] I use the term "regulatory welfare state," rather than simply "worker protection," to underscore that these policies, similar to welfare provisions, are integral to decommodification (Esping-Andersen 1990) because they reduce the extent to which workers' quality of life is determined by market forces alone. Like welfare provisions, regulatory policies reduce risk—not income loss, perhaps, but the many other risks associated with dependence on wage labor, including physical and developmental harm, insufficient pay, loss of leisure time, and the inability to provide care at critical times.

Worker protection limits capitalists' capacity to exploit their labor forces. Particularly for low-skilled workers with little bargaining power, it makes wage labor bearable where it otherwise would not be. Regulatory welfare saves lives and helps ensure that life is worth living. It is therefore an important but understudied feature of the modern welfare state.

Agents of Reform

What is puzzling about the regulatory welfare state is that it emerged in continental Europe and the United States when there was little demand for it from either above or below. Marx's (2011, 330) contention that labor protections come about when workers "put their heads together, and, as a class, compel the passing of a law," does not apply to most child labor laws enacted in the 1830s and 1840s.[6] Indeed, the laws' intended beneficiaries, working children and their parents, viewed them as harmful restrictions on family earning capacity, colluded with employers to evade the rules, and sometimes protested openly against them. Even if workers *had* wanted limits on child labor, they did not exercise the political power needed to effectively demand them until much later. Child labor laws came at a time when the working class was still politically marginalized; in most places, it did not even have the right to vote, and efforts at collective action were ad hoc and fleeting. Neither were these laws the result of top-down administrative priorities. Early mid-nineteenth-century states did not yet have agencies devoted to labor issues, and nowhere had the idea that government should actively intervene in the relationship between worker and employer been institutionalized. In short, modern institutional channels through which a countermovement against market fundamentalism could be mounted did not yet exist.

Instead, the push to protect (and control) child workers came primarily from middle-class and elite reformers—men and women who pursued child labor legislation largely on their own initiative, not at the behest of popular constituencies or state mandates. Child labor reformers laid the groundwork for a new conception of the proper relationship between state, market, and worker. In doing so, they connected the problem of child labor with indirectly related state priorities—economic prosperity, social order, and military readiness—seeking to convince policy makers that these aims could not be achieved as long as poor children's minds, morals, and bodies were being ruined by excessive and premature industrial employment.

The regulatory welfare state owes its emergence primarily to these individual "agents of reform." Accordingly, this book explains how these reformers exercised decisive causal influence over social policy outcomes through a *pragmatist field theoretical approach* to institutional change in which reformers are conceptualized as strategic, creative actors whose influence is conditioned

TABLE 1.1. Major Provisions of First Child Labor Laws in Britain, Prussia, France, and Massachusetts, and Belgium's Bill

	UK 1833 (1844 and 1847)	Prussia 1839	France 1841	Massachusetts 1836 and 1842	Belgium's Bill 1848
Targeted employers	Textile mills, except lace and some woolen mills	Mills, factories, mines, and quarries	Mills, factories, and workshops using mechanical power / continuous fire	Manufacturing establishments	Factories, mills, mines, and all other industrial establishments
Minimum age	9, except in silk mills	9	8	None	10; 12 for boys in mines (no females in mines)
Hours/age, exclusive of breaks	9 hours/day for children 9 to 12, except in silk; 12 hours/day for children 13 to 17 (6½ hours/day for children 8 to 12; 10 hours/day for children 13 to 17 and adult women, except lace and silk)	10 hours/day for children 9 to 15	8 hours/day for children 8 to 12; 12 hours/day for children 12 to 15	10 hours/day for children under 12	6½ hours/day for children 10 to 13; 10½ hours/day for children 14 to 17; 8 hours/day for boys 12 to 17 in mines; 12½ hours/day for adults 18 and over
Night work	Prohibited for children under 18	Prohibited for children under 16	Prohibited for children under 16	No regulations	Prohibited for children under 18
Education	2 hours/day, 6 days/week for working children under 13	3 years of schooling, or ability to read and write, before working	Working children under 12 must attend school regularly	At least 3 months full time per year for children under 15	Working children under 14 must attend school regularly
Religious instruction	None required	Required until confirmation	Must be made available to working children, but not required	None required	None required
Health/safety	Children to be examined by physician before working; factories to be limed and whitewashed annually (Certain machinery to be fenced)	1½ hours of break time per day, with opportunity to exercise outdoors	Local authorities to ensure health/safety of child workers; physicians may accompany inspectors	None beyond hours regulation	None beyond hours regulations
Enforcement	By government-appointed, salaried, professional factory inspectors	By local officials alongside existing duties	By unsalaried government-appointed inspectors	By local school committees alongside existing duties	By government-appointed, salaried inspectors and mining engineers

Sources: Anderson (2018, 175); Weissbach (1989, 231–34); Kastner (2004, 177–78); Massachusetts Acts and Resolves, c. 245, 1836, 950–51; Massachusetts Acts and Resolves, c. 60, 1842, 517–18; Belgium Ministère de l'Intérieur (1848, CXCII–CCI); Factories Act 1833, Ch. 103, http://www.educationengland.org.uk/documents/acts/1833-factories-act.html (accessed October 18, 2020).

by the structure of the policy field and their positioning within it. Methodologically, it adopts a *genetic approach* (Ermakoff 2019) to uncovering the causal processes through which child labor and factory inspection reforms came about. I trace over time the microlevel relational processes whereby regulatory welfare policy was forged and enacted. In doing so, I show that dominant theories of welfare policy development cannot adequately explain the origins of nineteenth-century regulatory social policy because they do not appreciate the causal influence of individual middle-class and elite reformers. It was these actors who did the crucial work of putting the child labor problem on the policy agenda and pushing legislative responses through to enactment.

This book develops this claim through seven case studies set in nineteenth-century continental Europe and the United States. The case studies in part I are 1820s–30s Prussia, 1830s–40s Massachusetts, 1830s–40s France, and 1840s Belgium. Whereas Prussia, Massachusetts, and France were all pioneers in industrial child labor regulation, roughly contemporaneous reform efforts in Belgium failed. Part I focuses on explaining these divergent outcomes as well as why states enacted a particular law and not another (for the major provisions of these laws and bills, see table 1.1). Chapter 2 traces how Prussia became continental Europe's first state to intervene in children's factory employment and compares two rival reformers to demonstrate why one prevailed over the other. Chapter 3 shows that Belgium's failure stemmed from strategic mistakes made by its leading social reformer—mistakes whose significance becomes clear in a close comparison with the lead reformer in France. Chapter 4 presents a case in which opposition to child labor regulation was nonexistent, rendering Massachusetts child labor crusaders' influence nearly superfluous. Thus chapter 4 begins to establish scope conditions under which individual reformers are most important.

Whereas part I is devoted to explaining the success or failure of early child labor reform efforts, part II seeks to elucidate why states later adopted different approaches to child labor law enforcement. Over the mid-nineteenth century, it became evident that labor rules do not enforce themselves and that new state administrative structures were needed to implement worker protections. Fledgling administrative entities, foremost among them factory inspection departments and departments of labor statistics, granted middle-class reformers new institutional opportunities to alter the relations of economic power by harnessing the interventionist authority of the state. The analysis presented in part II—drawn from 1870s Imperial Germany, 1860s–70s Massachusetts, and 1880s–90s Illinois—shifts the focus from legislation to implementation and shows why states adopted different models of factory inspection. Individual reformers' ideas and strategies continue to be featured, but changing institutional and political conditions—including the opening up of the polity to new kinds of political actors—require the analysis to adopt a wider lens.

In particular, organized labor plays an increasingly important role in the narratives presented in part II. In Germany, the advent of universal male suffrage and rise of the Social Democratic Workers' Party motivated a senior state official there to advocate mandatory factory inspection throughout the Reich. Chapter 5 relates how this reformer partially overcame the most powerful of opponents, Otto von Bismarck, and analyzes why Germany adopted a conciliatory model of inspection aimed at securing employers' voluntary compliance with labor laws. In Massachusetts and Illinois, grassroots labor movements organized to demand factory inspection and had more direct influence over policy outcomes. As chapter 6 describes, Massachusetts workers managed to push factory inspection through the state legislature but could not control how it was implemented. The middle-class party loyalist appointed to lead the inspection department pursued a conciliatory approach that secured the department's long-term bureaucratic survival at the expense of rigorous child labor law enforcement. Finally, chapter 7 demonstrates how organized labor and progressive middle-class women—working as policy advocates and, later, as factory inspectors—partnered to bring about a strict enforcement model of inspection in Illinois.

These episodes illustrate the historically evolving nature of child labor reform: the changing reasons for regulation, entry of new types of advocates into the policy field, and adoption of new strategies to navigate increasingly complex political and institutional landscapes. They highlight the birth and dramatically expanding capacities of the regulatory welfare state—not only the political origins of the first modern worker protection laws, but the forging of administrative infrastructures designed to carry them out. Most important, they show that individual reformers—those pursuing policy change largely on their own initiative—were essential for regulatory welfare's emergence and evolution in nineteenth-century Europe and the United States.

It is no coincidence that most reformers profiled in this book were middle class. The middle class was, no less than the haute bourgeoisie or proletariat, a creation of the modern capitalist order. By the mid-nineteenth century, middle-class actors were well positioned in terms of their economic security and social-institutional locations to exercise political influence. As public intellectuals, professionals, civil servants, and legislators, they enjoyed a measure of access to policy making that the working class still lacked. Not surprisingly, the policy interventions they pursued were designed to address what they *thought* would benefit labor and the general public—not necessarily what labor actually wanted. The regulatory welfare policies they promoted sought to preserve the existing social order, and their place within it, through moderate reforms that aimed at both protecting and disciplining the poor, but left the capitalist profit imperative intact. Still, variation among them was considerable in regard to why they thought child labor was a problem and precisely what they believed should be done about it. Their influence was a product of their class position as well as their individual ideas and actions.

The claim that individual reformers were central to the birth of regulatory welfare needs to be qualified two ways. First, this account of the causal significance of individual agency for institutional change does not offer a "great man" theory of history in the sense of attributing actors' influence to their exceptional aptitudes, moral righteousness, or other personal attributes. Middle-class reformers' agency did not manifest itself in an exercise of extraordinary freedom at the margins of a set of social structural constraints (Martin 2003, 25, 37; Bourdieu 1988, 149–50; Emirbayer and Mische 1998, 1004) but instead was constituted by and through social structural and field-specific factors. Large-scale economic and social transformations gave rise to the conditions reformers interpreted as requiring state responses. Culturally embedded discourses informed their definitions of these problems. Political institutions defined their legitimate pathways to influence. Field dynamics shaped their coalition-building opportunities and requirements. These factors did not *determine* reformers' understandings and actions; interpretation and strategic decision-making were always involved. But contextual factors such as these are causally significant to the extent that they influenced the motivations, opportunities, and strategies of the social actors who did determine the policy outcomes under analysis (Ermakoff 2008, xxiii; see also Mudge 2018, 25).

The second qualification is that the causal significance of individual middle-class reformers for policy outcomes varied. By making use of two negative cases—1830s–40s and 1870s Massachusetts—I show that whether middle-class and elite reformers were necessary for regulatory welfare development hinged on two conditions: the degree of cultural consensus around the need for regulation and working-class strength. The Massachusetts cases are negative in the sense that although labor reforms were enacted in both, the influence of individual reformers on these outcomes was less significant than the other two factors. Thus individual reformers were most essential for labor policy development when labor was weak and opposition to regulation was strong. Where working-class voters were still by and large excluded from politics, and where labor parties and politically engaged unions were absent or marginalized, middle-class and elite actors were the ones to take the lead in the cause for protective legislation. Where opposition to labor regulation was fierce, individual reformers' efforts were central to explaining policy outcomes. Their strategic and creative actions, including efforts to forge coalitions and circumvent veto players, determined whether labor reform succeeded and what type of law was passed in their state.

This does not mean that middle-class reformers played *no* role when labor exercised the power resources needed to make protective legislation happen. In 1870s Massachusetts, middle-class reformers contributed to the campaign for factory inspection, although they were not directly responsible for its legislative victory. In 1890s Illinois, when labor was at the height of its political power, middle-class reformers nevertheless had a decisive impact on policy outcomes. They harnessed a grassroots antisweatshop movement to mount a campaign for a factory inspection bill drafted by a middle-class activist. In both states, middle-class actors took the helm of newly created factory inspection departments and shaped the implementation models these agencies adopted. The point is that when labor is institutionally and politically empowered, it may not *need* middle-class leadership to successfully promote policy change; middle-class reformers, however, may still contribute to labor-driven policy change in substantive and significant ways.

Theories of the Welfare State and Institutional Change

Why do social policies emerge and change? Over the past sixty years, most answers emphasize structures, institutions, and collectivities rather than individual actors. The welfare state scholarship of the 1960s and 1970s posited that modern social policies, including worker protections, were a natural byproduct of industrialization (see, for example, Wilensky 1975; Kerr et al. 1960; Pryor 1968; Rimlinger 1971; for a succinct overview of this literature, see Myles and Quadagno 2002). This view assumed a deterministic relationship between economic development and policy change, with social actors playing no significant mediating role. Although it points to a necessary condition for child labor law development—these laws always began as restrictions on employing children in factories—the theory is far from adequate. That Belgium, Europe's most industrialized country by the mid-nineteenth century, did not enact child labor regulations until 1889—decades after its biggest rival, Great Britain did so—is a case in point. Likewise, the Kingdom of Saxony, despite industrial conditions similar to neighboring Prussia, did not regulate child labor until 1861 (Feldenkirchen 1981), and the state of New York, despite industrial development comparable to Massachusetts, did not regulate children's working conditions until 1886 (Ensign 1921). In short, the "logic of industrialism" can do little to explain important variations in the timing of child labor policy enactments.

By the late 1970s, the economic structural-determinist view had come under fire and a new generation of social scientists turned their attention to politics. These scholars focused their explanations on class-based interest groups fighting for or resisting policies designed to protect workers and the poor. Welfare state theorists in the power resources vein argued that major social policy changes are typically a result of working-class mobilizations, the growing strength of labor unions, and the political ascendance of labor parties (Castles 1982; Korpi 1978, 1983; Hicks and Misra 1993; Huber, Ragin, and Stephens 1993; Hicks 1999). Others asserted that capitalists are the most decisive class group when it comes to the welfare state. Employers often successfully block welfare expansion (Quadagno 1996; Hacker and Pierson 2002), but may sometimes support social policies they see as furthering their interests in some way (Stryker 1990; Esping-Andersen 1996; Swenson 2002). Scholars working in the "varieties of capitalism" perspective have shown that employers may advocate (or at least not oppose) labor regulations they see as reining in competition, or as enhancing workers' skill, productivity, or complacency (Hall and Soskice 2001; Mares 2003).

Although attention to class-based interest groups is essential, such groups varied widely in their approach to child labor. For example, whereas workers advocated forcefully for child labor laws and factory inspection systems in two of the later cases (1870s Massachusetts and 1890s Illinois), they were otherwise marginal. Likewise, employer influence was not consistent across cases. Whereas manufacturers put child labor on the policy agenda in France, they effectively blocked it in Belgium. Explaining this variation requires paying attention to the fractured and undetermined ways in which class actors come to understand and act on their interests. In the absence of labor mobilization, moreover, we must turn our attention to other kinds of promoters of social policy change.

Another variation of the class-based approach contends that states enact social policies to assuage poor and working-class people's grievances when elites feel threatened by collective social disorders (Piven and Cloward 1971; Tilly 1975). In this way, workers and the poor exercise influence even when they are not organized into parties or unions. This perspective is relevant to early cases of child labor reform in which spontaneous lower-class social disorder raised alarm and contributed to elites' sense that labor protections were needed. Nonetheless, it does not explain child labor policy outcomes. Not all countries with significant unrest enacted a child labor law during the early phase of their industrial development; Belgium and Saxony are, again, cases in point (C. Tilly, L. Tilly, and R. Tilly 1975, 210; Bazillion 1985). Moreover, that child labor laws were intended to assuage rioting workers' grievances makes little sense because workers protested for other reasons. In fact, most did not want restrictions on child labor because it was a vital source of family income (Schmidt 2010; Kastner 2004, 208–9, 212–13; Weissbach 1989, 57–58; Heywood 1988, 231). To understand why policy makers responded to social disorder by enacting child labor laws, we need to pay closer attention to the motivations and understandings of the key reformers involved.

The theory that comes closest to explaining nineteenth-century labor reform is the state-centered scholarship of the 1980s. In this view, semiautonomous states pursue social protections to mediate between the interests of competing social groups, or perhaps even to further their own state-building, economic development, or social welfare agendas (Evans, Rueschemeyer, and

Skocpol 1985; Orloff and Skocpol 1984; Weir and Skocpol 1985; McCarthy 2017). For example, states may adopt various social policies to enhance their military capacity or promote domestic tranquility. But with some noted exceptions, the classic state-centered literature treats "states as actors" (Skocpol 1985, 9) that are conceived rather monolithically.[7] To be sure, the new sociology of the state describes its "many hands," disaggregating it into multiple organizations and agencies (Morgan and Orloff 2017, 18). Yet even this work tends not to focus on individual state actors. In the cases that follow, legislators and bureaucratic officials were often the key movers behind the emergence of child labor laws and factory inspection departments, but they were never mere conduits of state interests or lower-level administrative prerogatives. Instead, they were acting on their own initiative according to their own interpretations and objectives, encountering both opposition and cooperation from other state actors in the policy field. Further disaggregation of the "the state"—all the way down to the level of individual actors—is therefore necessary for understanding the politics of nineteenth-century labor reform.

More recently, historical institutionalism, which arose from explorations into how government structures shape social politics, has come to dominate welfare states scholarship. Institutionalist scholars point to the effects, both constraining and enabling, of states' institutional arrangements on policy making (see, for example, Immergut 1992; Thelen and Steinmo 1992).[8] Institutionalist explanations of the weakness of the US welfare state, for instance, focus on how US government institutions (federalism, the separation of powers, the congressional committee system) generate veto points that opponents can exploit to block social legislation (see, for example, Steinmo 1994; Orloff and Skocpol 1984; Hacker and Pierson 2002). Institutionalist scholars also often stress how policies generate positive feedbacks that reproduce policy trajectories over time (Weir 1992; Pierson 1993; Skocpol 1992; Huber and Stephens 2001; Orloff 1993). Relatedly, the influential concept of path dependence argues that social policy, once it is set on a certain course, can become locked in and "virtually impossible to reverse" (Pierson 2000, 251; see also Krasner 1988; Mahoney 2000). As many critics have pointed out (Blyth 2002; Lieberman 2002; Thelen 2003; Streeck and Thelen 2005; Steinmo 2008), the emphasis on veto points, positive feedbacks, and path dependence makes it difficult to explain institutional change.

In response, the latest generation of institutionalist scholars has theorized how change occurs—including the emergence of new policies and administrative infrastructures. Moving beyond the "punctuated equilibrium" model, which treats change as a result of exogenous shocks (Krasner 1988), this literature stresses incremental endogenous processes (Hacker 2002, 2005; Thelen 2003; Mahoney and Thelen 2010). Individual agency has still not been incorporated into historical institutionalism's theoretical tool kit, however. As a result, the theory is still ill-equipped to explain abrupt breaks from the past that result from endogenous processes rather than exogenous shocks (Anderson 2008).

All these approaches offer insights relevant to the cases of child labor reform presented in this book. Class-based mobilizations, whether spontaneous or organized, informed reformers' motivations for pursuing labor legislation; in some cases, organized labor even took a leading role. Although states with vastly different governmental institutions adopted legislation at similar times, institutional arrangements were still important. For instance, whereas women could leverage the increasingly institutionalized power of voluntary associations and labor unions to exercise significant policy influence in the late nineteenth-century United States, their access to politics was far more restricted in Germany, where in some states they were legally barred from participating in political associations and meetings (Anderson 2000, 297–98). There, by institutional necessity, bureaucratic civil servants took the lead in pushing for labor reforms. In these and many other ways, institutional conditions constrained who could exercise influence over social policy making while also shaping reformers' coalition-building opportunities and requirements.

Moreover, child labor laws clearly built on the positive feedback that policy precedents generated, particularly in the area of public education. At the core of reformers' appeals was the argument that the state could not rear productive, peaceable, and hardy citizens if poor children did not go to school. Such claims rested on and reinforced states' preexisting efforts to promote popular schooling, including compulsory education laws and laws requiring localities to build primary schools. Decommodification involved not only removing children from factories but also putting them into classrooms; the institutional development of regulatory welfare and public education are therefore tightly bound up with one another. The case studies in this volume illustrate this interconnectedness, and thereby contribute to a growing literature on how the welfare state and education intersect (Marshall 1964; Allmendinger and Leibfried 2003; Iversen and Stephens 2008; Busemeyer and Nikolai 2010; Busemeyer 2014).

Despite their relevance, though, class-based, institutionalist, and state-centered theories are inadequate for this analysis because they overlook four important aspects of social policy origin and change. First, although many institutionalist scholars contend that both institutional continuity and change depend on the actions of historical agents (see Thelen 2004, 286; Mahoney and Thelen 2010), their empirical analyses still tend to portray actors as organized collectivities or their representatives.[9] This tendency to portray actors as carriers or conduits of social structure, rather than as agents of social transformation in their own right, makes it easy to overlook the differential impact that distinct individuals may have on policy outcomes. Second, in both class-based and institutionalist approaches, actors tend to be construed as pursuing material or power interests deterministically derived from their social and class locations.[10] This leaves out actors pursuing goals other than narrow self-interest. Where do social reformers acting on behalf of marginalized others or the general social good fit in? Third, questions of how actors *arrive at particular understandings* of their interests and goals, and how they translate them into particular policy plans, are often sidelined. Why, for instance, might state actors situated in similar positions in the same ministry or department have radically different conceptions of what sorts of policies might best serve the interests of "the state" or general public? Fourth, these perspectives do not tell us much about the microlevel interactive processes through which actors develop their policy programs and strategically build alliances around them. In short, the interpretative and microinteractive dimensions of policy making are black boxed.

A Pragmatist Field Theory of Institutional Change

This book addresses these issues by analyzing and theorizing the impact of individual agents on social policy enactment and implementation. Focusing on individuals requires the researcher to recognize not only the diversity among similarly situated political actors' ideas and goals; it also leads to a recognition that political actors' motives are frequently complex, involving a mix of both altruism and self-interest (Wolfe 1998). The middle-class reformers featured in the case studies that follow were acting on behalf of marginalized and disadvantaged children. They were genuinely appalled by working children's suffering and sincerely wanted to ameliorate it. Yet they also believed that protecting such children was in the broader interest of the state, society, and by extension, themselves. Their precise articulation of this mix of interests varied not only by sociopolitical context but among similarly situated reformers acting within the same context too. Thus focusing on individuals allows the researcher to empirically discover actors' culturally informed understandings of social problems, interests, and goals—rather than imputing to actors whatever understandings, interests, and goals it seems logical they should have based on their position in society.

Most important, the analyses presented in this book show that there are cases in which policy outcomes, in terms of both legislative content and its practical implementation, cannot be explained without taking into account the causal impact of individual middle-class reformers. To reiterate, my contention is that where opposition was strong and labor was weak, it was the strategic and creative action of these reformers that pushed states to adopt certain kinds of child labor and factory inspection laws at certain times. In some cases, the fact that a state enacted one law and not another is traceable to the differential impact of rival reformers. In others, states might have enacted policies if not for the mistakes these actors made. Even in cases where labor was politically powerful, middle-class reformers contributed to policy outcomes and exercised decisive influence over how labor policy was practically implemented.

This emphasis on individuals as agents is new, not because scholars of the welfare state have not taken individuals into account, but because they have no general theory of individual reformer influence. As a result, important figures in the history of the welfare state—Bismarck, William Beveridge, Franklin Delano Roosevelt, and so on—are often handled in one of two ways: either as residuals whose effects lie beyond theoretical explanation or as avatars of more fundamental forces (class-based power resources, economic imperatives, state-building prerogatives, and so on). The pragmatist field-theoretical approach aims to reconcile these extremes by developing a theory of how and under which conditions individual reformers matter, situating them in the context of a policy field that constrains and enables their influence.

POLICY AND ADMINISTRATIVE ENTREPRENEURS

Calls to pay greater attention to the influence of individual agency on institutional change (such as Katznelson 2003) have not yet enjoyed broad resonance, but one way social scientists *have* smuggled the individual into social change theory is through the concept of social entrepreneurship. Types of social entrepreneurs are of course numerous.[11] They share several characteristics that justify the common term, however. First, like business entrepreneurs, they take the *initiative* to promote products. These products could be commodities, ideas, policies, or organizations, but regardless of the type of product, social entrepreneurs try to secure support for or investment in it. Second, social entrepreneurs invest their own *resources*—money, perhaps, but also effort, time, and reputation—into promoting these products. Third, they take on *risk*: if the products fail to catch on, the invested resources will be lost.

I highlight two types of social welfare reformers: policy entrepreneurs and administrative entrepreneurs. Both attempt to influence policy outcomes by developing and promoting certain products: either policies, or administrative agencies and implementation models to carry out policies. The main goal of *policy entrepreneurs* is to influence legislative outcomes. To that end, they interpret social structural conditions as problems, craft policy solutions, seize political and institutional opportunities, build support around their programs, and push legislation toward enactment. Depending on the institutions governing policy making in their state, policy entrepreneurs may be government officials, elected representatives, nongovernmental policy experts, interest group lobbyists, social movement leaders, or civil society advocates. To the extent that a policy is the initiative of a particular individual who invests resources in promoting and building a coalition around it, we have a case of policy entrepreneurship.

Administrative entrepreneurs come onto the scene after policies have been enacted; they determine how those policies are practically implemented. Particularly when policies are new, administrative entrepreneurs can exert long-term influence by forging durable institutions and practices. Relative to policy entrepreneurs, they tend to occupy a narrower set of positions; typically they are mid- to high-ranking officials in the state bureaucracy. They often strive for some measure of bureaucratic autonomy—that is, the ability to set their agencies along courses of action in accordance with their priorities (Carpenter 2001, 14). Sometimes, the same actor can take on the role of both policy and administrative entrepreneur; more often, the two are not the same person.

THE POLICY FIELD

Child labor policy and administrative entrepreneurs were constrained agents. They exercised influence in strategic and creative ways, but their goals, strategies, and effectiveness were shaped by their social context and position within it. A theory that can usefully conceptualize their social significance and explain their varying degrees of influence must balance these two facts. To that end, I combine insights from Bourdieusian field theory and US pragmatism to build a novel approach to policy reform that highlights individual actors.

Although I do not adopt a Bourdieusian perspective wholesale, I borrow his concepts of field and capital to make sense of political contestation and institutional change.[12] Often thought of as a theorist of reproduction rather than change (Gorski 2013, 1), Bourdieu in fact contended that field theory was a useful analytic tool for explaining change because the competitive dynamics within fields are themselves sources of social transformation (Bourdieu and Wacquant 1992, 101–2; Bourdieu 1983, 312, 335–39; see also Gorski 2013, 1–13). In a given field, such as the field of politics, actors struggle over common stakes in a rule-based dynamic akin to a game (Bourdieu and Wacquant 1992, 95–101, 107; Martin 2003). These struggles enable actors to change their field positions, but can also lead to endogenous institutional or structural change. Thus, by throwing into relief individual actors and their relational struggles, field theory offers more analytic leverage for explaining pathbreaking policy change than mainstream institutionalist theory, with its emphasis on stability and incrementalism.[13]

Policy and administrative entrepreneurs maneuver within a policy field in which the stakes of the game are policy outcomes: both legislation and its practical implementation. The rules of the game are the political institutions that structure policy making and implementation. Fields are like ordinary games except that one of the stakes of the game is the rules themselves (Bourdieu and Wacquant 1992, 99, Martin 2003, 31); hence political actors may act in accordance with political institutions, or attempt to change or subvert them. Actors in the policy field struggle to influence outcomes by trying to build coalitions—the political equivalent of social capital. Allies can be anyone, from kings to voters, who has the ability to influence policy outcomes; who they are—and relatedly, the boundaries of the policy field—thus varies from case to case, depending on political institutions as well as the policy at stake.

In relation to others in the policy field, actors occupy positions that shape their goals and ability to achieve them. Field positions matter in at least three ways. First, the political institutions relevant to the policy field (rules of the game) empower actors in different positions differently and unequally. Second, field positions tend to shape (but not fully determine) policy-relevant goals and strategies (Swartz 2013, 30–31, 2014; Bourdieu and Wacquant 1992, 105). Third, field positions are unequally endowed with resources, including political capital and the chance to increase it. Particularly important is the idea that actors positioned at the overlap of the policy field with another field may enjoy strategic advantages when it comes to leveraging resources and building alliances. I return to this point in a moment.

Reformers' ability to effect institutional change is of course conditioned by their position within the field, and their related powers and resources. Position and resources, however, are not all that matter; how reformers take advantage of their positions and leverage their resources matters too. Reformers' strategic action can be classified into two broad categories: strategic alliance building and creative problem-solving.

STRATEGIC ALLIANCE BUILDING

In the policy field, as elsewhere (Latour 1987, 1988), influence requires allies.[14] To get past political veto players (Immergut 1992; Tsebelis 2002)—that is, actors institutionally empowered to block policy change—reformers must either build alliances with them directly, or circumvent or defeat them through alliances with others. At the same time, opponents of reform will try to prevent it by building alliances too. Fields are therefore characterized not only by competition but also by cooperation; indeed, to compete for influence, policy reformers must first build networks of support.

I identify six observable relational strategies that policy and administrative entrepreneurs use to build alliances. These strategies can succeed or fail depending on how audiences receive them. They are the causal mechanisms specifying how entrepreneurs transform audiences into allies and thereby build the political capital needed to realize their goals. By identifying these strategies, demonstrating how they are used, and pointing to conditions under which they may succeed or fail, the case studies in this book lend precision to the claim that under certain conditions, individual reformers' strategic action matters greatly for policy outcomes.

First, rhetorical *framing* refers to presenting proposed policy changes in ways intended to resonate with the existing ideas, interests, and identities of audiences to win their cooperation (Fligstein and McAdam 2012, 50–51; see also Snow et al. 1986). The likelihood of frames achieving positive resonance with audiences in the field depends on the degree to which they fit the field's discursive opportunity structure (Koopmans 2004; Koopmans and Statham 1999a, 1999b; Snow 2008). In other words, frames that tap into either dominant or institutionalized discourses, or elite interests, are more likely to be regarded as legitimate than those that tap into marginal or counterhegemonic discourses (Ferree 2003; McCammon et al. 2007). Nevertheless, a frame may fit with the discursive opportunity structure—that is, invoke hegemonic, institutionalized, or elite discourses/interests—and yet still be rejected if audiences do not deem it empirically credible or if it does not accord with their experiences (Snow and Benford 1988).

When entrepreneurs construct their policy and administrative programs, they often borrow and recombine the ideas of others.[15] These ideas may simply be "out there" in the policy field or already be institutionalized in law. Borrowing itself does not win allies unless combined with the second strategy, *citation*: giving public credit to those whose ideas are borrowed in order to give the impression that goals are shared or valued (Latour 1987; Anderson 2013). To this end, reformers may also simply cite either people who agree with them, or domestic and foreign policy precedents. Citations are more likely to be deemed legitimate, and thus facilitate alliance building, when they reference actors who are respected or powerful in the policy field, or policy precedents deemed relevant by others in the field. Citing foreign actors and policy precedents is therefore generally riskier than citing domestic sources.

Third, *compromise* involves changing the content of policy programs in response to the opinions and demands of potential allies, and is perhaps the most important of all the alliance-building strategies. Compromise is effective when it involves giving potential allies something they want without seriously undermining the reformer's goals. If the latter occurs, the reformer runs the risk of co-optation or capture.

Fourth, *piggybacking* occurs when reformers try to maximize alliances by attaching their preferred policy programs to other, more popular or more viable policy demands or programs. For example, they may attach their program to an existing piece of draft legislation that has a high chance of passage or insert it into the agenda of a policy-oriented social movement.

To win allies, reformers must convince their audiences that they are credible by *signaling expertise or competence*. How they do this varies with social context; for instance, referencing research-based facts and statistics rather than anecdotal evidence became more common toward the end of the nineteenth century. Referencing facts and statistics can backfire, though, if audiences deem the information to be irrelevant or questionable. Other ways in which reformers signal expertise and competence include invoking relevant personal experience or accomplishments, and demonstrating a firm grasp of a subject when under questioning.

Finally, *expanding jurisdiction* is a strategy specific to administrative entrepreneurs that they may use to help secure bureaucratic autonomy and long-term agency survival. Expanding jurisdiction to new areas of administrative responsibility enlarges an agency's base of constituents. Constituents are potential allies; when agencies have broad and diverse constituencies—particularly, in democracies, if those constituencies include large swaths of the voting public—then politicians will have a harder time defunding or otherwise weakening the agency. Expanding jurisdiction can backfire, however, because it is difficult to satisfy every constituency equitably, and disgruntled constituencies may become opponents.

In the case studies that follow, it will become clear that the success or failure of policy entrepreneurs is in large part attributable to not just whether but also how they used the first five strategies—namely whether they used them in accordance with the ideas, expectations, and priorities of potential allies. Similarly, the effectiveness of administrative entrepreneurs was related to their ability to signal expertise, compromise with key stakeholders, and expand jurisdiction in ways that did not alienate core constituencies. Entrepreneurs who used these strategies effectively can be described as having what sociologists Neil Fligstein and Doug McAdam (2012, 46) call "social skill," or the ability to win cooperation by creating shared goals and understandings.

CREATIVE PROBLEM-SOLVING

What happens when initial attempts at alliance building fail? How might reformers respond when blocked by veto players in the policy field? As the case studies presented in this book demonstrate, successful policy entrepreneurs frequently show considerable creativity of action (Joas 1996) in the face of obstacles. When one set of alliances fizzles out or fails, they forge new ones; when one route to change is blocked, they find alternatives. Fligstein and McAdam (2012, 47) gesture toward this in their discussion of social skill: socially skilled actors "will do whatever it takes to induce cooperation, and if one path is closed off, they will choose another." Similarly, political scientist Adam Sheingate (2007) argues that entrepreneurs get things done by creatively exploiting the ambiguity of rules.

The theoretical tradition most strongly associated with theorizing creativity in social action is US pragmatism. Pragmatism sees humans as problem solvers whose strategies are alternately routine and creative (Gross 2009). As actors move through their daily lives, they largely follow tried-and-tested routines. Most of the strategies outlined are examples of such routines—framing, citation, compromise, and signaling expertise are all ordinary, everyday strategies deployed in the course of normal policy making. This does not mean that they are unreflective or automatic, only that they tend to fit customary patterns of political action and communication. When routine strategies fail, though, actors experience doubt or perplexity (Peirce 1877, 4–5; Addams 1902, 13–70) to which they respond with greater deliberation and creativity (Dewey 2002, 207–8; Whitford 2002, 340–41; Emirbayer and Maynard 2010, 227–29; Schneiderhan 2011, 596; Jansen 2017, 20). They examine the situation inquiringly, revise their assumptions, devise new strategies for achieving their goals, and modify their goals to make them more achievable. They may bend the rules to get what they want.[16]

The ability and willingness to do this distinguished effective from ineffective child labor policy entrepreneurs. In certain cases of reform, such as 1830s–40s Massachusetts, reformers never confronted any perplexing or problematic opposition, and the path to reform was apparently so smooth that they never needed to exhibit any real creativity of action. They could follow routines and still win.[17] In other cases, however, reform efforts were met with potentially crippling opposition from veto players, and reformers had to exercise creativity if they were to get past this opposition. As several of the case studies demonstrate, effective child labor policy entrepreneurs recognized and opened unconventional windows of opportunity in the midst of such challenging situations. Those who did not, failed.

As pragmatist theory would predict, effective entrepreneurs are good situation readers, able to devise solutions that make sense given the immediate circumstances; they "keep their goals somewhat open-ended and are prepared to take what the system will give" (Fligstein and McAdam 2012, 47). At the same time, however, and often over years or even a lifetime, many stick to a core vision for policy change—sustained projects through which they persistently work toward an imagined future outcome (Emirbayer and Mische 1998, 991). Their goals may fall into abeyance for a time, but when the political situation shifts in their favor, they may bring the goal back onto the agenda again (Kingdon 1984, 181–82).[18] Effective political actors are thus both creative *and* goal oriented; indeed, the ability to steadfastly pursue long-term political goals requires just the sort of creative flexibility evoked by the pragmatist understanding of social action.

The most important mechanism through which child labor reformers exercised goal-directed creativity was *circumventing or subverting normal institutional channels of policy making in unconventional ways.* For example, in Prussia and Imperial Germany, state bureaucrats actually bent rules to get around veto players and push their programs forward. Subverting rules in this way can be risky; it can backfire if other actors in the policy field are aware of it and perceive it as unacceptable. In the two German cases, rule bending was conducted behind the scenes and succeeded in part because it was invisible to opponents. By contrast, ineffective policy entrepreneurs stuck close to institutionalized scripts and did not look for unconventional pathways to change when they encountered opposition. Instead, they repeated failed strategies or simply gave up.

FIELD ARCHITECTURE AND FIELD POSITION

The concepts of field architecture and field position are helpful for specifying conditions that shape actors' capacity for alliance building and creative problem-solving. Field architecture refers to the structure and extent of overlap between fields (Evans and Kay 2008) or subfields. Overlap can take the form of actors' *multiple membership* in more than one field or subfield; for instance, a legislator may be a wealthy businessman with significant ties to the business field. It can also entail *institutional penetration* of one field or subfield by another; for example, business groups may enjoy formal power to advise lawmakers on economic policy. In the analyses that follow, overlaps between the policy field and the intellectual field, business field, religious field, and social reform field are relevant, depending on the particular case.

The field position of child labor reformers relative to these overlaps is significant to explaining their understandings of policy problems, the strategies available to them, and their chances of success. Reformers who are members of more than one field may combine discourses across fields to develop new and potentially compelling problem definitions. Moreover, as many scholars note, actors who are positioned where fields or other semibounded groups (for example, networks or organizations) overlap may enjoy strategic advantages (Padgett and Ansell 1993, 1303; Emirbayer and Mische 1998, 1007; Sheingate 2003, 194; Vedres and Stark 2010; Campbell 2004, 74–75; Evans and Kay 2008; Eyal 2013; Mudge and Vauchez 2012). Such a positioning makes it possible for them to import allies, frames, or resources from the other field into the policy field to help them win new allies or overcome obstacles there. On the other hand, as I demonstrate in chapter 3, actors occupying "dual membership" positions may experience this as a liability if the overlap is weak. Moreover, given that they have other realms in which to achieve distinction, political actors who also belong to another field may have less incentive to exercise goal-directed creativity to accomplish aims within the policy field.

CULTURE, PROBLEM DEFINITIONS, AND PROGRAMS

Culture shapes social policy making in profound ways. For example, scholars have argued that the cultural values embedded in dominant political ideologies help explain variations in welfare state generosity, particularly the tightfistedness of the US welfare state (Steensland 2006, 2008; Somers and Block 2005). Religious beliefs and values shape national social policy trajectories; for instance, Christian Democratic parties have been major drivers of social policy progress in some European countries (Kersbergen 1995; Kersbergen and Manow 2010), and national religious differences have led countries to approach social provision differently (Gorski 2003; Kahl 2005; Morgan 2006).

The cases in this book contribute to our understanding of how culture and religion shape social policy, but do so using a microinteractive rather than macro "national cultures" lens. Culture—like all structures—is not an autonomous force that exerts influence on historical outcomes all by itself, like wind or earthquakes. Instead, culture affects policy making via individuals' social interactions. Like anyone else, policy reformers are culturally embedded actors. Through participation in the cultural discourses they encounter in the places of worship they attend, books they read, media they consume, teachers they study under, and associations they join, reformers develop culturally informed interpretations of social problems and how to address them. The same is true for the other actors with whom they cooperate and clash. Several child labor reformers profiled in this book, for example, were deeply motivated by religious beliefs they absorbed by engaging with religious movements and associations. At the same time, some encountered opposition from those who feared that child labor reform and especially mandatory schooling for working children would undermine their religious agendas. Church-state conflict thus influenced regulatory welfare development in certain cases, but did so because of the learned religious commitments of specific historical actors. In short, culture affects policy making through social interactions that inform political agents' policy-relevant *ideas*, which in turn shape their actions and interactions with others in the policy field.

Policy-relevant ideas can be sorted into two broad types. *Problem definitions* are theories about social conditions that explain why such conditions demand policy attention (Mehta 2011, 32–40). Typically, actors develop new problem definitions by drawing on and recombining elements of existing discourse in a process similar to bricolage (Campbell 2004, 69–74) or schematic transposition (Sewell 1992, 17). Problem definitions serve three core functions in policy and administrative entrepreneurship. First, they *motivate* entrepreneurs to take political action by connecting the problematic condition with entrepreneurs' interests or value commitments. Second, they can be deployed strategically as frames in which they become strategic *resources* for political action. It can be tricky to distinguish between problem definitions that motivate policy entrepreneurs and those used strategically as frames; the two may or may not have the same content. When reformers consistently express the same problem definition and use it with a variety of audiences, however, it becomes more likely that the problem definition is one they are sincere about and is actually motivating them. If, on the other hand, their articulated definition changes depending on their audience, it is more likely that it is only being used as a strategic frame (Anderson 2013, 91). Third, problem definitions provide the general road map that points the way forward in terms of what sort of policy should be pursued (Blyth 2002; Goldstein and Keohane 1993). Thus they undergird the content of policy entrepreneurs' concrete policy plans or *programs* (Campbell 2004, 98; Hall 1993).

Programs are the other broad type of policy-relevant idea. Grounded in problem definitions, they differ from them in that they comprise a concrete and specific set of policy prescriptions. Like problem definitions, programs are typically creative recombinations of existing ideas (Kingdon 1984, 124; Sheingate 2003). As others have pointed out (Hall 1993), however, programs are more malleable than problem definitions. This is yet another way that ideas serve as resources for political action; revising programs in the course of political compromise is a key way policy entrepreneurs recruit allies.

To review the theoretical framework developed so far, the macrostructural and institutional factors emphasized by existing theories of social policy development cannot fully explain the emergence of two major institutional innovations at the forefront of the modern regulatory welfare state, namely, child labor laws and factory inspection systems. While factors highlighted in existing welfare states theory—economic conditions, institutional frameworks, political dynamics, and cultural discourses—certainly did matter, they do not adequately capture the causal impact of individual reformers. Particularly when opposition to reform was strong and labor was institutionally disempowered, policy and administrative entrepreneurs exerted decisive influence on labor policy outcomes. To explain how this influence works, I invoked the policy field: a social dynamic akin to a game in which actors struggle over stakes—that is, policy outcomes and the alliances (or political capital) needed to affect them. Reformers' influence on policy outcomes is exercised through two types of empirically observable strategies: alliance building (manifested in six causal mechanisms through which audiences in the field are transformed into allies) and goal-directed creativity (a causal mechanism through which problematic veto players can be overcome). Finally, actors' likelihood of being able to effectively deploy these strategies is conditioned by the policy field's architecture and their position within it. This framework contributes to existing understandings of social policy development by systematically theorizing how individual actors contribute to institutional change, elaborating on the specific processes through which their agency is exercised, and taking into account how this influence is enabled and constrained by field dynamics as well as the broader social-cultural context.

Given that the framework explains institutional change in cases as diverse as 1830s Prussia and 1890s Illinois, it is conceived at a high level of abstraction. Yet the empirical application of the theory requires deep engagement with historical specificities, including macrolevel socioeconomic conditions, culturally specific discourses, diverse political institutions, and the dynamics of policy fields at particular times. Thus, though the framework may be broad and historically aspecific, how it is applied in the case studies is anything but.

Case Selection, Data, and Methods

For part I, the universe of cases is not especially large. Besides Prussia and France, four other European countries were early adopters of laws to regulate child labor in factories: Great Britain (1802, 1819, and 1833), Bavaria (1840), Baden (1840), and Italy (1843).[19] With the notable exception of New York, eight northeastern US states—Massachusetts, Connecticut, Pennsylvania, Rhode Island, Vermont, New Hampshire, Maine, and New Jersey—as well as Ohio established rudimentary child labor laws at some point before the Civil War (Otey 1910). The universe of late adopters was thus much larger.

Various considerations were taken into account when selecting Prussia, France, Belgium, and Massachusetts for the analysis in part I. The first was to select cases that exhibited both similarities and differences on dimensions theorized to be important in the welfare states literature. Accordingly, selection loosely followed a combined method of difference and method of agreement logic. This classic approach has been roundly criticized (see, for example, Goldthorpe 1997; Ragin 2014, 36–42), and rightly so, but I contend that it remains useful as a guiding rationale for case selection and way to rule out deterministic variable-based hypotheses, if not as an analytic method for generating positive causal claims. The Millian case selection logic was loose for two reasons. First, cases were not independent of one another given that states were aware of and to some extent emulated foreign labor policy precedents, particularly British ones. Second, because the similarities and differences were typically a matter of degree, not presence or absence.

Massachusetts and Prussia, despite their theoretically relevant economic, political, and institutional differences, both passed similar child labor laws at nearly the same time. The two states had different levels of industrialization

(Massachusetts being significantly more industrialized) and distinct political institutions, which in turn had implications for working-class strength. Whereas poor and working-class people exercised no political power in Prussia, working-class men had the right to vote in Massachusetts. In contrast, France and Belgium had many similarities. Both countries were liberal, semidemocratic constitutional monarchies in which all but the wealthiest property owners were excluded from the franchise, and the commercial and industrial bourgeoisie enjoyed increasing political power. Both had national legislatures empowered to introduce and enact legislation. Neither had a well-developed public education system, compared to Massachusetts and Prussia, which were already quite advanced in this regard by the 1830s and 1840s (see figure 2.1). In spite of this, France enacted a child labor law in the early phase of its industrialization. Belgium did not.

This case selection was intended to uncover theory-based patterns—that is, causal factors that Prussia, Massachusetts, and France had in common, but Belgium lacked. Preliminary analysis yielded no definitive findings. None of the factors that existing welfare state theory would predict to be causally relevant (a high level of industrialization, certain set of institutional arrangements or policy precedents, politically powerful industrial bourgeoisie, mobilized working class, or recent history of popular unrest) were consistently present in early adopting states and consistently absent in the late-adopting one (see table 1.2). A different analytic approach, one capable of closer analysis of causal processes as they unfold, proved necessary.

A somewhat different logic guided selection of the second set of case studies on the origins of factory inspection. Whereas two of the three cases (1870s Massachusetts and 1890s Illinois) were similar on various theoretically relevant institutional and political dimensions, one (1870s Imperial Germany) was quite different (see table 1.3). In the traditional sense, part II includes no negative cases; factory inspection systems were successfully adopted in all three places. Yet the *type* of inspection system in each state varied in important ways. Germany and Massachusetts, despite their differences, adopted conciliatory models in which factory inspectors aimed at securing voluntary compliance by serving as friendly mediators between labor and capital. Illinois, in contrast, created a strict enforcement model in which inspectors could and did rigorously prosecute and punish violators. The case comparisons in part II were intended to identify causal factors that contributed to the adoption of factory inspection systems, but could also explain this variation in the type of system that each state implemented. Again, no consistent patterns in terms of macrolevel causal variables were evident.

In light of the absence of variable-based patterns and the well-known shortcomings of a simple variable-based approach to small-N comparative-historical analysis (Ragin 2014, 36–42; Ermakoff 2019, 7–11), the analytic method I

TABLE 1.2. Similarities and Differences across Cases in Part I

	Prussia	Massachusetts	France	Belgium
Industrializing	Somewhat	Yes	Yes	Yes
Democracy	No	Yes	Partial	Partial
Powerful legislature	No	Yes	Yes	Yes
Commitment to public schooling	High	High	Low	Low
Politically empowered working class	No	Somewhat	No	No
Working-class unrest	Yes	Yes	Yes	Yes
Politically empowered capital	No	Yes	Yes	Yes
Early adoption of child labor law	Yes	Yes	Yes	No

TABLE 1.3. Similarities and Differences across Cases in Part II

	Imperial Germany	Massachusetts	Illinois
Industrializing	Yes	Yes	Yes
Democracy	Partial	Yes	Yes
Powerful legislature	Somewhat	Yes	Yes
Politically empowered working class	Somewhat	Yes	Yes
Politically empowered capital	Yes	Yes	Yes
Factory inspection model	Conciliatory	Conciliatory	Enforcement

eventually settled on was along the lines of the genetic approach outlined by sociologist Ivan Ermakoff (2019). This involves an in-depth and historically contextualized tracing of the temporal sequence of events that led to the outcome in question (Ermakoff 2019, 14–16). The genetic approach focuses on microlevel processes—the actions and interactions of key actors—to explain macrolevel outcomes. It emphasizes the need to uncover actors' motives and understandings to explain their action and its social effects (Ermakoff 2019, 15, see also Weber 1978, 4–5). It explains why an outcome occurred, not by detecting correlations among variables, but by carefully documenting how it came about. Its goals include the identification of generalizable causal mechanisms or processes as well as the conditions under which those are likely to occur. To avoid retrospective bias or teleological thinking, the genetic approach pays particular attention to situations of indeterminacy where counterfactual outcomes were possible and to explaining why actors took one path rather than another (Ermakoff 2019, 12–15).[20]

My analysis began with a close reading of secondary historical literature, approached inductively and involving only a general theory-driven expectation that microlevel processes among political actors were important. Deeply researched studies of the origins of child labor and factory inspection reform in Prussia, France, Imperial Germany, and Illinois exist.[21] Less has been written on the Belgian case, but it has been addressed to some extent.[22] The two Massachusetts cases have not been researched comprehensively by historians to my knowledge. In each of the cases for which secondary sources existed, a consensus emerged that one or two individuals—not part of the working class, but elite or middle-class state or civil society actors—had taken the lead in developing and advocating for a child labor law, or implementing a new factory inspection system. This was the basis for a broad working hypothesis that elite and middle-class *policy or administrative entrepreneurship* was the missing link between the structural and institutional factors emphasized by existing welfare state theories and labor policy outcomes.

Although secondary historical accounts were in general agreement on who the leading reformers were in each case, they could not systematically explain why some were successful, but others were not; why some states enacted child labor laws early in their industrial development, and others did not; or why states adopted different models of factory inspection. To answer these questions and refine the working hypothesis, I analyzed archival and published primary materials to develop a genetic account of the causal processes that led to divergent outcomes. The types of primary materials available varied from case to case. For example, backstage communications between government officials were most copious for the two German cases, whereas for the two later US cases, newspaper articles were abundant. The relative absence of backstage materials for some cases (the two Massachusetts cases and the Belgian one) means that relevant interactive dynamics among key players possibly went undetected. The policy entrepreneurs in these cases may, for instance, have displayed more behind-the-scenes creativity of action than I give them credit for. Still, public documents (news articles, records of legislative proceedings, published legislative drafts and investigative reports, and published books and essays by lead reformers) provided substantial insight into their how they went about developing and promoting their policy programs in interaction with other political actors.[23]

The genetic analysis proceeded abductively (Timmermans and Tavory 2012; Tavory and Timmermans 2014). I had a broad working hypothesis that the unexpected variations in policy outcomes had something to do with policy and administrative entrepreneurship, and some theories of action to draw on, such as John Kingdon's theory of policy entrepreneurship (1984, 179–83), Fligstein and McAdam's theory of social skill in strategic action fields (2012, 45–53), and pragmatist action theory. Close, repeated reading and summarizing of the primary sources alongside the secondary historical literature allowed me to re-create in detail the temporal sequence of social interactions and events that generated particular policy outcomes in each case.

The genetic analysis leverages three types of comparison. All three rely on negative cases, though the nature of these negative cases and the purpose they serve vary. First, I compare cases with different outcomes. The negative case of failed child labor reform in part I is conceived in the traditional way, as the absence of a particular historical outcome. It obeys the "possibility principle" (Mahoney and Goertz 2004) in the sense that although Belgium failed to adopt a child labor law, it could very well have done so, as I show in chapter 3. The inclusion of this crucial negative case allows me to rule out deterministic variable-based explanations, such as those that would treat industrialization, working-class power resources, or institutional precedents as sufficient causes of child labor reform. In place of such accounts, the comparative genetic analysis leads me to explain variations in outcomes by focusing on the strategic and creative action of key reformers, and by pinpointing the particular relational strategies through which they tried to build alliances and solve problems.

Second, I compare actors using three paired comparisons, each between a successful and unsuccessful policy entrepreneur who strove for labor reform under the same or similar social and institutional conditions. Here, negative cases of failed policy entrepreneurship help identify the distinguishing attributes of successful policy entrepreneurship, and the conditions under which alliance-building and problem-solving strategies are more likely to succeed. They also point to the significance of field position in determining the likelihood that actors can and will adopt effective strategies. Furthermore, these paired comparisons allow me to imagine plausible counterfactuals: how unsuccessful reformers could have acted in a given situation had they been more skillful, and what outcomes would have transpired had they behaved differently. Counterfactual thinking highlights missed opportunities, such as moments where policy entrepreneurs could have compromised with potential allies but chose not to, contributing to their eventual failure. Such counterfactuals are valuable because they strengthen my assertion that policy outcomes were not purely the result of structural determinants; had policy entrepreneurs acted differently, labor policy outcomes likely would have turned out differently as well.

Finally, I compare cases in which policy entrepreneurs mattered greatly for policy outcomes with those in which their influence was less decisive than other factors. Here, the negative cases, the two in Massachusetts, are those in which the outcome is present, but the hypothesized causal process leading to it—middle-class policy entrepreneurship—is absent or weaker than other factors. These comparisons allow me to theorize scope conditions under which the contributions of individual middle-class and elite reformers may be especially important for social policy development.

One last note on case selection is warranted here. The United Kingdom is not among the cases in this book, even though it was the first country—with the passage of its 1802 Health and Morals of Apprentices Act, and the 1819 and 1833 Factory Acts—to regulate child labor in factories and establish a national factory inspectorate. The 1833 act in particular set an important international precedent, serving as a model for subsequent reform efforts on the continent and in the United States. I omitted the United Kingdom for two reasons. First, because it industrialized so early and tackled child labor in factories more than three decades before any other state, Britain is an outlier and thus direct comparisons with it are problematic. Second, the British factory acts have received nearly all the English-language scholarly attention to nineteenth-century labor regulation; the cases I cover are less well known to English-speaking audiences but equally deserving of attention. The extensive literature on the British case, however, suggests that though it differs from the cases covered in the first half of this book, it is not entirely incompatible with the theory developed here. It is different in the sense that the 1833 Factory Act arose directly from a massive labor movement in which tens of thousands of Lancashire and Yorkshire mill operatives marched to demand restrictions on children's working hours. But, lacking the franchise, labor's power resources would have been futile without an alliance with sympathetic elites in Parliament, foremost among them Michael Sadler and Lord Ashley of Shaftesbury. The nucleus holding this cross-class alliance together was the "Tory radical" Richard Oastler, a middle-class estate steward who became the movement's leading strategist and orator (Driver 1946; see also Smelser 1959; Thomas 1948; Kirby 2003). Thus, although labor supplied the grassroots pressure that pushed Parliament to act, middle-class and elite reformers took on essential roles as social movement organizers and policy entrepreneurs in the British case as well.

Looking Ahead

The chapters that follow describe the political events leading to the passage of child labor laws or factory inspection systems in Germany, France, Massachusetts, and Illinois well as the failure of child labor reform in Belgium. Each chapter concentrates on answering four sets of questions.

1. What contextual factors created an impetus for middle-class labor reformers to pursue child labor laws and factory inspection systems? To answer this question, I provide a brief overview of the social conditions that reformers responded to and connected with child

labor, such as industrialization, collective social disorders and labor unrest, and primary school truancy.

2. What problem definitions motivated middle-class labor reformers, and how did these definitions shape the programs they pursued? Furthermore, where did these ideas come from—how were they related to the broader cultural context? To answer these questions, I explicate discourses that influenced policy and administrative entrepreneurs' thinking about the child labor problem and how to address it.

3. Both across and within sociohistorical contexts, why did some child labor policy entrepreneurs succeed while others failed? To answer this question, I trace in detail policy entrepreneurs' alliance-building efforts and problem-solving approaches. Wherever possible, I use paired comparisons between a successful and unsuccessful reformer to tease out what distinguished the two.

4. Relatedly, how was reformers' influence shaped by political context, the policy field's institutions and architecture, and their own field position? To answer this question, I pay attention to the major political players with whom reformers cooperated and clashed. I outline the relevant political conditions and basic institutional arrangements that structured policy making in each case. Further, I identify significant overlaps between the policy field and other fields, reformers' positioning relative to those overlaps, and the ways these overlaps facilitated or impeded their entrepreneurship.

The seven case studies in which I answer these questions cover a great deal of ground. Each contains many specificities that make it irreducibly complex and in some ways unique. But the task of comparative historical social science is to unearth the common patterns—causes, processes, and conditions—lying beneath such profusions of historical detail. This book reveals that elite and middle-class reformers contributed to the birth of the modern regulatory welfare state to an extent so far underappreciated by scholars. By leveraging three types of negative cases, it moreover demonstrates the alliance-building and problem-solving strategies through which their influence was carried out as well as the conditions under which they mattered most.

Part I

Introduction to Part I

Children have always worked. Whether as free or enslaved agricultural laborers, artisan apprentices, industrial homeworkers, helpers in retail establishments, domestic servants, or street vendors, children played an integral role in the early modern economy. But around the turn of the nineteenth century, as the Industrial Revolution spread from England to the European continent and into the New World, the nature of some children's work changed. Whereas industrial production in the putting-out system had largely been carried out within family homes under the supervision of parents, it now moved into workshops and factories, where children toiled for wages alongside strangers and dangerous new machines. Working days had always been long and tiring, but now they stretched to fourteen hours or more, and grew increasingly regimented and inflexible. It was no longer possible for working children to make enough time for learning, recreation, and rest without losing their jobs. A minute division of labor rendered children's tasks monotonous and stultifying. Overwork, malnourishment, unsanitary conditions, and lack of physical exercise in fresh air caused ill health and shortened life spans. Beyond this, each sector carried particular risks to health and safety—risks to which frail and incautious children were especially vulnerable.

Throughout the nineteenth century (and even today), agriculture relied most heavily on child labor, but children could be found in manufacturing sectors as well.[1] The sector most reliant on young workers was textiles, and when nineteenth-century reformers spoke of the need to regulate child labor in factories, the textile mills were foremost in their minds. Girls and boys, some as young as six, worked in large numbers in the textile mills of every industrializing country. Their tasks in the mills varied, but their work was always integrated with that of the adults who operated the spinning frames and weaving looms. In

FIGURE I.1. English cotton mill, c. 1830. Women tend carding, drawing, and roving machines. In the foreground, a bobbin girl. *Source*: Alamy Stock Photo.

the spinning mills, young children were typically employed as "piecers" tying together threads that broke as they were being spun, "doffers" who replaced spools of thread as they emptied, and "bobbin girls/boys" carrying spools between frames (see figure I.1). Children also picked up cotton waste from the floor, prepared fibers for carding, and cleaned machines (Scholliers 1995, 208; 2009). Older children operated the willowing and scutching machines (which removed coarse impurities from the fibers), carding machines (which combed the fibers into parallel strands), and combing machines (which prepared the carded fibers for spinning) (Herzig 1983, 340). Although regarded as light, workdays were long, from a minimum of twelve hours per day to as many as fourteen or even sixteen hours during spikes in demand (Persons 1971, 6–7; Mareska and Heyman 1845, 246; Herzig 1983, 339; Villermé 1837, 3). Given the need to boil yarn or fabric for bleaching and dying, mills were often hot and humid, with temperatures rising to 120 degrees Fahrenheit (de Herdt 2011, 183). The air was thick with cotton and woolen dust, and respiratory ailments were common. Further, because cleaning was usually performed while machines were running, accidents were frequent, sometimes resulting in severe injury or death (Herzig 1983, 342). Toward the end of the nineteenth century, textile manufacturing, particularly ready-to-wear clothing, moved into sweatshops operating out of tenements and private homes. Children who worked in sweatshops were even younger than those who worked in factories, and sanitary conditions were often worse.

FIGURE I.2. Boys operate lathes in the J. A. Maffei locomotive factory near Munich, c. 1849. *Source*: Wikimedia Commons.

Children also worked in machine making—for example, operating lathes to turn out machine parts (see figure I.2) or affixing fine wire hooks onto carding machine brushes—but were more widely used in small metal goods manufacture, where they were prized for their small fingers and ability to manipulate tiny parts. In the Rhineland, children worked in needle factories, where they hammered eyes into needles, hammered on pinheads, bent fish hooks and hairpins, and sorted, weighed, and packed finished goods (Herzig 1983, 333–34). The work was highly repetitive and routinized, as an observer of a pin factory near Aachen noted: "The instruments and machines that the children operate are ingenious, while the children themselves, who work seated in rank and file, now forward and now backward leaning, but always rhythmically performing the same motions and making the same noises, remind the observer of machines." Similar to work in the textile mills, these were jobs that required dexterity rather than physical strength, and were thus regarded as "light work," though working hours were as long as in the mills (340–41). Respiratory ailments were common because metal workshops were completely sealed and unventilated to prevent oxidation (342).

Another manufacturing industry that relied heavily on child labor was glassmaking. Young assistants were kept trotting all day and night, carrying molten or finished glass from one stage of the production process to the next.

FIGURE I.3. Boys assist glassblowers, France, c. 1880. *Source*: Alamy Stock Photo.

"Mold boys" sat hunched at the feet of the glassblower, closing and opening the molds; "napping-up boys" took items out of the mold to a finisher; and "carrying-out boys" transferred finished items to an annealing oven (see figure I.3). Like the textile mills, glassworks were hot, ranging from 100 to 130 degrees Fahrenheit (Fones-Wolf 2009, 468–69). Production was carried out in continuous shifts, so glassmaking, more than other industries, relied on night work. Aside from respiratory ailments, burns were the most common occupational hazard. As we will see in part II, glassmakers were able to successfully lobby governments for exceptions to child labor rules in some cases, arguing that the continuous nature of the glassmaking process, and integration of adult and child labor, precluded limits on children's working hours.[2]

In general, mining did not rely as heavily on child workers, but its unique horrors attracted particular attention and condemnation. In 1813, Napoléon outlawed the labor of children under the age of ten in mines in France, the Netherlands (including Belgium), the Rhineland, and all other French territories, but children did work underground in mines. Belgium was unusual in that coal mining there was a family enterprise. The youngest children were charged with opening and closing trapdoors to allow coal carts to pass, and

FIGURE I.4. Child labor in an English coal mine, c. 1843. *Source*: Alamy Stock Photo.

older children hauled carts through cramped, dark, airless tunnels (see figure I.4). It was common for them to spend more than twenty-four hours underground (de Herdt 2011, 177). In 1848, a coal mine manager near Liège described the use of children in older mines (not his own) this way: "The child is obliged to drag heavy loads along pathways lacking proper wooden supports, where he slips onto his back whilst struggling with a hard sled which is constantly threatening to crush him" (Belgium, Ministère de l'Intérieur 1848, 1:xxxvi).[3] After hauling, the most exhausting and dangerous part of a child mine worker's shift was the descent and ascent into the mine by ladder. A 300-meter ladder took about twenty minutes to climb down and forty minutes to climb up. By 1856, the average Belgian mine was 380 meters deep, and in the dark on slippery rungs, tired children sometimes fell to their deaths (Hilden 1993, 111–12). Child labor in mines was less pervasive in the United States. Beginning in the 1860s, however, children were widely employed in the Pennsylvania anthracite coal mines. Perched precariously on ladders beside the chutes, these "breaker boys" plucked slate and dirt out of the mounds of moving coal; injuries were, of course, common (Offiong 2009, 466–67).

The dire conditions endured by child workers in factories and mines did not go unnoticed. In the 1830s and 1840s, continental European and US states tentatively embarked on their first forays into regulatory welfare policy making when they established minimum ages, maximum working hours, and schooling requirements for children working in factories, workshops, and mines. In doing so, they were following in the footsteps of the world's runaway industrial leader, the United Kingdom, which had already begun in 1819 to regulate "free" (nonapprentice) child labor in textile mills. A more robust Factory Act, which included the establishment of a national factory inspection department, followed in 1833. European and US reformers were keenly aware of the United Kingdom's efforts, which they regarded as evidence that the state could, to some extent, interfere in industrial working conditions without bringing the manufacturing economy to ruin. After all, England was flourishing. At the same time, they regarded the condition of England's industrial working class as a warning: while most believed that working people in their own country would never succumb to the intense moral and physical degradation they imagined infesting the slums of Manchester, they were nevertheless alarmed by what they saw around them. The new factories were a wonder, generating output and riches that vastly exceeded the cottage industry of the previous generation, but they were increasingly staffed by a pauperized class of workers whose physical, intellectual, and moral development had been severely neglected.

Factory children, in particular, were worryingly overworked, and in danger of coming under the influence of adults who seemed uncouth, unchaste, and unsober. Most concerning, they were growing up entirely untouched by the civilizing influence of the primary school. Although states varied in the degree to which they had made public education a priority, many had started to take steps toward expanding educational opportunities for the poor. Prussia had mandated primary schooling already in the eighteenth century. By the 1830s, Prussia, Massachusetts, France, and Belgium all had laws on the books requiring localities to build primary schools. If poor children were too busy working to take advantage of these opportunities, they would reach adulthood fully unprepared for higher-skilled employment, and utterly lacking the knowledge and principles required for good citizenship. Even scarier, if left undisciplined by the mainly moral and religious primary school curriculum, then they might begin to harbor resentments that they would one day violently unleash on society. These children seemed to pose a threat to the social stability, national security, and long-term economic prosperity of the state. Something needed to be done.

In the following three chapters, I present four case studies of the first phase of child labor legislation in continental Europe and the United States. Chapter 2 traces the political origins of the first child labor law in continental Europe: Prussia's 1839 Regulative on the Employment of Young Workers in Factories. It uses a within-case paired comparison of two policy entrepreneurs to show how the problem definitions motivating the two reformers shaped their proposed programs, and to demonstrate how alliance-building and problem-solving strategies contributed to the success of one over the other. The two rival reformers were the minister of education, Karl vom Stein zum Altenstein, and the appointed governor of the Rhineland province, Ernst von Bodelschwingh. The eventual passage of Bodelschwingh's plan is significant because it foreclosed Altenstein's more holistic and grassroots approach to child labor regulation in Germany. Bodelschwingh's success is primarily attributable to his ability to round up political allies through citation, framing, and especially compromise. Further, he exhibited goal-directed creativity in the face of setbacks, bending the normal rules of policy making to get around veto players—a strategy facilitated by his position at the intersection of the central and local policy fields. Using these strategies, he was eventually able to overcome the institutional barriers erected by the collegial structure of decision-making at the top of the Prussian bureaucracy. I argue that without Bodelschwingh's policy entrepreneurship, Prussia would not have adopted the child labor law that it did when it did.

Chapter 3 presents a negative comparative case in which child labor reform was seriously attempted yet failed. A cross-case paired comparison of child labor policy entrepreneurs in 1830s and 1840s France and Belgium shows that the failure of reform in Belgium stemmed from strategic mistakes made by its leading child labor policy entrepreneur, Inspector General of Prisons Édouard Ducpétiaux. His proposed program failed primarily because he did not compromise with institutionally empowered stakeholders—specifically Belgium's local-level chambers of commerce. In France, chambers of commerce were similarly powerful, but the policy entrepreneur behind the French child labor law, Chamber of Peers member Charles Dupin, recognized this and made sure to compromise with them as well as others in the policy field. Furthermore, Dupin used frames and citations in ways that fit with the ideas and priorities (while flattering the egos) of potential allies, whereas Ducpétiaux used frames that contradicted the Belgian policy field's discursive opportunity structure and cited actors deemed irrelevant by potential allies. These differences in alliance-building skill are partly attributable to differences in the architecture of the Belgian and French policy fields, and in each man's positioning within that architecture.

Chapter 4 documents the passage of the first child labor legislation in the United States. It is the first of two negative cases in which reform happened, but the causal influence of individual middle-class reformers was less significant than other factors. In 1836, Massachusetts required children working in "manufacturing establishments" to attend school for at least three months per year. Six years later, it restricted the working hours of children under age twelve to ten per day. In both instances, Massachusetts reformers benefited from a strong complementarity between their proposed plans and the prevailing discursive opportunity structure. Cultural consensus around the importance of education for safeguarding democracy and expanding opportunity was so strong that the plans experienced no apparent opposition—neither bill required a roll call, an indication of clear majority support, and both were enacted within a few weeks of introduction. Moreover, a well-developed common school infrastructure meant that child labor regulation could build seamlessly on existing institutional precedents. Thus, the causal impact of individual reformers—their particular alliance-building or problem-solving strategies—mattered less for policy outcomes than these other factors.

Each case study includes an overview of the macrostructural conditions (industrial development, class dynamics, and institutional arrangements) that informed, enabled, and constrained reform in each case. In particular, class-based social disorders drew reformers' attention to the need to "do something" to both help and discipline the children of the poor. Further, each case study explicates the cultural discourses that shaped policy entrepreneurs' problem definitions and policy programs, paying special attention to debates around education reform. In all four cases, child labor regulation was intimately bound up with the development of public primary schooling and conceived as a piece of education policy. Prussia and Massachusetts were exceptional in regard to their strong commitment to universal education, but even in France and Belgium, countries with comparatively low school enrollment rates and undeveloped school systems, working children were seen as in need of the civilizing and disciplining influence of a primary education. As a result, the first child labor laws always included a compulsory education component—even in those places where schooling was not yet mandated for the general population.

To get a sense of similarities and differences in how leading reformers used framing and citation to recruit allies, I analyzed a selection of primary documents. A single document was chosen for each reformer—namely the key memo or report in which the reformer explained and defended his bill. These statements were similar enough in terms of context and purpose to be amenable to fine-grained comparative analysis. I used coding software to categorize and quantify citations and frames. I divided citations into two main categories: insiders (actors in the domestic policy, intellectual, or business fields, or domestic legal precedents) and outsiders (foreign actors and laws). I likewise divided frames into two types: simple, referring to immediate, obvious reasons for child labor reform (nearly always, these were the need to protect children's health, promote their education, or safeguard their morality), and fundamental, which invoked deeper, less immediately apparent reasons for reform. Fundamental frames either connected child labor regulation to the essential interests of the state, society, or economy (such as national security, social order, or economic prosperity), or connected it to core values such as children's rights.[4] Whereas the simple health, education, and morality frames were ubiquitous and invoked frequently across all three cases—sometimes all three in the same sentence—fundamental frames varied somewhat from case to case. This analysis allowed me to assess whether the unsuccessful policy entrepreneurs differed systematically from those who were more effective with regard to the frames they used and people they cited.

Additionally, in Prussia, France, and Belgium, governments queried chambers of commerce about their attitudes toward child labor regulation (though in the Prussian case, this was not carried out comprehensively or systematically—a significant finding in itself). I was therefore able to conduct a comparative analysis of employer attitudes toward various aspects of child labor regulation in these three countries. By comparing employer attitudes with the content of the programs that policy entrepreneurs proposed, I was able to test the possibility that reformers' (un)willingness to compromise with key stakeholders contributed to their success or failure. In the cases of France and Belgium, I was further able to conduct a prosopographical analysis of dual membership in the policy and intellectual fields by counting the number of people who belonged to each country's learned society, while also serving in their national legislatures or executive branches. This analysis lent insight into why lead reformers in the two countries adopted particular citation and framing strategies, and helped explain why their strategies did or did not resonate in the policy field. Finally, the genetic analysis of the relational processes leading to institutional change (or the lack thereof) allowed me to identify other manifestations of alliance building and creative problem-solving in each case. The picture that emerged is that unsuccessful reformers were significantly different from the successful ones when it came to their alliance-building and creative problem-solving strategies. It is these differences that explain why states adopted the child labor laws that they did, when they did—or in the case of Belgium, why they failed to adopt any child labor law at all.

2

Securing the Social Order

THE POLITICS OF CHILD LABOR
REGULATION IN PRUSSIA

In 1839, Prussia became the first country in continental Europe and the second in the world after the United Kingdom to pass a law restricting child labor in factories, mines, and quarries.[1] The law set the minimum employment age at nine, prohibited young people under sixteen from working more than ten hours a day, and required children to have three years of schooling before starting a job (for details, see table 1.1). As Prussia's first attempt to regulate the employment conditions of the new industrial proletariat, historians have designated it the "beginning of social policy in Prussia" (Kastner 2004, 181; see also Köllmann 1966, 39; Gladen 1974; Schulz 1996). In legitimating state intervention into the "free" labor market in an era when laissez-faire dominated economic policy and doctrine, the law set an important precedent. It became the institutional foundation for additional protections for child and adult workers later in the century, and served as a model for child labor policy interventions in other countries.

This chapter describes why Prussia enacted a child labor law and adopted the particular one it did. It compares two contemporary child labor policy entrepreneurs, one successful and one not, to tease out what distinguished the two. One difference was in the problem definitions that motivated them, which in turn led them to propose different programs. The failed program, proposed in 1828 by Karl vom Stein zum Altenstein, minister of religious, educational, and medical affairs (minister of education), was grounded in a view of industrial child labor as undermining the physical, intellectual, and moral quality of working-class Prussians. Consequently, it placed equal weight on protecting children's physical health, moral purity, spiritual development, and educational opportunities. The successful program, initially drafted in 1835 by Ernst von Bodelschwingh, *Oberpräsident* (governor) of the Rhineland, was based on a view of child labor as a barrier to schooling, and hence a potential contributor to disorder and immorality among the poor. Relative to Altenstein's plan, it was more narrowly focused on ensuring that working children received the modicum of education and religious instruction required to mold them into obedient, peaceable subjects. Moreover, Altenstein's plan included clear guidelines for local implementation; Bodelschwingh's did not. Had Altenstein emerged victorious, Prussian child labor policy would have taken a more holistic approach and put in place new grassroots institutions to implement regulations.

Altenstein's plan was clearly more ambitious than Bodelschwingh's. I argue, however, that the success of latter over the former cannot be simply chalked up to their content, since there were, after all, multiple opportunities to *change* that content. Rather, it has to do with variation in their alliance-building capacities and creativity in the face of political obstacles. Whereas Bodelschwingh used citation and compromise to amass a coalition of supporters, Altenstein's failure to seize alliance-building opportunities left him isolated and ineffective. Bodelschwingh also exhibited far greater creativity of action, evident in his ability to circumvent normal institutional channels of policy making when his initial efforts were blocked. These differences are important not only for explaining the two men's differential impact but also in accounting for Prussia's child labor policy outcomes over the long term.

Differences between the two men's alliance-building and problem-solving strategies were influenced (though not determined) by their positions within the policy field, which in absolutist Prussia was largely synonymous with the state. In terms of its architecture, the Prussian policy field overlapped little with other fields, and thus was insulated from civil society and other influences. The state was centralized and hierarchical, with the king and his ministers occupying the top rungs. The ministry was a collegiate body of officials, each with his own department (war, interior, education, finance, justice, and foreign affairs). The king's power was limited by the ministers; in practice he governed with, not over, them (Nipperdey 1983, 24). The country was divided into twelve provinces further divided into districts (*Regierungsbezirke*). The district governments were organized into departments whose heads were appointed by and subordinate to the central administration. Between the two was the Oberpräsident, the province's top-ranking representative of the crown, whose role was to mediate between the central and district governments.[2] The only source of political power operating outside this hierarchical administrative structure was the provincial legislatures (*Landtage*), whose members were elected by landowners. These bodies were merely advisory, however.

One might expect Altenstein, as a minister at the highest level, to have had an easy time building alliances. This turned out not to be the case. Decision-making at the top of the Prussian bureaucracy was carried out collegially, with each minister empowered to approve or block legislation relevant to his respective domain. This structure created challenges for Altenstein, who repeatedly found his child labor reform efforts thwarted by hostile colleagues. Altenstein had long been associated with a cohort of liberal reformers who briefly gained control of the royal government following the Napoleonic Wars. By the mid-1820s, though, most had been replaced by socially conservative reactionaries. As a result, it had become lonely at the top for the progressive education minister; he found it difficult to make alliances with fellow ministers and even lower-ranking officials in his own department. In comparison, Bodelschwingh was lower in rank than Altenstein, but more centrally positioned. He used his mediating position as Oberpräsident to "reach down" (White 1992, 262–65; Lachmann 2003, 355) for allies at the municipal level, to reach across for allies in the provincial legislature, and to reach up for allies in Berlin. By steadily amassing new and different allies at multiple levels of government, he was eventually able to push a revised version of his plan through to enactment.

Existing Explanations

The Prussian child labor law of 1839 has received substantial attention from historians, whose explanations emphasize either state-building priorities or class relations. A classic argument is that of the Marxist historian Jürgen Kuczynski (1968, 92), who maintains that the law arose from concerns that premature factory work yielded sickly, deformed young men unfit for armed service. This theory has been discredited (Preller 1954, 302–6; Feldenkirchen 1981, 2; Kastner 2004, 73–74), but it survives in the literature (Nipperdey 1977, 161; Bucher 1983; Brose 1993, 176, Steinmetz 1993, 135) and the popular consciousness; if one were to ask a historically informed German about the origins of child labor regulation in the country, she would be likely to mention some version of this so-called cannon fodder thesis.

Kuczynski's bellicist argument is a variation on the state-centered approach outlined in chapter 1. In this view, child labor reform was part of Prussia's efforts to improve its standing vis-à-vis its European rivals in the wake of the Napoleonic Wars. The argument mirrors sociologist Charles Tilly's (1990, 16) contention that European state building occurred at the juncture of capital and coercion: just as the "wielders of coercion" extracted monetary resources from the "manipulators of capital" to grow their standing armies, they also asserted control over the physical bodies of young people. When children's wholesale appropriation by capital came to be perceived as undermining national security and military ambitions, child labor laws were deemed necessary. The regulation of a male child's employment and education, instituted to pave the way for his subsequent military conscription, was just another form of resource extraction for state building through war.

The cannon fodder thesis rests primarily on evidence that in 1828, Frederick William III ordered his ministers to develop a child labor law in response to reports that conscription quotas were going unmet in the kingdom's industrial areas because local men were physically stunted from premature and excessive factory labor.[3] This evidence may at first glance appear conclusive, but I join other critics in arguing against the militarist view (Preller 1954; Thies 1988; Kastner 2004; Dörr, Grawe, and Obinger 2020). A closer look reveals that the political origins of child labor reform actually preceded the king's order by about a decade and the subsequent reforms were not directly attributable to the decree. Moreover, the king was not a politically powerful player in the child labor movement. In the age of bureaucratic absolutism that characterized pre-1848 Prussia (Rosenberg 1966), top ministers could and did ignore the king's demands. The officials who spearheaded the reform effort were not in fact motivated by military concerns; at most, they cited military issues as a pro forma framing device when presenting their proposals to the king. They also did not distinguish between girls and boys, which they likely would have done if they were mainly interested in protecting future soldiers. In short, Frederick William's military priorities may have facilitated the passage of a child labor law, but they did not drive it.

A second set of arguments portrays child labor regulation as a tool to advance class interests (Bülter 1953). The first such formulation contends that top Prussian bureaucrats, most of whom were aristocrats, pushed through regulations to stem the rising power of the bourgeoisie. Little evidence supports this claim. Many Prussian ministers had been schooled in liberal economic theories, and were sympathetic to industry and sensitive to the potential impact of the law on factory output (Beck 1992, 1995; for a similar assertion pertaining to the later nineteenth century, see Steinmetz 1993). Most viewed the advancement of industry as critical to Prussia's national interests. The liberal Chancellor Karl August von Hardenberg, for example, called industrialization the source of "culture and welfare in the flourishing lands."[4] Another such official, Interior Minister Friedrich von Schuckmann, blocked the passage of child labor legislation for years because he feared it would threaten Prussian industrialists' ability to withstand British competition. One important exception is Interior Minister Gustav von Rochow, who belonged to a minority camp that opposed large-scale industrialization and regarded factories as immoral (Brose 1993, 53). Still, the final law was deferential to capital; its authors were careful to ensure that its provisions did not exceed those of England's 1833 Factory Act and inserted language stipulating that its educational requirements be implemented so as to "disturb factory operations as little as possible."[5] In short, little evidence suggests that the law was intended to advance the interests of the aristocracy by harming Prussian capitalists—though one key supporter, von Rochow, may have been to some extent motivated by such hostility.

The second formulation contends that the child labor law was enacted to assuage working-class discontent and mitigate any impetus for a potentially disruptive workers' movement. The suggestion that policy entrepreneurs in the 1830s, like Bismarck in the 1880s, pursued social legislation because they felt threatened by a protosocialist movement has little merit simply because such a movement did not exist in Germany at the time.[6] The political threat that Prussian elites were concerned about, however, was the spread of a French-style political revolution to German-speaking lands. In this context, the working-class "rabble" (*Pöbel*) was to be feared, not because it was politically organized, but because it might use any incipient bourgeois-intellectual revolutionary agitation as an opportunity to rise up against brutal working and living conditions (Conze 1954; Tilly 1980). Child labor reform would be a way to redress the grievances underlying these disruptions by mitigating some of the worst abuses of the factory system. This argument mirrors the version of class-based welfare state theory that contends that social policies arise to preserve economic and political order in the face of working-class unrest, or perceived threats thereof (Piven and Cloward 1971; Tilly 1975).

Evidence does support the interpretation that early Prussian child labor regulations were seen by some proponents as a way to prevent uprisings. Many elites were indeed worried by the rumblings of discontent they felt from below. Political protests, food riots, and revolts against unfair labor practices were relatively common, especially during the hunger crises of 1816–17 and 1830–31 (Tilly 1980; Bass 1991; Brophy 2007; Kocka 1986). More generally, the lower classes posed a threat of "inchoate social disorder" in the form of pauperism, crime, begging, banditry, and gangs of ragged children who roamed and roughhoused in the streets (Steinmetz 1993, 46; see also Herzig 1983, 346–47). Still, reformers did not pursue child labor laws to redress workers' grievances. Workers did not in fact *want* restrictions on children's labor and were unhappy with the law, once passed, because it took away an important source of income from poverty-stricken families. At factories along the Sieg River in the Rhineland, for example, parents held demonstrations to protest the new rules (Kastner 2004, 209).

Child labor reformers, then, were not responding directly to pressure from either the aristocracy or workers. Even if they had wanted restrictions on child labor, workers had no organized way to express their grievances or make demands, and capital was still largely unorganized beyond the local level and had little influence on the policy debate.[7] Political parties and a national legislature did not yet exist. Neither was reform simply another manifestation of the state's coercive or extractive priorities. Worker protection did not fit with any preexisting administrative or policy mandate, and regulating employment conditions was not yet part of the state's institutional framework. Prussia had no Ministry of Labor, no factory inspection department, and no independent Ministry of Commerce. At this point no electoral or procedural channels through which to address the social problems of industrial capitalism had been established. Under these conditions, entrepreneurial reformers proved necessary for regulatory welfare policy development.

In 1830s Prussia, the policy field was circumscribed, and such reformers were state actors almost by default. The early period of child labor legislation came at the zenith of Prussian bureaucratic absolutism, when the collective power of civil servants outstripped that of all other political actors (Rosenberg 1966; Beck 1995). Hence the key players in early Prussian child labor reform were top bureaucrats at both the central and provincial government levels. Unique among the reformers profiled in this book, several were landed aristocrats, but they were also devoted servants of the state. Acting as mediators between labor, capital, and the aristocracy, they represented the narrow interests of none of these groups. In this sense, the case fits with state-centered theory, but this alone does not tell us much about what these policy entrepreneurs wanted or how they went about getting it. Some powerful officials opposed child labor regulation outright; even among supporters, opinion varied about why reform should happen and what it should look like. We therefore need to go further and unpack their thinking, what motivated them, and how they managed to make reform happen. Explaining why this law passed rather than some other version of it requires disaggregating "the state," and paying attention to the ideas and actions of the individuals involved.

The Stein-Hardenberg Reform Era: Free Trade and Primary Schooling

In 1806, Napoléon's army decisively defeated Prussia at Jena-Auerstedt. Prussia lost half its territories and population, and was saddled with impossibly huge war reparations. This humiliating defeat shook Prussia's conservative society to the core and ushered in a brief but consequential period of far-reaching domestic reforms. Led by Chancellor Karl von Stein and his successor, von Hardenberg, a new cohort of Enlightenment-educated, liberal bureaucrats gained control of the highest positions of the Prussian civil service. They believed that to survive, Prussia needed to be revitalized, not by a bloody revolution from below, but by an orderly revolution directed from above by the most educated and enlightened members of society (Nipperdey 1983; Clark 2006). Combining Kantian ethics with fervent nationalism, these reformers embraced the idea that the monarchical state could ensure its longevity and prosperity by educating citizens to embrace free and selfless devotion to the public good, unleashing their energies in the service of king and country (Levinger 1998). Two central pillars of the reform agenda were freedom of trade and public schooling. Whereas the former domain saw the abolition of serfdom along with the lifting of age-old obligations and protections for the lower classes, the latter saw the expansion of their educational opportunities and requirements—at least in theory, if not always in practice. Both sets of changes were relevant for child labor.

FREEDOM OF TRADE AND CHILD LABOR

In the eighteenth century, industrial child labor took the form of apprenticeship. Children typically began their three- to five-year training at the age of twelve. They boarded with their masters, and were fed and cared for by their masters' wives (Kocka 1990, 337). For the most part, the mutual obligations between masters and apprentices, including wages and the duration of training, were set by the guilds. Practically speaking, it was the guilds' responsibility to oversee the training of apprentices and ensure that children were being properly treated. Certain basic, if highly general, protective requirements were established by law, however. The Prussian Civil Code (*Allgemeines Landrecht*) of 1794 stipulated that only master artisans and craftspeople who were guild members could take on apprentices. Masters were required to ensure that their apprentices developed "good morals," attended church regularly, avoided vices, and acquired basic elementary and religious instruction. Masters were allowed to discipline apprentices, but not to exceed the severity permitted to fathers; in other words, punishment was not to endanger the child's health or life. Apprentices who were "abused" by their masters were to be reassigned by the guild elders to another master.[8]

In 1810, the Stein-Hardenberg reforms established freedom of trade in Prussia. Craftspeople were no longer required to belong to a guild or undergo an apprenticeship; all that was required to enter a profession was the payment of an occupational tax. The reforms ended the monopoly of the guilds over occupational training, and anyone, including nonguild members, could now take on apprentices. The stated reason for the reform was not only the need to liberate industry from its "oppressive shackles" but also the state's need for new sources of tax revenue.[9] The liberal bureaucrats who spearheaded the reforms had accepted Adam Smith's logic that policies and institutions that hampered free markets necessarily undermined the wealth of nations (Koselleck 1967, 158, 168). Guilds, which artificially limited the entry of labor into various industries, and hence kept production low and inflated market prices, needed to be broken (Smith 1976, 132–45). Economic growth required freedom of trade and contract.

Rules enacted in 1811 left "free" apprenticeship unregulated by either a guild or the state; the duration of the apprenticeship, compensation, board, and employment conditions were all matters of voluntary agreement between the employer and apprentice, or more likely, his parents. Local authorities were charged only with seeing to it that no morally unfit or incompetent person take on apprentices.[10] This move weakened the formal power of the guilds, but did not eliminate their relevance. Consumers were loath to trust craftspeople who had not undergone the lengthy and rigorous apprenticeship training, and apprentices did not want to risk working for someone who did not belong to a guild. Most trainees therefore still apprenticed themselves to guild masters, to whom laws regulating the relationship between masters and apprentices within guilds still applied. Thus the guilds retained a practical control over craft training (Bergmann 1980), and children apprenticed to guild masters retained the customary protections.

Factories were different. The Prussian Civil Code explicitly excluded factory workers from the protections and privileges granted to guild members and their apprentices. The conditions of their employment were to be set by free contracts between them and their employers.[11] Children who worked in factories thereby enjoyed none of the legal protections that craft apprentices did. Moreover, their routinized tasks required little skill and none of the prospects for upward mobility that traditional craft training promised. This issue would soon occupy the attention even of liberals who had championed deregulation and free markets—particularly when they came to realize that factory children were growing up not only untrained in a practical craft but also with little or no basic elementary or religious schooling.

COMPULSORY SCHOOLING: REFORM AND REACTION

Before the rise of the Protestant religious movement known as Pietism, Prussian primary schools "sought primarily to train good Christians, not necessarily literate ones" (Melton 1988, 13). This began to change in the eighteenth century, when Pietist pedagogues, with the blessing of Prussian kings, took on leadership roles in school reform. Pietism stressed the importance of living a rigorously devout life characterized by "loving one's neighbor" (*Nächstenliebe*) and reading the Bible. Pietist schools were the first to teach children in groups rather than individually, use standardized textbooks, and require their teachers to be formally trained; they became the model for the reformed Prussian primary schools (*Volksschulen*) and inspiration for the spread of teacher training institutes (normal schools). Aiming to reconcile moral autonomy and coercion, the Pietist approach to education attempted to teach voluntary submission to God and one's superiors; the God-given inclination to discipline and obedience was to be discovered within the self through conscientious self-cultivation, not imposed from without. This ideology appealed to the abso-lutist rulers of the eighteenth and early nineteenth centuries, and contributed to their increased focus on popular schooling (Melton 1988).

Frederick II, better known as Frederick the Great, was less enamored with the movement than his father and grandfather had been, but it was he who appointed the Pietist theologian and school reformer Johann Julius Hecker to draft the famous General-Landschul-Reglement of 1763. Protestant children in rural areas were required to attend school from age five until thirteen, year-round, six hours a day, except in summer, when only three hours were required. Parents who failed to educate their children were subject to a fine. Teachers were appointed by provincial authorities; schools were to be inspected annu-ally and visited twice weekly by the local pastor. The curriculum was largely religious, but children were also taught to read, and emphasis was on incul-cating piety and obedience. In practice, this ambitious program went largely unrealized; its goals were undermined by an inadequate supply of trained teachers, inadequate funding and enforcement, resistance from petty nobles who feared a literate peasantry, and sporadic attendance by children whose help was needed at home (Melton 1988; Neugebauer 1985, 120–34, 178–89; La Vopa 1980, 12–13).

The compulsory schooling provision promulgated by Frederick's nephew, Frederick William II, as part of the Allgemeines Landrecht of 1794 established that all children be educated from the age of five until their pastor (*Seelsorger*) deemed them to have acquired knowledge sufficient for their station in life.[12] In practice, for children of the lower classes, this was usually around seven or eight (Luxem 1983; Meyer 1971). The Landrecht placed all public and private schools under the supervision of the local secular and religious authorities, required teachers to pass an examination, and required each householder, regardless of parental status, to pay a school tax toward the maintenance of the local teachers and school buildings.[13] The Landrecht established once and for all that schools were institutions of the state, but the law went largely unenforced (Herbst 2002). Prussia simply lacked the capacity to implement universal schooling, and it was actually Catholic Austria that had the most developed school system in Europe at the end of the eighteenth century (Melton 1988).

Prussia's primary school system began to improve in the nineteenth century with the Stein-Hardenberg reformers' renewed commitment to popular edu-cation. The reformers were spurred by long-standing concerns about social disorder and national disunity deepened by the immediate crisis of war. The perception that Prussian subjects had responded passively to French aggres-sion suggested to the Prussian leadership that a common sense of patriotism was essential for creating a no longer merely obedient, but also participatory citizenry willing to labor and sacrifice for the homeland. Alongside univer-sal military conscription, educational reforms were intended to build up and deepen this sense of national loyalty (Ramirez and Boli 1987; Kocka 1990, 24–26; Schleunes 1989; La Vopa 1980, 37–44). To ensure that the curriculum advanced these ends, supervision was enhanced with the appointment of local school committees (*Schulvorstände*), made up of town magistrates and councillors, private citizens, and the local priest or pastor (Anderson 1970, 262–65; La Vopa 1980, 41). The Ministry of Religion, Education, and Medical Affairs (Ministry of Education) was established in 1817. By 1820, the ministry was allocating some central government revenue to the construction and maintenance of school buildings and teacher training (Zilch 2014, 32; Anderson 1970, 275), although school funding and administration continued to be a largely local affair (Herbst 2002, 328).

Schooling reform was also conceived as a vehicle for combating the social disorder resulting from crisis-level overpopulation and economic transformation. Between 1750 and 1850, German population growth surpassed that of most other European countries (Kocka 1986, 292). The demise of the social commitments embedded in feudalism created a large population of vulnerable free laborers. Dislocations caused by the end of serfdom, rise of large-scale commercial agriculture, and nascent industrialization spurred the mass migration of agricultural workers and formerly independent craftspeople into the urban centers as well as mass emigration to the United States (Hubert 1998). Together with rapidly rising living costs, these demographic upheavals and economic changes brought about widespread unemployment, poverty, and various accompanying social ills (Conze 1954; Gray 1986). The new uprootedness of the lower classes contributed to what was widely perceived as "moral decline and psychological dissolution" among them (Nipperdey 1983, 198). Elites became panicked about "pauperization" and the social unraveling they saw, and many turned to public education to restore morality (*Sittlichkeit*) and order to lower-class life.

At first, under the leadership of Chancellors Stein and Hardenberg, who interpreted Prussia's crushing defeat by Napoléon as an indictment of its traditionalism, the direction of educational reforms took a progressive, enlightened, liberationist turn (Meyer 1971; Schleunes 1989). Stein, whose brief tenure ended when Napoléon forced him into exile in 1808, wrote in his final address before fleeing Berlin that his aim had been to "lift the disharmony among the people, to quash the unhappy conflict between the estates, so that each person may freely develop his capabilities in a moral direction, and in this way to compel the people to love their King and Fatherland and to gladly sacrifice their property and lives for them." For Stein (1960, 992), the key was education: "The best results can be expected from educating and instructing the youth. If their every intellectual ability is developed from the inside out on the basis of their natural human capacities . . . and if their impulse to love God, King and Fatherland, which has heretofore been neglected and met with shallow indifference, is carefully cultivated, then we can hope for the birth of a physically and morally vigorous generation and a better future."[14]

Stein and his appointees to the education division of the Ministry of the Interior—including the famous education reformers Wilhelm von Humboldt and Johann Wilhelm Süvern—were inspired by J. H. Pestalozzi and Johann Gottlieb Fichte. Pestalozzi was a Swiss pedagogue deeply influenced by Jean-Jacques Rousseau who pioneered a child-centered teaching method that stressed active learning along with the integration of intellectual, physical, and moral training. One of his most prominent disciples in Germany was Adolph Diesterweg, a pedagogue who published widely on the Pestalozzian method and passionately denounced industrial child labor. In his articles, Diesterweg decried the spiritually and intellectually stultifying effects of factory children's highly routinized tasks as well as the cruelty and futility of sending them to evening schools at the close of a twelve-hour workday. The system, he argued, violated the nature of the child—the natural inclination to physical movement as well as the need for varied activity and outdoor play (Diesterweg 1826, 167–73; Diesterweg 1828).[15]

Pestalozzi also influenced the thinking of Johann Gottlieb Fichte, a neo-Kantian idealist philosopher who popularized the view that mass education was essential for rebuilding Germany following the war. In an influential series of lectures delivered in 1807 and 1808 at the Academy of Sciences in Berlin, Fichte argued that "a total change of the existing system of education" was the "sole means of preserving the existence of the German nation" (Fichte, Jones, and Turnbull 1922, 13). The education system he called for should aim to fashion a new German subject—one no longer motivated by materialism and self-love, but instead by love of "the good" (21, 23), one capable of applying his imagination and independent thinking to the pursuit of "the social order of mankind as it ought to be . . . for the sake of the community" (32, 34). The newfound capacity for "living thought" and "clear knowledge" would bring the person into "immediate contact with God," and thus "education to true religion is . . . the final task of the new education" (37–38). Fichte exhorted his audiences to include the working masses in the new system of education "so that it is not the education of a single class, but the education of the nation"; otherwise, he said, the masses would "desert us and be lost on us" (15). Fichte's contention that freethinking yet "moral" people would constitute the new German nation expressed the ideological basis for progressive school reform, and later, Education Minister Altenstein's attempts to further compulsory schooling and protect working children.

Fichte's followers believed that education could simultaneously liberate the masses and elicit their loyal service to king and country (Meyer 1971). Like the Pietists of the previous century, they saw no contradiction between intellectual freedom and obedience to divine and secular authority, because a properly educated person would by necessity freely choose to live in harmony with their king and in accordance with God's plan (Levinger 1998, 263). This view was not shared by everyone, however. Conservatives in the king's administration had long feared that the type of mass education the reformers championed would foment disrespect for authority and tradition, popular discontent, social unrest, and possibly even revolution (Nipperdey 1977; Schleunes 1989; Kuhlemann 1992; Anderson 1970). These fears seemed validated in the late 1810s when student protests against a conservative resurgence in both academia and government culminated in the murder of a conservative playwright, August von Kotzebue. After a commission appointed by the king concluded that "the growing moral corruption" had emerged from "the school and educational system of the Prussian state," the administration began to clamp down (Schleunes 1989, 94). An 1822 order restricted the normal school curriculum to basic subjects. This order was drafted by a leader of the conservative reaction in the 1820s, Ludolf Beckedorff, who until 1827 was the Education Ministry official in charge of public primary schools. For conservatives like him, primary education was not supposed to cultivate the inherent human capacities of the masses; it was supposed to uphold the natural inequality of the estates, restrict intellectual freedom, and impose order.

Even in the midst of these debates, primary education reform proceeded steadily. Altenstein, a progressive member of the Stein-Hardenberg reform party and close friend of Fichte, had been appointed head of the new Education Ministry in 1817. In 1825, he issued an order extending the compulsory education provisions of the Allgemeines Landrecht to the recently created Rhine Province. Normal schools proliferated under his tenure, and the number of teachers grew 40 percent between 1816 and 1846 (Schleunes 1989, 110). Standardized teacher examinations were instituted in 1826 (Keller 1873). Even primary school (Volksschul) teachers were trained to cultivate pupils' knowledge, understanding, engagement, and capacity for independent thinking rather than rote memorization (Barkin 1983). These efforts seem to have had a positive impact on education among the general population. School enrollment increased steadily and, until 1870, exceeded that of other European nations (see figure 2.1). By 1850, 80 percent of adults in Prussia could read versus about 55 to 60 percent in England and France (Flora 1972, 304). The quality of the primary schools varied dramatically, however, and generally remained poor in rural areas, particularly in the east (Anderson 1970, 269–71). Education was still in the hands of local governments, and advances depended heavily on local will and tax revenue (Lindert 2004, 121). Still, the Prussian education system developed an international reputation for excellence, and French, British, and US school reformers journeyed from afar to study the administration and pedagogy of the Prussian Volksschulen, high schools (*Gymnasien*), and normal schools (Barkin 1983, 38).

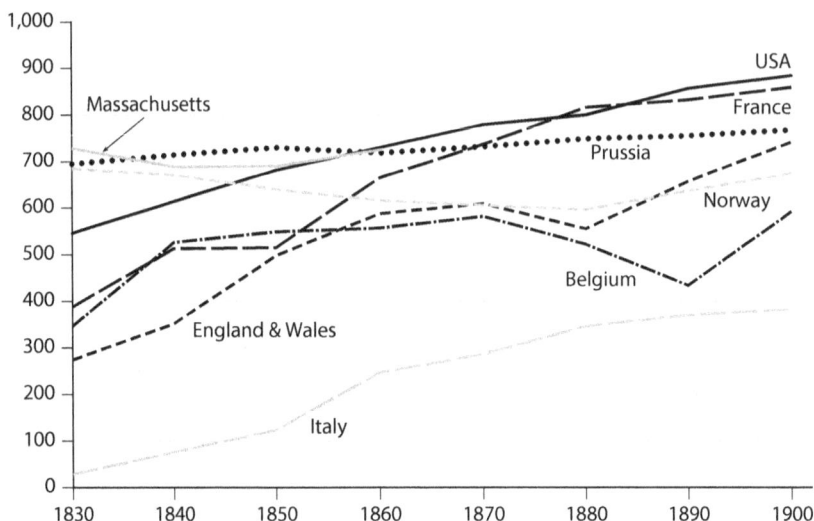

FIGURE 2.1. Primary school enrollment, per one thousand children. *Sources*: Lindert 2004, 90; Fishlow 1966, 43; Vinovskis 1972, 512.
Note: Massachusetts figures are children ages five to nineteen for 1830 and 1840, and children five to fifteen for 1850 and 1860. All others are children five to fourteen. Norwegian and US figures are for public schools only; all others are for both public and private schools. Data for Italy 1840 and the United States 1840 and 1860 are missing.

In sum, different ideological motives underlay early nineteenth-century Prussian educational reform. Progressives saw universal education as a way to liberate and invigorate the masses by cultivating their human capabilities while inspiring their loyalty to king and country. Conservatives thought popular education should impart only basic knowledge and teach lower-class children to accept unquestioningly their lot in life. Both sides, though, thought mass education was essential for instilling in Prussia's geographically, religiously, and culturally fragmented population a common sense of national identity and patriotism. Both sides viewed public education as a powerful tool for creating moral and loyal Prussian subjects. To reap the full benefits of this, the state would have to ensure that its educational system reached everyone—even the poorest children who toiled in mills and factories instead of going to school.

Child Labor Policy Reform in Prussia, 1817–39

The first phase of Prussian child labor reform spanned 1817 through 1839, and despite the oft-vaunted efficiency of the Prussian bureaucracy, was marked by false starts and delays. Highly aware of reform in England yet hesitant to initiate changes that would compromise Prussia's economic competitiveness, officials limited themselves to investigation at first. Liberal economic philosophies had taken hold, and leading Prussian officials tended to view market regulation skeptically. Furthermore, the assumption that work was normal and actually beneficial to children predominated. The Allgemeines Landrecht formalized this tenet in clauses qualifying compulsory education requirements with the caveat that children who were needed to help with industrial homework or farming could attend special Sunday schools rather than regular Volksschulen.[16] Industrial schools operated on the assumption that early labor instilled in poor children the work ethic they needed to achieve self-sufficiency and contribute to economic growth (Thies 1988). Nineteenth-century children's literature was replete with stories and images that valorized industriousness and condemned idleness, even for the very young (Nassen 1988; Pech 1988). Even progressive Education Minister Altenstein asserted that factory work encouraged children to develop diligence, endurance, and a sense of order early on, and maintained that it should be tolerated if it could be combined with school attendance and was not abusive.[17] He and his contemporaries by no means wished to abolish child labor in factories, they merely wanted to regulate it. The cultural shift to viewing children as "priceless" objects of parental love, universally unfit for gainful employment (Zelizer 1985), was still on the distant horizon.

INVESTIGATION AND INACTION, 1817–28

The Prussian government conducted surveys of the child labor situation in 1817 and 1824. The first was initiated by Chancellor Hardenberg. In September 1817, Hardenberg surveyed the Oberpräsidenten of five industrializing provinces to collect information on factory conditions.[18] These inquiries were conducted during the severe economic downturn of 1816–17, "the year without summer," when crop failures compounded existing economic hardship following the lifting of Napoléon's continental blockade (Webb 2002). In 1816, poor harvests caused food price increases just when many industrial workers could least afford them; the result was widespread hunger (Bass 1991; Rowe 2003). It was this lack of self-sufficiency that first turned Hardenberg's attention to industrial working conditions. One of the roots of the current crisis, he argued, was child labor: "Each child is an additional tie that binds the worker to the factory, and these people, who have been raised by the factory, soon become accustomed to their dependence on it."[19] According to the reform-minded chancellor, the factory system had created a whole new stock of people whose factory training had come at the expense of their civic and human education. The state must step in on the basis of two prerogatives: education and military conscription. Factory owners must be made aware that they would no longer be able to count on the state's support if they continued to undermine its basic interests. Thus the problem definition motivating Hardenberg's inquiry was

FIGURE 2.2. Karl vom Stein zum Altenstein, Prussian minister of religious, educational, and medical affairs. *Source*: Österreichische Nationalbibliothek.

the notion that the de-skilling effects of industrial child labor eroded the state's human resources. Despite detailed and thoughtful responses from the five governors, however, Hardenberg neglected to push forward the child labor issue as a conservative backlash forced him to abandon much of his reform agenda (Hermann 2003).[20]

After Hardenberg's death in 1822, Education Minister Altenstein took up the cause. A wealthy member of the Franconian landed aristocracy, Altenstein had risen rapidly through the ranks as Hardenberg's protégé; in 1808, at the age of thirty-eight, he was appointed finance minister, only to be forced to step down two years later, in part for his failure to raise enough funds for the war reparations demanded by France. Characterized by historians as enlightened and thoughtful, but mild mannered, reclusive, and indecisive, he seems to have been somewhat unsuited for the contentious politics of postwar Prussia. After becoming education minister in 1817, he enjoyed greater success, particularly in advancing the kingdom's higher education institutions (Goldschmidt 1893; Hömig 2015).

A longtime member of the Stein-Hardenberg reform party, Altenstein viewed public education as a crucial engine for a revitalized, productive, and unified postwar Prussian nation (Schuurmans 1998). During the Napoleonic era, he had accompanied the temporarily exiled Hardenberg to Riga, where the two men each wrote their own memorandums (*Denkschriften*) outlining their respective visions for the future of Prussia. Altenstein's memo makes it clear how much the statesman was influenced by his friend, mentor, and sometime collaborator, the philosopher Fichte. Prussia, Altenstein wrote, was a state without a nation, an administration without a community (Altenstein 1931, 393). To construct that community would require tapping into the Prussian people's productive and creative potential. In addition to various economic and social reforms, Altenstein stressed the need to improve the education system so that it would "train [pupils'] ability to think, leading them to the higher and the intellectual" (458). Nearly twenty years later, as education minister, he echoed this sentiment when he observed that elementary school teachers should strive to "awaken" their pupils' "latent powers" (quoted in Hömig 2015, 234). As minister, he supported the progressive reformist education agenda and promoted the spread of Pestalozzian teaching methods (241–42).

This does not mean that Altenstein did not prioritize inculcating piety and morality in lower-class children. Like Fichte, he argued that the state should regard the advancement of "religiosity as its highest goal" and focus on cultivating pupils' innate spiritual receptiveness (Altenstein 1931, 490). Only a broad spiritual awakening would yield a true Prussian nation, which Altenstein (370) defined as "a union of people inspired by the same spirit"—a spirit that would replace narrow self-interest with a collective dedication to a higher good. Later, as education minister, he stressed that the schools should ensure that the people "can and should serve God, the king and the fatherland, as well as themselves, with a strong, intelligent love, awakened spirit, and good feelings" (quoted in Hömig 2015, 238). The Pietist idea that obedience should be freely given—not exacted by force or dull indoctrination—is the clear subtext here (see also Hömig 2015, 241). In sum, the problem definition motivating much of Altenstein's domestic reform agenda was the idea that the Prussian people lacked a moral and cohesive sense of nationhood, and that achieving this would require them to acquire a humanist-Christian education that would awaken feelings of piety, patriotism, and commitment to the greater good of the community. These ideas, which he shared with the Stein-Hardenberg reform party, remained stable throughout his career and would strongly influence his approach to the child labor problem.

Altenstein first turned his attention to child labor in 1824. Appalled to learn that a spinning mill near Düsseldorf was working children through the night (Anton 1953, 21), he sent a survey to the governments of ten industrializing districts to determine whether such abuses were common.[21] The questions reflected a holistic interpretation of the child labor problem. Altenstein paid particular attention to whether the health of working children was being compromised, but also addressed the impact of early employment on children's education and moral condition. The results of the survey revealed that conditions were variable, but extremely bad in some places, especially the Rhineland.[22] Numerous health problems were observed: on the one hand, general ill health was brought on by poverty, hunger, and neglect; on the other, there were workplace-specific ailments, including respiratory problems caused by breathing bad air and poisoning caused by handling hazardous materials. The Cologne government reported that children began working in cotton mills at age six and worked from thirteen to fourteen hours per day; their physical condition appeared "miserable," and their moral condition was "raw." Children in Aachen also started factory work at age six, endured up to twelve-hour days, and exhibited "dull eyes, sallow appearance, [and] scrofulous disorders." Working with the opposite sex corrupted their moral purity, leading to premature sexual development and carnal "trespasses."[23] The picture painted by the Düsseldorf government was equally bleak. Some employers had established factory schools, but children typically attended either sporadically, or only one or two hours a day, and usually after a full day in the factory.

After the first two survey responses, Altenstein approached Interior Minister Schuckmann with his intention of drafting a child labor law.[24] Decision-making in the upper reaches of the Prussian bureaucracy was carried out collectively, with each minister and sometimes his top deputies weighing in on decisions relevant to their domains. Each responsible minister had to approve a new policy proposal before it could be presented to the king for his assent. Essentially, each was empowered to act as a veto point on change (Tsebelis 2002). The result was an institutional governance structure vulnerable to political impasses, blocking, and stalling (Weber 1978, 222, 271–82; Müller 1984, 135; Kiser and Schneider 1994; Beck 1995, 128). In the case of child labor policy, the responsible parties included the minister of education, interior minister, and finance minister, and so Altenstein needed to win their approval to proceed with his legislation.

Despite his privileged field position at the top of the state hierarchy, Altenstein faced significant difficulties recruiting allies to his reform agenda. One reason is the institutional barriers erected by collegialism; it was easy for the ministers to block one another. Another is the reactionary political culture that followed the Stein-Hardenberg reform period. After the death or departure of most of the progressive reformers, the upper bureaucracy came to be dominated by conservatives and orthodox economic liberals, both of whom rejected the humanistic ideals of their predecessors. Altenstein was increasingly surrounded by ideological opponents, even within his ministry. For example, when Beckedorff (1827b, 174, 177), who had been appointed to the Education Ministry in 1821 as a counterweight to Altenstein, read the survey responses that Altenstein viewed as demanding legislative intervention, he concluded that child labor conditions outside the Rhineland were generally not so bad and publicly opposed a general child labor law of the kind Altenstein was now seeking.

Another leading figure of the reaction was Interior Minister Schuckmann. By the mid-1820s, the relationship between Altenstein and Schuckmann had been tense for years.[25] The latter's sensibilities were authoritarian and regressive; he agreed with the reformers that society had become dangerously amoral and atomized, but believed that the solution was to return to the paternalism of the past (Müsebeck 1918, 124–25). Yet like many, he combined this social conservatism with economic liberalism and was influenced in his economic thinking by his deputy, the staunchly liberal commerce councillor Peter Beuth (Preller 1954). Citing concerns that any child labor regulation would undermine Prussia's ability to withstand English competition—a worry that deeply preoccupied Beuth (1826)—Schuckmann stalled. He wanted, he said, to wait for additional reports.[26] Several months later, after seeing more reports, he tersely announced that he wanted Beuth to gather information about the economic impact of recent child labor legislation in England and the child labor situation in the Rhineland.[27] These delay tactics stymied reform for the next three years.

THE ALTENSTEIN PROGRAM

In 1828, the child labor issue was resurrected by an unexpected party. In a report to Frederick William III, Lieutenant General Heinrich Wilhelm von Horn noted that the industrial regions of the monarchy had failed to meet their military draft quotas, and that as a result, their shortfalls had to be made up by agricultural districts. Horn connected this failure with the pervasive "evil" that many children in the factory districts were forced to work at night, thus causing them to grow up feeble and unfit for military service. Horn's observations dismayed the king: "I can tolerate such practices even less given that the physical education of our tender youth is thereby undermined, creating the danger that, in the factory regions, the future generation will be even weaker and more crippled than the current one reportedly is." He ordered Altenstein

TABLE 2.1. Citations and Frames in the Writings of Prussian Child Labor Policy Entrepreneurs

	Altenstein proposal (1828)	Bodelschwingh proposal (1835)
CITATIONS		
Insiders	100%	100%
Local government / officials	35%	57%
National government / officials	28%	8%
Chambers of commerce / individual industrialists	–	15%
Domestic law	42%	24%
Outsiders	0%	0%
FRAMES		
Simple frames	100%	100%
Health/safety	43%	–
Education	47%	91%
Morals	26%	21%
Fundamental frames	3%	24%
Social order/criminality	–	12%
Economic prosperity/competitiveness	–	12%
National security/defense	3%	–

Note: Percentages refer to the amount of total citation or framing text devoted to the particular category of citation or frame. Category percentages do not add up to 100 percent because text portions were often coded in more than one way.

and Schuckmann to look into how the problem might be addressed through legislation.[28]

Altenstein responded to the directive with enthusiasm and lost no time preparing a proposal for a child labor law. His detailed plan offers a revealing picture of how he translated his definition of the problem into a concrete policy program. Altenstein argued that the issue lay not with child employment per se but instead with excessive and abusive forms of it. Acknowledging that the responses to his survey had revealed conditions that were not uniformly bad, he nevertheless asserted that on the whole, the "dark side" of child labor had emerged as dominant. Altenstein defined abusive child employment as that which was premature, unhealthy, or overly arduous; taking place in the company of immoral adults; or causing the neglect of the child's religious and intellectual upbringing. Relying mainly on simple health, education, and morality frames (see table 2.1), he presented factory labor as damaging in several important ways: it made children physically weak and unhealthy, undermined their spiritual and intellectual capacities by creating barriers to school attendance, spoiled their childlike cheerfulness, encouraged them to engage in mischief and brutality, and morally corrupted them by tempting them to smoke, drink spirits, and commit "carnal sins."[29]

Altenstein's policy plan centered on establishing local commissions made up of local officials, factory owners, and "several of the most diligent, prudent and righteous factory workers." The proposed commissions would be responsible for implementing regulations on factory child labor in accordance with local conditions and needs, and were clearly modeled on the local school committees established during the Hardenberg reform period. But although he placed great stock in granting flexibility to accommodate local circumstances, Altenstein's proposal nevertheless included numerous requirements and restrictions. For example, it set the minimum working age at eight (with limited exceptions); allowed only half-day employment for children age eight to fourteen (again with limited exceptions); prohibited night work for children; mandated that time be set aside every day for eating, recreation, and schooling; required factory owners to ensure that children were clean and properly fed; mandated that children be able to read and write, and undergo a medical examination before being allowed to work; and (reiterating existing rules) required children to receive religious instruction and attend school until their priest or pastor (Seelsorger) deemed them to have acquired knowledge sufficient for their station in life. It also required factory owners to keep their buildings ventilated and clean, and suggested a system in which child workers would monitor one another's behavior to enforce discipline as well as prevent cursing, smoking, and drinking spirits. Altenstein's proposal was unusual relative to British laws, and later Prussian and French proposals, not only in its detail but also in proposing measures to safeguard children's morality, shield them from uncouth adults, and combat inappropriate behavior.

Altenstein's plan reflected his human development definition of the child labor problem by placing equal weight on protecting children's minds, bodies, and souls. Whereas Hardenberg had conceived the problem primarily in economic terms, and the king conceived it as a military issue, Altenstein viewed excessive child labor as a threat to the overall spiritual, moral, physical, and intellectual quality of working-class Prussians. For him, protecting working children was part of the larger agenda of creating a new and improved citizen-subject. Elementary education for factory children was not a method of thought control but rather part of a holistic program to foster intellectual and moral development among them, and create a productive and spiritually unified nation.

After a six-month delay, Interior Minister Schuckmann responded to Altenstein's proposal. His reaction was mixed, but uncooperative overall. Schuckmann began by arguing that not only factories but also elite Gymnasien produced weaklings unfit for military service—a charge that must have rankled Altenstein given that the development of the Gymnasien was one of his signature achievements. Although Schuckmann expressed a general willingness to support a child labor law that included some of the sanitation, minimum working age, and education requirements that Altenstein had proposed, he declared that now was not the time to draft a bill. This job should instead be handed over to the Ministry of State, which was a consortium of all the separate ministries.[30] This proposal was an attempt to wrest control over the contents of the law from Altenstein's hands.

Altenstein had failed to secure a productive alliance with the interior minister. Building alliances with conservatives like Schuckmann and economic liberals like Beuth would have been difficult in any case, but the rhetorical strategies that Altenstein used did not help. First, aside from a pro forma summary of the king's order and the military concerns expressed in it, Altenstein deployed no fundamental frame. His argument was limited to simple health, morality, and education frames, and neglected to directly link these concerns with the interests of elites or the state.[31] He did not, for instance, contend that regulating child labor might enhance human capital and thus be good for the economy—a line of argument that Schuckmann and Beuth might have been receptive to. His near-exclusive use of simple frames must have given the impression that he either regarded poor children's holistic well-being as an end unto itself or was still motivated by the now-defunct progressive ideology of the Stein-Hardenberg era. In either case, Altenstein's framing was out of sync with the prevailing discursive opportunity structure.

Second, Altenstein failed to take advantage of citation opportunities. He did cite the king's order as well as Prussia's mandatory schooling law as justifications for taking action. And he cited in general terms the survey responses from the municipal governments in Aachen, Arnsberg, Cologne, Düsseldorf, and Potsdam. Yet he did not specifically credit the local officials whose ideas he borrowed for his policy program. For example, the commission idea originated with the Düsseldorf government's report (Anton 1953, 42–43), but Altenstein did not say so. Neither did he mention that the idea that younger children be restricted to half-day employment had come from the Erfurt and Merseburg governments (45), or that the notion that working children should undergo medical examination had come from Münster, Arnsberg, Cologne, and Erfurt (44–45). By failing to cite the sources of these ideas, Altenstein was missing an opportunity to rhetorically "reach down" (White 1992, 262–65; Lachmann 2003, 355) for allies at the local level, choosing instead to present the proposal as his brainchild alone. This only isolated him and allowed his opponents to dismiss his plans without addressing the fact that on-the-ground officials had deemed them necessary.

Finally, Altenstein missed a valuable opportunity to compromise with Schuckmann. The latter had, after all, expressed a grudging willingness to support child labor regulation, even while trying to remove the matter from

Altenstein's control. Altenstein could have come back to him with a more modest plan, framed in a way that fit with Schuckmann's priorities. Instead, Altenstein's response was oddly feeble. Ten months after receiving Schuckmann's letter, he finally responded, surrendering on all points and asking Schuckmann to take the lead on bringing child labor legislation to the Ministry of State.[32] This was evidently never done, and reform stalled again. In sum, although collegialism and resurgent conservatism created challenging hurdles, Altenstein's failure to compromise, cite allies, and use frames in ways that fit with the discursive opportunity structure made success unlikely.

ERNST KELLER'S FACT-FINDING TRIP, 1833-34

Despite neglecting to pursue legislation in a goal-directed way, Altenstein continued collecting information on the child labor problem. In 1833, he sent one of his deputies, Ernst Keller, on a fact-finding investigation to the Rhineland. The Rhineland, which included the cities of Koblenz, Cologne, Düsseldorf, Trier, and Aachen, was the most industrialized region in Germany in the nineteenth century. Its territory was granted to Prussia at the Congress of Vienna in 1815. Before that, Napoléon had introduced major political and economic reforms to the region, many of which disadvantaged the landed aristocracy while strengthening the political and economic position of the bourgeoisie.[33] Most important, Napoléon's continental blockade greatly stimulated industrial production—especially textile manufacturing—in the Rhine region.[34] Although many of the Napoleonic reforms were reversed after the Congress of Vienna, the class of landowning capitalists created under his reign retained voting rights and representation in local and provincial governing bodies, including the provincial legislature (Landtag) (Boch 1991, 39; Kitchen 2006, 15). After the Napoleonic Wars, aided by a German customs union (*Zollverein*) and new protective tariff, the region entered the early phase of the Prussian "takeoff" period. Production, trade, capital accumulation, and investment all began to ramp up (R. Tilly 1990). The textile and small metal goods industries, both of which relied heavily on child and female labor in both factories and cottage industry, were particularly successful.

Keller's report provides a rich and detailed picture of child labor conditions in the Rhineland in the early 1830s.[35] In the absence of any type of uniform regulations, conditions proved highly variable. For instance, one of the worst factories that Keller visited was a textile mill in the town of Gladbach, owned by the brothers Busch, two well-known Protestants with a reputation for piety. Keller reported that the mill resembled a prisoners' pit (*Mördergrube*) more than a factory. The ceilings were so low that one had to bow one's head while walking, and rooms were so crowded that getting one's clothes caught in the machinery was a serious concern. The air was thick with particulate matter, and the walls and furnishings were covered with dust. The children, hollow eyed and pale, were the epitome of suffering. But Keller's impression of many of the other factories was more positive. At a cotton mill in Bonn, for example, 150 workers, including 60 to 70 children age eight and older, worked in well-lit and spacious rooms. The children appeared healthy and comfortable, and though they did not attend school, some were released to attend catechism class daily from 11 a.m. to noon.[36]

One issue that concerned Keller deeply, even in the better factories where children appeared reasonably healthy, was the lack of educational opportunities for them. In Düsseldorf in 1834, nearly 23 percent of school-age children attended school only intermittently and nearly 10 percent did not attend at all (Luxem 1983, 75). Many of the children with whom Keller spoke seemed quite ignorant. At the Bonn cotton mill, Keller questioned a few of the more "open and alert-looking" children about a few aspects of daily life and general knowledge. The children were either unable to understand his questions or unable to formulate an articulate reply. Alarmed by what he called the "brutalization [*Verwilderung*] of the next generation," he raised the issue with the factory's foreman and a local professor. They confirmed that no effort was made to enforce mandatory school attendance in Bonn, and lamented that lower-class youths were succumbing to beggary and demoralization. The professor had been trying for years to no avail to interest members of Bonn's upper class in establishing schools and mutual aid societies for these children and their parents. But in Bonn, "a largely Catholic city," the local population was "used to beggary" and failed to sense any urgent need for change.[37]

In addition to the lack of education for working children, Keller was, like Hardenberg before him, alarmed by the de-skilling effects of monotonous factory labor. The division of labor in most modern establishments limited children's work experience to extremely repetitive tasks and precluded a more well-rounded training program. In nearly all the factories that Keller visited, children were so narrowly trained that their ability to do any other type of work in the future was seriously compromised. In the factories, he argued, "one person is assigned to function as a lever his whole life long, and another person a hook or crank. It is completely dispensable and coincidental, that this lever or hook or crank also happens to possess a human nature; technology awaits the moment when it can replace the human beings, who represent levers, hooks and cranks, with actual levers, hooks and cranks" (Keller, quoted in Kastner 2004, 95). The best these children could hope for was to avoid losing any of their five senses and developing thoroughly "worm-eaten" souls and bodies.

Although concerned about the human consequences of the division of labor and child employment, Keller was at bottom an economic liberal who saw changes in the mode of production brought on by industrial capitalism as necessary and inevitable. In spite of the tragic conditions he acknowledged, Keller, like Beckedorff before him, concluded that the state's role in protecting child laborers should be limited (Kastner 2004, 81–82). In this time of conservative reaction and orthodox liberal ascendency, Altenstein's progressive reform agenda received little support, even from colleagues in his own ministry.

THE BODELSCHWINGH PROGRAM

In 1835, it had been eighteen years since Chancellor Hardenberg first broached the need for child labor legislation in Prussia, yet no legislation had been passed. In the midst of this inertia, Bodelschwingh decided to pursue a child labor law for his province. A member of the Westphalian landed aristocracy and a Lutheran liberal who could "quote Adam Smith as easily as the Bible," Bodelschwingh was concerned about the impact of child labor on the education of working people (Kastner 2004, 98). He was among those German liberals who rejected absolute laissez-faire and instead saw the state as bearing a responsibility to stem the rising tide of popular discontent through positive measures (Sheehan 1978). He was, ultimately, a political moderate at heart. Later, as interior minister during the revolution of 1848, he convinced Frederick William IV to make certain democratic concessions, but remained steadfast in his loyalty to the king and opposition to the revolutionary agitators. His writings from that time reveal him to be sympathetic to demands for a constitution and press freedoms, but disdainful and afraid of the working-class "rabble," which had seized the opportunity to protest employment conditions, poverty, and joblessness (Clark 2006, 469–71; Bahne 1996).[38]

As an appointee of the royal government, the Oberpräsident represented both the central government to the province, and the provincial and local officials to the royal administration. Bodelschwingh was thus responsible for carrying out Berlin's decrees in the Rhine Province, but he could also recommend provincial legislation to the royal ministers—although only in a supplicating or advisory capacity (Koselleck 1967, 222; Unruh 1985). Where appropriate and only with the ministers' approval, he could also propose legislation to the provincial legislature, which could in turn appeal to the central government for permission to enact new laws. His role was established by official protocol and supported by formalized channels of communication (Gräff et al. 1839). Through these officials, then, the central governmental policy field institutionally penetrated the local policy field, and vice versa. Bodelschwingh's position at the overlap of the local and central policy fields was therefore different from Altenstein's. The latter was relatively isolated at the top; the former was enmeshed in a dense network that spanned multiple levels. His field position would soon prove advantageous.

In keeping with Bodelschwingh's long-standing interest in primary schooling, the initial program that he articulated was largely an education measure;

FIGURE 2.3. Ernst von Bodelschwingh, Oberpräsident of the Rhineland. *Source*: Friedrich Jentzen / Stadtarchiv Trier, Lith 12 GR.

it would have required children to attend three years of school before commencing a factory job, limited their working hours to ten per day, and required them to attend school for eight hours per week if employed. Before sending the proposal to Berlin, Bodelschwingh solicited comments from the district administrations in Aachen, Cologne, and Düsseldorf.[39] In his letter to the district officials, he framed child labor squarely as a problem of education; regulation was needed because early employment was making it impossible for poor children to fulfill their compulsory schooling requirements. This simple education frame was grounded in a prevalent discourse that treated primary schooling as a solution to various social ills, including a perceived lack of morality among the poor (Fichte, Jones, and Turnbull 1922; Kocka 1990, 471; Ramirez and Boli 1987; Schleunes 1989; Stein 1960).

Bodelschwingh used his field position as mediator between the local and central policy fields to create an alliance with district officials in support of child labor reform. After revising his plan to reflect some of their suggestions—in particular, reducing the daily working hours from ten to seven and replacing the requirement that children attend school while working with a prohibition on their working while religious instruction was taking place in town—he sent it to the appropriate minister in Berlin. This was none other than Education Minister Altenstein, whose permission Bodelschwingh needed to take his next planned step: presenting the bill to the provincial Landtag.[40] Bodelschwingh included an introduction in which he emphasized the district officials' input and support; this represented more than half the text he devoted to citations (see table 2.1). In stark contrast to Altenstein, his citation of these actors' contributions created the impression that he had allies at the local level.

Bodelschwingh did not, however, directly solicit employers' opinions about his proposed law. During their occupation of the Rhineland, the French had introduced chambers of commerce (*Handelskammern*) to inform government about economic matters. The chambers' role was advisory, and though they persisted in the Rhineland after 1815, their influence declined markedly (Zeise 1976). In Prussia's absolute monarchy, then, the business field had little overlap with the policy field; policy making was insulated within a largely autonomous state controlled by bureaucrats. Bodelschwingh thus had little reason to solicit the chambers' input. Acting on its own, however, the Aachen government asked the Aachen and Eupen Handelskammern for their opinions. The two chambers took opposite stances.[41] The Aachen chamber declared wholehearted support; it even went further than Bodelschwingh by recommending that all children be prohibited from working before age nine, and that children between nine and twelve be allowed to work only half days.[42] A solid elementary education for working-class children would serve bourgeois interests, it argued, by improving popular morality, creating opportunities for individual workers, and combating social disorder, idleness, and begging. In contrast, the Eupen chamber opposed many of Bodelschwingh's proposals because it believed them "highly damaging to industry." If children were to work only ten hours per day, the chamber contended, they would "spend the rest of the time playing in the streets or swarming about doing mischief, ripping their clothes, whereas currently they help to support the household of their parents."[43]

This divergence of opinion warns against assumptions about capitalists' attitudes toward child labor regulation in early nineteenth-century Prussia. The capitalist class had not yet formed any unified agenda in regard to state intervention into employment conditions, and in any case, the new industrial bourgeoisie did not yet exert strong and direct influence over policy making. Bodelschwingh was free to accept or ignore the chambers' recommendations. Hence, though he followed the Aachen chamber's suggestion to reduce his proposed limitation on children's daily working hours from ten to seven, he utterly ignored the Eupen objections. Skeptical employers exercised no direct influence over the first round of child labor legislation in Prussia. As we will see in chapter 3, this was not the case in France or Belgium.

In his introduction to his revised proposal, Bodelschwingh deployed two fundamental frames that linked child labor regulation with elite interests. For one, a law was needed to protect the economic interests of employers who were unwilling to exploit little children, but were being undercut by their more ruthless competitors. More fundamentally, reining in child labor was a matter of security. Connecting the simple frame of education to the fundamental frame of social control, he wrote, "only a thorough religious and moral education of the youth will save the factory regions from an overpopulation of crude individuals, drawn to every excess, who, as recent experiences have repeatedly demonstrated, will sooner or later avenge themselves through violent uprisings against those who abused them irresponsibly in their youth."[44]

Bodelschwingh probably did not choose this social order frame in a strategic way; instead, this statement likely expresses the problem definition actually motivating him. First, the framing was unlikely to resonate with his primary audience, Education Minister Altenstein, whose progressive view of popular schooling was well known. Second, Bodelschwingh used no other fundamental frames in any of his related writings; in other words, he did not tailor his frames to audience expectations or changing situations in a calculated way. Third, his interest in promoting popular education to instill morality in the lower-class population appears to have been consistent and of long duration. Earlier in his career, as mayor of Trier, he had made schooling one of his top policy priorities (Gerhardt 1950, 38); moreover, he stuck to the notion that a child labor law should be fundamentally an education measure throughout the reform process. Furthermore, like many elites, he was deeply concerned about threats to social order posed by the increasingly pauperized lower classes—a situation exacerbated in the Rhineland by hostility on the part of the Catholic majority toward the mostly Protestant (and often nonnative) ruling class. In 1839, in reference to the security situation in the Rhineland, he wrote that "the lack of restraint over the lower popular classes . . . encourages minor excesses which, if they were to become commonplace, could all too easily lead to greater excesses" (quoted in Lüdtke 1989, 77, 185). If a greater military and police presence was needed to quell disturbances, a religious and moral education would help prevent such disturbances from arising in the first place.

Whether strategically chosen or not, Bodelschwingh's social control frame fit with the prevailing discursive opportunity structure, which was at the time dominated by fear around the perceived threat posed by an increasingly restless underclass (Nipperdey 1996, 212; Schleunes 1989, 115–18; Steinmetz 1993, 55–69; Tilly 1984, 2–3). His comment about "recent experiences" refers to an upwelling of riots and clashes with authorities in Germany, and particularly the Rhineland, in the 1820s and early 1830s (Dowe 1970, 28–35; Bass 1991; Sperber 1991; Brophy 2007; Tilly 1980). These uprisings were frequently political, led by students and intellectuals against repressive government policies, but many also included workers protesting high grain prices and unfair labor practices (Tilly 1980, 154). The weaving centers around Aachen and Eupen formed the northeastern segment of the so-called triangle of trouble, which extended south into Belgium (Haase 2000). For example, a major riot erupted in August 1830 when the wages of workers at an Aachen textile factory were docked for supposedly shoddy workmanship. The civic guard was called in, the rebellion was quelled, and 150 participants were arrested (Rowe 2003, 276–77). A smaller riot broke out in the town of Elberfeld, near Düsseldorf, the following night (Bass 1991, 328). Because disturbances such as these came on the heels of the 1830 July Revolution in France, some elites feared that they could evolve into a full-blown revolution. Political scientist Robert von Mohl (1835, 151–52), for instance, warned of a proletariat becoming "embittered against the prevailing order," and conspiring to commit violence against employers and potentially the state as well. Similarly, Cologne officials worried that factory children "will not only fail to realize the purpose of their own lives, but will also prove dangerous to human society as a whole."[45] A "religious and moral education" for working children was one way of addressing these new threats.

ALTENSTEIN THE VETO PLAYER, BODELSCHWINGH THE CREATIVE PROBLEM SOLVER

After Bodelschwingh sent his proposal to Berlin, progress again stalled. Even after several reminders, Altenstein did not respond.[46] Historians have long puzzled over Altenstein's strange neglect of Bodelschwingh's proposal (Preller 1954; Adolphs 1972; Meyer 1971; Thies 1988; Kastner 2004). It becomes less mysterious when we recognize that even though both Altenstein and Bodelschwingh wanted to regulate child labor, their definitions of the problem and their practical solutions were quite different. Altenstein not only envisioned a holistic approach to tackling child labor but also was firmly committed to creating local enforcement commissions that would include representatives of capital, labor, and the state. Bodelschwingh's plan, in contrast, narrowly stressed education—especially religious education—and included no new enforcement mechanisms. For these reasons, an alliance with Bodelschwingh may have seemed unattractive to Altenstein. Still, his decision to ignore Bodelschwingh rather than work with him shows a lack of alliance-building skill. Bodelschwingh was a willing compromiser who would likely have been happy to take many of Altenstein's suggestions if it meant securing a valuable alliance; it was Altenstein who had no interest in compromising with the Oberpräsident or joining forces with him—and through him, the Rhineland Landtag. It was a major missed opportunity for the education minister. Had Altenstein behaved differently, child labor regulation would likely have come about sooner, and a more comprehensive law would quite possibly have been passed.

Despite repeatedly running up against Altenstein's veto power, Bodelschwingh did not give up. When an opportunity to form a different alliance presented itself in March 1837, he was quick to seize it. That month, a textile manufacturer named Johannes Schuchard published an article in a Rhenish newspaper in which he passionately called for legislation to protect children in factories. Schuchard represented Barmen from 1826 until 1843 in the Rhineland Landtag, where he ardently defended the interests of the dwindling group of manufacturers to which he belonged that still relied on the putting-out system (Boch 1991, 75–84). He thus clearly had a strong financial stake in imposing regulations on factories, which were rapidly displacing organized cottage industry. His article painted child labor in factories in the direst terms: "The humanitarian shudders, when he looks to the future and sees . . . the huge, massive buildings multiplying, in which a mass of children are locked in from early morning till late at night," deprived of air, sun, and everything else that children need to "thrive and be happy," often because their "work-averse parents" choose begging over fulfilling their parental responsibilities. "The spirit of the age has befriended industry . . . lifting it, like in England, onto an iron throne, to rule like a mighty despot over the land: since such a power cannot be resisted, so I beg you, friends of humanity and of the King, to ask our lawgiver[s] to have mercy upon the little ones."[47]

Schuchard's intervention soon turned him into an essential ally for Bodelschwingh. For more than a year, the Oberpräsident had been awaiting a response from Berlin regarding his legislative proposal. Citing Schuchard's article and characterizing it as evidence of a general "public outcry," he once again pressed Altenstein for permission to present his law proposal to the Landtag.[48] Yet again Altenstein failed to respond. This ongoing silence put Bodelschwingh in a perplexing, problematic situation—one in which the normal course of action was not panning out. A creative new course was required.

When Schuchard (seemingly unexpectedly) sent a child labor law proposal to the stalemated Oberpräsident, this move opened up a new possibility that Bodelschwingh eagerly exploited.[49] Knowing Schuchard's proposal had little hope of success in Berlin, Bodelschwingh instead submitted it directly to the Landtag (Kastner 2004, 125). This was legal because Schuchard was a Landtag member, not a representative of the royal government, which Bodelschwingh was. The gears of the provincial legislature started moving. A committee was assigned to evaluate Schuchard's bill. But then Bodelschwingh passed on his *own* proposal to the committee as well (Kastner 2004, 126)—probably not as an official bill, but as one document among others on the child labor problem.[50] Bodelschwingh needed Berlin's permission to put his bill forward, but he had repeatedly written Altenstein for approval and the minister had ignored him. That he submitted his proposal to the committee anyway shows that Bodelschwingh was willing to breach protocol to circumvent Altenstein's veto power; in other words, it is evidence of his creativity of action. The gamble worked. The Landtag's legislative committee combined the two proposals into a revised joint bill that included elements from each.[51] Bodelschwingh and Schuchard's de facto alliance was now solidified in a common legislative product.

On July 6, 1837, the Landtag met to debate a composite bill that combined the key features of Bodelschwingh's and Schuchard's proposals. Schuchard was the first to speak. After he rose to argue that working in factories—those "dens of misery"—robbed children of their health and happiness, a prominent cotton manufacturer countered that conditions in certain factories were actually quite good, and the law would reduce families' earnings and undermine Prussian manufacturers' ability to compete with England.[52] Despite these and similar objections from other members, the Landtag voted unanimously to require three years of schooling before children could begin factory employment, but to allow exceptions, to be granted by the local authorities, if necessitated by local conditions. The members also voted unanimously to support provisions setting the minimum working age at nine and giving children two-hour breaks in fresh air at midday.

By far the most controversial provision of the bill sought to restrict children's working hours to ten per day. Some representatives contended that the allowable hours should be reduced even further, to eight, to protect children from developing physical defects. In response, a representative vehemently argued that factories, far from heaping suffering on their workers, actually reduced the hardships they faced: "Factories that employ children, which you judge so harshly, do not produce the misery you have depicted with such vehemence, but rather mitigate it. A surplus of workers, who can no longer be absorbed by the agricultural sector, is streaming into these establishments in search of work, in search of bread. The factories can only exist in places where people can find no other useful work." Another representative pointed out that the English Factory Act of 1833, which set children's maximum daily working hours at nine, had also been found to be too ambitious to be enforced; he maintained that the law should be made flexible to allow exceptions if local conditions required. Someone called for a vote, and after the representative reiterated his objections, Schuchard arose with the plea, "If you could only imagine, esteemed gentlemen, that piteous scene wherein these poor, delicate children, with tears and reluctance, are dragged from their mothers at 5 in the morning, in cold or wet weather, only to be locked in such a jail, then your hearts, too, would break." The vote was again called, and the assembly overwhelmingly endorsed the ten-hour restriction (the vote was sixty in favor, and nine against). The bill was then sent in the form of a petition to the king.[53]

Again Bodelschwingh found himself in a perplexing situation. On the whole, he liked the bill, but it failed to prohibit children from working at night and allowed an overly broad exception to the three-year schooling requirement wherever "local conditions" required. Again he responded to this dilemma with goal-directed creativity. Less than a month after the Landtag submitted its petition, Bodelschwingh sent an "expert opinion" (*Gutachten*) to Berlin supporting the Landtag's petition, yet requesting that its bill not be considered on its own but instead be merged with his original 1835 proposal. Displaying a willingness to compromise, he asked that his own proposal be modified to include two of the Landtag's key measures: a minimum working age of nine and ten-hour days broken up by breaks in fresh air. At the same time, however, he requested that features of his original bill that the Landtag had not endorsed—particularly the prohibition on night work—be retained. He also asked that the Landtag's provision for exceptions to the three-year schooling requirement be eliminated.[54] In these ways, he sought to preserve his alliance with the Landtag while undermining parts of its bill in favor of his own ideas, especially the full strength of the education measure, which was after all at the heart of his definition of the child labor problem.

At long last Altenstein responded, but his reply was disappointing: he informed Bodelschwingh that the king had requested a child labor law for the entire monarchy and a provincial law was therefore no longer an option.[55] Altenstein was developing a new bill of his own and did not intend to stand in the shadow of the provincial governor; he continued to treat Bodelschwingh as a rival rather than a potential ally and attempted to shut him out.

Altenstein's new bill, which he completed and shared with the Interior Ministry in July 1837, contained most of the same measures as his old one, and again framed child labor regulation simply as a matter of protecting children's health, morality, and intellectual development without connecting these goals with the interests of elites or the state.[56] In contrast to Bodelschwingh, Altenstein continued to pass up opportunities for productive collaboration. When Beuth sent him detailed comments on his plan, Altenstein failed to compromise and simply let the matter drop—even though the Ministry of the Interior was now evidently willing to help him produce a child labor bill broadly in keeping with his ideas.[57]

A NEW INTERIOR MINISTER, A NEW ALLY

Even though his alliance with Schuchard and the Landtag had not borne immediate fruit, Bodelschwingh persisted. After waiting a full year for news, he wrote again to Altenstein and this time also to the new interior minister, von Rochow, to urge them to get moving.[58] In Rochow, Bodelschwingh finally found an ally through which he was able to subvert Altenstein's veto power. Rochow was a hard-line conservative cut from a similar cloth as Beckedorff.[59] He had replaced the more economically liberal Schuckmann as interior minister in 1834 and is best known for his staunch opposition to the creation of a national representative assembly. Nostalgic for the corporatist order of the past, he regarded the industrialization of Prussia with deep unease (Brose 1993, 53). Of all the characters involved in Prussian child labor reform in the 1830s, he came the closest to fitting the argument that reform was motivated by aristocratic hostility toward the industrial bourgeoisie's economic and political ascendance. A supporter of the reaction's social control approach to popular schooling, he expressed great enthusiasm for a pamphlet authored by Daniel Legrand, an Alsatian manufacturer, urging child labor regulation in France. Legrand's pamphlet stressed in particular the need to ensure that poor children received a moral and religious instruction. Referring to Prussia, which had recently defeated France in war, Legrand (1838, 17) wrote, "Do we wish to know the principal cause of the power and the civilization of the nation whose borders touch ours over such an extended line? Let us visit its schools and we will see that the education of its youth is moral and religious." Small wonder that Rochow concluded that the pamphlet's author must be a "highly benevolent, wise and knowledgeable man."[60]

In the conservative climate of the 1820s and 1830s, an authoritarian like Rochow exercised greater sway than a progressive like Altenstein. It was fortunate for Bodelschwingh, then, that Rochow effectively wrested control over child labor legislation from the Education Ministry and proceeded to sideline Altenstein from future discussions on the matter.[61] Bodelschwingh's good fortune was doubled when, in November 1838, Rochow asked him—not Altenstein—to draft a new child labor law. In his writings, Rochow indicated that it was the petition of the Rhineland Landtag that prompted him to push for child labor legislation, not only for that province, but for the entire monarchy.[62] Bodelschwingh's alliance with Schuchard and the legislature had proven useful after all, and yielded an even more advantageous alliance with the powerful new interior minister.

Bodelschwingh's direct involvement in this final stage of the policy process was made possible by his field position as mediator between the Rhineland Landtag and central administration. But though it made sense to involve Bodelschwingh at this point, doing so was not required. Provincial governors were not put in this position every time a Landtag petitioned the king for new legislation. So it was thanks to his goal-directed creativity—particularly his move to submit an expert opinion that subtly drew power and attention from the Landtag back to himself—that Bodelschwingh had come to be seen as the most appropriate person to craft the bill. Moreover, Rochow most likely read Bodelschwingh's 1835 memorandum and bill, in which he framed child labor as a threat to social order. Such a framing would undoubtedly have appealed to him.

With Rochow's invitation, Bodelschwingh finally had his chance to secure the law he had so long been seeking. Reflecting his continued focus on education, he lost no time in writing a new bill titled "an Ordinance to secure sufficient schooling and religious instruction for children employed in factories, mines and quarries."[63] The draft privileged Bodelschwingh's definition of the child labor problem as an issue of religious and moral education, but also incorporated ideas from the provincial actors who had weighed in on the issue over the past three years.[64] In other words, it was fully a compromise measure; Bodelschwingh had heeded and incorporated other actors' calls for a minimum working age, prohibition on night work, midday breaks in fresh air, and more.

Soon, a conference of representatives from the Ministries of Education, Finance, and Interior met in Berlin to discuss both the Landtag petition and Bodelschwingh's bill, and to hammer out a final draft. Bodelschwingh was brought to Berlin to take part in the deliberations. Notably, Altenstein was not in attendance. The resulting bill followed Bodelschwingh's suggestions, including all his education measures, much more closely than the Landtag's, though his proposal was amended slightly to strengthen its health aspects.[65] The participants also opted to change the name of the law because they did not want to imply that its aim was exclusively educational. Again, the meeting minutes indicate that Bodelschwingh was a willing compromiser on all points.[66]

Now that Bodelschwingh had managed to circumvent the education minister's veto power and, thanks to an alliance with Rochow, helped to produce a draft that was poised to become law, Altenstein made a last-ditch effort to put forward some of his ideas. He wrote to Rochow that the Bodelschwingh bill was not holistic enough: "In my opinion [it] neglect[s] . . . the sanitation of the workplaces, discipline within them, and [fails to provide for] daily sustenance of the children in special cases where the remoteness of the factory from the homes of their parents makes it necessary." He also reiterated the need for local commissions to ensure that the law was implemented and enforced: "Without proper control, the good intention of the regulations would remain without their intended consequences."[67] Rochow as well as the finance minister reacted to these suggestions dismissively.[68] In the end, all of Altenstein's ideas were sidelined.[69]

On February 15, the Royal Cabinet met to discuss the bill. Present were the crown prince, Minister Rochow and Councillor Hesse from the Interior Ministry, the finance minister, and the justice minister. Bodelschwingh was also there; Keller represented the Education Ministry. A few minor changes were made, and the cabinet agreed to submit the bill to the king with the recommendation that it be applied to the entire monarchy.[70] In his presentation to the king, Rochow began by summarizing the king's 1828 order, including the health and related military concerns that had prompted Frederick William to call for child labor legislation more than a decade earlier.[71] He cited "provincial officials" to make the case that large numbers of young children were employed in factories to the detriment of their health and physical development as well as their "intellectual and moral development." To show the king that the proposed measures had arisen at the provincial level and thus enjoyed bottom-up support, he repeatedly cited the Rhineland Landtag's petition as well as Bodelschwingh as the main contributors to the bill. To assure the monarch of the bill's moderate approach, he also stressed the ways in which it resembled but did not exceed English precedent.[72] The king ratified the law in full soon after, and the Regulative regarding the Employment of Children in Factories went into effect on March 9, 1839.

What was the impact of the 1839 law on working children in Prussia? Unfortunately, general statistics documenting the extent of child labor in factories do not exist before the 1840s, making it impossible to compare the overall extent of child labor before and after the 1839 law was passed. Yet the number of children working in factories did indeed drop dramatically in the decades that followed—from 31,064 children under fourteen in 1846 to 21,945 in 1852, to 12,592 in 1858 (Feldenkirchen 1981, 18). The proportion of the workforce composed of children declined too (see table 2.2).

Was this decline, as historian Karl-Heinz Ludwig (1965) argued, and as economist Clark Nardinelli (1980) claimed to explain similar trends in England, simply the result of children being rendered redundant by new technology? This question is difficult to answer. Historian Wilfried Feldenkirchen (1981) maintains that the decline cannot be wholly attributed to technological changes because child labor increased during the same time period in the neighboring Kingdom of Saxony, where identical technology was in place, but child labor regulations were not passed until 1861 (see also Kocka 1990, 470; Wehler 1987, 258). In 1846, for example, 5.1 percent of spinning mill workers in the Prussian province of Saxony were children, whereas the figure was 13.4 percent in the neighboring kingdom. Overall, 1.12 percent of children in the kingdom worked in factories, whereas only 0.21 percent did so in the province. Feldenkirchen concludes from this evidence that the child labor law must have had some deterrent effect on the spread of industrial child labor in Prussia. Moreover, anecdotal evidence that many Prussian factory owners, rather than dealing

TABLE 2.2. Percentage of Total Workforce under Age Fourteen in Selected Prussian Industries

Year	Textiles	Needle factories	Pin factories	Glass	Tobacco
1846	27.3 (cotton)	32.3	41.6	15.0	17.6
1849	11.4	31.0	41.5	15.2	14.2
1852	9.1	24.2	35.6	14.6	11.9

Sources: Feldenkirchen 1981, 21; Herzig 1983, 330.

with the regulations, stopped hiring young children altogether, supports this conclusion. Anecdotal evidence also indicates that by the 1870s, the notion that children under twelve did not belong in factories had become taken for granted by Prussian industrialists, but not by factory owners elsewhere in Germany.[73] I return to this subject in chapter 5, where I consider another crucial phase in German child labor policy development: the creation of mandatory factory inspection throughout the German Reich.

Alliance Building and Creativity

Previous analyses of the 1839 Prussian child labor law argue that it was developed in response to the conscription needs of the Prussian Army, the aristocracy's desire to thwart the ascendant bourgeoisie, and the state's need to appease a potentially revolutionary working class. The first of these explanations, possibly because of its conformity with popular images of Prussian militarism, has been particularly enduring and influential. My analysis shows, however, that all three explanations are inadequate. They each attribute to various actors—the aristocracy, state bureaucrats, and workers—motivations and goals derived deterministically from their structural positions. They also fail to pay close attention to the microlevel political processes that led to reform. My analysis corrects this error by disaggregating "the state," and offering a close reading of key state actors' definitions of the child labor problem and their programmatic plans to address it. It demonstrates that in the absence of institutionalized administrative or electoral channels to address the social problems that industrial capitalism introduced, the Prussian child labor law of 1839 was to a large extent the strategic and creative accomplishment of an entrepreneurial reformer, Bodelschwingh.

   Two competing definitions of the child labor problem emerged in 1820s and 1830s Prussia. The first, embraced by Education Minister Altenstein, conceptualized child labor as a threat to poor children's overall human development, which undermined Prussia's capacity to build a unified, moral, and robust nation. This definition reflected his progressive political education as a young member of the Stein-Hardenberg reform cohort. Accordingly, his bill placed equal emphasis on protecting working children against physical, moral, and intellectual harm. In contrast, Bodelschwingh's initial plan focused narrowly on religious and moral education, and defined child labor as a problem of social control. This focus reflected the times: Bodelschwingh embarked on his campaign in a context of increasing lower-class unrest in the Rhineland in the early 1830s brought on by a hunger crisis as well as yet another revolution in neighboring France. In addition, he was responding to institutional opportunities presented by Prussia's already relatively well-established primary education system alongside the apparent failure of Prussia's compulsory schooling law to achieve its goals in manufacturing regions. But although class dynamics and institutional conditions laid the groundwork for his policy entrepreneurship, they did not guarantee his success.

Altenstein's and Bodelschwingh's different problem definitions inspired them to propose policy programs that varied in important concrete respects. Overall, Altenstein's plan was the more ambitious. It went beyond Bodelschwingh's by requiring that children be examined by a physician before working, restricting children under fourteen to half-day workdays, and demanding that factories be kept clean and ventilated. His schooling requirements were also more extensive than Bodelschwingh's. And whereas Bodelschwingh's law included no special oversight mechanism, local child labor commissions would have been established under Altenstein's plan to enforce the law in accordance with local circumstances.[74] By comparing the law that passed to the law that might have been, we can see that the ideas motivating political action do indeed have real policy consequences. To put it bluntly, Prussia's working children would have received better protection under the Altenstein plan.

But that Altenstein failed to see his program enacted into law while Bodelschwingh succeeded has more to do with differences in their alliance-building skill and creativity of action than with the content of the laws they proposed. The two men differed significantly in their ability to recruit allies and solve problems. Whereas Altenstein ended up isolated and marginalized, Bodelschwingh progressively forged new alliances at every stage. In pursuit of allies at multiple levels of government, he reached down to the municipal level, across to the Landtag, and up to Berlin. Bodelschwingh's coalition building was facilitated by his field position at the institutionalized overlap of the local and central policy fields, but ultimately it was the result of his alliance-building initiative and goal-directed creativity of action.

The alliance-building strategies most relevant to this story are citation, framing, and especially compromise. Altenstein, in his 1828 proposal, failed to use citation strategically, making it seem like the plan was his work alone and that he lacked allies at the local level. Furthermore, by neglecting to present a prominent fundamental frame, he failed to connect his reform agenda with the interests of elites or the state, thereby rendering it out of sync with the prevailing discursive opportunity structure. In contrast, by invoking elite fears about lower-class social disorder, Bodelschwingh's frames—whether strategically chosen or not—fit with the reactionary discursive opportunity structure of the 1820s and 1830s. We do not know precisely how his social disorder frame was received by officials in Berlin, but given what we know about Rochow's political sensibilities, it is likely that he found it compelling. Stronger evidence of Bodelschwingh's alliance-building skill was his use of strategic citation. Although both he and Altenstein built their policy programs by borrowing and combining ideas suggested to them by others, Bodelschwingh was the only one to publicly credit the sources of these suggestions. These citations signaled that he had allies at the local level—most important among them, the Rhineland Landtag.

The most consequential difference between Altenstein and Bodelschwingh, however, relates to their willingness to compromise for the sake of winning allies. Both men faced considerable opposition—not from capitalists, who had little direct power over the insulated Prussian policy-making field, but from other state actors. Altenstein was forced to contend with conservative Interior Minister Schuckmann and his liberal deputy, Beuth, who took advantage of collegialism to stall and block the education minister's program. But even after Schuckmann and Beuth changed their minds and expressed willingness to collaborate, Altenstein repeatedly passed up the opportunity. Moreover, when presented with the chance to form an alliance with the young Rhineland governor, he chose to block rather than work with Bodelschwingh. Altenstein was evidently uninterested in compromise if it would result in a less than ideal law. His refusal to collaborate with others resulted in a string of missed opportunities. Despite the ambition of his plan, some version of it could have become law had he cooperated with potential allies; the counterfactual outcome was a real possibility.

Bodelschwingh, on the other hand, was an eager compromiser. Although he stayed true to his core commitment to ensuring a modicum of religious and moral instruction, he revised his bill five times between 1835 and 1838, with each revision reflecting input from new allies picked up along the way. This willingness to work with others was crucial to his eventual success. It meant that the bill proposed by the Landtag was truly an amalgamation of both Schuchard's and his ideas. It meant that he retained influence even after the Landtag petitioned the government for a law. It was that Bodelschwingh credibly presented himself as the Landtag's ally that ensured that it was he—not Altenstein, Keller, or Beuth—who was asked to draft the version of the child labor bill that was finally enacted into law.

Finally, Bodelschwingh, unlike Altenstein, exhibited a great deal of goal-directed creativity when it came to circumventing veto players. As pragmatist theory would predict, Bodelschwingh initially embarked on his quest in a routine, tried-and-true manner. But soon he found himself in a problematic situation when Education Minister Altenstein ignored his requests. He ignored him from November 1835 to August 1837, despite repeated attempts by Bodelschwingh to solicit a response. Rather than give up, though, Bodelschwingh looked for unconventional alternative pathways to change. After each setback, he kept his child labor plan on the back burner, waiting for a turn of events (Schuchard's intervention and later Rochow's appointment) that created new political opportunities. His greatest creativity came in May 1837, when he submitted two proposals for a child labor law to the Rhineland legislature—one that he had received from Schuchard and one written by himself. This was a breach of protocol, but he did it anyway, and it worked.

This case comparison demonstrates the importance of policy entrepreneurs' ideas and individual agency for shaping policy outcomes. Of course, ideas and agency do not exist in a vacuum; they are conditioned by the broader social, institutional, and political context as well as by actors' field positions within a given field architecture. Actors positioned at the intersection of fields or subfields, as Bodelschwingh was, may have greater incentive and opportunity to forge alliances in ways that those at the top of a field do not. Mediation was not part of Altenstein's job description in the same way that it defined the Oberpräsident's role. Nonetheless, the minister's refusal to seize opportunities for collaboration and his defeatist response to problem situations are not reducible to his field position, but instead indicate his personal failure to exercise creativity and alliance-building skill.

3

A Tale of Two Reformers

SUCCESS IN FRANCE, FAILURE IN BELGIUM

Child labor burst onto the national policy agenda in Belgium and France in the 1840s.[1] In France, calls for regulation began in 1828, when a group of industrialists in the textile town of Mulhouse began petitioning the state for regulations on the employment of children in factories. In 1837, these petitions finally captured the government's attention, and a child labor law was enacted in 1841. On the heels of this development, the king of neighboring Belgium, Leopold I, called for a similar law and a major investigation was undertaken. Yet the proposal that resulted was quickly defeated. Partly as a consequence of this early setback, Belgium did not enact a child labor law until 1889. Comparing the French and Belgian cases, this chapter explains why, despite social and political conditions favorable to reform in both countries, France succeeded in regulating child labor early in its industrial development while Belgium did not.

Some have argued that Belgium failed because it embraced economic liberalism with extreme fervor and granted capitalists great influence over policy (Gubin 2011; Scholliers 2009; for this assertion applied to social reform in general, see Witte 2020, 260). Both characterizations are correct. Yet a closer look at the historical record reveals that child labor regulation was nevertheless a political possibility in 1840s Belgium. The social conditions that contributed to elites' embrace of labor regulation in Prussia and France were also in effect there. Concerns about popular unrest and social disorder were at least as prevalent in Belgium as elsewhere. Further, the political power of capital was similarly considerable in France under the July Monarchy, yet France passed a child labor law and Belgium did not. In fact, Belgium's politically influential chambers of commerce were more open to modest child labor regulations than the equally influential French chambers were. Why then did the Belgian chambers unanimously reject the proposal in 1848, thereby derailing that country's child labor reform prospects for the next fifty years?

This question cannot be answered without paying close attention to the microlevel political processes that led up to the drafting of the Belgian proposal and its defeat. Comparing France with Belgium shows that the key difference between them was neither institutional nor political. Instead, their divergent outcomes hinged on the alliance-building strategies and goal-directed creativity of each country's leading child labor policy entrepreneur. Whereas the French reformer, Charles Dupin, exercised skill in building alliances as well as creativity in circumventing veto points, his Belgian counterpart, Édouard Ducpétiaux, made significant strategic errors, squandering a rare window of opportunity. Ducpétiaux failed to compromise with key stakeholders, framed his proposal ineffectively, and tended to cite foreign actors and policy precedents that audiences deemed irrelevant. Moreover, in the face of roadblocks to institutional change, Ducpétiaux exhibited neither Dupin's nor Bodelschwingh's creativity of action. These differences were conditioned, but not determined, by differences in the two actors' field positions, which were in turn shaped by differences in the architecture of the policy field—particularly the extent to which it overlapped with the intellectual field—in the two states. In short, the failure of Belgian child labor reform was in large part a failure of policy entrepreneurship.

The Revolutions of 1830, and Political Liberalization in France and Belgium

Both France and Belgium underwent liberal revolutions in 1830, resulting in political institutions that were broadly similar in both countries. In France, the July Revolution swept away the reactionary Bourbon monarchy and replaced it with the more liberal "king of the French," Louis Philippe. Belgium, meanwhile, was born of revolution that year. The Congress of Vienna had awarded the Belgian provinces to the United Kingdom of the Netherlands under the rule of William I of Orange. This fragile union lasted until 1830, when Belgium gained its independence.

In both countries, the revolutions produced new constitutions that reaffirmed (in France) or established (in Belgium) parliamentary monarchies in which legislative power was exercised jointly by king and parliament. In France, the upper house of parliament, the Chamber of Peers, was no longer hereditary; members were instead appointed by the king. The lower house, the Chamber of Deputies, was elected by the highest taxpayers, or approximately

0.5 percent of the population (Collingham 1988, 71). This constituted approximately a doubling of the franchise—a development that largely benefited the bourgeois elite.[2] In Belgium, members of both the upper and lower houses were voted on directly by the wealthiest citizens, amounting to approximately 1 percent of the population (Witte, Craeybeckx, and Meynen 2009, 27). In both countries, the executive branch was made up of the king, his ministers (whom he could nominate and dismiss at will), and their staffs. In France, the revolution divested the king of his exclusive right to introduce legislation, which became the shared power of the king, Chamber of Peers, and Chamber of Deputies. Likewise in Belgium, both the king and parliament possessed the power to introduce and veto bills. The prefects of France's eighty-six departments and governors of Belgium's nine provinces were appointed by as well as subordinate to the minister of the interior; in addition, each department or province had an elected council. The result in both cases was a highly centralized yet liberal state.

In both France and Belgium, the revolution was led by the liberal bourgeoisie (Witte, Craeybeckx, and Meynen 2009, 21; Clark 1984). They were joined by lower-middle- and working-class people who took to the streets in hope of better living conditions and a greater share of political power. These desires were largely in vain. Although the French and Belgian Constitutions enshrined liberal rights, including freedom of expression, religion, and association, the rights of ordinary people were still restricted in various ways. They could not vote. France, in response to labor unrest in the early 1830s, launched a policy of repression against organized labor, effectively abolishing freedom of association for workers (Sewell 1980, 217). Similarly in Belgium, labor unions were outlawed and freedom of the press was undermined by a high stamp tax (Lademacher 2000). These institutional constraints put limits on labor's political and economic power resources. It was the commercial and industrial bourgeoisie, and to some extent the bourgeois intelligentsia, that disproportionately reaped the benefits of revolution in both countries. Although the landed aristocracy continued its political dominance after 1830, the bourgeoisie gained a stronger foothold on the rungs of power, particularly in the lower houses of parliament as well as all levels of the civil service and judiciary (Collingham 1988).

Another way in which capitalists in both countries were institutionally empowered to influence politics was via their chambers of commerce, which played a much greater role in economic policy making than in Prussia. In France, the political role of these bodies, which had existed in some form since the seventeenth century, was formalized in 1832 when their advisory functions were clearly spelled out by royal ordinance. The French chambers were frequently asked by the government to comment on existing and proposed economic policies, and as a result of this official consultative role, they enjoyed considerable political influence (Lefèvre 1977; Lemercier 2003). Under the July Monarchy, for example, they successfully resisted calls to lift tariffs on imported goods such as Caribbean sugar (Collingham 1988, 353). The Belgian chambers of commerce were granted official status by the Dutch government in 1815 and survived the 1830 revolution intact. A royal ordinance clearly defined their objectives, rights, and duties in 1841. The mandate of the Belgian chambers was to advise the government on matters of industry and commerce, and they regularly did weigh in on matters of economic policy making and exercised considerable influence (Vanthemsche 2004).[3] Thus to a degree not yet heard of in Prussia, the French and Belgian business fields had institutionally penetrated their countries' policy fields through these bodies' formalized roles and privileges.

Both Belgium and France were Catholic countries in which political conflict between secularist and Catholic factions persisted throughout the nineteenth century. In France, the 1830 revolution was anti-Catholic, and the authority that emerged from it was liberal and secular; advocates of political Catholicism were forced into a position of opposition to the state and society, from which they were nevertheless able to wrest concessions from liberal policy makers. The question of who should control primary schooling, the state or church, was one of the most fraught areas of conflict (Collingham 1988, 50). In Belgium, the legislative and top ministerial posts were initially filled by a coalition of secular liberal and Catholic elites. This unionist Catholic-liberal government lasted more than a decade. The coalition hinged on liberal concessions to church power in exchange for Catholic support for business interests, particularly unfettered exploitation of the labor market. Over the course of the 1840s, however, it became increasingly clear to secular liberals that they no longer needed nor wanted an alliance with the Catholics. Liberal hegemony was more decisively established under Prime Minister Charles Rogier and Finance Minister Walthère Frère-Orban in 1847 (Gooch 1963; Shelley 1990). This government survived the disruptions of 1848—minor in Belgium—intact, though it granted some concessions to "radical" democrats, including a reduction in the electoral tax and consequently a doubling of the urban electorate. The government's successful handling of the incidents of 1848 solidified liberal control, and a new era of political tension between anticlerical liberals and religious Catholics began in Belgium. This tension centered most intensely on the ongoing issue of church involvement in public education.

Primary Schooling in Belgium and France

Child labor legislation in Prussia built on policy achievements in public schooling. A compulsory schooling law had been in place since the eighteenth century, more was spent on public schooling than in any other country, and attendance rates were among the world's highest (Lindert 2004, 91). Accordingly, child labor reform was in large part conceived by reformers like Bodelschwingh as a way to accomplish the state's existing education goals. Things were different in France and Belgium. Neither had adopted compulsory schooling by the first half of the nineteenth century.[4] In 1830, roughly 35 to 40 percent of Belgian and French children were enrolled in school, compared to nearly double that in Prussia (Lindert 2004, 90; Fishlow 1966; see figure 2.1).

This lag is attributable to the ongoing conflict between Catholics and secular liberals for control of the schools. Still, both countries found ways to increase education access and state control over schools by striking compromises with the church. In France, the Guizot law of 1833 required each commune to establish and fund a public primary school—either secular or parochial—for boys, set standards for curricula and teacher training in both public and private schools, and established local school committees to oversee both public and private schools (Nique 1990; Collingham 1988, 309–10). Church influence was still pronounced, however. Localities could set up a private parochial school if they chose, the state-sanctioned curriculum emphasized religious components, and the local priest belonged to the local school committee (Curtis 2000; Meyers 1985). A similar law, modeled on the French precedent, was enacted in Belgium in 1842 (Gontard 1980). It required all local districts to set up at least one primary school—whether public, publicly funded private ("adopted"), or independent private—and mandated religious instruction, overseen by the local church authorities, in all schools. Publicly funded schools were administered by local governments and subject to inspection. Unlike in France, though, independent private schools were free to appoint teachers and manage their affairs without government oversight. Whereas the Guizot law contributed to a sharp increase in school enrollment rates in France, in Belgium the 1842 law had less of an obvious impact (see figure 2.1). Despite these reforms, school quality continued to be generally quite low in both countries, particularly in rural areas. It remained typical for parents to send their children to school for only a few months before their first communion—just long enough to memorize the catechism (Weber [1976] 2007, 307, 319).

Pestalozzian pedagogy did not make its way into Francophone education debates in the same way that it shaped reformist discourse in Prussia. Discussion in these countries centered more on state versus church control over schooling, and how to enhance the reach and quality of mass education. Despite delayed progress, elites in both France and Belgium viewed educating the children of the poor as important, and advocated improvements. In both countries, they spoke out against the neglected condition of the primary schools and decried what they perceived as their country's failure to keep up with the Germanic states. They lamented children's ad hoc attendance, the lack of appropriate school buildings and resources, and the paucity of properly trained teachers (Heywood 1988, 65; Maynes 1985, 70–73). As in Prussia, education was, for many elites, primarily a tool for social control. It was an essential bulwark against popular moral decay—besides the church, the only institution that could prevent the morals and manners of the poor from degenerating into total depravity (Maynes 1985). For conservative Catholics like the Abbé de La Mennais (1828, 148), elementary schooling should be religious, and "introduce . . . emerging generations to the hierarchy of beings united by justice and truth." In the words of the bishop of Liège, religious schooling was essential because "there is no security for those who command unless they are loved by those who obey" (Van Bommel 1840, 4). For girls, popular schooling would instill the "virtues" of the subordinate sex: obedience, sweetness, and modesty (Curtis 2000, 93).

Liberals, too, saw schooling as an essential social control mechanism, and by the 1830s some, like Inspector General of Prisons Ducpétiaux, who later became Belgium's most important child labor policy entrepreneur, began calling on their governments to enact a Prussian-style compulsory schooling law. No less than for conservative Catholics, political radicalism among the working classes was a major concern for liberal elites (Shelley 1990). In the words of the president of the University of Liège, for instance, elementary schooling was "a guarantee against political conflagrations" (Gubin 2011, 197). French education minister François Guizot maintained that "ignorance renders the people turbulent and ferocious; it makes them an instrument at the disposal of the factious." National education would promote "between the government and the citizens, or among the various classes of society, a certain community of opinions and feelings which will become a powerful link, a guarantee of calm, and a more effective basis for order than all legal prohibitions" (Guizot 1816, 5, 11). His successor, Victor Cousin (1832, 20), argued similarly: "The mission of the state is also to spread morality . . . to protect the social order both inside and outside; and it cannot be denied that of all the means of internal order, general education is the most powerful."

Some education reformers saw beyond social control objectives, and optimistically proclaimed that primary schooling would tap into and cultivate the as yet neglected human capital of the lower classes. In France, members of the Société pour l'instruction élémentaire—including the future child labor reformer Joseph Marie, baron de Gérando—imported the Lancastrian school system from England in hope of tapping into this latent potential.[5] A poster announcing the opening of a new monitorial school in Bolleme in 1831 declared, "It no longer suffices to know how to babble a few words in a lamentable tone or to trace a few lines. It is necessary that children who are entering the era of equality, of industry and of emulation be capable of gaining knowledge extensive enough to get out of the rut in which they unavoidably find themselves with the old methods of instruction" (quoted in Maynes

1985, 7–8). Extending popular schooling to the poorest children would not only improve their life chances but also serve the interests of capital by instilling self-discipline, obedience, and diligence in the future workforce (Gubin and Lefèvre 1985; Curtis 2000, 101). Moreover, it would inculcate a new sense of national identity and patriotism in the still hyperlocal lifeworld of the common people (Weber [1976] 2007), and "implant everywhere . . . the spirit and unity of French nationality" (Guizot 1889, 98–99). Similar rhetoric prevailed among liberals in Belgium, where elementary schooling was further linked to the country's ability to preserve its newly won independence (Visschers 1838, 47–48).

Industrialization and Child Labor

Both France and Belgium began industrializing in the first half of the nineteenth century; Belgium was more industrialized, but France was not far behind (Bairoch 1982; Broadberry, Fremdling and Solar 2010, 172). As integrated members of the global capitalist economy, both experienced plenty of economic volatility, especially the transatlantic financial crisis of 1837–39 and the recession coinciding with the potato famine of the mid-1840s. Belgium experienced greater volatility than France, but more rapid growth overall. Furthermore, whereas French workers remained dispersed in smaller-scale family-owned enterprises, Belgian workers, particularly those in the cotton and woolen textile industries, were increasingly concentrated in large-scale enterprises, and experienced more drastic proletarization and immiseration as a result.

France has long been portrayed as an economic laggard, but this characterization does not hold if the comparison is with continental Europe rather than Great Britain or the United States. In the first half of the nineteenth century, France's economy grew steadily and sometimes rapidly, despite being predominantly agricultural, continuing to rely on small-scale farming and industry, and experiencing a shortage of natural resources like coal (Cameron and Freedeman 1983; Heywood 1992). Slow population growth meant that the country's overall economic progress did not match England's, but if measured in terms of GDP growth per capita, it compared well. France was continental Europe's leading producer of textiles: in 1850, it had about the same number of mechanized cotton spindles as the rest of the continent combined (Milward and Saul 2012, 316–17). The textile industry was more characterized by small family firms than elsewhere in Europe and was highly regional. Cotton spinning and weaving were concentrated in Rouen and the Alsace, and linen and cotton mills proliferated in the Norde, particularly in and around the city of Lille, near the Belgian border. Lyon was Europe's center of silk manufacture. Technological change was slow in France, and industry remained labor

TABLE 3.1. Workers in Belgian Factories by Age and Sex, 1843–48

Age	Male	% of workers	Female	% of workers	Total	% of workers
Under 9	532	1.0%	164	0.3%	696	1.3%
9–11	1,615	3.0%	684	1.3%	2,299	4.2%
12–15	5,638	10.4%	1,881	3.5%	7,519	13.9%
16–20	5,768	10.6%	3,377	6.2%	9,145	16.9%
21+	29,520	54.5%	5,002	9.2%	34,522	63.7%
Total	43,073	79.5%	11,108	20.5%	54,181	100.0%

Source: Belgium, Ministère de l'Intérieur 1848, 1:iv.

intensive; mechanized spinning coexisted with a rural weaving cottage industry until around 1850 (Heywood 1992; Caron and Bray 2011).

The term "Industrial Revolution" was first coined to describe Belgium, not England (Clark 1984; Mokyr 1976, 237). Belgium was a small country with a small economy, but it was the most industrially advanced in Europe by 1850 (Mokyr 1976, 232). Large-scale industry evolved in regions where protoindustry had long flourished: mechanized cotton manufacturing concentrated in Ghent; the linen cottage industry survived well into the nineteenth century in rural Flanders; woolen manufacturing centered in Verviers; and heavy industry (coal, iron, and steel) flourished in Liège and the Borinage. As in Prussia, the French occupation (1795–1814) proved beneficial to industrial capitalism in the southern Low Countries. Within a decade, Ghent cotton manufacturing grew tenfold (Mokyr 1976). A similar transformation occurred in woolen production in Liège. But after the lifting of the continental blockade in 1814, the textile industry's fortunes declined, and the leading Belgian industries became iron and metallurgy. Over the 1830s and 1840s, textile mills stayed afloat by modernizing technology and concentrating business in the hands of fewer, larger manufacturers (Scholliers 1996). The industry's survival also hinged on low wages relative to other industrializing European countries (Scholliers 1996; Gubin 2011). In this economic climate, industrial workers constantly teetered on the edge of pauperism.

As it did everywhere, child labor existed in all industrial sectors, but predominated in Belgium's textile towns.[6] A government survey (*Enquête*) and census, both conducted in the 1840s, reported that about one-fifth of Belgium's industrial workforce was children younger than sixteen (see tables 3.1–3.2).[7] Most of these were teenagers; the 1848 *Enquête* found that just 1.3 percent of Belgium's factory workers were younger than nine, 4.2 percent were between nine and eleven, and 14.4 percent were between twelve and fifteen.[8] The census data break down the number of workers by age group in various major industries—in some cases treating factory and craft industries separately

TABLE 3.2. Workers in Selected Belgian Industries by Age and Sex, 1846

Industry		Number of establishments	Adults (16 and over)		Children (under 16)		Total per sex		General total	Percent of workers by age	
			Men	Women	Boys	Girls	Male	Female		% adults	% children
Mineral industries	Coal and coke	202	31,742	4,105	7,378	2,961	39,120	7,066	46,186	78	22
	Metallurgy — Primary establishments	243	18,390	1,100	1,447	175	20,037	1,275	21,312	91	8
	Secondary establishments	2,176	3,548	436	760	222	4,308	658	4,996	80	20
	Craft enterprise	12,028	13,460	123	2,393	35	15,853	158	16,011	85	15
	Quarries, slate, ceramic — Industrial establishments	1,613	13,249	1,118	2,982	627	18,234	1,745	19,976	72	18
	Craft enterprise	6,786	10,696	147	928	18	11,624	165	11,789	92	8
	Glass — Industrial establishments	35	2,718	318	539	119	3,257	437	3,694	82	18
	Craft enterprise	595	235	1	29	–	264	1	265	89	11
Manufacturing industries	Linen and hemp — Industrial establishments	2,401	7,006	6,585	1,491	2,147	8,497	8,732	17,229	79	21
	Craft enterprise	18,732	11,559	10,828	2,361	18,046	13,920	28,874	42,794	52	48
	Wool — Industrial establishments	768	10,134	4,686	2,076	1,257	12,210	5,943	18,153	82	18
	Cotton — Industrial establishments	330	7,551	3,029	2,491	1,247	10,042	4,276	14,318	74	26
	Craft enterprise	43	1	100	3	258	4	358	362	28	72

Silk		27	380	58	208	29	588	87	675	65	35
Hosiery, ribbons, trimmings		1,074	1,497	675	501	337	1,998	1,012	3,010	72	28
Fabric		10,036	5,817	2,641	1,352	1,247	7,169	3,888	11,057	76	24
Various industries	Heating (peat)	12	45	16	8	2	53	18	71	86	14
	Lighting	1,690	2,624	186	176	147	2,800	333	3,133	90	10
	Food Industrial establishments	8,434	18,454	2,057	1,329	567	19,780	2,624	22,404	92	8
	Food Craft enterprise	7,928	6,291	434	688	44	6,979	478	7,457	90	10
	Wood Industrial establishments	1,032	1,524	53	135	10	1,659	63	1,722	92	8
	Wood Craft enterprise	20,636	16,960	169	2,060	46	19,020	215	19,235	89	11
	Leather Industrial establishments	968	2,292	180	157	63	2,449	243	2,692	92	8
	Leather Craft enterprise	14,841	8,039	218	2150	52	10,189	270	10,459	79	21
	Stationery and printing Industrial establishments	142	1,202	904	380	183	1,582	1,089	2,674	79	21
	Stationery and printing Craft enterprise	611	2,034	20	632	49	2,666	39	2,705	76	25
	Chemical products Industrial establishments	417	1,262	62	126	3	1,385	63	1,453	91	9
	Chemical products Craft enterprise	1,240	1,484	16	125	2	1,609	18	1,627	92	8
	Other	2,694	5,393	408	1451	164	6,844	572	7,416	78	22
Total		114,754	207,784	40,673	36,356	30,029	244,140	70,702	314,842	79	21

Source: Belgium, Ministère de l'Intérieur 1851, x.

(see table 3.2). These data provide a clear picture of which Belgian industries relied most heavily on child labor. The top five were all in textiles, with the craft industry being most reliant; whereas the craft cotton processing workforce was 72 percent children, industrial cotton processing was 26 percent.[9] The largest industry in Belgium in terms of the raw number of workers employed was coal mining. The country was unusual in that mining was traditionally a family enterprise (Hilden 1993, 87); as a result, 22 percent of the country's mine workers were under sixteen.

According to a French government inquiry conducted between 1839 and 1845, about 12 percent of France's industrial workforce were children under sixteen. The French textile industries (excepting silk) employed large numbers of children and women: children made up over 18 percent of the cotton, woolen, and mixed-fiber textile workforces. Children did not work in the French coal mines like they did in Belgium; the only nontextile industries in which children comprised more than 10 percent of the workforce were ceramics, metalworking, and paper (see table 3.3).

The accuracy of all these historical statistics is no doubt dubious. Still, differences between the Belgian figures and contemporaneous ones collected in France are large enough that it seems likely that industrial child labor was somewhat more prevalent in Belgium than in France.

Labor Movement and "la question sociale"

Workers were not the drivers of child labor regulation in France or Belgium, but working-class unrest in both countries contributed to the social structural backdrop against which child labor policy entrepreneurs mounted their campaigns for reform. France is well known for having had, since its revolution, an especially self-confident and defiant working class. Certainly before 1848, working-class formation was more developed there than in Prussia. Because of the relative absence of large-scale industry, French workers were less proletarized than elsewhere, but more precocious in developing a class consciousness. Gathered into craft-based corporate associations that joined forces when necessary, they were organized, unified, and ideologically socialist (Sewell 1980; Shorter and Tilly 1974; Katznelson 1986, 25).

The July Revolution brought the industrial bourgeoisie to power, but was fought and won in the streets by artisans and workers. The failed promise of the new regime to improve the lot of working people stimulated insurrections throughout the 1830s. Between August and December 1830, Paris-based printers, spinners, tailors, shoemakers, and carpenters mounted strikes as well as petitioned the government for a normal working day and wage increases (Dolléans 1848; Bron 1968; Robert 2014). In 1831, silk weavers in Lyon staged

TABLE 3.3. French Industrial Labor Force by Age and Sex, 1839–45

| | Number | | | | Percentage | |
Industry	Men	Women	Children (under 16)	All workers	Women and children	Children (under 16)
Textiles						
Cotton	109,344	90,647	44,828	244,819	55.3%	18.3%
Wool	72,678	44,668	26,800	144,146	49.6	18.6
Linen and hemp	33,067	15,868	7,232	5,6167	41.1	12.9
Silk	109,662	46,127	9,326	165,115	33.6	5.6
Mixed fibers	47,062	21,471	15,803	81,336	44.2	18.7
Mines, quarries	69,243	5,786	6,256	81,285	14.8	7.7
Basic metallurgy	63,066	3,287	6,340	72,693	13.2	8.7
Metalworking	41,864	4,458	6,315	52,637	20.5	12.0
Leather	11,751	9,320	751	21,822	46.2	3.4
Wood	5,150	425	262	5,837	11.8	4.5
Ceramics	25,187	4,222	4,089	33,498	24.8	12.2
Chemicals	7,547	930	606	9,083	16.9	6.7
Construction	26,825	2,449	2,930	32,204	16.7	9.1
Lighting	1,239	262	71	1,572	21.2	4.5
Clothing	4,147	1,945	410	6,502	36.2	6.3
Food	115,368	14,163	6,889	136,420	15.4	5.0
Transport	4,838	13	223	5,074	4.7	4.4
Paper, publishing	13,518	8,370	2,841	24,729	45.3	11.5
Luxuries	1,199	57	95	1,351	11.3	7.0
Miscellaneous	5,153	4,369	1,598	11,120	–	–
Totals	767,908	278,837	143,665	1,190,410	35.5	12.1

Source: Heywood 1988, 104.

a major uprising and took over the city for several days; in 1833 and 1834, strikes became a common occurrence once again as skilled urban workers staged mass insurrections in Lyon and Paris. After that wave, the government responded with repression, outlawing all workers' associations that had formed since the July Revolution. The workers' movement was driven underground, and not until 1839 and 1840 did it remobilize. In 1839, Auguste Blanqui's Society of the Seasons instigated an uprising in Paris, and cotton workers in Lille organized strikes to protest high bread prices. The following year witnessed another major strike wave among the skilled trades (Moss 1976; Sewell 1980, 206–8, 219; Collingham 1988, 349). Workers' demands centered on the regulation of the working day and higher wages; child labor did not feature on their agenda.

Belgium's labor unrest in the first half of the century more closely resembled that of Prussia than it did France: disorganized, ad hoc, and occasionally violent. According to the standard political history of Belgium, the first generation of the factory proletariat—people uprooted by the declining cottage industry and agricultural overpopulation—did not have the necessary capacities to form a class consciousness (Witte, Craeybeckx, and Meynen 2009, 51–52; see also Brepoels 2015, 40; d'Hondt 1960, 179). Unions were outlawed in Belgium until 1866 (Witte, Craeybeckx, and Meynen 2009, 71). Artisans formed mutual aid societies, but factory workers remained unorganized. Protests consisted mainly of spontaneous strikes and attacks on factory buildings and owners, and did little to legitimize workers' grievances. For example, in October and November 1830, looting and machine smashing took place in the Borinage and Ghent to protest wage cuts, changes to work organization, and the introduction of power looms (Kuypers 1960). In January 1831, workers at the Voortman cotton mill in Ghent looted buildings, smashed machinery, and beat up the owner (Scholliers 1995, 212). Tension culminated in 1839 with a "cotton revolt," instigated by a mass meeting to hear the fiery labor leader Jacob Kats that ended in troops opening fire and killing a number of workers (Brepoels 2015, 38–39).

The 1840s returned to relative quiet (Scholliers 1996). Still, the decade was not disturbance free. Coal miners in the Borinage protested the imposition of work booklets (*livrets*), a social control mechanism imported from France to blackball workers not in good standing with previous employers (Hilden 1993, 121). In 1843, Jacob Kats founded one of the first people's societies (*Volksmaatschappij*). In 1846, at the height of the Hungry Forties, one of these associations organized a hunger march on Brussels, but like the 1839 Ghent uprising, it was quickly suppressed (Witte, Craeybeckx, and Meynen 2009, 53; Brepoels 2015, 40). Criminal statistics indicate that although Belgians did not strike and riot as often in the 1840s as they did in the 1830s, they resisted their impoverishment in other ways. Between 1844 and 1847, the number of criminal cases in Belgium increased by 50 percent. The biggest increases came in begging, vagrancy, petty theft, trespassing on public land, and stealing crops—all crimes of poverty (Vanhaute 2007, 136–37).

In response to these upheavals, a rich discourse on the social problems of industrial society emerged in France and crossed the border into Belgium. It took many directions—from the radical anarchist to the utopian socialist to the social Catholic. The school of thought most engaged with "la question sociale" was utopian socialism. In 1817, Henri de Saint-Simon published his manifesto critiquing of the parasitic wealthy "idling class" and advocating an industrialized state directed by modern science. Attempting to bring religion to bear on the suffering of the masses, he advocated a "new Christianity" that would "guide society towards the great goal of the most rapid improvement possible in the lot of the poorest class" (Saint-Simon 1825, cited in Gattone 2006, 16). Saint-Simon's contemporary and rival, Charles Fourier, avoided an explicitly religious agenda and saw civilization as a destructive force. Fourier rejected the idea that further industrialization would resolve social problems and advocated instead the construction of utopian agricultural cooperatives called phalanxes, where people would be free to pursue their interests and all manner of passions. Anticipating Marx's theory of alienation, he regarded modern industrial employment as unbearably dehumanizing; in its stead, he promoted the idea of "attractive labor" that the phalanxes would make possible by allowing people to perform jobs suited to their inclinations and frequently switch tasks (Beecher 2001, 34–37).

A new flowering of French socialist thought occurred at the end of the 1830s. In influential tracts both published in 1839, the utopian Etienne Cabet and socialist Louis Blanc advocated self-sustaining workers' cooperatives. The anarchist Pierre-Joseph Proudhon followed in 1840 with *What Is Property?* in which he declared private ownership to be theft and advocated collective ownership of the means of production. These writings made their way into the discourse of ordinary workers. According to historian William Sewell (1980, 220), "In the course of the 1840s, ideas about cooperation, about the reorganization of labor, about joint ownership of the means of production, were discussed, debated and assimilated by thousands of French workers."

Before midcentury, Catholic thinking had not yet recognized the problems of poverty and pauperism as endemic to industrial capitalism. More concerned with saving souls than with social welfare, Catholic attention to the social question was slow to evolve (Gould 1999, 114). Priests preached to their well-off parishioners that the rich depended on the poor as much as vice versa because it was through voluntary almsgiving that the privileged would ensure their salvation (Misner 1991, 16; Kahl 2005). This perspective, however, began to be challenged by French and German Catholics in the decades after Napoléon. Alarmed by the spread of deep and persistent poverty, and dismayed by the apparent social atomization brought on by the breaking up of old corporate forms, the new social Catholics sought a third way between liberalism and socialism. They searched for new institutions that could hierarchically organize and integrate individuals from different classes, much the same way the guild had once done. In their view, what was missing in the new liberal, postrevolutionary order were local social organizations, standing between the individual and state, that could revive social solidarity while addressing the needs of the poor.

One of the most important of the French social Catholics was Viscount Alban de Villaneuve-Bargemont. In the 1820s, he served as prefect of the Département du Nord, an area on the border with Belgium that encompassed

Lille and other industrial towns. After extensive study of the French and British economies, in 1834 he published *Économie politique chrétienne*, a study of French pauperism in which he concluded that France would be ill advised to follow in Britain's footsteps and should, as much as possible, preserve the pastoral traditions on which Christian bonds of mutual responsibility were founded. The state, he thought, should take an active role in alleviating pauperism by promoting new institutions such as mutual aid societies and credit unions for poor workers (Misner 1991, 50–52). Arguing that capitalists must not be allowed to enrich themselves by speculating on the "strength, needs and feelings" of their workers, he demanded that children under fourteen be barred from factories, and that employment be conditional on the ability to read, write, and calculate.[10] In 1841, now a member of the Chamber of Deputies, he was one of the key supporters of the first French child labor law (Misner 1991, 60–62; Solari 2009, 2010).

Social Catholicism and utopian socialism were more fertile in France than in Belgium, but French ideas and individuals did permeate the border. Fourier's most ardent disciple, Victor Considerant, brought his ideas to Belgium in the 1840s, giving a series of lectures in Brussels and having a significant impact on the thinking of Belgium's leading child labor policy entrepreneur, Ducpétiaux. Another social Catholic in Ducpétiaux's immediate circle was Adolphe Bartels, a Dutchman who made his way to Belgium via France to join the revolution in 1830. A socialist who nonetheless converted to Catholicism, Bartels represented the left wing of social Catholicism. In 1842, he published *Essai sur l'organisation du travail*, a Fourierist treatise on the merits of cooperatives, and from 1844 to 1846 was the editor of Belgium's leading leftist newspaper (Misner 1991). Also in the 1840s, charitable organizations seeking to put social Catholicism into concrete practice spread from France to Belgium, and the first Belgian Saint Vincent de Paul society was founded in Brussels in 1842 (Moody 1953).

Thus in the 1830s and 1840s, the Francophone intellectual milieu was rich with ideas about the structural causes, social consequences, and political solutions to the social question. Still, most French and Belgian elites regarded the problems of industrial society in terms of a supposed lack of morality among the new industrial proletariat and poor. Indeed, this was the primary lens through which they viewed the social question in these years (Cross 1989; Lynch 1988; Sewell 1980; Vleugels 2016). Historian Katherine Lynch (1988) describes the emergence of a "moral economy" discourse that sought to address the problems of industrial capitalism primarily by imposing bourgeois moral standards onto proletarian families. Although socialists were also deeply concerned about the moral dissolution they perceived among the lower classes, most elites eschewed the socialists' systemic or structural explanations for it. In their view, the solution to the social question lay in reforming the attitudes and behaviors of the poor.

This moral opprobrium is on clear view in the writings of the public intellectual physician Louis Villermé (1840), who wrote a widely read book on the physical and moral condition of textile workers in France. He drew attention not only to the wretchedness of workers' living conditions but also their dirtiness, sexual immodesty, drunkenness, and improvidence. These prejudices were likewise reflected in the writings of Daniel Legrand (1838), an industrialist in the Vosges who decried the immorality of the textile mill operatives—especially young workers' smoking, drinking, and premature parenthood. Such observers saw no contradiction in lamenting the extreme poverty of working-class families in one breath, and in the next, condemning the dissoluteness and improvidence of parents who sent their children into the factories (Villermé 1837).[11] Moreover, they linked this supposed moral degradation to the threat of rebellion and revolution against bourgeois property. For instance, the Belgian physicians Daniel Mareska and J. Heyman (1845, 243) warned, "In moments of unrest and popular effervescence, manufacturers, instead of finding in the workers they employ as many defenders of their lives and their belongings, encounter rather their foremost and bitterest enemies." Such thinking dominated elite attitudes toward poverty and proletarization in mid-nineteenth-century Belgium and France.

Child Labor Policy Entrepreneurship in France

As shown, France and Belgium were similar in many significant respects. They were both constitutional monarchies with similar state institutions. Both were Catholic countries mired in conflict between liberal secularists and conservative Catholics. Although laggards in public schooling compared with Prussia and Massachusetts (see chapter 4), both had recently enacted legislation to further the building of primary schools. Industrialization in both countries was ramping up, liberal economic doctrines were hegemonic, and the liberal bourgeoisie was growing in both economic and political power. Chambers of commerce exercised significant influence over economic policy, and workers were still politically marginalized. Both countries experienced high levels of unrest and similar sets of discursive approaches to the social question. These similarities suggest that we must go beyond a variable-based approach to explain why France enacted child labor legislation in the 1840s and Belgium did not. A comparative genetic account detailing the relational processes through which policy entrepreneurs responded to these conditions and pursued child labor reform is needed.

In France, child labor reform involved a larger and more diverse constellation of actors than in Prussia. Although reform occurred against the backdrop of a militant (though repressed) working class, the French child labor law of 1841 was not a direct response to workers' grievances or demands; it was instead the product of sustained advocacy by a loosely allied group of elites. Because France had a constitution, the architecture of its policy-making field was quite different than that of absolutist Prussia. It not only included the state but also overlapped significantly with the business and intellectual fields. With the "parliamentarization of contention" after 1830 (Tilly 1997), the state-society divide grew more permeable, and members of the intellectual and business fields, often organized into associations, frequently petitioned the parliament for legislative reforms. These institutional conditions meant that unlike in Prussia, actors other than state civil servants could exercise significant influence over child labor reform in France. It also meant that French policy entrepreneurs needed to take stakeholder interests—in particular, those of employers—more explicitly into account than their counterparts in Prussia did.

France went through what Kingdon (1984, 127–30) calls a lengthy "softening up" period in which the child labor problem was discussed within the policy field and beyond. Political advocacy on behalf of child labor regulation began in the late 1820s and was initiated by members of the capitalist class. The manufacturer Jean-Jacques Bourcart (1828, 327–28) of the Société industrielle de Mulhouse framed child labor regulation as a matter of interest for both employers and the state:

> The principal advantage to be drawn [from a child labor law] will be the health of the children . . . as well as their greater moral development. The master should have a choice of robust workers; he should have workers who are more intelligent and easier to guide. France, when necessary, will find *men* amongst them, defenders of the fatherland, whereas if she does not take certain energetic measures, she risks greatly that the workers . . . will become miserable, weak and morally depraved, incapable of preserving the glory of their country.

Bourcart proposed that the Mulhouse Society petition the government to demand limitations on child labor, which it did in 1828, and again in 1834 and 1837 (Weissbach 1989, 30–31, 36), arguing that French "society finds itself threatened by a weakly and degenerate population without principles" (Société Industrielle de Mulhouse 1837, 499).

In 1837, Commerce Minister Martin du Nord finally responded to the Mulhouse Society's pleas by sending a survey with questions about industrial child labor conditions as well as potential legislative responses to the *département* prefects and various bodies representing industrial interests, including the chambers of commerce, *chambres consultatives* (which represented the smaller towns and cities), General Councils of Commerce and Manufacturing, and the *conseils des prud'hommes* (labor courts). The ministry's inquiry revealed general (if not enthusiastic, consistent, or unanimous) acceptance among much of the French business elite of the need for some type of restriction on child labor (see table 3.4).[12]

TABLE 3.4. Employer Attitudes toward Child Labor Regulation in Prussia, France, and Belgium

	Minimum age	Maximum hours	Schooling before employment	Schooling alongside employment	Health exam	Ban night work	No regulations at all	No age/ hours regulations
Prussian Handelskammern (n = 2)	1 (50%)	1 (50%)	2 (100%)	1 (50%)	—	—	0 (0%)	1 (50%)
France, 1837								
Chambers (n = 24)	13 (54%)	11 (46%)	6 (25%)	12 (50%)	7 (29%)	7 (29%)	2 (8%)	5 (21%)
Council of manufacturing (n = 1)	1 (100%)	1 (100%)	—	—	—	—	—	—
Council of commerce (n = 1)	1 (100%)	1 (100%)	—	—	—	—	—	—
French chambers, 1840 (n = 20)	10 (50%)	13 (65%)	—	9 (45%)	—	8 (40%)	4 (20%)	8 (40%)
Belgian chambers, 1848 (n = 15)	12 (80%)	5 (33%)	10 (66%)	—	—	9 (60%)	2 (13%)	3 (20%)

Sources: LHA, Koblenz, Best. 403, Nr. 8082, 24–34; National Archives of France, F12–4705, F12–4706; Belgium, Ministère de l'Intérieur 1848, vol. 2.

Note: Chambers did not definitively answer every survey question; only explicit expressions of support are counted.

FIGURE 3.1. Charles Dupin. *Source*: Julien Leopold Boilly / Smithsonian Libraries, SIL-SIL14-D5-12.

Whereas the Council of Manufacturing wanted the minimum age to be seven and the Council of Commerce wanted it to be eight, the chambers were more humane. Of the thirteen chambers that endorsed a minimum working age, twelve proposed age nine or older. As for children's working hours, preferences ranged from no regulation at all to as few as eight, up to as many as thirteen hours per day.

Despite sizable, though certainly not overwhelming, support among capitalists for modest child labor regulations, du Nord did not seize the opportunity to pursue legislation. In the absence of government initiative, child labor reform advocacy was once again taken up by various nongovernmental actors. In 1838 and 1839, the Mulhouse Society as well as industrialist Legrand (1838) and others sent petitions to Paris demanding child labor legislation.[13] These advocates began picking up new allies in the state field—the most important being Chamber of Peers member Dupin. Dupin formally presented the Mulhouse Society's latest petition to the Chamber of Peers, and soon became the leading child labor policy entrepreneur in the period leading up to the adoption of the 1841 law (Anceau 2009; Heywood 1988, 228; Weissbach 1989, 64–65).

TABLE 3.5. Dual Membership in the Intellectual and Policy Fields in France and Belgium

	Legislators	Ministers	Public administrators	Total
France, 1831 to 1841 (n = 237 in 1840)	45 (19.0%)	9 (3.8%)	22 (9.3%)	60 (25.4%)
Belgium, 1838 to 1848 (n = 114 in 1848)	8 (7.0%)	3 (2.6%)	8 (7.0%)	17 (14.9%)

Sources: Institut Royal de France (1840) and Académie Royale des sciences, des lettres et des beaux-arts de Belgique (1848) were used to make a list of learned academy members. Numerous sources were used to determine academy members' policy field position, if any.

Notes: Figures refer to the number/percentage of Institut Royal de France members and Académie Royale de Belgique members who were also legislators, ministers, or high-ranking public administrators at the national level. Membership in the intellectual field was defined as belonging to a national learned society in the year that the law was passed/defeated. Learned society membership was derived from Institut Royal de France (1840) and the Académie Royale de Belgique (1848). Membership in the policy field was defined as being a national legislator, government minister, or national-level public administrator during the decade leading up to the child labor law's passage/failure (1831–41 in France, and 1838–48 in Belgium). Individuals who occupied more than one role are included in every category that applies to them, but the total column does not double or triple count anyone.

Dupin, the son of a lawyer, initially rose to prominence as a naval engineer and was a member of the Académie des Sciences morales et politiques, one of the five academies of the Institut de France, France's premier learned society. In 1819, he accepted a chair at the Conservatoire des Arts et Métiers in Paris and was made a baron in 1824. He thus belonged to both the policy and intellectual fields, which was quite common in France at the time. A prosopographical analysis of dual membership in the Institut de France and national government reveals that between 1831 and 1841, forty-five (19 percent) institute members were also legislators, nine (3.8 percent) served as government ministers, and twenty-two (9.3 percent) served in high-level public administration positions (see table 3.5). According to sociologist Corinne Delmas (2006, 155), during the July Monarchy, fully 70 percent of the members of the Académie des Sciences, including Dupin, were also legislators at some point in their careers—a situation that she describes as akin to osmosis. Because of this robust overlap between the two fields, not only were intellectual credentials, expertise, and discourses valued in the French policy field, but actors who belonged to both fields were embedded in a large community of politician-intellectuals from whom they could learn how to play by the rules of both fields.

Following a state-sponsored research trip to England, Dupin had become an enthusiastic advocate of the French adoption of policies that he believed were responsible for that country's industrial might. These included not only economic liberalization tempered by protectionism but also public investment in infrastructure, transportation, and human capital (Bradley 2012; Bradley and Perrin 1991; Démier 2009; Henderson 1982). Worker education was of particular interest to him; by the time of his appointment to the Chamber of Peers in 1827, he had written several academic textbooks for polytechnical students as well as political tracts on the importance of worker education (Grattan-Guinness 1984). Despite this advocacy, Dupin was impervious to most workers' grievances; he proselytized the benefits of mechanization, endorsed protectionism (which raised living costs), despised socialism, believed workers' associations and strikes should be illegal, and—most tellingly—opposed any sort of government regulation of the hours or wages of adult males (Anceau 2009; Bradley 2012). Unmoved by the utopian socialist and social Catholic discourse of the day, he was nonetheless not indifferent to the suffering of the working poor. His motivation for pursuing child labor regulation was grounded in a patriotic commitment to improving France's economic and military strength, alongside elitist concern about working-class vice. Accordingly, he defined the child labor problem as both a cause of human capital erosion and threat to working-class morality. As Lynch (1988, 33, 78–79, 190–99) documents, the latter concern placed him among the leading contributors to the French moral economy discourse.

In January 1840, sustained pressure exerted by the Mulhouse Society and other advocates finally pushed the new minister of commerce, the wealthy businessman Laurent Cunin-Gridaine, to introduce a child labor bill. Cunin-Gridaine may also have been moved to act by the first major workers' uprising in six years, which took place in Paris in May 1839. Staunchly liberal, he was not favorably disposed toward economic regulation, so his bill merely sought to empower the Commerce Ministry and departmental governments to impose industry-specific child labor rules, and thus fell far short of what advocates wanted.[14] A Chamber of Peers committee—led by Dupin and the social Catholic philosopher (and fellow Académie des Sciences member) Joseph Marie, baron de Gérando, and including five other legislators (two of whom were also members of the Académie des Sciences)—rejected the minister's bill, and in a report authored by Dupin, called for national regulation modeled after Great Britain's and Prussia's laws.[15]

Dupin's report is a masterpiece of alliance-building rhetoric, replete with strategic citation and framing. First, he referenced child labor laws already enacted by Britain and Prussia as models for French legislation, arguing that allowing France to be surpassed by other countries in this regard would "dishonor" the nation. Citing the policy precedents of France's rivals made it possible for him to contend that the committee "cannot . . . be reproached with sacrificing the interests of the French manufacturers to those of foreign competitors."[16] Whereas about 40 percent of Dupin's citations were of foreign laws and actors, more than 60 percent were of French politicians, intellectuals, and industrialists (see table 3.6). First, he mentioned the interventions of

TABLE 3.6. Citations and Frames in the Writings of Prussian, French, and Belgian Child Labor Policy Entrepreneurs

	Altenstein proposal (1828)	Bodelschwingh proposal (1835)	Dupin committee report (1840)	Ducpétiaux commission conclusion (1848)
CITATIONS				
Insiders	100%	100%	61%	7%
Local government / officials	35%	57%	—	0%
National government / officials	28%	8%	21%	
Chambers of commerce / individual industrialists	—	15%	11%	4%
National legislators	—	—	6%	—
Experts/intellectuals	—	—	10%	3%
Other domestic actors	—	—	16%	—
Domestic law	42%	24%	—	2%
Outsiders	0%	0%	40%	93%
British legislators	—	—	3%	4%
British factory inspectors	—	—	—	13%
Other British actors	—	—	5%	4%
British law	—	—	23%	11%
French legislators	—	—	—	30%
Other French actors	—	—	—	2%
French law	—	—	—	9%
Prussian law	—	—	5%	5%
Other country law	—	—	7%	17%
FRAMES				
Simple frames	100%	100%	60%	71%
Health/safety	43%		39%	26%
Education	47%	91%	9%	44%
Morals	26%	21%	28%	16%
Fundamental frames	3%	24%	55%	34%
Social order / criminality	—	12%	7%	1%
Economic prosperity / competitiveness	—	12%	31%	11%
National security / defense	3%	—	4%	—
National honor / strength	—	—	3%	—
Childhood happiness / suffering	—	—	4%	4%
Humanity	—	—	5%	—
Public interest	—	—	4%	2%
Rights	—	—	7%	18%

Notes: Percentages refer to the amount of total citation or framing text devoted to the particular category of citation or frame. Category percentages do not add up to 100 percent because text portions were often coded in more than one way.

several prominent Frenchmen who, like him, had dual membership in both the policy and intellectual fields. This included an address by Gérando to the Conservatoire des Arts et Métiers as well as Villermé's publications. Second, he drew particular attention to the "enlightened and generous" advocacy of the Mulhouse Society.[17] Third, he cited various national and local government insiders, including government officials, members of the Chambers of Peers and Deputies, chambers of commerce, labor courts, and General Councils of Agriculture, Commerce, and Manufactures, all of whom had expressed support for child labor regulation. This retinue of citations created the impression that intellectual, professional, government, and business elites all stood behind the committee's recommendations.

Dupin presented a three-pronged framing that adroitly blended academic and political language. First, exercising his fondness for statistics, he presented figures on Britain's industrial output before and after the passage of its child labor laws to frame regulation as compatible with economic growth. Second, he reported military statistics showing that disproportionately high numbers of French Army recruits from industrial areas were being rejected for being "infirm" or "deformed." From there, Dupin connected child workers' poor health to the fundamental frames of national defense and economic prosperity, asserting that overwork not only caused "individual suffering of the most afflicting kind" but also rendered "the country weak in military powers, and poor in all the occupations of peace." Third, Dupin connected working children's lack of school attendance to the moral degeneration of the working class. To support the need for mandatory schooling—especially "moral training"—he reported additional statistics purporting to demonstrate that unmarried birth and crime rates were higher in the industrial areas of France than in the agricultural districts. In light of these worrisome trends, mandatory schooling was needed to "bring back the working classes . . . to principles of order and morality, to a respect for the security of persons and property, and to a reverence for the laws and for religion." These fundamental concerns as well as the simple need to protect the health and lives of children trumped the right of fathers to "sell" their children into industrial servitude.[18]

Dupin's framing drew on a hegemonic moral economy discourse of alarm about the working class's assumed lack of virtue, and a patriotic discourse about the need to cultivate its physical and mental capacities to restore France's military and economic power. These social order, national security, and economic prosperity frames tapped into dominant discourses and appealed directly to elite interests. Further, his use of social scientific evidence and citation of intellectuals fit well with the discursive opportunity structure of the overlapping French policy and intellectual fields. Accordingly, his contentions were referenced and reiterated by various Chamber of Peers members during floor debate. Count de Montalembert, for example, praised "the splendid work of the recorder [Dupin]," and argued, "Can we close our eyes to the alarming symptoms which are displayed in all quarters, and which attest to, through the [statistical] figures, the deep corruption, the physical and the moral decrepitude of the working classes? Should we not fear for the future when we see, in the richest regions of France, the population, weakened by the precociousness of vice no less than by the excess of work, offering almost no resources to [military] recruitment?"[19] Such statements are evidence that Dupin's frames resonated and were deemed legitimate.

In place of the weak Ministry of Commerce bill, Dupin's committee proposed a program with a minimum employment age of eight, restrictions on children's working hours based on age, and the requirement that children either acquire two years of schooling before working or attend school while working.[20] With regard to the minimum age and maximum hours rules, Dupin claimed to have taken into consideration both foreign precedents and suggestions made by the General Councils of Commerce and Manufacture, striking a compromise between them. With regard to the minimum age, for example, Dupin said the committee would have recommended nine, but "feared the great inconvenience in the woolen factories."[21] Evidently, he and his fellow committee members recognized that in the liberal French policy field, given its institutionalized penetration by business, disregarding capitalist interests would be unwise.

The Chamber of Peers debated the merits of the government's and committee's proposals in March. It fell primarily to Dupin to win allies over to the committee's bill, and his influence was apparent from the outset. The first to speak was Commerce Minister Alexandre Gouin, who had in January presented the government's proposal, and had defended it on the grounds that it allowed for flexibility and sensitivity to differences among children, industries, enterprises, and regions. In February, however, Dupin had submitted the committee's report and proposal to the Chamber of Peers. By March, Gouin had changed his mind in favor of the committee bill because, he explained, he did not want to see France fall behind England and Prussia in social legislation. This change of heart suggests that Dupin's citation of foreign legislation had served its purpose and he had already turned a major veto player into an ally.[22]

Throughout the March debates, Dupin vigorously defended the committee bill's core provisions while expressing a willingness to compromise on its details. In his first statement before the Chamber of Peers, he said, "The recorder [Dupin] thus persists, in the name of the Committee, with the principal proposals it has submitted to the Chamber, whilst reserving the right, as far as clauses dealing with matters of detail are concerned, of benefitting from the insights which might arise from the discussion."[23] After each full day of debate, Dupin's committee met to make revisions to its proposal. The revisions were relatively minor, but demonstrate a readiness to adjust to the

Chamber of Peers' suggestions so long as the ideas did not undermine the bill's main components.[24]

Dupin and his allies succeeded in winning the Chamber of Peers' support for every major element of the committee bill save one: compulsory schooling for working children. After six days of discussion, the Chamber of Peers approved the amended bill and sent it to the Chamber of Deputies.[25] Dupin now found himself in a problematic situation. He considered removal of the education rules a grave mistake, but had no institutionalized path to push for their reinstatement. The bill was out of his hands; it was up to the deputies to decide what to do with it. Rather than letting the defeat go, however, Dupin seized the opportunity to formulate a creative and unconventional response. He mobilized resources that he had accumulated in the intellectual field, namely his long-standing relationship with the publishing house of the École Polytechnique, and hastened to release a tract that he addressed directly to his "non-political [open-minded] friends of the Chamber of Deputies" to urge them to not only support the bill but also restore the education rules (Dupin 1840, xi). This strategy—essentially an effort to piggyback mandatory schooling onto child labor legislation—was possible because of his dual membership position at the intersection of the policy and intellectual fields.

A Chamber of Deputies committee was formed to consider both the government's and the Chamber of Peers' bills, propose revisions, and write a report to justify them. In his report, the chair, the lawyer Charles Renouard, explained that the committee members had carefully considered the merits of both bills and decided to endorse the Chamber of Peers' bill.[26] He recapped Dupin's earlier arguments, mentioning the statistics that Dupin had presented, and invoking similar social order, national security, and economic prosperity frames. Child labor, he argued, was "not solely an individual ill, it is also a deep wound inflicted on the country, which has need of vigorous men for its works and its armies, intelligent men for the development of its national activity, upstanding and conscientious men for the preservation of general order and public peace."[27]

The correspondence between these and Dupin's assertions indicates that Renouard and the other members of the Deputies' committee regarded Dupin's framing of the child labor problem as legitimate. These potential veto players had become Dupin's allies. Renouard diverged from the Chamber of Peers, though, in that he offered an extensive defense of the state's duty to protect children's rights against abuses by parents and employers.[28] In addition, although Renouard and his fellow committee members endorsed the bill, they proposed two important amendments: a special factory inspectorate and, heeding Dupin's call, mandatory schooling for working children.[29] Compulsory education would fulfill society's most important obligation to its citizens, Renouard maintained: it would ensure the "moral existence" of the rising generation.[30] Moreover, he noted that the Guizot law of 1833, which required each commune to establish a public elementary school, had created the institutional precedent on which the child labor law merely sought to build.[31]

With this new bill in hand, Commerce Minister Gouin conducted another inquiry to gather opinions regarding the three proposals now on the table—those of the government, Chamber of Peers, and Chamber of Deputies—from the chambers of commerce and other bodies representing industrial interests.[32] This inquiry did not reveal any significant change in general opinion since the 1837 survey; the attitudes of the chambers of commerce were mixed, but the slim majority supported regulation of some kind (see table 3.4).

At the end of 1840, the deputies debated their commission's bill.[33] Capitalist interests were more strongly represented among the Chamber of Deputies members than among the Chamber of Peers members, and several representatives from centers of manufacture spoke in opposition to what they viewed as a threat to French economic competitiveness as well as an improper infringement on the liberty of workers and employers. In the end, these voices had little influence. The Chamber of Deputies voted to reinstate the education provisions and otherwise support the bill. The Chamber of Peers overwhelmingly approved the revised measure with little debate in early 1841, and it went into effect six months later (Koepke 1992; Weissbach 1989, 80–81).[34]

In summary, the French child labor law of 1841 was a response to macrostructural and institutional conditions that reform advocates then connected to child labor. The immiseration of the new industrial proletariat aroused pity and fear; moral economists like Villermé, Legrand, Bourcart, and Dupin argued that educating the children of the poor would make them less prone to licentiousness, crime, and rebellion. The continuing rivalry between France and its European neighbors stimulated economic liberalization, but also raised concerns about the relative "quality" of the French populace. Accordingly, reformers contended that raising a militarily fit and economically competitive population required intervening in children's industrial employment. Finally, past institutional changes and policy precedents created a platform for reform. Political liberalization ushered in by the July Revolution opened up opportunities for organized interests, such as the Mulhouse Society, to exert influence over policy making. British and Prussian child labor laws generated a positive policy feedback effect, providing a model for France to emulate and reassurance that regulation would not undermine economic growth. Closer to home, the Guizot law of 1833 supplied an institutional infrastructure to support the bill's mandatory school attendance provisions.

These macrosocial and institutional conditions laid the groundwork for a loosely allied group of industrialists, intellectuals, and legislators to advocate for child labor reform. Drafting five petitions over twelve years, the Mulhouse Society deserves credit for putting child labor on the national policy agenda. Its advocacy fits with the varieties-of-capitalism argument that employers support social legislation when they see it as a way to cultivate a better-skilled but also more pliant (in Bourcart's words, "easier to guide") workforce. The willingness of the majority of the chambers of commerce to support basic child labor rules suggests that capitalist buy-in helped pave the way for child labor reform under the procapitalist July Monarchy. Still, that France passed a real child labor law, rather than the commerce minister's weak enabling bill, is primarily attributable to the policy entrepreneurship of Charles Dupin.

Defeating the ministry's bill required a sustained alliance-building campaign—one in which Dupin's alliance-building skill and goal-directed creativity were essential. Dupin cited many prominent and respected French insiders in his report. He also cited foreign policy to make the case that France must not fall behind its rivals in social legislation. His framing of child labor as a problem of morality and social control drew on a dominant moral economy discourse, and his emphasis on economic prosperity and national security spoke directly to elite interests. His frames and citations thus fit with the discursive opportunity structure of the French policy field, and were deemed legitimate by Chamber of Peers members like Montalembert and Chamber of Deputies members such as Renouard. Perhaps most important given the French business field's institutional penetration into the policy field, Dupin compromised with employers, keeping the bill's provisions within the bounds of what most chambers would tolerate—a fact that he referenced repeatedly. Finally, his creativity of action is best exemplified by how he responded to the Chamber of Peers' rejection of the education provisions. Rather than let the defeat go, he rushed to publish a book in which he exhorted the Chamber of Deputies to reinstate the education requirements. This move was within the bounds of legislative protocol, but nonetheless highly unconventional.

In short, as in Prussia, it is difficult to imagine that France would have passed the law that it did, when it did, in the absence of a skilled and creative policy entrepreneur. Dupin's agency mattered. Yet in several ways, his policy entrepreneurship was both facilitated and constrained by his field position as well as the architecture of the French policy field. First, Dupin was part of a large community of academics that had crossed into politics and learned to play by the rules in both fields. Accordingly, several of his strategies—use of social statistics, citation of intellectuals, and publication of a book with an academic press—were made possible and appropriate by his position at the overlap of the intellectual and policy fields. Second, because of the business field's institutional penetration into the policy field, Dupin needed to compromise with capital and could not ignore the chambers' views as Bodelschwingh had done in Prussia. As a result, the French law was slightly less ambitious than it otherwise might have been, particularly in regard to the minimum employment age.

The Failure of Child Labor Policy
Entrepreneurship in Belgium

The first political intervention into the problem of child labor in Belgium came in 1842, when on the heels of the French law and likely in response to it, King Leopold I stated in opening the parliamentary session that the legislature should take seriously the "perfecting of the legislation and the protection of childhood in the factories" (Loriaux 2000, 20). A year later, the liberal prime minister, Jean-Baptiste Nothomb, ordered a special commission to investigate child labor in factories and mines, and to propose draft legislation. The investigation lasted several years. Factory owners' responses revealed that a small yet significant percentage of the workforce was young children (see table 3.1). The responses also revealed widespread alarm about the "deplorable" intellectual and moral condition of the workers. Illiteracy, drunkenness, promiscuity, prostitution, illegitimacy, and improvidence were all reportedly rife among the Belgian industrial working class.[35]

Employers were asked, "What is your opinion concerning a measure that would fix, depending on their ages, a maximum work period for work carried out by children? What limit should be established?" Forty employers among the sixty-seven responding supported some sort of limitation. Many did not give reasons, but those who did generally mentioned either protecting children's health and physical development, or giving them time to attend school, or both. Others mentioned safeguarding children's morality by shielding them from uncouth adults, or ensuring they had opportunity to receive a moral and religious education. The remaining twenty-seven opposed hours regulations for various reasons, including the necessity of integrating adults' and children's labor, and the impact it would have on children's earnings.[36]

Chambers of commerce were surveyed too. The Belgian policy field overlapped extensively with the business field, much as in France. A small but growing number of capitalists occupied political office (Clark 1984), and the chambers of commerce enjoyed significant policy influence. As part of the investigation, chambers were asked to comment on various possible policy interventions. Their responses reveal that as in France and Prussia, employers' attitudes on regulation were mixed. They were as a whole quite suspicious of the regulation of working hours, yet in comparison to their French counterparts, they were more supportive of a minimum working age (see table 3.4). Moreover, the age that Belgian employers proposed in their responses was generally higher than that established by French law (eight); of the fifteen chambers, ten wanted the minimum age to be nine or older. Belgian employers were also more favorably disposed than the French toward education requirements.

These results suggest that moderate child labor regulations, encompassing age and education rules but excluding hours restrictions, were within the realm of possibility in Belgium. Why, then, were no regulations enacted there until 1889? A commonly proposed answer is that the government was particularly sympathetic to capitalist interests and opposed child labor regulation for economic reasons (Gubin 2011; Scholliers 2009). This answer is incomplete, as we now see. True, the government was highly responsive to capital, yet most chambers were willing to accept minimum age and mandatory schooling rules for young workers. Why were these provisions not adopted in 1848?

That year, the Belgian child labor commission published the last of its findings and presented its proposal for a child labor law. The proposal closely resembled ideas developed elsewhere by the commission's de facto leader, Ducpétiaux (1843, 313–20). A liberal unionist and devout Catholic, Ducpétiaux was the son of a prominent Brussels lace manufacturer. As a young university graduate, he had embarked on a career in a law and journalism, and had avidly promoted the revolutionary cause in his writings. In 1830, he was appointed inspector general of prisons and charitable institutions—a position he held until 1861. A social policy expert in the early nineteenth-century mold, by the 1840s Ducpétiaux had built a well-established reputation as a prison reformer and anti–death penalty advocate (Aubert 1964). Like Dupin, he belonged to both the policy and intellectual fields. In Belgium, however, these fields did not overlap significantly. Whereas forty-five Institut de France members (19 percent) also belonged to the French legislature in the decade before it enacted a child labor law, only eight members (7 percent) of the Institut de France's counterpart, the Académie Royale de Belgique, were legislators too. Three Académie Royale members (2.6 percent) were government ministers during that time, and eight (7 percent), including Ducpétiaux, occupied high-level public administration positions (see table 3.5). The overlap between the Belgian policy and intellectual fields was thus significantly weaker than in France.

Ducpétiaux belonged to the Académie Royale and ranked among Belgium's leading public intellectuals. Nevertheless, because Belgium lacked a robust community of policy experts active in both fields, Ducpétiaux found his main intellectual home in the transnational penology field. He belonged to a well-networked, pan-European group engaged in a lively debate about how the ideal prison should be organized (Leonards and Randeraad 2014; Vanhulle 2010). He participated in this field by publishing numerous reports in which he presented copious criminal statistics as well as information about prisons and their reform in various countries. His leading field position was confirmed in 1846 when he helped organize the first penal congress in Frankfurt. Dupin's outward-looking orientation toward this transnational field is also evidenced by his vast library, in which texts by non-Belgian policy experts and philosophers are heavily represented.[37]

Ducpétiaux penned numerous quasi–social scientific tracts on a wide array of policy issues, ranging from primary education to pauperism; public health to

FIGURE 3.2. Édouard Ducpétiaux, Belgian inspector general of prisons and charitable institutions. *Source*: Joseph Demannez / *Annuaire de l'Académie des sciences, des lettres et des beaux-arts de Belgique*, 196–97.

savings banks. He initially became interested in child labor because of its connection with problems that had long concerned him. In his mind, the matter was largely one of education. In *De l'état de l'instruction primaire,* he commented that promoting the education of the working class would require limits on child labor (Ducpétiaux 1838, 290). Lack of schooling condemned the child laborer to ignorance, lifelong poverty, moral degeneration, and often criminality. This perspective also prevailed among child labor reformers in Prussia and, as we will see in chapter 4, Massachusetts; the difference is that in those states, child labor regulation was clearly linked to a broader social consensus on the importance of public schooling. Indeed, in Prussia and Massachusetts, child labor regulation essentially grew out of an effort to promote universal schooling. In Belgium, a segment of the elite shared Ducpétiaux's concerns, but a consensus had not yet emerged.

Ducpétiaux first tackled child labor directly in 1843 with the publication of *De la condition physique et morale des jeunes ouvriers et des moyens de l'améliorer*. This book makes it clear that compared with Bodelschwingh in Prussia and Dupin in France, Ducpétiaux had a more philosophical definition of the child labor problem—one strongly influenced by French utopian socialism and social Catholicism (Beecher 2001). Works by Saint-Simon, Fourier, Blanc, Blanqui, Cabet, and Proudhon feature in Ducpétiaux's personal library.[38] Although he reportedly had some personal connection with the Saint-Simonian church in Belgium (Dupont-Bouchat 1988), he was, for a time at least, more profoundly influenced by Fourier.

Fourier's impact is evident in *De la condition physique*, not only in Ducpétiaux's (1843, xii) direct endorsement of the Fourierist journal *Le Phalange* ("We cannot recommend enough the reading of this gazette to those who take an interest in the lot of the labouring class and the solution to social questions"), but in his call for a "special administration" to initiate social welfare projects as well as an international body to regulate trade, develop land, organize work, eliminate pauperism, and preserve peace. Fourier's influence is also obvious in the moral centrality that Ducpétiaux placed on "attractive labor" as a tool of human development and emancipation:

> The goal of man, no matter the position he occupies on the ladder of humanity, is the free and complete development of his physical, intellectual and moral faculties. Society, constituted in the interests of all, must give him the means to achieve this goal. Work is the most important of these means. Every man is obliged to work, and, by a necessary corollary, every man has the right to work. As a no less strict consequence, the work must be organized and remunerated in such a way as to ensure . . . his development and the satisfaction of his legitimate needs. Thus, it must foster health instead of harming it; it must be reconcilable with exercise and intelligence, the needs of education and the task of the moral improvement of individuals. . . . [It must] eliminate, through the variety and the succession of occupations, the monotony and the boredom ordinarily brought about by uniform and extended work (v).

For Ducpétiaux, industry needed a wholesale restructuring; child labor legislation—he included a law proposal in his book—was merely a first step: "The improvement of the condition of young workers must lead to the improvement of the condition of the laboring class in general; the bill on child labor must serve as an introduction to a regulatory bill on national labor" (v).[39]

The other strand of thought evident in *De la condition physique* is social Catholicism. Ducpétiaux's library contains many key works by early French-speaking social Catholics along with their intellectual predecessors and successors.[40] In the opening paragraphs, Ducpétiaux demonstrates unambiguously that he was inspired by deeply held Catholic convictions: "God had said to man: 'You shall work by the sweat of your brow,' but he also gave him cause to hope that following the work he would have received a fair remuneration, the satisfaction of a duty fulfilled, prosperity and peace. We have made of work a curse, an instrument of torture and of death. Who is to blame? And how has the goal which Providence had assigned to human activity found itself so deformed?" (ii). With arguments such as these, Ducpétiaux established himself as a pioneer of Belgian social Catholic thought, but in the 1840s, his was still a relatively isolated voice—one of the few of any significance in Belgium.

Ducpétiaux defined child labor as a threat to human development in a holistic sense and violation of God's plan for humanity. Like Bodelschwingh and Dupin, though, he was also motivated by a more conventional elite problem definition that emphasized the threat that the popular classes posed for social order: "Let us then heed this long cry of suffering rising up within the laboring class as a vigorous protest, a deafening appeal! . . . It is our duty, [but] it is also in our interest. Because let there be no mistake about it: the edifice of our domination is less solid than we might think. . . . It is impossible to be ignorant of the warning signs of a new revolution . . . of the proletariat against property" (xiii–xiv). Elementary education, in his view, was the best means for securing the social stability on which bourgeois society relied: through it, society could exercise a "deep, intimate domination; a domination all the more powerful in that it establishes itself little by little by habits, and seeps into souls secretly without their being aware of it" (Ducpétiaux 1838, vi). As in Prussia and France, this ominous rhetoric was a reaction to the uptick in working-class social unrest in the 1830s and 1840s. Elites had come to view workers with fear and suspicion, and the arguments Ducpétiaux adopted in his book accorded strongly with elite interests. When it came time to defend the commission's child labor bill in 1848, however, he prioritized a different—far less effective—framing.

The child labor commission's bill—clearly Ducpétiaux's brainchild, given its similarity with the law he had proposed in *De la condition physique*—was ambitious. It included a minimum age of ten for industrial employment, a year above that in Prussia, and two years above that in France. In other respects, the bill went far beyond legislation in other countries (see table 1.1), and certainly far beyond what the Belgian chambers were willing to countenance (see table 3.4).[41] Ducpétiaux had one big chance to defend this proposal and recruit allies: a seventy-seven-page conclusion—authored by himself and Director of Mines Administration Auguste Visschers—that attempted to justify the proposed measures.[42] Table 3.6 presents an analysis of this document's frames and citations. Two results stand out. First, rather than using the social order frame that Ducpétiaux had presented in the past, child labor is framed as fundamentally a matter of children's rights. Ducpétiaux and Visschers argued that the state had not only the duty but also the authority to promote liberty—not just the liberty of the strong, but of the weak as well. Defending the rights of the child required circumscribing to some degree the liberty of employers and fathers. Such intervention, "far from being a violation of freedom, on the contrary serves as an auxiliary and a guarantee to it."[43]

In making this principled argument, the authors heavily cited French legislators, including Deputy Renouard: "If the father has his rights conferred on him by nature, the child also has his; if the father infringes the rights of the child, it is up to the state to protect him."[44] This rights frame was risky, though. The notion of children's rights certainly had appeared in discussions around child labor in Prussia, France, and England, but this was the first time it was used as the main fundamental frame in the major outlet in which a child labor law was being proposed and defended. Unlike other fundamental frames, the children's rights frame was controversial. By law, throughout Europe, the rights of the paterfamilias were paramount; state intervention into the familial sphere was regarded with deep suspicion. The idea of children's rights as such only gained wide legitimacy in Belgium at the end of the nineteenth century (Dupont-Bouchat 2004). In short, the concept of children's rights was neither dominant nor legally institutionalized, and thus did not fit neatly with the Belgian policy field's discursive opportunity structure.

The other major frame that Ducpétiaux and Visschers used appealed more directly to elite interests and did evoke hegemonic discourses, but it was consigned to a footnote in which they maintained that evidence from England countered the concern that labor regulation undermined economic prosperity. British exports had grown significantly since the Factory Acts had been in place, leaving no reason to believe that regulating child labor would undermine the Belgian economy.[45]

This points to the second finding presented in table 3.6: like Dupin and Bodelschwingh, Ducpétiaux and Visschers made ample use of citation. Yet the difference in whom they cited is marked. Bodelschwingh tended to cite local government officials and occasionally the Aachen chamber of commerce. Dupin cited a mix of French intellectuals, legislators, and employers as well as foreign (mainly British) policy precedents. Ducpétiaux and Visschers overwhelmingly cited foreigners. A mere 7.3 percent of their citations were of Belgian actors—this even though they had at their disposal an extensive report with favorable statements from a wide variety of Belgian employers, health professionals, and government officials. This was in keeping with the practices of the transnational penology field in which Ducpétiaux was active, but whether it would resonate with the expectations of domestic audiences was less clear.

By August 1848, Ducpétiaux and Visschers had finalized their report and sent it to Prime Minister Rogier. We do not know what Rogier thought about the commission's bill, but in August 1849 he sent it and the conclusion to all fifteen chambers of commerce to solicit their reactions.[46] This was normal practice with regard to economic legislation and a move that Ducpétiaux should have anticipated.

Not surprisingly, the Belgian chambers overwhelmingly rejected the bill's key provisions.[47] Of the eleven responses that survive, all but two—those of Ostende and Bruges, which had no manufacturing to speak of—were largely negative.[48] Eight of the remaining nine chambers opposed the proposed regulation on the working hours of children; many argued that due to the integration of child and adult labor, this would be impractical and raise production costs. In the name of freedom of contract, seven opposed any limitations on the working hours of adults. The only child labor provision that received wide support was a minimum working age of ten; eight of the eleven chambers endorsed or did not oppose this idea, and two—Tournai and Verviers—even thought the minimum age should be raised to twelve years. The Tournai chamber contended that children younger than twelve should be expected to attend school and should not be employed without a schooling certificate. Besides Tournai, only the Brussels chamber explicitly endorsed a mandatory schooling requirement, but none of the others explicitly opposed such a measure.

By far the most extensive response came from the chamber in Liège, a major mining center. In a volley of attacks, it bitterly denounced the bill, accusing Ducpétiaux and Visschers of being overly intellectual: in their well-intentioned but naive and misguided attempt to protect children, these "men of study and of the office" would only cause harm to the very people they were trying to protect (Liège Chamber of Commerce 1860, 8). The chamber's counterframes explicitly reject Ducpétiaux's and Visschers's frames and citations; these had resonated—elicited a strong reaction—but had definitely not been deemed legitimate (Koopmans 2004).

The largest share of the counterframes (34.5 percent) attacked the citation of foreign actors and precedents; the "authors have found themselves in [an] . . . awkward position, because they have been obliged to draw their inspiration from foreign sources" (Liège Chamber of Commerce 1860, 8). Economic arguments accounted for another 22 percent of the counterframes. Although the commissioners' economic frame had evoked hegemonic discourses and spoke to elite interests, and in this respect fit well with the policy field's liberal, procapitalist discursive opportunity structure, it was received as illegitimate. Liège employers did not consider the commission's claim that regulation would not harm industry empirically credible because it did not square with their direct experience of intense economic struggle (Snow and Benford 1988). On the contrary, they argued that productivity would be harmed and poor families would suffer.

Finally, in some of its most forceful passages, the Liège Chamber of Commerce (1860, 17–18) threw the rights frame back into the commissioners' faces (13 percent of counterframes), asserting that child labor regulation was an egregious violation of the rights of fathers: "[The commissioners] want to enslave and govern [the father]. . . . By what right are the authors of the bill confiscating these precious liberties? Has the worker abdicated his status as a citizen, have the laws ceased to be impartial? Is this not an insult to our laboring classes, and to class them with a cast of pariahs unworthy of possessing and exercising civil rights?" These employers considered the argument that children's rights trumped fathers' rights to be illegitimate. This was unsurprising given that the idea of children's rights was still marginal and not institutionalized in law. In the midst of this full-throated attack, however, the Liège chamber reiterated its support for establishing a minimum age of employment (22).

Ducpétiaux's bill's defeat is mainly attributable to his failure to compromise with industrial interests, not to cite or frame effectively. Nevertheless, the citations of foreigners and the children's rights frame provided the Liège chamber with easy ammunition for a strong counterargument. Ducpétiaux's errors helped the chamber defend its position, and its forceful attack likely helped convince the government to drop the bill. In any case, its and the other chambers' opposition killed the bill; no further action was taken (Gubin and Lefèvre 1985; Loriaux 2000).

By the late 1840s, then, macrostructural and political conditions were reasonably favorable to child labor reform in Belgium. Working-class social disorder was as much a concern there as elsewhere. Like France and Prussia, Belgium was engaged in intense economic competition with England, and had as much at stake in fostering a vigorous, skilled workforce as any industrializing country. The policy field was also ripe for reform. Following France's lead, the king had urged the legislature to enact a child labor law, and the government had commissioned a major investigation. Powerful stakeholders—the chambers of commerce—were favorably disposed toward minimum age and education requirements. Yet in the absence of a policy entrepreneur capable of taking advantage of these promising conditions, reform failed. Unlike Bodelschwingh and Dupin, Ducpétiaux was unable to forge alliances in the Belgian policy field. Like Altenstein, his main error was to pursue an ideal bill rather than a compromise, but his framing and citation strategies did not help.

Ducpétiaux's failures as a child labor policy entrepreneur in some ways mirror his difficulties as a prison reformer and education policy advocate. In a revealing article, Bert Vanhulle (2010) analyzes Ducpétiaux's successes and failures as inspector general of Belgium's prison system. In one sense, Ducpétiaux was more effective as a reformer of prisons than as a child labor advocate. His main policy goal was a cellular system that would segregate prisoners from one another, which was thought to block moral contagion. Although he was unable to get a law passed, he did manage to implement the system in newly built institutions, and older institutions were reformed to group prisoners by age, sex, and severity of offense. He was able to see through pieces of his desired prison reforms because his official position granted him latitude over prison administration, and opponents did not have the power to block him (Aubert 1964).[49] As Vanhulle illustrates, however, the actual implementation of these measures was often incomplete because lower-level prison officials found them impractical and ineffective. Despite his self-presentation as someone whose recommendations were grounded in empirical realities, Ducpétiaux's reform program was in fact based on an idealized model. He did not listen to local prison officials' concerns, compromise with them, or seek to reach down for allies who might have facilitated implementation. Rather, he exhibited the same single-minded, purist vision—immune to opposing perspectives of those with direct experience with the problem—that he displayed as a child labor reformer. His efforts at education reform were marked by similar liabilities. An ambitious bill he drafted in 1838 was modeled after the best legislation in other countries and exceeded a contemporaneous government proposal by forty-nine clauses (Ducpétiaux 1838, xvii–xviii); it was also a political nonstarter.

The point is not that Ducpétiaux would have definitely succeeded in passing a child labor law in Belgium had he used compromise, framing, and citation in ways that fit with the priorities and ideas of others in the policy field. Many hurdles separated his bill from enactment, and as director general of prisons his impact on legislative outcomes was limited by institutional constraints. He was not a lawmaker. Moreover, like France under the July Monarchy, Belgium was notoriously friendly to capital, and any social legislation there faced an uphill battle. The point, rather, is that given the absence of a strong labor movement, effective middle-class policy entrepreneurship was necessary (not sufficient) for child labor law enactment in mid-nineteenth-century Belgium. Given his failure to exercise alliance-building skill and goal-directed creativity, Ducpétiaux squandered a unique window of opportunity for regulatory welfare development in Belgium.

The point is also not that Ducpétiaux was inherently stupid, or intrinsically lacking in skill and creativity. He could be an intelligent and effective actor in other contexts; he was, after all, a highly successful player in the transnational penology field. His problem was simply that he misrecognized the rules of the game of the policy field, inappropriately importing strategies into it from the intellectual field in which he excelled. These mistakes were "his fault," to be sure, but the likelihood of his making them was increased by the absence of a robust overlap between the two fields in Belgium.

In any case, Ducpétiaux played no further role in child labor reform efforts there; he was not, for instance, at all involved in a second attempt to enact a child labor law initiated by the Ghent Chamber of Commerce in 1859. By that time, though, child labor regulation had become even more politically challenging. In the 1840s, it was still possible to combine support for mandatory schooling with proclerical social Catholicism. This began to change after 1847 when an all-liberal government, under the leadership of Rogier and Frère-Orban, came to power. This government initiated an explicitly anticlerical program, focusing on ending the church's grip on public schooling. A new "young liberal" movement in the 1850s vehemently advocated both compulsory schooling and the removal of the Catholic church from public education at all levels. For this movement, school reform was the weapon through which the secularization and democratization of public life could be accomplished. The conservative Catholic majority fought back bitterly (Gubin and Lefèvre 1985; Gubin 2011), and moderates, including Ducpétiaux, reluctantly abandoned their previous support for compulsory instruction. Mandatory schooling thus became a political lightning rod inextricably linked with anticlericalism. In this context, the Ghent chamber's proposed child labor measure, which included compulsory education for working children, was a nonstarter.[50]

Belgium was thus unable to pass a child labor law until the relatively late date of 1889. This long-overdue measure was precipitated in 1886 by a violent strike wave, which stoked the growth of the newly formed Belgian Labor Party. The party's central rallying cry was universal suffrage, but compulsory schooling and the abolition of child labor were among its explicit demands.[51] These developments "forced" the government to enact protective labor legislation, including not only child labor rules but regulations on female employment, workers' housing, and wages as well (Witte, Craeybeckx, and Meynen 2009, 119; see also Deneckere 1993; Dubois 1902; Strikwerda 1997). According to Belgian labor historian Gita Deneckere (1993, 359), the 1889 reforms "cannot be attributed to the enlightened insights of the upper classes" but were instead the direct result of "collective action from below." This characterization suggests that the country's first child labor law can be regarded as one of several (partial and limited) concessions to workers spurred by their growing political and economic power resources.

Field Position and Alliance Building

In the 1830s and 1840s, France and Belgium were in many ways similar in terms of their state institutions, religion, education systems, and discursive approaches to the social question. In both countries, macrostructural conditions—industrialization, proletarianization, social unrest, and international economic and military competition—laid the groundwork for child labor reform, but did not guarantee reformers' success. In the absence of a politically empowered working class, a socially skilled, creative, and goal-directed policy entrepreneur was the necessary link between these conditions and institutional change. The limited development of representative institutions in both countries meant that this reformer would not necessarily have to be a state civil servant, as in Prussia; it also meant that he would need to take greater account of diverse interests, particularly those of organized capital.

In providing a genetic analysis of the course of child labor politics in two countries, this tale of two reformers demonstrates that their differential impact is attributable to differences in their relational and problem-solving strategies. Dupin exhibited considerable alliance-building skill, as evidenced by his citation of respected insiders, use of frames that fit with the prevailing discursive opportunity structure, and willingness to compromise with potential allies. Ducpétiaux, in contrast, cited the wrong people, used the wrong frames, and— most consequentially—refused to compromise with influential stakeholders. Dupin exercised significant creativity of action too, turning to unconventional methods in a problematic, perplexing situation. Ducpétiaux did not. Finally, Dupin exhibited a clear sense of goal directedness, facing setbacks by sticking to his core vision of reform even while compromising on details. His policy entrepreneurship was characterized by both flexibility and steadfastness—two sides of the same course of action. In contrast, not only was Ducpétiaux a rigid idealist, but he let the child labor issue fade from the agenda after one defeat, squandering a narrow window of opportunity for reform.

These differences are to some degree matters of personality irreducible to social context. The two men's field positions, however, as well as the architectures of their respective policy fields, played an important role. Like Dupin, Ducpétiaux belonged to both the policy and intellectual fields, but because the overlap between the two fields was weak in Belgium, the country did not have the robust community of politician-intellectuals that France had. Ducpétiaux therefore had little opportunity to learn how to play by the rules of both fields. Instead, when he drafted his proposal, he abided solely by the norms of the transnational penology field in which such "best practices" thinking, grounded in cross-national comparison and utopian social philosophy, was valued; while ignoring the realities of the domestic policy field in which compromise, especially with industrial interests, was required. In contrast, Dupin understood the need to compromise with capital and cite French political insiders.

Moreover, because the intellectual and policy fields overlapped so heavily in France, the frames and citations Dupin imported from the former were actually appropriate to the latter. When Dupin deployed social statistics to frame child labor, he was speaking a positivist discourse that enjoyed legitimacy among French policy makers. When he cited French intellectuals like Villermé, he was dropping names that carried weight in policy-making circles. Ducpétiaux's extensive citation of foreign actors and legal precedents, on the other hand, was far more suited to the transnational intellectual field than the Belgian policy field. It is no surprise, then, that he was derided as a man "of study and of the office" who was inspired by irrelevant foreign models and did not understand Belgian industrial realities. Finally, in the face of defeat, Ducpétiaux exhibited no creative response or goal directedness. This is a marked contrast to Dupin's refusal to give up on the education requirements, and his creative move to publish a book aimed at influencing the Chamber of Deputies' votes.

Alongside the Prussian case study, this comparison provides strong evidence that the origin of regulatory welfare—both the emergence and content of early child labor legislation—depended on the ideas and agency of individual policy entrepreneurs. In the 1830s and 1840s, European states still lacked the institutionalized capacity to respond to the dislocations of industrial capitalism in routinized ways. Administrative entities like ministries of labor did not yet exist, and child labor laws did not emanate directly from preexisting state mandates. Moreover, labor was still too weak to advocate effectively for labor legislation. Under these conditions, elite and middle-class reformers had to take the lead. When they were successful, these actors skillfully forged alliances around their reform agendas and creatively overcame barriers to enactment. The laws that were passed embodied, in large part, their particular definitions of the child labor problem and foreclosed alternative approaches. Policy entrepreneurs like Altenstein and Ducpétiaux, who refused to compromise with stakeholders, or use frames and citations that fit with the discursive opportunity structure, failed. In Belgium, this meant that child labor regulation was delayed for nearly forty years.

These case studies tell us less, though, about the scope conditions under which policy entrepreneurs' ideas and agency matter more or less. Progressive policy change is not always mainly attributable to elite policy entrepreneurship. Under certain conditions, other factors can be more important. In the next chapter, I explore such a case. When a policy proposal benefits from both complementarity with existing institutions and cultural consensus, and as a result, faces no opposition in the policy field, then reformers' individual capacities and actions are far less consequential.

4

Defending Democracy

CULTURAL CONSENSUS AND CHILD LABOR REFORM IN MASSACHUSETTS

Early nineteenth-century Massachusetts, France, and Prussia were characterized by radically different political systems, institutional structures, and social worlds. France was a constitutional monarchy in which democratic rights were restricted to the upper echelon, whereas Prussia was an absolute monarchy where policy making was controlled by a powerful, centralized bureaucracy. Both countries were industrializing but still largely agrarian (Bairoch 1982; Dennison and Simpson 2010, 149). Massachusetts, on the other hand, was a rapidly urbanizing and industrializing democracy in which political participation was widespread, and social mobility was a real possibility for many. Despite these differences, all three produced broadly similar, pioneering child labor laws at roughly the same time (for a comparison, see table 1.1). Even more strikingly, all three enacted these laws even though no broad-based political or economic faction demanded them. In 1836, Massachusetts became the first US state to regulate child labor when it required children working in "manufacturing establishments" to attend school for at least three months a year. Six years later it restricted the working hours of children under twelve to ten per day.

Although the democratic institutions structuring the early nineteenth-century Massachusetts policy field were robust, the field was in other respects undeveloped compared with the European states described earlier. The field's boundaries were vague, and its membership unstable. The state administrative apparatus was still bare bones; this was the time of the state of "courts and parties," as Stephen Skowronek (1982, 39) famously put it. Terms of office for the governor and state legislators were one year only. Career politicians were still a rarity, and most elected officials had their primary occupations in law, commerce, manufacturing, banking, education, ministry, or agriculture. Thus few were primarily in the policy field, and because dual membership was commonplace, the field overlapped heavily with various professional and civil society fields. This would shape the ideas and strategies of Massachusetts child labor policy entrepreneurs.

Just as in Prussia, Massachusetts's first reforms were conceived primarily as a way to ensure that working children received some measure of formal schooling. Low attendance rates, particularly in industrial towns, spurred reformers to pursue new regulations to compel working children to attend school. The education field generated ideas—especially about the dangers that lower- and working-class children posed, and how to address them—that strongly influenced how Massachusetts reformers defined the child labor problem. Indeed, the author of the 1836 law, James G. Carter, was a leader in both the education and policy fields, playing an active part in an elite discourse on the perils and promises of the state's common schools. Moreover, existing educational infrastructures provided reformers like Carter with institutional resources on which to build their plans for child labor regulation. As in Prussia, a comparatively well-developed primary education system ensured that children barred from factory employment would not be consigned to the unruly streets but could instead be placed in schools to learn appropriate skills and values.

Because Massachusetts child labor reformers' programs were so closely aligned with existing education policy priorities and discourses, they faced no opposition, and therefore did not have to engage in strategic compromise or creative problem-solving. These reformers' agency mattered simply because *someone* had to articulate a culturally appropriate response to low attendance and fears about popular social unrest. But compared to French and Prussian policy entrepreneurs, who faced significant pushback against their policy plans, Massachusetts reformers' individual attributes and actions mattered less for policy outcomes than their programs' institutional complementarity and cultural fit. This finding helps to establish one of the scope conditions—namely the existence of political opposition—under which policy entrepreneurs' alliance-building skill and goal-directed creativity are more important for explaining policy outcomes.

Education Reform and Discourse in Massachusetts

In early nineteenth-century Massachusetts, attitudes toward children were still strongly colored by the Puritan belief that they were born inherently "depraved" and required strict discipline to break their sinful natures. Moralistic tracts written by self-styled child development experts abounded, warning of dire consequences should children fail to fully submit to earthly authorities and to God. Heman Humphrey, a conservative Congregationalist minister and president of Amherst College from 1823 to 1845, urged parents to establish "complete subjection" of their children by their first birthdays, and to rigorously implement a course of social, moral, and intellectual training in early childhood. He warned that lax discipline would produce "stubborn" children ruled by "evil passions" who would ultimately commit crimes and succumb to "licentiousness" in adulthood (Humphrey 1840, 22–23). Other contemporary moralists, more lenient than Humphrey, rejected authoritarian discipline in favor of more gentle methods adjusted to the child's natural capacities and individual inclinations. By the 1850s, the doctrine of infant depravity had been called into question and began to be replaced by a conception of the child as a highly susceptible blank slate. But even these more progressive commentators regarded the undisciplined child as a deep threat to the social order and survival of democratic institutions (Wishy 1968; Kuhn 1947). Given that poor and immigrant parents' child-rearing practices could not be trusted, it was essential to ensure that their children benefit from the edifying influence of the state's common schools.

The commonwealth's long-standing commitment to education had Puritan roots. As early as 1647, the Massachusetts Bay Colony ordered every small township to appoint a teacher to instruct children in reading and writing, and every larger one to set up a grammar school at the public's expense. Such steps were necessary to thwart Satan, "that old deluder," whose chief project was "to keep men from the knowledge of the Scriptures." Promoting the literacy required to acquire religious knowledge and inculcate Christian morality was the chief goal, but it is clear that colonial lawmakers envisioned schooling as a gateway to higher learning and upward mobility too. To that end, the local schoolmaster was required to be "able to instruct youth so far as they may be fitted for the university" (Emerson 1869, 13). The common school curriculum's Puritan religious underpinnings grew less overt, but remained in place throughout the eighteenth and nineteenth centuries. As immigration from Ireland and eventually southern Europe ramped up, elites clung to the common school as the chief way the state could impose Anglo-Saxon Protestant values and mores on an increasingly diverse (read: Catholic) population (Fraser 2016).

By the 1820s, however, the common school was already reputed to be in serious decline. Private academies proliferated, and the wealthier and native born lost interest in maintaining institutions for poor and immigrant children. A common school reform movement emerged. In 1830, the American Institute of Instruction was founded in Boston, and began to lobby the legislature for normal schools and a state board of education. Its members, including James Carter, George Barrell Emerson (headmaster of a Boston girls' school), and the Unitarian minister Charles Brooks, were inspired by the example of the

Prussian teacher seminaries and primary schools. Emerson and Brooks—as well as Horace Mann—even made "Atlantic crossings" (Rodgers 1998) to study the Prussian system, and Brooks was in touch with French education reformers such as Victor Cousin (Barnard 1851, 151; Emerson 1869, 31–32; Cousin 1838). Schools were supported by local taxes, but in 1835 the state established a fund "for the aid and encouragement of common schools"; by 1866, it had reached $2 million (Emerson 1869, 33). Emerson estimated that by the mid-1860s, Massachusetts was spending an average of $12 in state and local funds on education per school-age child—an enormous sum compared with other states and countries, such as France, where the average expenditure in 1856 was about $2 per child (34–35).

The Massachusetts Board of Education was created in 1837 with Mann as its secretary. The board originated as a sort of clearinghouse for the collection and dissemination of statistics and information about the problems faced by the common schools as well as recommendations for how to address these issues. In addition to collecting data and publishing reports, the board established two state-funded teacher training (normal) schools in 1839. Beyond these roles, Mann exercised little institutional power, but he marshaled his considerable rhetorical skills to exert great influence over education policy in the state. In his reports and lectures, he paid particular attention to the dilapidation, poor design, and overcrowding of schoolhouses; lack of adequate teacher training and examination; poor quality of instruction at some schools; high rates of absenteeism; and indifference of parents and the community toward what he perceived as the common schools' decline.

Even though compulsory schooling was not adopted in Massachusetts until 1852, when children between eight and fourteen were required to attend school for at least twelve weeks each year, enrollment rates were still quite high. Nearly 73 percent of the state's white children between five and nineteen were enrolled in public school in 1830 (Fishlow 1966, 43; see figure 2.1), and this figure does not include those enrolled in private institutions. Enrollment, however, did not guarantee attendance, and reformers agonized over the high rate of absenteeism in some school districts. Early school returns suggest that absenteeism was indeed a problem in some towns. During the winter 1837 session, for example, 79 percent of the enrolled pupils could be found in school on any given day.[1] Attendance rates at schools in manufacturing towns seem to have fallen well below this cumulative average, however. In Lowell, 69 percent of school-age children were enrolled, but only 55 percent attended school on any given day during the winter session; in Fall River, these figures were 83 and 52 percent, respectively. Mann declared the number of students absent and tardy "deplorable."[2] Accordingly, one of his top goals as secretary of the board was to increase enrollment and attendance rates, particularly in the manufacturing districts. In this he seems to have been moderately successful: under his leadership, the average schooling that children between four and sixteen received increased from 140 days in 1840 to 154 in 1848 (Vinovskis 1972, 521).

An old but still influential body of literature has connected nineteenth-century US education reform with economic transformation, arguing that the development of a universal and increasingly bureaucratized public school system was aimed primarily at preparing children for the punctuality, routinized discipline, and basic intellectual skills required in the new industrial labor market (Katz [1968] 2001; Tyack 1974; Field 1976; Rury 2002). According to economists Samuel Bowles and Herbert Gintis (2011, 29), "Education was to help preserve and extend the capitalist order. The function of the school system was to accommodate workers to its most rapid possible development." An examination of Mann's and Carter's writings, though, suggests that at least at this early period, reformers were far more concerned with readying children for membership in a (semi)democratic republic than preparing them for participation in the nascent industrial economy (Vinovskis 1970). More influenced by the pedagogy of Pestalozzi than the ideas of Joseph Lancaster (Chambliss 1968; Hutchinson 1943), reformers such as Mann and Carter (1826, 41) explicitly rejected schooling modeled after the factory system as better suited to "training young animals" than teaching children.[3] These men viewed free, universal elementary education as the foundation of US democracy. As in Prussia and France, education was seen as a tool for creating a virtuous citizen—but in this case (if he was male, anyway), a citizen who was also a voter, jury member, and exerciser of a broad slate of civil rights.

Beyond rhetoric, the numbers do not support the notion that early school reform was primarily geared toward preparing children for factory work. School enrollment rates were already high in Massachusetts before industrialization, and higher in rural than in urban manufacturing areas (Kaestle and Vinovskis 1980; Rubinson 1986). Further, many employers were consistently uncooperative with regulations requiring working children to attend school. Evasion tactics and resistance only grew stronger as industrialization advanced; many employers evidently did not find a basic education necessary or desirable for their young workers. Thus the early proponents of schooling were more often political and social leaders, not capitalists, and the expressed aims were more frequently civic than economic. Although the reformers' philosophy was bent on imposing uniform, middle-class, Anglo-Saxon norms and values on an increasingly diverse population, it was not intended to justify turning children into docile worker drones (Kaestle 1983).

A mixture of optimism and fear motivated reformers such as Mann and Carter to address these issues through common school reform. On the one hand, they believed in the promise of public education to lift children out of poverty and allow them to achieve their potential as human beings as well as citizens. They had great faith in US institutions, especially the common schools, to counteract poor parents' supposedly negative influence on their children and to develop such children into responsible, productive, peaceable citizens. According to Emerson (1869, 26), a founding member of the American Institute of Instruction, the function of the common schools was to raise "the gifted children of the indigent . . . to better opportunities, and thence to the highest stations of society." In his *Essays upon Popular Education*, Carter (1826, 20) argued that if properly invested in, the common schools would still make upward social mobility possible: "Every generation . . . will bring its quota of new men to fill the public spaces of distinction—men who owe nothing to the fortunes or the crimes of their fathers, but all . . . to their own industry and the common schools." Carter optimistically envisioned a truly fluid society in which merit, not inherited wealth, would determine a child's future—a line of thinking quite different from the views that motivated education reform in Germany, where upward mobility for the children of the lower working class was generally unthinkable. Beyond making it possible for children of all backgrounds to fulfill their potentials, reformers viewed public education as the wellspring of Massachusetts's economic prosperity: "Having no other mines to work, Massachusetts has mined into the human intellect" (Mann 1849, 150). Universal education, they believed, would rain fortune down on individual citizens and the state as a whole.

Carter's and Mann's extensive writings on education, though, are equally characterized by a sense of apprehension toward what would become of Massachusetts society if the common schools were to continue their apparent decline. For them and other contemporary commentators, an uneducated mass posed several serious dangers (Block 2012). These were particularly salient for Whig leaders, including Carter and Mann, who were concerned about the rise of populist Jacksonian democracy, which seemed to threaten the foundations of the social order by elevating the uncouth and uneducated to positions of power and influence (Groen 2008). This was not only the view of the Whigs; the idea that the common schools were an indispensable requirement for social stability was "virtually unopposed" by northeastern elites in general—an "undisputed good" that all could get behind (Kaestle 1976, 178, 182). The value of the school for social order and democratic stability was a hegemonic feature of the discursive opportunity structure across multiple social fields. Common schools were to serve as preservers of the status quo while giving poor children "legitimate" opportunities to improve their intellectual capabilities and material life chances (Block 2012; Kaestle 1983; Cremin 1980).

The first of the threats that schools were believed to combat was crime. School reformers frequently connected a lack of education with criminality; indeed, they often seemed to believe that ignorance directly caused "immoral" behavior and delinquency. In his annual report for 1847, for example, Mann (1868, 573–74) made this connection clear: "In modern times, this relation of early education to adult character has been more clearly and generally recognized as being . . . a relation between cause and effect. . . . [C]rime recedes as knowledge advances." Carter (1824, 48–49), in his letters to the historian William Prescott, quoted extensively from Senator Daniel Webster of Massachusetts: "We regard [public instruction] as a wise and liberal system of police, by which the property, and life, and the peace of society are secured. We seek to prevent, in some measure, the extension of the penal code, by inspiring a salutary and conservative principle of virtue and of knowledge, in an early age . . . and to turn the strong current of feeling and opinion . . . against immorality and crime." Without the dissemination of virtue through public schooling, Carter warned, the lives and property of the wealthy would be put "in jeopardy . . . by the rapacity of the hungry, the destitute, and unprincipled" (51). According to these reformers, education would prevent crime not only by improving the objective life chances of the poor but also by inculcating in them a respect for the law and an abhorrence of deviant behavior.

The second threat was class conflict. School reformers were especially concerned that the decline of the common schools was contributing to an increasing reliance by middle- and upper-class families on private, tuition-charging academies. The resulting lack of contact between poor and wealthier children was dangerous because it bred hostility between them. According to Carter, educating children of different classes together would serve to "harmonise and bind together all those different and distant classes of the community" (49). But when "nineteen-twentieths" of the population must rely on inferior free schools while the wealthy attend private academies, then "the several classes, being educated differently and without a knowledge of each other, imbibe mutual prejudices and hatreds" (25). Such prejudices might turn destructive when "an ignorant and naturally jealous populace . . . impatient of the influence and authority, which property naturally bestows," decides to take its revenge by seizing the property of the wealthy through violence or by abusing its political rights (51). Educating all children together would address these dangers by fostering solidarity across the classes and inspiring poor children to emulate the morals and manners of their middle-class peers.

Finally, democratization was also a source of worry for education reformers, even if they supported it in principle. Beginning in 1820, when the property requirement was abolished, all white adult male taxpayers in Massachusetts could vote; those too poor to pay taxes could pay a poll tax of $1.50 (Williamson 1960). Sixty-five percent of the state's white men voted in 1840 versus 42 percent in 1820 (Pole 1957, 589–91). In light of this expansion, Mann and Carter repeatedly expressed concern that ordinary citizens, if left undereducated, would use their democratic rights to attack the wealthy and destabilize society. In his first report, Mann (1891, 417) warned that if the education of poor children continued to be neglected, the wealthy would become "vulnerable at every point, and utterly incapable of finding a hiding-place for any earthly treasure, where the witness, the juror and the voter cannot reach and annihilate it!" Mann and Carter both maintained that mass ignorance also threatened democracy itself: "A government like our own can only exist among a people generally enlightened; the only question as to the permanency of free institutions being, whether it be possible to make and keep the *whole* population of a nation so well educated as the existence of such institutions supposes and requires" (Carter 1826, 48). Carter went further. The poor and ignorant members of the community multiply faster than the more "enlightened" members, he wrote; if left unchecked, they would soon "have a preponderance of physical power." When this happens, "what hinders a revolution, and an arbitrary government, by which the mind of a few can control the physical strength of the many . . . ? The ignorant must . . . be made to learn, at least, enough to make them peaceable and good citizens" (48).

He was not the only one who thought this way. A lengthy review of a collection of Carter's essays echoes his thoughts: "In our frame of government, we are trying a grand political experiment, which, in the hands of other mighty and opulent nations, has totally failed . . . [and] led to a state of disorder more terrific and appalling, than any despotism that can be imagined. On what, then, rest our hopes of safety?" The answer was universal education, "the only thing which can prepare men for the enjoyment of liberty." Without it, popular "licentiousness" would yield a social unraveling so terrible that the people, finally "weary of the fruitless exercise of their own destructive powers," would surrender themselves to some tyrant "more oppressive and galling than any which mere despotic sovereignty could possibly impose upon them" (Anonymous 1827, 347–48). US republicans, like Prussian bureaucrats, trembled at the thought of what might happen if the masses were left undisciplined by the public school. In both places, universal education was seen as the bulwark between the state and its ruin. "Such an event as the French Revolution never would have happened with free schools," Mann (1872, 41) proclaimed; "the mobs, the riots, the burnings, the lynchings, perpetrated by the *men* of the present day, are perpetrated, because of their vicious or defective educations, when *children*."

As in Prussia, Massachusetts education reformers' fears about the threats of lower-class crime and rebellion were not paranoid fantasy but rather based in local history and lived experience. Shays's Rebellion was half a century in the past, but had not been forgotten (Kaestle 1976, 187). Small riots and acts of collective violence were still commonplace (Tager 2001). Some were about slavery, such as an 1835 antiabolitionist riot initiated by elite Bostonians with textile industry interests; others were directed at violators of social norms, such as brothels; and others were fueled by nativist anti-Catholic and anti-Irish sentiments, such as the mob attack on the Ursuline Convent in Charlestown in 1834. On June 11, 1837, shortly before taking up his job as secretary of the Board of Education, Mann (1865, 74–75) reported in his private journal that yet another bloody melee between Irish residents and volunteer firefighters—later dubbed the "Great Broad Street Riot" (Dickinson 1838, 39)—had been raging in Boston's streets for several hours. That May, he had written of an attempted arson at his residence: "A gang of incendiaries infest [*sic*] the city. . . . Is it possible that such things could be, if moral instruction were not infinitely below what it ought to be?" (72). In both cases, Mann connected the disorder with the failures of public education and declining public morality. He did not seem to notice that these disturbances were occurring amid not only increasing religious and ethnic tension caused by Irish immigration but also an economic depression and high unemployment in the wake of the financial panic of 1837 (Rezneck 1935; Roberts 2012, 172).

According to Mann and Carter, education would do more than prepare children for life and work; it would create the type of law-abiding, thoughtful, restrained, productive citizen that Massachusetts needed to survive and thrive as a democratic state. In Massachusetts, as in Prussia, reformers had strong faith in the ability of government institutions to shape individuals into citizens suited to the state's needs and goals. Government had the power to mold the population to suit its purposes. In his famous second essay—a classic in American educational thought—Carter (1826, 13) invoked admiringly the example of Sparta, where male children were removed from their families, and placed in strict military training regiments to "form the passions, sentiments, and ideas, to that tone which might best assimilate with the constitutions of the state." Noting approvingly that "the Spartan Law-giver made his nation what he wished it to be" (13), he argued that Massachusetts should strive to do the same: "If the Spartan could mould and transform a nation to suit his own taste, by means of an early education, why may not the same be done at the present day?" (16). Just as Sparta could use military training schools to create perfect warriors, Massachusetts could use its common schools to mold perfect citizens ready to exercise their rights with wisdom and restraint.

Elite reformers were not the only ones demanding improved common schools; working people did as well. The Boston Working Men's Party listed on its 1830 platform "the establishment of a liberal system of education, attainable by all," as "among the first efforts of every lawgiver who desires the continuance of our national independence" (Commons et al. 1910, 188). The New England Association of Mechanics, Farmers, and Other Workingmen, an organization of skilled laborers founded in Providence in 1832 to advocate for the ten-hour day, soon formed a committee on education to investigate the schooling situation in the manufacturing districts of Massachusetts, Rhode Island, and New Hampshire. It too called for "some wholesome regulations with regard to the education of children and youth employed in manufactories," not to protect the elites from the barbarism of the unschooled masses, but to protect the masses from the "final prostration of their liberties at the shrine of a powerful aristocracy" (198–99). For these workers, public schooling was to secure the political independence of working people so that they could democratically and peacefully transform society in their favor.

Among elites, the central impetus behind the movement to improve and expand educational opportunities in Massachusetts was a deep fear that the masses, if left ignorant, would undermine the social order, harmony between classes, and potentially democracy itself. Given that children who worked in factories typically came from the poorest, most "dangerous" families, and usually received little or no schooling, reformers soon came to see them as a population requiring special legislative attention.

Industrialization and Child Labor in Massachusetts Factories

Massachusetts was on the cusp of a profound social and economic transformation. At the beginning of the nineteenth century, the state's mostly native-born, rural population was still able to eke out a modest but largely self-sufficient living from New England's poor soil. By the 1820s, declining soil fertility and population growth forced many to begin relying more heavily on monetary exchanges to secure necessities. For a time, a self-regulating putting-out system allowed women and older children to earn supplemental income by producing consumer goods at home, such as cloth, buttons, hats, and shoes (Prude 1983; Dawley [1976] 2000). This system was dealt its first major blow in 1815, when industrialist Francis Cabot Lowell, with the support of a group of wealthy Boston investors known as the Boston Associates, built a water-powered textile factory—the Boston Manufacturing Company—along the Charles River at Waltham, about ten miles northwest of Boston. Unlike the mills operating on the older Rhode Island system, where mechanized spinning in factories was integrated with home-based weaving by women on nearby farms, spinning and weaving were integrated in Lowell's mill (Dublin 1979, 17). With the help of the Tariff of 1816, it succeeded spectacularly. In 1823, the mill's owners expanded to a new site near the New Hampshire border. Three years later, they built the nation's first true company town there and named it Lowell. By 1828, the town had thirty-five hundred residents, and by midcentury nearly ten times that (Dublin 1979, 21; Brown and Tager 2000, 125).

Lowell's success mirrored a broader transformation in work and production in Massachusetts. Thirty-two percent of the state's workforce was reportedly employed in manufacturing by 1837—almost as many as those still in agriculture (34 percent). By 1845, manufacturing exceeded agriculture (34 to 24 percent) to become the state's largest source of livelihood. Throughout this period, by far the two largest manufacturing sectors were textiles and leather goods, particularly shoemaking. Also by 1845, most of Massachusetts's population lived in urban areas (Siracusa 1979, 33, 46). Massachusetts was well on its way to becoming the most "thoroughly industrialized" and among the most urbanized US states (22).

Two models of workforce recruitment emerged during this time. In Lowell, most workers were unmarried young women and girls—or in some cases widows with children—who had migrated from the surrounding countryside to work in the mills. These "respectable" Anglo-Saxon Protestants typically worked in the mills only for a few years, often just long enough to earn money for a hope chest, pay off a farm mortgage, or raise funds for a brother's college tuition. Because of the scarcity of labor, they were well paid, earning far more than teachers or domestics (Dublin 1979, 66). They were protected yet also tightly controlled by boardinghouse keepers as part of the mill owners' paternalist approach to employment relations. They lived in clean but crowded company-owned boardinghouses, and participated in various social and enrichment activities during their off-hours, including attending school (workers under fourteen were required by most companies to attend school three months of the year), prayer meetings, lectures, and choir practice; reading library books; playing the boardinghouse's piano; and writing stories and poems for the *Lowell Offering*, a literary newspaper written and published by women (Robinson 1898; Ware 1931, 64–65, 256–58; Rosenberg 2013).

An alternative model originated in Rhode Island. The first water-powered spinning mill in the United States was erected at Pawtucket in 1790 by Samuel Slater. It started with nine employees, all children between seven and twelve who initially worked twelve hours a day, six days a week (Dublin 1979, 43). Slater supervised them personally, reportedly whipping and sprinkling water on them to keep them awake while they toiled (Tucker 1984; Mintz 2004, 136–37). He undoubtedly preferred children because they were cheap and docile, but labor shortages also made it difficult to find adults willing to work for meager wages. Within a few decades, however, the Irish-born population increased, and the Rhode Island system evolved to include entire immigrant families. For example, a contract drawn up in 1829 in a Massachusetts mill near the Rhode Island border reads, "Agreed with Abel Dudley for himself and family to work one year from the last day of March past at the following rates: self, four shillings threepence per day to tend picker, Mary eight shillings per week, Caroline four shillings per week. Mary and Caroline have the privilege of going to school two months each, one at a time, and Amos is to work at four shillings per week when they are out" (Ware 1931, 260).

The families lived in company housing surrounding the mills, obtained their provisions at the company store, and were often paid in store credit (Bremner 1970, 146). Fall River, which was to surpass Lowell as the state's largest textile producer by the end of the century, was home to ten such mills by 1837. These relied on children like Mary and Caroline to help spin cotton yarn, which was then put out for weaving by local homeworkers (Blewett 2000, 24, 48). The working hours seem to have been longer in Fall River than elsewhere too, particularly in summer; an 1825 US Senate investigation found that Fall River's factory children worked from sunrise until 7:30 p.m. in winter, and from sunrise to sunset in summer, and were "allowed half an hour for breakfast, and three quarters of an hour for dinner, and take their supper in winter and summer after they have done their working in the evening" (Persons 1971, 7). Fall River mills also paid less than mills elsewhere in Massachusetts; whereas children under ten typically earned fifty cents a week, the Troy mill at Fall River paid the youngest children between ten and twenty-five cents (Bremner 1970, 147). These were miserable wages. For comparison, adult female factory operatives in Lowell were paid around two dollars per week, not including board, in the 1830s (Ware 1931, 239). Not surprisingly, Fall River's factory owners became notorious for their indifference toward their workers' welfare. In 1855, the owner of a large Fall River mill reportedly said, "As for myself, I regard my work-people just as I regard my machinery. So long as they can do my work for what I choose to pay them, I keep them, getting out of them all that I can. What they do, or how they fare, outside my walls I don't know, nor do I consider it my business to know. They must look out for themselves as I do for myself. When my machines get old and useless, I reject them and get new [ones], and these people are part of my machinery."[4] It is perhaps not surprising, then, that the impetus behind Massachusetts's 1842 child labor law, which restricted the working hours of children under twelve to ten per day, originated in Fall River.

By the mid-1830s, this harsh approach to industrial relations became more prevalent as the paternalist model in Lowell proved unsustainable. Employers lowered wages to deal with declining prices and growing competition from new mills in other parts of Massachusetts, New York, and Pennsylvania, and conditions worsened during the depression of 1837–40. Taking their cues from protests organized by male workers in other industries, female mill operatives organized under the banner Daughters of Freemen to dispute wage cuts and increases in boardinghouse fees. One of the first walkouts occurred in October 1836 in Lowell. As many as two thousand operatives participated (Dublin 1979, 98–100). As Harriet Jane Hanson Robinson (1889, 83), who at age twelve led the walkout on her floor, later recounted, "When it was announced that the wages were to be cut down, great indignation was felt, and it was decided to strike, en masse. . . . The mills were shut down, and the girls went in procession . . . and listened to 'incendiary' speeches from early labor reformers. One of the girls . . . gave vent to the feelings of her companions in a neat speech. . . . This was the first time a woman had spoken in public in Lowell, and the event caused surprise and consternation among her audience." A decade later, the conditions in the Lowell mills had not improved, and employers continued to cut wages. An 1845 petition to the Massachusetts General Court, penned by Sarah Bagley of the Lowell Female Labor Reform Association, lodged a complaint demanding a ten-hour legal workday and decrying "the evils already come upon us, by toiling from thirteen to fourteen hours per day, confined in unhealthy apartments, exposed to the poisonous contagion of air, vegetable, animal and mineral properties, debarred from proper *Physical* exercise, time for *Mental* discipline and *Mastication* cruelly limited; and thereby hastening us on through pain, disease and privation, down to a premature grave" (quoted in Ware 1931, 251).

Despite the occasional strike, working conditions continued to deteriorate as the makeup of Massachusetts's industrial workforce changed. Native-born girls and women left the mills, and were replaced by impoverished Irish immigrants who, as labor shortages turned into labor surpluses, had little choice but to accept meager wages and bad working conditions. Whereas only 3.7 percent of the employees of one large Lowell mill were foreign born in 1836, 38.6 percent were by 1850 (Dublin 1979, 26, 139). The boardinghouse system practiced in the northern part of the state collapsed as the composition of the workforce shifted from single women and girls to immigrant families (Ware 1931). Irish workers were segregated into lower-skilled, lower-paying jobs within the mills, lived in segregated housing (Dublin 1979, 145–49), and sent their children to segregated schools—if at all.[5] By midcentury, the typical factory town was a dismal and slum-ridden place. Overcrowded and dilapidated housing became a serious problem; in Lawrence, for instance, so-called shanty Irish lived in cramped, dirt-floored wooden huts along the banks of the sewage-filled Merrimack River. Scores succumbed to a typhoid fever epidemic in 1850 (Cole 2002, 29). In a few decades, immigration and industrialization had together created a proletarian underclass in Massachusetts.[6]

Early Criticisms of Industrial Child Labor: State, Religion, and Labor

Although most early nineteenth-century observers agreed that children should work, not all were sanguine about the prospect of small children toiling in factories for twelve or fourteen hours a day. Early critics—including state actors, ministers, and labor organizers—connected excessive industrial child labor, and the educational neglect that accompanied it, with the destruction of children's health and happiness, and more frequently, with delinquency, pauperism, and democratic decline. This commentary provided child labor policy entrepreneurs with the raw materials with which they could develop their own definitions of the child labor problem and craft arguments to frame their proposed interventions.

In general, the state paid little attention to the problem of child labor, but in 1825, the Massachusetts Senate Committee on Education conducted an investigation of children working in factories. The investigation revealed that the employment of very young children was rare, but that working hours were long and prevented young people from attending school. The ensuing report discussed the consequences of factory employment for children, and noted that young workers had "little opportunity for instruction" and were therefore unlikely to "become proprietors of these establishments, or at least greatly to influence their affairs." Their "moral habits and chaste manners," however, were at least protected by the "American sentiment" that prevailed in the factories. Warning that "wisdom & learning as well as virtue, diffused generally among the people, are necessary to the preservation of their rights and liberties," and that this required the state to "preserve, improve and extend public provisions for the education of children & youth," the committee nonetheless refrained from taking legislative action (cited in Commons et al. 1910, 57–61; see also Abbott 1947, 277–78).

Although he never became directly involved in child labor legislation, Mann did incorporate observations on industrial child labor into his annual reports. Strongly condemning callous factory owners for turning their young employees into "thorough-made products of ignorance, and misery, and vice," and unscrupulous parents for selling their children into "ransomless bondage," Mann (1868, 6) concentrated his critique on the deleterious impact of early employment on children's "intellectual and moral growth" as well as on social order and stability. The concentration of families relying on their children's earnings in manufacturing districts, he asserted, would turn those areas into dens of pauperism and criminality (7). He invoked the image of filthy and vice-filled Manchester, and predicted that Massachusetts's factory workers would end up similarly degraded if child labor laws and other social welfare measures were not implemented as well as enforced. Even worse, Mann argued, children "steadily worked in our manufactories without any schooling" while temporarily kept under control by the rigid discipline of the workplace would eventually "pass from the condition of restraint to that of freedom . . . for which they have secretly pined . . . not merely as a period of emancipation, but of long-delayed indulgence." When these morally and intellectually stunted children reached adulthood and achieved the "political sovereignty of a man," he warned, they would become a social menace, and "then, for that people, who so cruelly neglected and injured them, there will assuredly come a day or retribution" (8–9). This last statement is uncannily similar to the language Bodelschwingh used in 1835 in the preface to his proposed Prussian child labor law. On both sides of the Atlantic, working children were regarded as prone to immoderation and self-indulgence, and hence potentially dangerous.

Massachusetts's religious leaders also sometimes protested certain types of child labor while advocating the "right" type of work for children. Unitarians and Universalists—religions of the reform-minded cultural elite—were particularly active in this regard. Joseph Tuckerman, a Unitarian minister who worked with the poor in Boston, argued that children's employment should be for their own benefit, not that of their parents; "three fourths of [delinquents] are from families, which have looked to these children for *a part of their means of support*," Tuckerman (1827, 23) noted with alarm. Working children were likely to grow up without an adequate education and were in danger of being corrupted by "vicious" persons. It was vital, then, that children younger than fourteen attend school, both to secure a "moral education" as well as to prepare for an apprenticeship "at some useful employment" to combat crime and pauperism among the lower classes (Tuckerman 1874). William Ellery Channing (1848), one of the foremost Unitarian preachers of the early nineteenth century, echoed Tuckerman's call for improved education for the working classes in an 1837 essay; although common schools were adequate to preventing crime and disorder, Channing believed that special vocational schools and other private institutions might go further in enabling poor children to realize their intellectual potential, cultivate their moral sensibilities, and fulfill their civic responsibilities.

Finally, labor organizers folded protections for children into their broader platforms, which at the time concentrated on establishing a ten-hour legal working day (English 2006; Zonderman 2011). In 1832, the New England Association of Farmers, Mechanics, and Other Workingmen denounced the conditions that working children endured. According to its investigations, 40 percent of industrial workers in Massachusetts, New Hampshire, and Rhode Island were under sixteen. Further, children reportedly could not be removed from factories for any length of time to attend school without being dismissed; if one child were withdrawn to attend school, employers would retaliate and dismiss any siblings as well. Like elites, labor leaders drew a connection between working-class ignorance and tyranny, but a tyranny of the aristocracy rather than of the mob. Early democratization made them regard schooling as a right of participatory citizenship instead of an imposed method of social control (Skocpol 1992, 89). Accordingly, the association resolved to promote state legislation to regulate the hours of labor and advance the education of working children (cited in Commons et al. 1910, 195–99; Zonderman 2011, 33).

The same year, Seth Luther, a former mill worker and labor activist involved in the ten-hour movement, made a similar critique. Observing that it was impossible for children who worked thirteen hours a day to obtain an education, Luther (1832, 21, 29) warned that the resulting "moral and political degradation" of working people would lead to disorder, crime, and eventually tyranny: "Without the assistance of the common people a free government cannot exist. . . . [T]he capability to govern depends on intelligence and learning; . . . Let us not think we are free until working-men no longer trust their affairs in the hands of designing demagogues." In 1834, Frederick Robinson, a radical Democratic state legislator, delivered a rousing Fourth of July speech to the Trades' Union of Boston on the value of unionism and the ten-hour day. He called on the assembled to use their legislative power to "make it a crime to work our daughters or our children in the mills of these Philistines more than six hours a day" (Robinson 1834, 28). The thrust of these commentaries was that child labor was a problem because it interfered with poor children's intellectual and moral training. In short, elementary schooling was a universally accepted good in nineteenth-century Massachusetts society (Kaestle 1976, 178, 182).

Policy Entrepreneurship and the Legislative Response to Child Labor in Factories

Carter was the policy entrepreneur behind Massachusetts's first child labor law. In the 1830s, he was the state's leading education reformer—"more intimately identified with the cause of education" than any other man (Messerli 1965, 16; see also Martin 1894). The son of a farmer, Carter was born into modest circumstances, but managed to work his way through Groton Academy and then Harvard (Barnard 1858). He subsequently taught in both public and private institutions, authored textbooks, and penned two widely read education reform tracts, the *Letters to the Hon. William H. Prescott* (1824) and *Essays upon Popular Education* (1826). For seventeen years, he advocated for the expansion of public schools, establishment of a normal school, and creation of a state board of education (Martin 1894). Following work as an editor of various education journals, he was elected to three terms in the Massachusetts House of Representatives (from 1834 to 1836) and then Massachusetts Senate (1837 and 1838), where he served as chair of the Education Committee (Barnard 1858). Carter enjoyed considerable political influence at a time when the state legislature was dominated by his own party, the Whigs (Formisano 1983). His brief tenure at the statehouse was typical at a time when elections occurred annually and professional politicians were still a rarity. For five years, Carter straddled the educational and policy fields, and not surprisingly, brought the priorities and discourses of the former field into the latter. Accordingly, his definition of the child labor problem focused squarely on its impact on poor children's education, which he regarded as a prerequisite for social order under a democratic form of government.

On March 17, 1836, Carter issued a report on behalf of the House Education Committee in which he examined the child labor situation in Massachusetts and recommended legislation to require children working in manufacturing

FIGURE 4.1. James G. Carter. *Source*: Barnard 1858.

establishments to attend school. The report reiterated many of his previous arguments in support of school reform generally. It framed child labor squarely as an issue of education and morality, and connected these simple frames with the fundamental frame of social order (see table 4.1). Carter began by framing universal education as the key to social stability, and with it, Massachusetts's status and influence: "Upon what, but these same provisions for universal education . . . can we rely for our domestic social, and moral well being? Upon what but these can we rely for our relative political consequence in the Union, or even for our political existence as free and independent communities?" Because of a variety of ecological factors and technological changes, he argued, the state was becoming industrial—a situation inimical to educational attainment. Although industrialization brought prosperity, it was not without its problems, for "it requires no spirit of prophesy to foresee . . . that a change in occupation, from those diversified employments which characterize a sparse and agricultural population, to the simple operations consequent upon that

TABLE 4.1. Citations and Frames in the Writings of Prussian, French, Belgian, and Massachusetts Child Labor Policy Entrepreneurs

	Altenstein proposal (1828)	Bodelschwingh proposal (1835)	Dupin committee report (1840)	Ducpétiaux commission conclusion (1848)	Carter report (1836)	Battelle petition (1842)
CITATIONS					None	
Insiders	100%	100%	61%	7%	—	100%
Local government / officials	35%	57%	—	0%	—	—
National government / officials	28%	8%	21%	—	—	—
Chambers of commerce / individual industrialists	—	15%	11%	4%	—	—
National legislators	—	—	6%	—	—	—
Experts/intellectuals	—	—	10%	3%	—	—
Other domestic actors	—	—	16%	—	—	—
Domestic law	42%	24%	—	2%	—	100%
Outsiders	0%	0%	40%	93%	—	0%
British legislators	—	—	3%	4%	—	—
British factory inspectors	—	—	—	13%	—	—
Other British actors	—	—	5%	4%	—	—
British law	—	—	23%	11%	—	—
French legislators	—	—	—	30%	—	—
Other French actors	—	—	—	2%	—	—
French law	—	—	—	9%	—	—
Prussian law	—	—	5%	5%	—	—
Other country law	—	—	7%	17%	—	—
FRAMES						
Simple frames	100%	100%	60%	71%	97%	71%
Health/safety	43%	—	39%	26%	—	25%
Education	47%	91%	9%	44%	86%	66%
Morals	26%	21%	28%	16%	46%	17%
Fundamental frames	3%	24%	55%	34%	26%	45%
Social order / criminality	—	12%	7%	1%	18%	9%
Economic prosperity / competitiveness	—	12%	31%	11%	4%	19%
National security / defense	3%	—	4%	—	—	—
National honor / strength	—	—	3%	—	2%	—
Childhood happiness / suffering	—	—	4%	4%	—	—
Humanity	—	—	5%	—	—	—
Public interest	—	—	4%	2%	4%	6%
Rights	—	—	7%	18%	—	6%

Notes: Percentages refer to the amount of total citation or framing text devoted to the particular category of citation or frame. Category percentages do not add up to 100 percent because text portions were often coded in more than one way.

minute subdivision of labor, upon which the success of manufacturing industry depends, is not a circumstance favorable to intellectual development." This de-skilling was particularly damaging to working children, whose "ignorant and groveling" parents had to be forcibly compelled to do the right thing by their offspring. To support this view, he cited figures from the previous year's school returns, including the statistic that in "four large manufacturing towns" (not including Lowell), 1,895 children between four and sixteen "do not attend the common schools any portion of the year."[7]

Repeating claims he had made elsewhere, Carter contended that uneducated working-class people were a threat to democracy. The more ignorant a population, the faster it multiplied, "and consequently, being themselves degraded, unless their children be rescued from their exclusive influence and educated, the more dangerous they become to the peace of the state. . . . If this be true generally, it is a truth which has peculiar and inestimable importance in this country, where, by our laws of universal suffrage, the government is thrown . . . into the whole mass of the people, without reference to their intelligence or their virtue." The legislature must therefore ensure that no class be allowed to remain uneducated. "For if a small part only of one generation, however employed, be suffered to become men in physical strength only, without something like a corresponding development of their heads and hearts, their intellects and affections, there is a disease,—a canker in the body politic, which will corrode and spread itself in every direction, to the final destruction of the system." Thus the key danger presented by industrial child labor was that by preventing lower-class children from receiving any education whatsoever, it created a class of people devoid of intellectual and moral capacity. This presented a particular danger in the United States because broad suffrage would allow these people to destabilize the republic.[8] Carter's repeated use of these democratic order frames over time and in front of different audiences suggests that they were not merely strategic but also honest expressions of the core problem definition motivating Carter's policy entrepreneurship.

Carter concluded the committee report with a proposed "Act to Provide for the Better Instruction of Youth Employed in Manufacturing Establishments." Unlike Bodelschwingh's similarly titled plan, Carter's really did focus exclusively on education. The proposal suggested that children under fourteen not be employed in "manufacturing establishments" unless they had received instruction at a public or private school for at least three of the preceding twelve months. Hence even though the Prussian and French laws established educational requirements too, the Massachusetts bill proposed a much more extended period of schooling. In Massachusetts, the goal was not to prepare children for their inherited "station in life," as in Prussia, but to train boys to "responsibly" exercise their democratic rights and prepare girls, as future mothers, to teach their children basic civic values.[9] Carter's bill was introduced in the House on March 17; after that body *raised* the age until which working children would be required to attend school from fourteen to fifteen years, both the House and Senate approved the final bill by a voice vote on April 14, less than a month after its initial reading.[10] The absence of a roll call vote indicates that a clear majority favored the law. It was signed by Governor Edward Everett, also a Whig, on April 16.[11]

Although the democratic policy field in which Massachusetts child labor reform took place was radically different from the bureaucratic absolutist policy field of Prussia, the exogenous pressures and opportunities that propelled reform in the two states were actually quite similar. In both places, recent social unrest and rioting instilled in elites a deep sense of unease. Furthermore, in both places, a relatively well-developed primary education system created positive institutional feedbacks: common schools provided a real institutional alternative to the factory or workshop. At the same time, the failure to fully achieve existing education policy goals, evidenced by less than optimal school attendance rates in manufacturing towns, created an impetus for further reforms to get working children through the schoolhouse doors. Carter, like Bodelschwingh, also defined child labor primarily as a problem of education and social control. In doing so, he drew on a discourse generated in various social arenas that established universal primary schooling as essential to morality and democracy. This logic, dating back to the colonial period, was remarkably unified and pervasive in Massachusetts. Carter's bill and the frames with which he justified it thus fit neatly with existing institutions along with the prevailing discursive opportunity structure. As a result, he encountered no apparent resistance, and the law was passed almost immediately.

Lacking any effective enforcement measures, the 1836 law was often disregarded. In 1839, the *Boston Daily Times* reported that it was being "evaded by cruel and mercenary owners of the children, who keep them nine months in one factory, and then take them directly to another, with a lie in their mouths, that the children have had three months of schooling" (quoted in Bremner 1970, 622). In 1840, Mann (1868, 5) remarked that although the law was obeyed in "the majority of cases," it was "uniformly and systematically disregarded" in certain towns. According to him, the worst offenders were not the big mills at places like Lowell and Waltham but rather smaller businesses and private individuals in search of short-term profits. Parents too—"not only of our immigrant, but of our native population"—were to blame for the law's disregard. Some parents, he asserted, had made a practice of migrating from town to town "seeking opportunities to consign" their children "to unbroken, bodily toil, although it involves the deprivation of all the means of intellectual and moral growth." Such parents were more interested in "pandering to their own vicious appetites" than in caring for their children, and their neglect was sure to make their offspring just as vicious as themselves (6).

In 1842, a group of three concerned citizens petitioned the General Court to pass a new child labor law. In Massachusetts, the citizens' petition was an institutionalized channel through which ordinary citizens could easily draw legislators' attention to various issues. Hezekiah Battelle was a prominent lawyer from Fall River who had served in the Massachusetts House of Representatives in 1838 and 1839. According to a brief biographical sketch published twenty-five years after his death, Battelle "was actively interested in the organization of the Unitarian Church of Fall River, and in all matters relating to the moral and religious welfare of the community [in which] he unselfishly participated" (Borden 1899, 676). He served on the Fall River school committee (Smith [1890] 2013), and in 1828 joined with other community leaders to establish the Fall River Institution for Savings. The bank's declared purpose was "to provide a mode of enabling industrious manufacturers, mechanics, laborers, seamen, widows, minors, and others in moderate circumstances" the opportunity to open savings accounts (Earl 1877, 170). These shards of evidence suggest that Battelle was a progressive community leader interested in promoting the welfare of Fall River's working population.

Battelle was joined by two other Fall River residents. The first was Thomas Wilbur, a prominent physician who had also served on the Fall River school committee (Fowler 1862, 97). A Quaker, he was remembered after his death for his religious devotion, "kind and affable disposition," and willingness to help poor patients at his own expense.[12] The second, H. N. Gunn, was a mechanic and member of the Unitarian church that Battelle helped found (First Congregational Society of Providence, RI 1867). Gunn was a coleader of a local labor organization called the Association of Industry that advocated for a ten-hour day on the logic that it would prevent "ignorance and vice" by allowing workers time for intellectual, religious, and moral self-improvement. In 1842, he helped author an appeal, "To the Employers of Fall River," in which, among other things, he exhorted factory owners to reduce hours and abide by the 1836 child labor law (Blewett 2000, 56–57). Later in life, he participated in an effort to establish an orphanage in Fall River.[13] By 1860, he seems to have joined the entrepreneurial class himself by opening a roofing company (Bishop, Freedley, and Young 1864, 683).

Together, the lawyer, physician, and mechanic represented a cross-class coalition of humanitarians standing in opposition to the abuses perpetrated by Fall River's notoriously ruthless industrial employers. In their petition, they framed child labor as a threat to children's education and morals, but also to their physical health, and used these simple frames to make the more fundamental argument that it undermined the peace and prosperity of the state of Massachusetts (see table 4.1). They began their succinct appeal for legislative intervention by blasting the shortsightedness of factory owners who, in the face of stiff international and domestic competition, placed short-term profits ahead of the "physical, intellectual and moral culture" of their workers. When employers "demand the most prolonged hours and the greatest speed, and pay the lowest rate of wages," they maintained, "they overlook the truth, that the energetic labors of free, intelligent, well-educated, well-paid, contented and thriving workmen, will ultimately prove more valuable to them than the nervous, exhausting toil, of ignorant, over-worked, discontented and degraded laborers." This was a situation inimical to the well-being of the working class, and by extension, the "political prosperity of the State and the nation." These generally awful working conditions were even more deplorable when they applied to children, the petitioners asserted, because they "prevent the proper and healthful development of their physical natures," and thwart the "mental education" essential for preparing them for their future civic, social, and domestic duties. Working children's opportunities for instruction were few, and the provisions of the 1836 law, requiring them to attend school three months out of the year, "are in but few instances carried into effect, and in most cases are wholly disregarded." Further state intervention was therefore necessary to "guard against the evils to which a manufacturing people are exposed."[14]

The petition, which was presented in the House on January 19, offered two policy recommendations. The first was that children's hours of labor be restricted. Second, it called for a board of commissioners to enforce school attendance and restrictions on working hours, and to collect and publish statistics on the number of industrial workers as well as their physical, intellectual, moral, and social conditions. The petitioners ended by articulating the hope that the information collected by such a commission would guide future legislation to protect the rights and well-being of all factory workers, not just children.[15] No record remains of the legislative response to this petition, with the exception of an act proposed by the House Committee on Manufactures on February 18 and enacted on March 3, again by voice vote. This law restricted the working hours of children under twelve employed in manufacturing establishments to ten per day—a first step in the state's legislative progress toward a ten-hour normal working day, not achieved for adult women until 1874. The law did not establish a child labor commission, but it did task local school committees with enforcing the 1836 law.[16]

Scope Condition 1: Strong Political Opposition

This case study has shown that basic child labor regulations were adopted in Massachusetts in 1836 and 1842 with swiftness and ease. The speed with which the bills made it through the legislature, apparent lack of opposition from employers or their political allies, and absence of media attention all suggest that the proposed measures and their framing fit with the prevailing discursive opportunity structure.[17] They also fit with existing institutional infrastructures, viz the state's common school system, which despite reformers' fears of decline, rivaled Prussia's in terms of its enrollment numbers and resources. Moreover, Massachusetts's early child labor laws were evidently deemed not threatening enough to industrial interests to warrant resistance. Perhaps Massachusetts manufacturers and their friends in the legislature knew they had little to fear from a state government that lacked the administrative capacity to rigorously enforce the new regulations (Skowronek 1982). In any case, the apparent lack of controversy around the bills contrasts starkly with child labor reform in Prussia and France (as well as England), where the earliest laws faced considerable skepticism from those who feared their impact on industry. We are left with the surprising outcome that it was in democratic Massachusetts, not authoritarian Prussia, where child labor regulation was enacted with little opposition, debate, or revision.

The upshot is that the causal processes in the theoretical framework outlined in chapter 1 are largely absent in Massachusetts. True, middle-class policy entrepreneurs were needed there to get the reform ball rolling; despite the state's high level of democratization, organized labor was still in its infancy and did not wield the necessary political power to effectively demand protective legislation. But aside from choosing appropriate frames, Carter and the Battelle group exhibited little of the alliance-building skill and none of the creativity that we saw in Bodelschwingh and Dupin. They didn't need to. This study thus helps establish one of the scope conditions under which policy entrepreneurs' individual capacities, actions, and influence matter more than other causal factors for explaining social policy outcomes. Individual elite and middle-class reformers matter more in the face of disagreement in the policy field about what problems are important, and how best to tackle them. With regard to child labor legislation, such opposition is more likely when employers and their political supporters mobilize to portray regulation as threatening to industrial interests. As we will see in part II, labor reformers in Massachusetts would have to contend with fiercer opposition from capitalists and their allies as the nineteenth century progressed.

Conclusion to Part I

The regulatory welfare state began with child labor laws, but the causal factors highlighted by existing theoretical approaches—industrialization, class-based mobilizations, social unrest, and institutional feedbacks—were not enough to generate these laws on their own. In the early and mid-nineteenth century, states outside the United Kingdom lacked labor movements with the will and resources to effectively demand protection for working children. They also lacked institutionalized administrative channels through which a countermovement against industrial capitalism's most extreme abuses could be mounted by the state from within. Instead, entrepreneurial middle-class and elite reformers took the lead in this era of regulatory welfare development. These individuals' ideas and strategies were instrumental to the passage or failure of early child labor laws. At the same time, social, political, and institutional context clearly constrained as well as enabled their political agency. The task is not to reduce institutional change to policy entrepreneurship but rather to clarify its interaction with other causally relevant factors in the policy field and broader society.

To that end, the genetic analyses presented so far suggest four field-level scope conditions that shape policy entrepreneurs' influence. First, as illustrated in chapter 4, their impact is conditioned by the degree of opposition to reform in the policy field, such that their influence is more important when opposition is strong and less important when cultural consensus around the need for policy change is widespread. Under these conditions, a policy entrepreneur may be needed to draft a bill or otherwise set reform into motion, but alliance-building and problem-solving abilities matter less for policy outcomes.

The remaining three scope conditions pertain not to conditions under which policy entrepreneurs are more or less important but instead to those that constrain who can be a policy entrepreneur, with whom they must compromise, and their likelihood of success. First, field position and field architecture, as shaped by government institutions, influence who is empowered to be a policy entrepreneur, but do not guarantee such persons' victory. Policy entrepreneurs are not randomly selected into their leadership roles. Actors occupying certain field positions within a given architecture are more likely than others to become policy entrepreneurs. It is not surprising, for instance, that in Prussia, where the policy field was highly insulated from civil society and dominated by aristocratic state officials, the two leading child labor entrepreneurs were high-ranking bureaucrats. Likewise, in Massachusetts, where the field was comparatively wide open and child labor was primarily an education issue, it makes sense that the leading policy entrepreneur would be a middle-class part-time legislator with an extensive background in education. But although field position may select certain people into leadership roles, it does not necessarily facilitate their political victory. This depends on the institutionalized powers and privileges associated with their position, but also on their alliance-building strategies and goal-directed creativity.

Second, field position and field architecture constrain as well as enable policy entrepreneurs' ability to pursue alliance building and creativity. Bodelschwingh and Dupin occupied strategically advantageous positions at the intersection of multiple fields. These positions created opportunities for them to cite actors, use frames, strike compromises, and creatively leverage resources across (sub)fields in ways that helped them build alliances and overcome veto players. In contrast, for Ducpétiaux, being positioned at a field overlap proved disadvantageous. Like Dupin, he attempted to import strategies from the intellectual field into domestic policy; the best practices program he articulated, however, was appropriate in one, yet backfired in the other. This error, though not preordained by his outward orientation toward a transnational intellectual field, was made more likely by the weakness of the overlap between it and the Belgian policy field. This finding suggests that being positioned at a field overlap is not always beneficial; it depends on the commensurability of the different fields' norms, discourses, and stakes. This, in turn, hinges on the overlap's strength in terms of the extent of multiple membership and/or institutional penetration.

Finally, field architecture influences the types of actors with whom policy entrepreneurs must compromise to build essential alliances. A prime example is the degree to which reformers needed to appease institutionally empowered capital. Bodelschwingh could proceed without taking chamber of commerce opinions into account (except where it suited him) because the insulated, state-controlled Prussian policy field was relatively autonomous in relation to the business field. In France or Belgium, however, the two fields overlapped considerably, not only by way of dual membership in business and government, but also because chambers of commerce had institutionally penetrated the policy field via their formal advisory role. A child labor bill to which many business leaders strongly objected would therefore be unlikely to pass. Dupin's commission took this into account and kept its recommendations within the bounds of what most chambers expressed willingness to tolerate. Ducpétiaux's bill did not. In short, capitalist penetration into the policy field was not all that different in Belgium and France; what differed was how leading policy entrepreneurs responded to this structural reality.

Beyond these field-level factors, broader social conditions, including those highlighted by existing welfare states theory, shaped child labor policy entrepreneurship in various ways. In particular, widespread social unrest motivated reformers to take political action and informed their problem definitions. An uptick in strikes, riots, and crimes of poverty deeply concerned reformers everywhere, and drove home for elites the need to "do something" about industrial working conditions. Thus the social disorder version of power resources theory applies even though it cannot on its own explain variations in policy outcomes. Every country experienced significant social disorder, but not every country enacted a child labor law in response.

Moreover, what existing welfare states literature generally overlooks is the extent to which social policy responses to working-class resistance, whether inchoate or organized, have focused on not only strengthening social provision but expanding the reach of public education too. Child labor laws were intended to not only protect but also discipline; to that end, they were as much education measures as protective ones. Whereas welfare state scholars have turned their attention to the "elective affinities" between welfare state and education regimes since World War II (Busemeyer and Nikolai 2010; Iversen and Stephens 2008), the case studies here show that regulatory welfare was to a large degree born of existing primary education goals. In the first half of the nineteenth century, these goals centered more on securing social order by inculcating norms and values of "good citizenship" than on developing poor children's human capital. Further, whereas welfare state scholars typically see education as buttressing workforce "activation," for nineteenth-century child workers, it served the opposite purpose. By mandating an alternative to workforce participation, public education and child labor laws worked together to promote the decommodification of early childhood.

Part II

Introduction to Part II

In the last quarter of the nineteenth century, states on both sides of the Atlantic began to not only legislate but also build their capacity to implement and enforce regulations on industrial employment conditions. The factory inspection systems that emerged from this administrative state building represented an important new stage in the development of regulatory welfare. No longer would governments content themselves with passing laws that set limits on the commodification of labor. The state would now actively insert itself into the relationship between industrial employers and "free" labor by sending eyes and ears into the closed-off spaces where this relationship played out. Although inspectors' powers and responsibilities varied from state to state, in all cases they were endowed with the unlimited right to enter private workplaces, at any time, unannounced, to unearth violations of labor laws. The state's role as regulator of ostensibly free and private market relationships achieved a newly forceful and interventionist form. More significant, labor protection became a regularized and routine government function.

In Germany and the United States, factory inspection was a response to the growing recognition that child labor laws had fallen short of their intended aims. Increasingly sophisticated efforts to collect and standardize social knowledge were central to this "political learning" process (Rueschemeyer and Skocpol 1996; Heclo 2010). The nineteenth century witnessed a revolution in the collection as well as application of social data that rendered previously obscure populations visible and reduced complex problems to straightforward quantities (Porter 1996; Hacking 1990; O'Connor 2001). The shortcomings of child labor laws were made evident in state-sponsored proto–social scientific investigations and statistics. Social data imperfectly captured the scope and nature of child labor along with the true extent to which children were illegally employed, but made it clear that illegal employment was rampant and, in the German Empire, enforcement was extremely uneven. Data revealed that enacting protective legislation did not guarantee social change; the state would need to forcefully implement social policy.

Middle-class professionals spearheaded this political learning process. In both Germany and the United States, they orchestrated efforts to collect statistics on child labor and other labor "problems," particularly female employment. Administrative agencies—including, in the US case, newly formed state and federal bureaus of labor statistics—endowed reformers with the resources and authority to gather extensive social data. As a result, they no longer based their programs solely on moral or ideological principles; instead, they claimed "expertise" and asserted "objective" knowledge of their policy areas. Expertise became a source of credibility and authority that policy and administrative entrepreneurs leveraged to build alliances, amass resources, and achieve influence. Lawmakers came to rely on the expert professionals who staffed statistical bureaus and factory inspectorates to identify problems, and to recommend how to better accomplish their administrative mandates. These new administrative entities opened channels through which state responses to industrial capitalism could become more proactive and routinized.

New labor protections came not only in reaction to new social information but also in response to the demands of an increasingly organized and powerful working class. Political elites recognized that in a context of mobilized labor and universal male suffrage, workers' grievances could no longer be ignored. In the United States, labor unions and associations gained momentum after the Civil War, launching campaigns for a standard working day. Even in the Republican-dominated northern states, the growing strength of the Democratic Party and various third parties made elections competitive. Party leaders tried to court working-class and immigrant votes without substantially challenging the status quo; the promise of moderate labor legislation—laws aimed at women and children, but not adult males—was integral to their strategic appeals. After winning new protections for women and child workers, labor harnessed the tools of mass democracy to demand strong, independent factory inspectorates to ensure that labor legislation did not remain a dead letter.

In Germany, fear of the industrial proletariat persisted, but the perceived threat was no longer spontaneous disorder and ad hoc rebellion. By the late 1860s, the democratic socialist movement was heating up. Universal manhood suffrage, first adopted in the North German Confederation's 1867 Reichstag election, continued after the empire's founding in 1871; the modern Social Democratic Party was formed just four years later. As the long economic depression following the Panic of 1873 helped give socialists as well as social Catholics ominous victories at the polls, government officials increasingly came to see the necessity—and potential payoffs—of accommodating at least some of labor's more "reasonable" demands.

Failed child labor laws in a context of intensifying industrialization, as well as the need to make concessions to politically mobilized labor, created the impetus for new labor reforms. But the factory inspection systems built toward the end of the nineteenth century were not simply reactions to these baseline conditions. Like the laws they were intended to enforce, they were the accomplishment of middle-class reformers: policy entrepreneurs who pressed for their enactment and administrative entrepreneurs who guided their early administrative development. In Illinois, these entrepreneurs worked in full partnership with organized labor; in Germany, their stance was paternalist and aloof. In one case—1870s Massachusetts—middle-class policy entrepreneurs were actually less important than labor when it came to getting factory inspection legislation passed. Nevertheless, middle-class reformers were the ones whose problem definitions had the most direct impact on what inspection regimes ended up looking like. Similar to the child labor policy entrepreneurs profiled in the first half of the book, their ability to translate these ideas into administrative practice hinged on their alliance-building strategies and creative problem-solving efforts.

At the same time, institutional arrangements and political context continued to condition which field positions could produce effective labor reformers. In Germany, the best-positioned political actor was still a high-ranking government bureaucrat. In the United States, progressive activists working outside government became increasingly influential. Moreover, reformers' field positions influenced the resources and powers at their disposal as well as the types of alliances they needed—and were able—to forge. Cultural discourses continued to constitute their problem definitions and inform the kinds of frames they could effectively use. In short, regulatory welfare state development continued to be the product of a complex interplay between individual agency and the political and institutional factors that conditioned the opportunities afforded by the policy field.

Although Imperial Germany, Massachusetts, and Illinois each mandated some form of factory inspection in the last quarter of the nineteenth century, the particular type of system each adopted differed significantly (see table II.1). Through genetic analyses of reformers' writings and the political processes leading up to policy enactment and implementation in each case, I trace these outcomes to interactions between reformers' ideas, on the one hand, and the political and institutional dynamics of their policy fields, on the other. Factory inspection models embodied reformers' definitions of the labor problem, but political/institutional conditions constrained what kinds of reformers with what kinds of ideas could rise to field positions from which they could exert policy influence. For example, whereas it was possible for a Marxist feminist

TABLE II.1. Three Models of Factory Inspection

State / year of adoption	Factory inspection model	Role of state vis-à-vis labor and capital	Policing power	Inclusion of women	Bureaucratic autonomy
Imperial Germany (1878)	Advisory conciliation	Mediation and education	None	Marginal	—
Massachusetts (1877)	Conciliatory policing	Mediation and education	Yes, but used sparingly	Marginal	Sustainable
Illinois (1893)	Feminist enforcement	Protecting labor against capital	Yes, used aggressively	Strong	Unsustainable

to shape factory inspection policy in Illinois, such actors were marginalized in the German policy field and labor reform was by necessity led by conservatives. At the same time, reformers' ability to translate their ideas into legislation depended on their adoption of alliance-building and problem-solving strategies that made the most of the political/institutional conditions in which they found themselves. Just because a reformer was well positioned to achieve policy influence didn't mean that they would necessarily succeed.

In the *advisory conciliation model* created in Germany, factory inspectors took on the role of friendly mediators between labor and capital to promote cross-class solidarity. Inspectors lacked autonomous policing power, but on the basis of their class position as well as professional expertise were supposed to exercise didactic and moral authority over employers and workers. The *conciliatory policing model* adopted in Massachusetts was similar in many respects. Although inspectors, being part of the state police force, did enjoy police power, they were expected to be reticent in using it, and to pursue a pedagogical and persuasion-oriented approach to labor relations. This approach was prefigured in law, but brought to fruition by the state's first chief factory inspector, the administrative entrepreneur who molded inspection's practical implementation. Finally, the *feminist enforcement model* adopted in Illinois required five of the state's twelve inspectors to be female; the state's first chief inspector and her top deputy were both women. Illinois's factory inspectors were conceptualized as tools through which labor could harness the power of the state in its struggle against capitalist exploitation. Accordingly, the Illinois inspectors rejected mediation and conciliation in favor of aggressive enforcement of child and female labor laws.

These approaches had implications for bureaucratic autonomy, which refers to agencies' ability to take sustained patterns of action in accordance with their leaders' independently crafted goals rather than at the behest of politicians or organized interests (Carpenter 2001). I use the Massachusetts and Illinois case studies to theorize the relationship between factory inspection models and bureaucratic autonomy. In brief, I argue that in the context of patronage politics and politically empowered capital, a strict enforcement model of inspection foreclosed bureaucratic autonomy because it garnered too much backlash from capital.

Chapter 5 demonstrates how goal-directed creativity can make it possible for a tenacious policy entrepreneur to overcome the most powerful of veto players. In 1878, in response to the growing power of democratic socialism and in light of data that disclosed the shortcomings of existing legislation, Germany mandated factory inspection throughout the Kaiserreich. Yet factory inspection cannot be seen as a direct outcome of these pressures. Significant political obstacles stood in the way. In particular, Chancellor Bismarck vehemently opposed new worker protections that he believed would undermine German economic recovery in the midst of a prolonged depression. Chapter 5 thus concentrates on the struggle between Bismarck and Prussian bureaucrat Theodor Lohmann, without whose persistent advocacy factory inspection could not have become a reality. Positioned at the overlap between the policy and religious fields, Lohmann combined ideas from both to develop a distinctive vision for social welfare reform—one that prioritized cross-class conciliation and self-help. A conservative steadfastly opposed to socialism yet deeply knowledgeable about labor issues, Lohmann had risen, with Bismarck's blessing, to a high position in the Prussian bureaucracy. Still, his ability to exert policy influence was constrained by Bismarck's institutionalized veto power. After five years of creative political maneuvering, including bold rule bending, he partially vanquished the chancellor by pushing through a compromise measure that established mandatory inspection but stripped inspectors of their police powers. As a result, German factory inspection followed a conciliation model in which the inspectors' role was aimed at mediating between labor and capital to guide the two sides toward mutual understanding.

Similarly, factory inspection was established in Massachusetts in 1877 in response to working-class political mobilization and data produced by proto–social scientific investigations. After finally winning a ten-hour working day for women and children in 1874, labor leaders set their sights on a factory inspectorate. But while labor was mobilized, no strong middle-class reformer emerged to promote factory inspection. This negative case, presented in chapter 6, indicates that labor protections are possible in the absence of sustained middle-class policy entrepreneurship when working-class power resources are mobilized. If labor lacks robust representation at the decision-making table, however, then legislators will try to appease their working-class constituents by adopting half measures unlikely to have the full desired effect. They will also appoint officials who do not represent labor's interests. This is what happened in Massachusetts. Factory inspection was put under the auspices of the state police rather than the independent board that labor leaders had pushed for. Furthermore, in keeping with the norms and practices of patronage politics, the Republican governor named a party loyalist with no labor experience, Rufus Wade, as chief of police and chief factory inspector. The conciliatory model that Wade put into practice manifested his view that the interests of labor and capital could be harmonized with the state's help. In an attempt to compromise between the two sides, he avoided prosecuting labor violations and instead tried to convince employers to voluntarily comply with labor standards. He also expanded the scope of the inspection department's jurisdiction to build a middle-class constituency. These moves were extraordinarily successful when it came to cultivating the department's bureaucratic autonomy, but less so in actually combating illegal child labor.

The book's final case study, which traces the politics behind a factory inspection law enacted in Illinois in 1893, further refines the "weak labor" scope condition for middle-class policy entrepreneurship. Labor was strong in 1880s and 1890s Illinois, and political conditions were ripe for reform. The election of a progressive Democratic governor and Democratic state legislature meant that the labor movement likely would have been able to push through new legislation on its own, without the help of a middle-class reformer. Nonetheless, middle-class actors played a vital role as social movement organizers and policy entrepreneurs. Chapter 7 revolves around a within-case comparison of Florence Kelley, a middle-class socialist intellectual and activist, and Elizabeth Morgan, a working-class socialist labor leader. The 1893 law was drafted and promoted by Kelley, who took advantage of a mass antisweatshop movement as well as the short-lived window of opportunity opened by Democratic political victories to establish a factory inspection system that labor activists had not envisioned on their own. Kelley's eventual success and Morgan's ultimate failure to pass a competing bill—one that lacked a factory inspection component—was due to Kelley's superior ability to signal the kind of expertise increasingly expected of reformers in the Progressive era (Rueschemeyer and Skocpol 1996; O'Connor 2001). Moreover, whereas infighting within the labor movement had left Morgan relatively isolated, Kelley's field position at the heart of the state's progressive social reform field helped her make inroads into the policy field and bring a broad set of allies along with her. Reflecting her Marxist definition of the labor problem, Kelley's law put in place a strict enforcement model of factory inspection in which inspectors exercised robust policing powers. Had Kelley not been involved, a weaker law would likely have been passed—one that applied new rules to sweatshops, but no way to enforce them. Thus this case suggests that when labor is strong, middle-class entrepreneurs may not be *necessary* for policy change, but they can nevertheless serve as valuable partners to labor by applying their skills and resources to strengthen the contents of regulatory welfare legislation.

5

Restoring Solidarity and Domesticity

CONCILIATORY FACTORY INSPECTION IN IMPERIAL GERMANY

As the driving force behind Germany's pathbreaking accident, sickness, and old-age insurance programs of the 1880s, Bismarck is a well-known figure in the birth of the modern welfare state. Equally well known is that he believed these innovations would dampen workers' attraction to democratic socialism and win their loyalty to the crown. But Bismarck was no supporter of regulatory welfare. In 1873, Germany, along with the rest of Europe and the United States, was plunged into a depression that lasted more than a decade, and Bismarck vehemently opposed any worker protections that might slow recovery. He considered factory inspectors to be petty bureaucrats who enjoyed imposing senseless rules that cut into industrialists' profit margins. Such interference, he feared, would provoke resentment among industrial capitalists and undermine their support for the imperial government.

Yet in spite of resistance from this most formidable of veto players, Germany enacted mandatory factory inspection across the Reich in 1878. This chapter traces how this surprising outcome came to pass. It focuses mainly on the political maneuvering of a high-ranking bureaucrat in the Prussian Ministry of Commerce, Theodor Lohmann, the architect and prime mover behind Germany's factory inspection law. Lohmann was emblematic of a new breed of bureaucratic specialist in whom the Prussian state increasingly invested toward the end of the nineteenth century (Wunder 1986; Süle 1988; Torstendahl 1991), but he was a policy reformer at heart. By mobilizing various coalition-building strategies and exercising remarkable goal-directed creativity, Lohmann was eventually able to circumvent Bismarck's veto power with the help of allies in the Reichstag. The 1878 measure was a compromise—crucially, it denied inspectors policing powers—but it still embodied Lohmann's definition of the labor problem. Lohmann wanted to use labor legislation to protect workers, particularly women and children, against capitalist exploitation, but he was even more concerned with promoting interclass harmony and self-help. German factory inspection realized this vision by constructing factory inspectors as expert mediators between labor and capital—people who would promote social reconciliation by commanding the respect of powerful employers while giving voice to workers' "legitimate" grievances.

Economic Crisis and Child Labor

Germany was in the midst of unprecedented economic growth when it unified in 1871. In the 1830s, when the first phase of child labor reform took place, Prussia was just beginning to see an uptick in industrialization and economic development, but it still lagged behind its key rivals, including France and of course England. Spurred by the pan-German customs union (Zollverein) of 1833, German industrialization began to accelerate in the following decades. Between 1850 and 1873, the factory workforce tripled (Kocka 1986, 296). By the early 1870s, mainly because of railway development in the midcentury and an accompanying boom in heavy industry, Prussia had become the dominant economic power in continental Europe as well as the leading state in the German Empire (R. Tilly 1990; Wehler [1985] 2005).

Germany's concerted effort to catch up with England, which did not happen until the turn of the century, was an obsession and primary goal of economic policy making. Accordingly, from 1866 through the mid-1870s, German economic policy was decidedly liberal. Liberal economic policy achievements, made possible by the left-wing parties' pragmatic alliance with Bismarck, included currency reform and the creation of a German central bank, loosened regulations on joint-stock companies, and an industrial code that guaranteed free trade (Sheehan 1978; Langewiesche 2000). During the first three years of the empire, known as the Gründerzeit, financial speculation reached a fever pitch. Many people from all social strata became suddenly rich, and Germany experienced a gilded age of previously unheard-of prosperity and conspicuous consumption. The working classes too enjoyed improvements in their standard of living (R. Tilly 1990). Strikes and protests spiked because the high demand for labor increased workers' sense of confidence and power.

The bubble burst in 1873. The financially unsound and legally corrupt foundations of the boom were revealed by leading liberal Eduard Lasker in a three-hour speech before the Reichstag. The ensuing depression lasted longer than any other known before in Germany; recovery did not even begin until 1879, and did not conclude until 1894 or 1895. In the short term, the crisis created an antiregulatory political climate in which anyone seeking stronger protections for workers faced an uphill battle. In the longer term, as the depression lingered and suffering mounted, the liberal economic orthodoxy was discredited. By the late 1870s, views had returned to protectionism, and a new window of opportunity for moderate worker protection reforms had opened.

In 1869, the major provisions of the 1854 Prussian child labor law (enacted as a set of amendments to the 1839 act) were incorporated into the Industrial Code (*Gewerbeordnung*) of the North German Confederation; in 1871, it became the Industrial Code of the German Empire. The basic rules governing child labor in factories, mines, quarries, and ironworks were as follows: the minimum working age was now twelve rather than nine; children between twelve and fourteen had to attend three hours of school daily, and could work only six hours per day; and youths between fourteen and sixteen could work no more than ten hours.[1] This age distinction formalized the difference between child and youth workers.[2] Workers under sixteen were also not allowed to work at night, on Sundays or holidays, or during their local church's catechism or confirmation classes. Local authorities could grant exceptions to all these rules for limited periods during labor shortages.[3] If special officials—aka factory inspectors— were employed by the locality to carry out the child labor laws, they were explicitly granted the same law enforcement powers that the local police had. Beyond child labor, the industrial code's regulation of "free" labor conditions was limited to requiring employers to pay factory workers in cash rather than in kind, and ensure their workers' health and safety on the job.[4]

Statistics on children working in factories are not available for the 1830s, when the first child labor law was passed, but by the 1840s Prussia had started to collect industrial data that provide a glimpse of the prevalence of child labor across various factory-based industries. The number of children working in factories in Prussia declined throughout the second half of the nineteenth century. In 1846, the figure was just over 31,000 children under the age of fourteen, or about 6.5 percent of all Prussian factory workers and 1.5 percent of all Prussian children in that age group. By 1852, this number had dropped to about 22,000, or about 3 percent of all factory workers. By 1875, the number had fallen to just over seven thousand (Feldenkirchen 1981, 18). This downward trend was driven primarily by the textile industry, which continued to employ the largest absolute number of children, but still saw a dramatic decline in child labor (Feldenkirchen 1981). As discussed in chapter 2, this decline can be attributed at least in part to child labor regulations.

The good news about the declining number was tempered, however, by four sobering countertrends. First, anecdotal evidence suggests that to avoid regulation, some employers simply moved young workers out of factory settings

TABLE 5.1. Number of Children (under Age Fourteen) and Youths (Age Fourteen to Sixteen) Working in Industry in the German Empire and Selected Member States, 1875–1913

	German Empire		Prussia		Bavaria		Saxony		Baden		Württemberg	
	Children	Youths	Children	Youths	Children	Youths	Children	Youths	Children	Youths	Children	Youths
1875	21,158	66,827	7,076	40,418	1,057	4,562	8,284	8,627	2,176	4,458	569	2,433
1880	—	—	4,795	49,920	—	—	—	—	1,332	5,511	363	4,616
1882	14,600	108,943	—	—	1,247	4,747	4,193	8,990	1,512	6,574	222	5,458
1884	18,895	134,472	5,667	80,146	1,160	8,658	8,666	20,543	1,519	7,342	281	6,701
1886	21,053	134,529	5,992	78,065	999	8,566	10,170	20,570	1,603	7,619	598	7,524
1888	22,913	169,252	6,225	98,014	1,597	11,573	11,479	27,900	1,589	9,010	356	8,252
1890	27,485	214,252	6,636	119,785	2,140	14,760	12,448	43,060	2,360	11,569	378	9,847
1892	11,339	208,835	2,347	115,260	1,642	15,419	5,428	33,331	593	10,887	227	10,445
1894	4,259	209,715	889	115,274	1,410	15,567	—	—	—	—	—	—
1896	5,312	239,548	1,050	132,592	—	—	—	—	—	—	—	—
1898	7,072	276,386	1,471	155,360	—	—	—	—	—	—	—	—
1902	8,077	316,303	1,834	177,619	2,408	25,816	1,665	43,780	388	15,585	759	16,175
1906	10,847	413,654	2,385	237,246	3,603	35,600	1,852	52,357	420	18,720	1,168	20,237
1910	12,870	476,326	2,765	268,969	3,884	43,324	2,474	59,790	532	22,798	1,469	24,893
1913	14,166	556,840	—	—	—	—	—	—	—	—	—	—

Source: Feldenkirchen 1981, 24.

and into private homes. The government did not collect data on children working outside factories, and did not regulate homework because such interference was deemed both infeasible and a violation of parental rights. Second, the number of children working in agriculture continued to be high and may have risen toward the end of the century (Quandt 1978). Third, the number of older children and teenagers in factories continued to increase. This was reflected in statistics collected in 1875 for the German Reich as a whole. Whereas about 21,000 children under fourteen worked in factories at the time, about 67,000 between fourteen and sixteen worked too. The number of teenagers in factories continued to rise over the following decades, reaching 316,000 at the turn of the century (Feldenkirchen 1981, 24; see table 5.1). Finally, although child labor laws may have been effective at reducing the number of young children working in Prussian factories, they were less effective in other German states, including Bavaria and Saxony, where laws were newer and less well enforced.

The Growing Complexity of Political Institutions

Understanding the constraints and opportunities that Lohmann faced as he navigated the Prussian policy field in pursuit of a factory inspection law requires some understanding of Imperial Germany's complex political institutions. By the 1870s, the political landscape had changed dramatically since the first child labor law was passed in 1839. Imperial Germany was a constitutional monarchy with a federal structure. Prussia remained the most powerful, populous, and industrialized German state, but with the conclusion of the Austro- and Franco-Prussian Wars, it had been united with twenty-four other states to form the German Empire. This union created a complicated administrative structure in which the semiautonomous German states coexisted (and sometimes clashed) with the imperial government. The policy reforms considered here were a matter of federal law because the Industrial Code applied to the entire Reich, and revisions to it required the approval of the imperial legislature, which was composed of the Reichstag (parliament) and Bundesrat (federal council). Yet both the Prussian and imperial administrations played leading roles in the reform. The civil servants who staffed the Prussian Ministry of Commerce, in particular, took charge of drafting early versions of the law. This in itself was not unusual because the federal bureaucracy was too small to handle all the responsibilities associated with imperial administration (Huber 1963, 834).

Imperial domestic policy-making institutions differed from the early nineteenth-century Prussian system in four ways relevant to the political course of the child labor and factory inspection reforms of the 1870s. First, the imperial chancellor—Bismarck from 1871 to 1890—was more powerful than any of the ministers or bureaucrats discussed in chapter 2. He was not, as he is sometimes portrayed, all powerful; neither he nor the kaiser had veto power over legislation passed by the Bundesrat and Reichstag, and they were bound to accept laws enacted by the legislative. But Bismarck wore many hats, and thus his power flowed through numerous institutional channels. As both chair of the Bundesrat and leader of the Bundesrat's Prussian delegation, he could strongly influence imperial legislation. It did occasionally happen that Prussia was overruled by the other states in the Bundesrat, but this was rare because Prussia had by far the most votes (seventeen, whereas the next largest, Bavaria, had six), and because Bismarck was adept at making coalitions with the smaller states (Craig 1978, 42). Further, the specification of a law's statutory regulations and administrative protocols was entrusted to the Bundesrat, not the Reichstag (Huber 1963, 860, 929–30). Hence, using his de facto dominance in the Bundesrat, the chancellor could exert strong influence over how legislation was practically implemented.

In addition, the chancellor was also the Prussian minister president (prime minister). When the Prussian child labor law was enacted in 1839, political power over domestic policy rested with a small coterie of cabinet ministers who kept one another in check through a system of collegial decision making. This power sharing persisted in the Prussian government even after German unification, but as minister president Bismarck occupied a position of authority that had not existed in 1839. In the imperial executive, moreover, he was unconstrained, except by the emperor, because he had no cabinet colleagues; the chancellor was the only imperial minister and controlled the appointment of the lower-ranking imperial officials (Hayes 1916, 401).[5] The closest thing to an imperial-level minister other than the chancellor was the Reich Chancellery president, who was supposed to manage internal affairs in accordance with Bismarck's decrees. In reality, the Reich Chancellery presidents—including Rudolf von Delbrück and Karl von Hofmann—were not Bismarck's toadies and sometimes attempted to push imperial policy in directions that Bismarck did not approve of.

Still, Bismarck had control over legislative proposals coming into the Bundesrat from the imperial government or the body's Prussian delegation. It was impossible for any imperial or Prussian official to present legislation before that body without Bismarck's approval. Under these rules, Bismarck was easily able to block factory legislation as long as those proposals remained within the imperial or Prussian administrations. As we will see, once such officials forged alliances with Reichstag members, however, they could circumvent his veto power.

The second major institutional difference was the imperial legislature, which had real power, even with respect to the chancellor (Huber 1963; Anderson 2000; Kreuzer 2003). In the 1830s, the Rhineland Landtag could recommend child labor legislation for its province, yet needed the approval of the

Prussian government to proceed. It had influence but little actual power. More-over, no national legislature was in place in Prussia at the time. In contrast, the imperial legislature had limited but real powers. The legislative branch consisted of the Bundesrat, composed of elite delegations appointed by the governments of the separate states, and Reichstag, which was elected via uni-versal manhood suffrage. The Bundesrat was hardly a source of independent power, being too much dominated by Bismarck. The Reichstag was another matter. The franchise was unrestricted by class and exercised via secret ballot. Only two other European countries, Greece and France, could claim such a broad electorate at the time (Anderson 2000, 5). The Reichstag had the power to initiate legislation, and approve, reject, or amend proposals brought to it by the Bundesrat (and vice versa). Thus the Reichstag had veto power over the Bundesrat and, through that, the chancellor. At the same time, the Bundesrat had veto power over the Reichstag, although the Bundesrat rarely used its veto power, and "few proposals for imperial legislation of any significance can be named that were defeated in the Bundesrat" (Huber 1963, 851). The Reichstag had many members who opposed Bismarck's policies and it sometimes served as a real counterweight to him. It was by way of this limited authority that over Bismarck's objections, it was able to enact significant changes to the German Industrial Code, including new child and female labor regulations, and more important, factory oversight provisions.

The third difference was the existence of organized political parties. When the Rhineland Landtag approved the child labor law in 1838, its members were not yet organized around coherent ideological platforms. Lacking an automatic faction of supporters, those few industrialists who opposed certain parts of the measure acted alone and ineffectively. In contrast, support for as well as opposition to child labor reform, factory inspection, and other labor regula-tions tended to be organized along party lines during the Reichstag debates of 1877 and 1878.

The Reichstag had six major parties.[6] On the Left were the National Liberal and German Progress Parties, which represented the educated urban elite, and received support from many members of the upper civil service and business. Both advocated Manchesterist laissez-faire economic policies, the centraliza-tion of government, the removal of the vestiges of feudalism and aristocratic privileges, press freedoms, anti-Catholicism, and secularization. Both factions tended to oppose worker protections and factory regulations, including child labor regulations, or to at least want to keep regulation to a minimum. The National Liberal Party was the larger of the two; in 1871, it received 30 percent of the votes and controlled nearly one-third of the seats in the Reichstag. In the 1877 election, it received 27 percent of the vote, but this percentage dropped precipitously to about 15 percent by 1881.[7] The Liberals' decline can be traced to the long depression that began in 1873, which called into question the prevailing liberal economic policies. The party's alliance with Bismarck dissolved around 1877 or 1878, after which came a return to protectionism, and new calls for economic regulation and worker protections.

On the Right were the German Conservative Party and Reichspartei. The Conservatives were the party of the East Prussian landed gentry, the Junkers; they had little strength in the Reichstag, but their policy interests were generally represented by the Bundesrat, where they dominated. Some Conservatives supported worker protection, seeking to establish a paternalist relationship between workers and the state, and win worker loyalty to the monarchy. The Reichspartei included both big landlords and big industrialists, and was the party of Bismarck and the bureaucratic elite, providing unwavering support for the chancellor's policies. Together, the conservative parties received about 23 percent of the Reichstag election votes in 1871 and about 18 percent in 1877.[8]

In the middle was the Catholic Center Party, which was broadly supported by the Catholic working classes. After the National Liberal Party, the Center Party was the most powerful one in the Reichstag in the 1870s, receiving 18 percent of the vote in 1871 and nearly 25 percent in 1877. Many of the party's virulent opponents believed its growth stemmed from the clergy's improper influence over the votes of the faithful (Anderson 2000). Bismarck blamed it for cultivating an unpatriotic allegiance to Rome and fomenting disaffection among ethnically Polish citizens in eastern Prussia. Between 1871 and 1879, he led a Kulturkampf (culture war), a systematic campaign of repression against the Catholic church, particularly Jesuits, in Germany. This crackdown only galvanized the Center Party, which continued to grow, superseding the Liberals as the Reichstag's largest party by 1881.[9] It tended to be traditional on issues of monarchal authority and the decentralization of power, but moderately progressive on worker protection and social policy (Nolan 1986, 390). The party embraced the social Catholicism championed by its founder, Wilhelm von Ketteler, and supported child labor regulation.

The sixth major party was the Socialist Workers' Party, renamed the Social Democratic Party in 1891. Ferdinand Lassalle had founded the General German Workers Association in 1863; in 1869, the Social Democratic Workers' Party was created under the leadership of Wilhelm Liebknecht and August Bebel. After a period of ideological and political rivalry, the two organizations joined in 1875 to form the Socialist Workers' Party. Drawing their support from the urban Protestant working classes, especially skilled factory workers and journeymen (Nolan 1986, 352), the Socialists remained a small but—in the midst of depression—growing minority party throughout the 1870s, winning 3 percent of the votes in 1871 and 9 percent in 1877.[10] The Socialists favored worker protections and child labor regulations, and advocated protective measures stronger than those that the Center Party favored (Nolan 1986). The prevailing attitude toward the Social Democrats was mounting hostility and fear. Finally branding the Socialists an enemy of the state, Bismarck pushed through a set of "socialist laws" in 1878 that outlawed socialist organizations and periodicals in Germany. The efforts backfired. Socialist candidates, running as independent "representatives of the whole people" and exploiting the moratorium on the socialist ban during election times (Anderson 2000, 287, 289), continued to attract ever-larger segments of the electorate throughout the 1880s. Beginning in 1890, Social Democrats started winning more votes than any other party, though this did not translate into the most seats until 1912.

The fourth relevant political-institutional difference between Germany in the 1870s and Prussia in the 1830s was the rise of organized interest groups. In the 1830s, Prussian workers had not yet organized, but this changed markedly by the latter third of the century. Following a phase of state repression in the 1850s, during which mutual aid societies were encouraged but heavily policed to stamp out any hint of politicization, unions began to reorganize in the late 1860s (Reidegeld 2006; Kocka 1986, 290–91; Tenfelde 1987, 100–122). In 1869, the Industrial Code of the North German Confederation positively affirmed the right of workers to organize in the interest of better wages and working conditions. This did not end police harassment, but it did facilitate further unionization (Nipperdey 1990, 364–65).

Business interests in the 1830s were represented almost entirely by local Handelskammern (chambers of commerce), which although sometimes asked to weigh in on policy debates, had little independent political clout and no unified political agenda beyond the local level. As industrialists found that the multisectoral Handelskammern did not adequately represent their interests, they started forming sector-based business associations (Schulz 1961). The politicization of industry reached a high point in 1875, when the Central Association of German Industrialists (Zentralverband Deutscher Industrieller) formed as an umbrella organization to represent the economic and political interests of heavy industry and big agriculture as a whole. In the 1870s, it responded to the economic crisis by concentrating its political activities on lobbying for protective tariffs (R. Tilly 1990), but had no role in discussions on revisions to worker protection policy. Several smaller sectoral groups, however—those representing glassmaking and iron smelting in particular—did seek to influence child labor rules.

In general, industrial interest groups such as these embraced a benevolent paternalist view, and expected workers to remain compliant and subordinate in return. The largest employers, at least, believed—for moral, economic, or political (antisocialist) reasons—that they bore some personal and discretionary responsibility for their workers' welfare, but they resisted state interventions into working conditions or safety standards in factories (Breger 1982; Kocka 1990, 429–30). Unlike in the 1830s, organized business was by the latter half of the nineteenth century united in opposing further restrictions. Some industrialists even sought to roll back existing rules, though most had come to accept—and even praise—the ban on factory employment for children under twelve.[11] Nevertheless, they resented regulations on older children and fought against new protections.[12]

These four factors—a powerful imperial executive, a less powerful but not powerless imperial legislature, semiorganized political parties, and class-based interest groups—constituted the political-institutional context of the policy field in which Lohmann along with his allies and opponents interacted. They created an array of opportunities as well as barriers that political actors grappled with as they struggled over the issue of mandatory factory inspection for the German Reich.

The Worker Question

In the 1830s, during the first round of Prussian child labor legislation, the expression "the social question" (*die soziale Frage*) was not yet common in German policy circles. This changed as industrialization and urbanization ramped up later in the century, and a new urban industrial proletariat arose en masse. Concerns deepened in the 1860s and early 1870s as strikes calling for higher wages and shorter hours increased dramatically (Kocka 1986, 328–29, 338; Nolan 1986, 379–80). Attention to the social question, now synonymous with the worker question (*Arbeiterfrage*), generated the discursive opportunity structure for new policy ideas, providing conceptual materials from which policy entrepreneurs could construct problem definitions while drawing boundaries around programmatic possibilities.

In politics, discourse around the social question emerged from both the Left and Right. Politicized labor's first priority was the regulated working day, but it also advocated for child labor and factory inspection legislation. In his 1866 instructions to the German delegates to the congress of the International Workingmen's Association at Geneva, Marx (2019, 769–77) called first for an eight-hour day, but improved child labor legislation appeared second on his agenda.[13] In 1869, the German Social Democratic Workers' Party demanded the elimination of all child labor.[14] In 1875, the Socialist Workers' Party called for the abolition of child labor as well as the appointment of inspectors, employed by the state but elected by the workers, to enforce labor laws in mines, factories, and workshops as well as in industrial homework.[15] For socialists, regulation was needed not only to protect children's physical health but also to allow working-class children to obtain the education they needed to be effective participants in the labor movement as adults.

Whereas socialist parties advocated for factory inspection and stronger labor laws, labor union attitudes were mixed. For instance, in 1867, a conference of forty unions declared employment to be harmful to children's physical, moral, and educational development, and a threat to family, community, and state. It urged kindergartens and other community institutions to be established to prepare poor children for future employment and political engagement, but did not call for protective legislation or factory inspection.[16] Other unions were more politically progressive. In 1873, for example, the German Tobacco Workers' Association demanded a prohibition on factory work for children under fifteen and called for a Reich-wide factory inspectorate.[17]

Conservatives, responding to both the perceived threat of socialism and the rising economic and political power of the liberal bourgeoisie, also turned their attention to the social question in the 1860s and 1870s. Even though the urban proletariat—factory workers and low-skilled laborers—played only a marginal role in the upheavals of 1848 (Kocka 1986, 322), conservatives began to portray it as a source of hostility to the state and prevailing social order. Their most prominent spokesperson was Hermann Wagener, the deeply religious, archconservative editor of the evangelical Protestant *Kreuzzeitung*, which was founded as a counterrevolutionary forum for the aristocracy and clergy during the 1848 revolutionary period. One of the founding members of the Prussian Conservative Party, he was appointed privy counselor in the Ministry of State in 1866 at Bismarck's behest. Until 1873, he was Bismarck's go-to man for social policy questions. Influenced by the conservative social theory of protosociologist Lorenz von Stein, Wagener despised the liberals and bourgeoisie, decried the dehumanizing and atomizing effects of industrialization, and romanticized the supposedly well-ordered, socially harmonious, estate-based agrarian, pre-industrial society. Recognizing, however, that regression was impossible, he looked for ways in which the situation of workers could be ameliorated, and their attraction to socialism and political Catholicism neutralized. Key to this would be the development of neocorporatist occupational associations and worker protections—including a minimum wage, normal working day, arbitration courts, and factory inspection—as well as universal manhood suffrage. Together, welfare and suffrage would cement an alliance between the people and crown, forming a powerful counterweight to political liberalism (Hornung 1995; Kraus 2002). Wagener's ideas encouraged Bismarck to open Reichstag elections in 1867 to all nonpauper males age twenty-five and up—a top-down decision made almost entirely free of popular agitation (Kraus 2002, 559–60; Anderson 2000).

The second center of reform advocacy and discourse was organized religion. Among Catholics, the leading social reform activist of the 1860s and 1870s was Ketteler, bishop of Mainz and cofounder of the Catholic Center Party. Ketteler made worker protection a central part of his policy agenda, stressing the corrosive effects of factory employment on women's and children's morality and sense of responsibility toward their families. The degradation of the family—caused primarily by working mothers—was, according to Ketteler, the direst threat that the German working class faced.[18] Children belonged at home with their mothers, not in factories amid strangers. "The child of workers, like every other child, [should stay] amid his family" and be able to enjoy like all children "the educational influences, which belong to a true human and Christian education" (quoted in Boentert 2007, 179–80). In 1873, he proposed a party platform for the Catholic Center Party that included a prohibition on the employment of children under fourteen, ban on the industrial employment of married women, separation of the sexes at work, and mandatory factory inspection or some other oversight organ (*Arbeitsamt*) to enforce the laws (Ketteler 1873, 89–94). Ketteler's message was transmitted to the broader public by young priests active in the Social Christian Associations, which were growing in popularity during the 1860s and 1870s.

Among Protestants, leading voices included Wagener's fellow conservatives Victor Aimé Huber and Rudolf Meyer. These social Protestants were products of the German Great Awakening, but differed from their predecessors in focusing not only on the spiritual but also the material well-being of the masses. Both were monarchist corporatists who forcefully rejected socialism and wanted to preserve a society organized by stable, harmoniously cooperating estates. At the same time, they were distressed by the suffering of the industrial proletariat and realized that charity alone was not enough to improve their lot. Huber advocated cooperative associations to enable workers to pool risks, enhance their bargaining power vis-à-vis employers, and build community. Cooperatives modeled after the famous English Friendly Societies became one of the most commonly prescribed remedies to the social question in the second half of the nineteenth century. Huber went further, though, arguing that worker cooperatives could produce their own commodities, competing with and eventually displacing capitalist-owned enterprises. Like Ketteler, these Protestant reformers emphasized the restoration of a wholesome, Christian, working-class family life as the most important social reform goal (Shanahan 1954).

The Protestant social reform ethic translated into direct political action soon after the founding of the Reich. In 1871 and 1872, two widely noted petitions were submitted to the Reichstag. The first was sent by a Protestant minister who advocated a ban on Sunday work to combat the threat of socialism: "The horror of the Paris Commune, the rallies of the International Workingmen's Association and the Social Democratic Party, the many contagious 'strikes,' etc. have revealed to even the stupidest eye, that we are standing on the edge of a precipice!"[19] A ban on Sunday work should be enforced, he asserted, to uphold the Sabbath, and "protect the working class and family life, the German youth and the entire folk life, and especially to protect the serving class from ensnarement and destruction" by socialist elements.[20] The second, more widely circulated petition was drafted by a minister too, and signed by thousands of clergy, teachers, businesspeople, civil servants, and other members of the middle class from across Germany.[21] It also called for a ban on Sunday work as well as the prohibition of night work and implementation of a normal twelve-hour day for all workers. This petition's stated motives were less dramatic: "Our folk life urgently requires reconsolidation and protection of its religious and moral foundations. The working classes . . . urgently require a protected Sunday."[22] In sum, Protestant social reform advocacy stressed the need for employment regulations to appease workers, restore comfortable domesticity and traditional gender roles to the working-class home, and stave off the threat of socialism.

A third major center of discourse was the academy. Marx is only the most well known of a slew of German intellectuals who, beginning in the 1840s, criticized the atomizing and immiserating consequences of industrial capitalism from a variety of ideological perspectives. In 1842, Stein had anticipated Marx by analyzing class conflict through the theoretical lens of the Hegelian dialectic; he regarded society as composed of antagonistic social classes whose interests were determined by their unequal access to property. Revolution was imminent, Stein (1842) cautioned, if the state did not step in with reforms to restore social harmony. The economist Johann Karl Rodbertus decried the immorality of the working classes, but blamed it on their poverty, advocating "state socialism" and minimum wages to enable workers to share in the fruits of their production (Reidegeld 2006, 71–72). Historian Leopold von Ranke warned of "a new power arising from the heart of European society . . . the populations of the factories" that wanted "to topple society or to rule it" (quoted in Steinmetz 1993, 61).

In 1872, a group of academics formed the Verein für Sozialpolitik expressly to research social and economic matters pertinent to the social question. Its early members included prominent professors such as Gustav von Schmoller, Lujo Brentano, and Adolph Wagner, but also journalists, civil servants, and others. Many of its academic members belonged to the German historical school, and believed that state and economy, and their relationship to one another, should be understood not as manifestations of natural law but instead as historically and culturally constituted constructions. The political purpose of the association was to oppose Manchesterist laissez-faire in social policy, and as Schmoller, put it, "On the basis of the existing social order [to] raise, educate and reconcile the lower classes so that they integrate themselves into the social organism in harmony and peace" (Verein für Sozialpolitik 2010). Nothing about these *Kathedersozialisten* (socialists of the chair), as they came to be called, was revolutionary.

The Verein für Sozialpolitik was the first organization to use systematic social data to expose the uneven enforcement of the child labor regulations in the Industrial Code. When the founding members met for the first time in Eisenach in 1872, the first item on their agenda was the reform of factory regulations specifically as they pertained to child labor. Brentano delivered a report in which he praised the Prussian child labor law as "surpassing the English in certain points," but lamented its widespread lack of implementation. Although the central government had been conscientious in routinely denying employers' petitions for special dispensations, Brentano's investigation revealed that local governments, which were charged with implementing the rules, had been far more lax. The situation was even worse in the other German lands, particularly Saxony, where child labor regulations "are generally only followed to the extent that they accord with the inclinations and interests of employers, parents, etc., and where therefore children under age 12 continue to be employed" in violation of the law. Given this deplorable situation, he remarked, it was no surprise that the center of socialist activity in Germany was Saxony. To address this lack of enforcement and help forestall a revolution, Brentano recommended establishing specialized institutions to oversee and report on the implementation of the factory laws (Brentano 1873, 11, 27). He thus joined the growing chorus of voices clamoring for mandatory factory inspection in Germany.

In sum, in the mid- to late nineteenth century, socialist and conservative politics, Catholic and Protestant religious awakenings, and academic inquiry generated new ideas about the social question. The workers' movement voiced grievances that suggested to policy makers not only concrete possibilities for reform but also the sense that something needed to be done to stem the rising tide of socialism. Social conservatives responded by advocating state action in response to workers' "legitimate" demands, with the goal being to win workers' allegiance to the crown. Social Catholics and Protestants pointed to the corrosive influences of female and child labor force participation, and the need to restore traditional gender and parent-child relations to the working-class home. Finally, academic discourse questioned the prevailing liberal economic orthodoxy; leading Verein für Socialpolitik members used social data to reveal the widespread failure of existing child labor laws and call for mandatory factory inspection. Conservatives, Christians, and academics all underscored the connection between abusive working conditions and the allure of organized socialism. These were the ideas from which Lohmann later drew to formulate his own definition of the child labor problem and response to the worker question.

State Responses to the Social Question in the First Years of the Reich

The German workers' movement and the International Workingmen's Association shifted the attention of the Prussian government. Lawmakers began to consider social and economic reforms that might forestall what many feared was becoming a coordinated international revolutionary crusade.

WAGENER AND LOHMANN

Within the Prussian bureaucracy, privy counselor Wagener was charged with formulating a policy response. In November 1871, he wrote a widely noted memo for Bismarck that recommended not only repressive measures but also recognition of "that which is justifiable in the socialist demands" to "reconcile the majority of workers with the current social order and harmonize the interests of workers and employers."[23] The following year, with Bismarck's blessing, Wagener organized a conference of experts from Prussia, Austria, and Hungary to discuss the social question along with how to counter the International. The principal problem of the day, the participants asserted, was that the state had ignored workers' legitimate grievances. This failure had driven them into the arms of a dangerous socialist movement. The state should shift course, and begin to devise positive interventions to address issues as diverse as housing shortages, worker protection, union rights, and cooperative associations. The conference also advocated repressive measures, including press censorship and restrictions on certain types of associational activities.[24] Further, it declined to endorse establishing a normal working day for adult males. Such regulations were appropriate for dependent persons—women and children—but otherwise amounted to an indefensible interference into freedom of contract. This position was a flat rejection of the principal demand of the workers' movement.

Although the conference's focus was on adult male workers—those most susceptible to socialism—child labor was a topic too. In fact, the first policy intervention addressed in detail was working-class education. Education was the state's first defense against socialism and corrosive female "emancipation," participants noted. Primary schools should stress a religious and moral education, teaching boys to reject socialism and preparing girls to fulfill their "natural calling as housewives." It is striking that the conference goers prioritized changing not social conditions but instead the beliefs and values of workers through elementary education. To that end, they insisted that elementary schooling be obligatory, and that wage labor should under no circumstances interfere with school. The participants also recommended that the rules governing the employment of children be applied to industrial homework, and that children under twelve be barred from factory employment without exception. Finally, they joined Brentano in recommending that factory inspectors be employed in all industrial districts to enforce these and other worker protection measures.[25]

Wagener was caught up in the financial scandal of 1873 and forced to resign, though his work continued to influence and be used as a resource by the next generation of officials working on social legislation. His successor as the leading government expert on the social question was Lohmann, who joined the Commerce Ministry in 1871 at the age of forty, after Bismarck, at Wagener's recommendation, directed the ministry to hire several officials with an understanding of workers' issues (Karl 1993, 93–94). A devout Lutheran raised in a pious middle-class home in Lower Saxony, Lohmann's religious convictions strongly influenced his career and reform work. Since his student days at Göttingen, he had played an active part in an evangelical movement known as the Inner Mission. Founded by Johann Hinrich Wichern, this was a nineteenth-century outgrowth of Pietism, the Lutheran movement that had inspired the education reforms of the eighteenth century. It aimed at rejuvenating Christian spirituality in German folk life through voluntary religious associations and charitable work.

Lohmann's religiosity carried over into his professional and reform career. At Göttingen, he cofounded an evangelical Protestant fraternity, Germania, and joined an Inner Mission student association. Before joining the Commerce Ministry, he served as an official in the Ministry of Culture of the Prussian province of Hanover, specializing in church-state relations and education policy. Later in his career he returned to Inner Mission work, serving as president of the Society for the Promotion of Christianity among the Jews as well as a leading member of the Central Committee of the Inner Mission, for which he wrote an important position paper on the relationship between the religious movement, state, and social question (Zitt 1997; Machtan 1995). Thus, even though Lohmann was a career civil servant and firmly entrenched in the policy field, he had strong intellectual and social ties to the evangelical religious field as well. Such a positioning was not unusual; many members of the Inner Mission's Central Committee, including its president and vice president, were high-ranking Prussian state officials (Gerhardt 1948, 6–7, 12), and several political parties, including the Conservative Party, Reichspartei, and Center Party, had long-standing ties to Protestant and Catholic religious movements. This dual membership in the policy and religious field would shape Lohmann's problem definitions about the causes of the social question, and how best to address them.

As a member of the Prussian bureaucracy, Lohmann's job was to draft worker protection and social welfare legislation in accordance with the directives he received from above. His unparalleled subject area expertise, however, led him to influence legislation to a degree that superseded his less specialized superiors—a pattern that Max Weber (1878, 224–25) recognized as typical for an advanced stage of bureaucratic state building. He worked tirelessly on behalf of policy initiatives he believed in. He mastered a sphinxlike inscrutability to hide his true feelings—his frustration with Bismarck and colleagues in the Commerce Ministry—to try to win alliances with them. He also secretly sought to influence policy through legislators and the press. These activities stretched and sometimes exceeded the boundaries of bureaucratic protocol (Tennstedt 1994, 543, 551; Hennock 2007, 81–83), and demonstrate Lohmann's capacity for creative and goal-directed action. Lohmann fit the modern bureaucratic

FIGURE 5.1. Theodor Lohmann. *Source*: BArch, N 2179 Bild-01.

ideal type in his expertise and outward deference, yet defied it with his partly concealed and borderline insubordinate missionary zeal.

INVESTIGATION

One of the first projects Lohmann undertook on joining the Prussian Commerce Ministry was to commission two studies of child and female labor to assess the extent to which existing laws were being followed and to determine whether new laws were needed. Both investigations were carried out in 1872. The first focused exclusively on female labor. The other aimed at assessing the degree of child labor violations.[26] It found that though employment of children under twelve had all but ceased in Berlin, it persisted elsewhere in Brandenburg. The requirement that children under fourteen work only six hours and attend school daily was "routinely" disregarded, largely because poor parents sought dispensations from the local authorities responsible for monitoring school attendance.[27]

In 1874, Lohmann's investigatory efforts were joined by the Bundesrat. This development came in response to conversations within the Prussian and imperial administrations that Lohmann himself had set in motion. In 1873, Lohmann had written a *Denkschrift* (memorandum) in which he called for a Reich-wide investigation into female labor conditions.[28] In July 1873, the Reich Chancellery, evidently with Bismarck's blessing, commissioned the Bundesrat to carry out such an investigation, extending it to child as well as female labor.[29]

The survey results provided the first comprehensive picture of child and female workers in the German Reich. Eighty-eight thousand young workers were employed in factories in the German lands, with 24 percent between the ages of twelve and fourteen, and 76 percent between fourteen and sixteen. Sixty percent were male, and 40 percent female. Forty percent worked in the textile industry, 17 percent in mines and smelting works, and 17 percent in tobacco and cigar factories. Ten percent of the empire's 880,500 factory workers were children and youths between twelve and sixteen.[30]

More than half of Germany's young factory workers—47,500—lived in Prussia, or roughly 1.8 percent of Prussia's population of twelve- to sixteen-year-olds. Child labor rules there had been in force the longest, and violations were less rampant, though they still persisted in some industries, especially glassmaking. The Bundesrat's investigation confirmed the earlier finding that factory child labor in Prussia had been all but eliminated among children under twelve, and the number between twelve and sixteen was getting ever smaller.[31] For example, a factory in Düsseldorf reported that between 1866 and 1867, the number of children under fourteen had dropped by more than 40 percent.[32] Instead, children barred from factories now likely worked at home, where conditions might be worse. This worry was a common theme throughout the 1860s and 1870s.[33] It was even used as an argument against strengthening or enforcing the factory laws.[34] At the same time, the idea that child labor regulations should be extended to industrial work being carried out in private homes began to gain limited traction.[35]

In the other German states, where regulations were newer or even more poorly enforced, children under twelve continued to work openly in factories. In Bavaria, for example, children as young as ten were reportedly found in brickyards as well as match and paper manufactories. Violations of the hours regulations were widespread too. Bavarian respondents remarked that owners and overseers of smaller establishments often did not even know what the rules were, much less enforce them. Laxity and confusion were similar in Saxony, where parents reportedly routinely lied about their children's ages, and underage children were hidden during inspections. Respondents typically blamed parents—not employers—for noncompliance, and argued that factory owners could not be held accountable for employees who lied or independently engaged children.[36]

Lohmann's investigations and the sweeping Bundesrat survey were the product of the German government's improved administrative capacity to collect social information. Together, they yielded the revelation that although fewer young children were working in factories, many aspects of the imperial regulations were routinely disregarded. That this information even existed was largely thanks to Lohmann's initiative. Moreover, it provided an impetus and rationale on which he could begin to formulate a concrete programmatic response. First, though, let us explore the ideas that inspired Lohmann to devote much of his career to labor reform.

Lohmann's Ideas on the Social Question

What motivated Lohmann's unusual reformist zeal? How did he define the labor problem? Like Wagener, Lohmann was no socialist, but he believed that the state should meet legitimate worker grievances with accommodation rather than repression. In Lohmann's view, the state disregarded these demands at its own peril. He often lamented that Bismarck and the commerce ministers under whom he served did not understand that authoritarian measures could not effectively combat socialism.[37] Bismarck, in particular, "was too used to expecting success through 'blood and iron,' and therefore want[ed] to eliminate unpleasant elements with a billy club even in domestic policy, instead of approaching them with reforms."[38] Workers needed to be listened to, not repressed, if they were to reconcile themselves with the existing economic order (Machtan 1995).

One set of discourses that motivated Lohmann came from evangelical Protestantism. The Inner Mission movement concentrated on helping the poor via proselytizing and individual charity, not by tackling the socioeconomic roots of the situation. Its theology, though, instilled in Lohmann the idea that Germany's social problems were primarily moral and cultural in nature. Thus the solution lay in a spiritual awaking of the masses, return to Christian piety, rebirth of brotherly love, rejection of wanton materialism, and regeneration of a wholesome family life (Zitt 1997; Machtan 1995).

But Lohmann also took seriously the material causes of working-class moral degeneration. He recognized that workers could not achieve spiritual enlightenment so long as they lived in squalor and were at the mercy of exploitative employers. Accordingly, his most important intellectual guide was actually the decidedly nonreligious social theorist Stein, with whom he initiated a private correspondence in 1878 (Machtan 1995; Zitt 1997). Stein's (1842) *Socialism and Communism in Contemporary France* had introduced Lohmann during his student days to a systematic analysis of the economic causes underlying

working-class poverty and alienation. Anticipating much of Marx's historical materialism, Stein traced the recurrent disorder in France to the division of labor, private property, workers' economic dependence on capital,
and resulting class conflict (Mengelberg 1961; Singelmann and Singelmann
1986). Yet he stopped short of Marx's radicalism by rejecting revolution and
the abolition of private property. He advocated instead a "social kingship"
(*soziales Königtum*) in which the monarchy would preserve itself by actively
promoting the social welfare of the masses, thereby winning their loyalty
and countering the lopsided power of the liberal bourgeoisie (Blasius 1971a,
1971b). The welfare state that Stein envisioned was oriented toward creating, through enlightened administration, the conditions necessary for each
individual to own property and achieve economic self-sufficiency. Most
important in this regard was the promotion of universal education (Kästner
1981). From his radical critique of class conflict under capitalism, then, Stein
produced fundamentally conservative conclusions and rather timid policy
recommendations.

Like Wagener and other social conservatives, Lohmann embraced Stein's
idea that economic conditions were the root cause of declining social solidarity and moral corruption in Germany. Combining the Inner Mission's moral
critique with Stein's historical materialism, Lohmann's reformist vision was
of a just and humane social order founded on traditional Christian principles,
but suited to the new realities of industrial capitalism as well. A moderate conservative, he rejected both liberalism and socialism, which he saw as equally
mistaken in attributing human happiness to material satisfaction rather than
spirituality and fellowship. Instead, he favored an approach that would create
an institutional and legal foundation for transforming the worker-employer
relationship. The problem was not just that workers were poor; it was that
people—both rich and poor—lacked the correct moral and religious world-
view. Because people prized material accumulation over everything else, they
regarded one another instrumentally. Because they did not understand their
mutual interdependence or recognize their moral responsibility toward one
another, they lived in a potentially explosive state of callous exploitation and
self-interested hostility. Employers, in particular, viewed their workers as
commodities, not as moral beings fulfilling the earthly task that God assigned
them. These destructive attitudes needed to be replaced with a cross-class
sense of "brotherly love" for social harmony to be restored (Brakelmann 1994;
Zitt 1997).

Lohmann agreed that the social question should be addressed through
state-led reform. At the same time, he had doubts that the problems of poverty and class conflict could be resolved by legislation from above, believ-
ing "that, which the governments can do in this regard, can accomplish very
little in the way of overall development. Essentially it is a question of cultural

development."[39] A central feature of Lohmann's theological thinking, which carried over into his social thinking, was that morality could not be imposed but instead needed to emerge spontaneously from within the individual and community (Brakelmann 1994). The state should step in, but its role should be limited to three core functions. First, it should regulate working conditions by imposing safety and sanitation measures on industrial workplaces as well as restrictions on the employment of women and children. Second, it should encourage the spontaneous development of cooperatives, mutual aid societies, unions, and other types of workers' associations so that workers would be empowered to help themselves (Brakelmann 1994). Finally, the state should create institutions to facilitate cross-class understanding and reconciliation.

In sum, Lohmann's definition of the labor problem combined elements of the discourse on the social question that pervaded the policy, academic, and religious fields. Like Wagener, Lohmann acknowledged the legitimacy of at least some workers' grievances and believed the state should respond to the threat of socialism with reform rather than repression. From social Protestantism, he gleaned that the gravest problems Germany faced—declining cross-class social solidarity and the erosion of the working-class family—were moral and cultural, and resolving them required a voluntary and spontaneous change in values. From Stein's work, however, he learned that the underlying causes of society's ills were material. Workers' material deprivation would need to be addressed for a change in values to emerge. The state should play a role in improving workers' situation, but in a way that avoided paternalism toward adult males, and instead granted them autonomy and self-determination. The state's role should be to create laws and institutions that facilitated a voluntary reconciliation between workers and employers, and that enabled workers to help and advocate for themselves in peaceful ways. These ideas underlay his future policy program, especially his quest for mandatory factory inspection and attempt to enact new regulations on the employment of women.

Lohmann's Policy Program

Lohmann's skepticism regarding the efficacy of social legislation stemmed in part from the lack of reformist political will in the upper reaches of the Prussian bureaucracy in the early 1870s. In a letter to his brother-in-law, for example, Lohmann recounted the reaction of Commerce Minister Heinrich Graf von Itzenplitz, his liberal boss, to the ideas he laid out at a May 1872 meeting to discuss positive state responses to the social question. The minister did not receive Lohmann's suggestions well: "Everything, which went beyond already-existing arrangements, was offhandedly dismissed as totally unfeasible or dangerous—essentially, one may like to think, as 'adventuresome'! . . . [T]he whole thing will run aground after a few weak steps forward."[40]

In 1877, the government's foot-dragging on social legislation gave way to frantic corrective action as the economic crisis worsened, unemployment and poverty deepened, and the Social Democrats won more than 9 percent of the vote (up from just under 7 percent in the previous election).[41] These pressures finally broke the liberal hegemony and created an opening for "doing something" about the social question. It was in this context that Lohmann was able to seize the opportunity to push forward a worker protection agenda. His labor policy agenda revolved around three concrete programmatic goals. The first was to create a Reich-wide mandatory factory inspection system, which he hoped would not only address the uneven enforcement of child labor laws and safety measures but also create a tool through which the state could mitigate class tension. The second was twofold: to enact special regulations for female workers (whom he considered too weak to defend themselves without paternalist protection), and to make existing labor regulations more flexible to accommodate the needs of specific industries. The third, enacting stronger educational requirements for working children and expanding educational opportunities for teenagers, soon fell by the wayside as Lohmann compromised with his allies. The other two, however, were addressed to some degree by revisions to the German Industrial Code in 1878, largely thanks to Lohmann's creativity of action.

FACTORY INSPECTION

Factory inspectors had in fact been in force in some parts of Prussia since the 1850s, when amendments to the child labor law of 1839 expressly required inspectors in heavily industrialized areas. Their primary responsibility was enforcement, but they also assisted local authorities in monitoring environmentally disruptive enterprises and ensuring industrial safety (Buck-Heilig 1989). Only three districts actually employed inspectors, though (Karl 1993, 64–65).[42] Outside Prussia, the only two German states that had any factory inspectors were Saxony and Baden.[43] Elsewhere in the empire, police departments and other local authorities had to enforce the child labor laws alongside their other duties. The police were generally ineffective not only because they lacked the time and resources but also because their personal relationships with local employers often compromised their impartial execution of the law (Karl 1993, 66–74).

In 1873, Lohmann and newly appointed Prussian commerce minister Heinrich Achenbach began pushing doggedly for funds to hire more highly qualified inspectors. Lohmann himself was responsible for hiring decisions. By 1876, the number of inspectors had risen from three to thirteen—five of whom possessed PhDs or medical degrees.[44] This new focus on credentials reflected the shared view that the role of the factory inspector needed to be professionalized and expanded. To command the respect and cooperation of wealthy factory owners, inspectors needed to be recruited from the upper-middle and aristocratic classes, have the technical expertise required to understand industrial methods of production, and be afforded the pay and status of the higher civil service.[45] Not only should inspectors enforce child labor rules, but they should actively promote occupational health and safety (Simons 1984, 27). They needed the ability to spot potentially dangerous mechanical defects, for example, or recognize the hazards posed by the improper handling of chemicals. The ideal candidate was a trained doctor, engineer, or scientist. The new hires helped elevate the status and influence of the Prussian factory inspectors, but the absence of legislation to mandate inspection, or spell out rights and responsibilities, rendered this administrative progress piecemeal and tenuous.

Improving the enforcement of child labor laws and promoting workplace safety were the two obvious reasons for mandating as well as expanding the role of factory inspectors. But Lohmann was perhaps even more committed to another rationale: mitigating the class tension, atomization, and erosion of social solidarity that seemed to define industrial capitalist society. Inspectors, he hoped, would help alleviate these ills by serving as beneficent mediators between labor and capital, bringing the two sides closer together until they recognized one another as partners (Machtan 1995). Through inspectors, the state could fill a moral-pedagogical role vis-à-vis the German people (Zitt 1997). As social peers of factory owners, inspectors could teach employers to "care more than they had before about the social aspects of industry."[46] As compassionate listeners to labor's grievances, they could help workers advocate for their reasonable interests in nondisruptive ways. As experts with technical expertise and experience, they would be able to disseminate information and friendly advice that would benefit both workers and employers. In short, advisory and conciliatory factory inspection by experts was for Lohmann the key programmatic answer to the social question. It was grounded in a problem definition that blended social conservatism's desire to rekindle the mythical social solidarity of the corporatist past with the Inner Mission's rejection of coercion. Factory inspectors were to help bring about a voluntary, spontaneous change in attitudes and social relations; ergo, their policing powers should be de-emphasized as much as possible (Machtan 1995; Tennstedt 1994, 1997).

Lohmann formally proposed expanding and professionalizing the factory inspectorate in an 1873 Denkschrift and 1876 follow-up. In these texts, he tended to invoke straightforward frames as well as citations of insiders that had a better chance of resonating with the economic liberals that still dominated the upper bureaucracy in the 1870s. In the first memo, he recommended that inspectors be appointed, and their responsibilities be expanded to include workplace safety. In justification, he cited the support of local governments, mentioning that several had asked for them in their responses to his inquiries. The primary frame he used was simple administrative efficacy. First, existing laws were going unimplemented for the lack of administrative capacity that expanding the factory inspectorate would address. Second, inspectors could improve employment conditions not only by enforcing the law but—perhaps even more important—also sharing information and making recommendations that employers could voluntarily implement. Lohmann used an economic prosperity frame too: inspectors would serve industrialists' economic interests because they would recognize and help employers rectify violations before they became so entrenched that fixing them would result in financial losses.[47]

In emphasizing benefits to employers, these frames fit well with the liberal discursive opportunity structure that prevailed in the early 1870s. Lohmann soon managed to win three important allies—Commerce Minister Itzenplitz, Finance Minister Otto Camphausen, and Chancellery President Rudolf Delbrück, all liberals—to his factory inspection program. They each reiterated the administrative efficacy frame in their writings on the matter, and at Itzenplitz's initiative, recommended further that in the interest of leveling the playing field to protect Prussia's economic competitiveness, inspection be made obligatory across the entire Reich.[48]

No new legislation came out of Lohmann's first Denkschrift. Disappointed but undeterred and goal directed, he submitted a second one on his own initiative (Tennstedt 1994, 552) three years later to advocate mandatory factory inspection for the entire Reich.[49] Skillfully deploying citation, Lohmann opened with a careful reckoning of all those insiders who had declared support for an expanded factory inspectorate in 1873, including the minister of commerce, minister of finance, and president of the Reich Chancellery.[50] In addition, he cited English legislative precedent, arguing that if the land of small government had deemed it necessary to employ state authorities to carry out the labor laws, then surely the same was needed in Germany.[51] Despite the change in political climate—due to the financial crisis, economic liberalism was under question—Lohmann did not noticeably change his framing strategy. Once again, the administrative efficacy frame was paramount: the state had enacted child labor and workplace safety laws that were going unfulfilled, and inspectors would solve this problem.

THE "POISONING" OF TEENAGE GIRLS

As reviewed, Catholic and Protestant clergy in particular articulated the fear that the early employment of females would damage them physically and morally, leading to the degradation of the entire working-class population. This discourse shaped Lohmann's thinking and prompted him to investigate. In 1872, he organized a survey of the district governments to assess whether special protections for girls and women in factories, similar to those in England, were warranted. In its introduction, Lohmann connected the simple health frame with a fundamental eugenics one: "Women's excessive exertion in factories produces negative effects far into the future, not only because its consequences include damage to their own bodies, but quite often also the degeneration of whole generations." He invoked gender role and related morality frames as well: full-time work prevented women from properly caring for their homes and children, and kept girls from learning the domestic arts, thereby undermining "the most important foundation for the economic, spiritual and moral elevation of the working class, . . . [namely] an orderly home and a satisfying family life."[52] At the same time, Lohmann acknowledged, such restrictions on female labor could undermine the competitiveness of German industry and deepen the impoverishment of working-class families. He therefore invited the respondents to express their opinions.

The responses revealed that opinions on the dangers of female factory labor and the feasibility of special regulations were by no means unanimous. On the one hand, some respondents agreed that factory labor was undermining the health and virtue of working-class girls in dangerous ways. The Düsseldorf government took this view. In its experience, women who had started working as young girls were so physically weakened by the experience that they were incapable of fulfilling their domestic and child-rearing responsibilities. Even worse, it maintained, was the moral damage done to working girls and women, especially teenagers, who were "more receptive [than grown women] to bad influences, which poison their souls for all time and which poison they carry home to their families." An outright ban on the factory employment of girls under sixteen was warranted.[53] In contrast, the Aachen government contended that girls and women, like anyone else, could leave exploitative employers and find employment elsewhere. With regard to female morality, it pointed out that out-of-wedlock births were more common in rural areas than in factory towns. Moreover, restricting female employment simply wasn't economically feasible. Families depended on the income of wives and daughters, and German factories depended on inexpensive female labor. Aachen officials concluded that other than prohibiting night work, special protections for females were neither necessary nor practicable.[54]

In Lohmann's 1873 Denkschrift, he cited prominent political insiders and academics—his survey respondents, the Verein für Socialpolitik, and Wagener's Prussian-Austrian conference on the social question—to make the case that the time had come to seriously consider regulations on female employment. Although he agreed with the Düsseldorf officials, he was nevertheless hesitant to recommend specific interventions. Noting that married women and women over twenty were only a tiny proportion of factory workers, he argued that the real problem lay with young, unmarried teenagers and girls.

These were more vulnerable than older women to the factory's negative influences: "The regular absence from home, the early independent income, the contrast between control [in the factory] and freedom [outside the factory] lead to [indulgence in] fleeting luxury; to frivolous, unthrifty attitudes; and to premature, frivolous marriages; in short, most factory girls are deprived of the natural relationships that form the necessary preconditions for the healthy development of the female character."[55] Lohmann's point was that teenage girls (but not boys) were incapable of responsibly handling the independence afforded them by factory jobs. Without constant familial oversight, working girls would squander their earnings and marry unsuitable boys; as a result, they would preside over disorderly and unhappy homes, further contributing to working-class discontent. Thus his social disorder frame was less about crime or class conflict—he did not invoke the socialist menace— and more about unfulfilled gender roles within the family and the resulting moral dissolution.

SPECIAL EXCEPTIONS: THE CASE OF GLASSMAKING

The third aspect of employment regulation that concerned Lohmann was the perceived need to relax the rules for certain industries. Foremost among them was glassmaking, which more than other industries engaged in organized interest group lobbying against child labor laws. Discussions about the special circumstances that glassmakers faced began in November 1874, when the German Association of Glass Industrialists submitted a petition to the Bundesrat complaining about the prohibition on night work for children under sixteen. The protest rested on five interrelated claims. First, glassmakers were not really factory workers; they were more like skilled craftspeople, and the children working under them should be considered apprentices and hence exempt from the factory rules. Second, the nature of glassmaking made it impossible to interrupt the work at regular intervals. Working through the night was essential to the production process. Third, excluding people under sixteen from night work meant that the glass manufacturers could not hire them at all; instead, young people would have to start their "apprenticeships" at sixteen. Fourth, beginning an apprenticeship at age sixteen was too late because military service would interrupt and prolong the apprenticeship period. Young people would simply choose another trade that allowed them to start training at age fourteen. Fifth, these factors created a dire shortage of skilled young workers in the glass industry. The high labor costs that resulted spelled doom for a business already facing stiff foreign competition.[56]

This petition—unlike most submitted by individual factory owners or industrial associations asking for dispensations—was taken seriously. Commerce Minister Achenbach sent a questionnaire to nineteen district governments asking their positions in regard to the claims, zeroing in on the assertion that the industry was under threat from foreign competition. Was it true that German glassmaking suffered because of restrictions on child labor, or was its weakness due to other factors, such as a failure to keep up with technological advancements?[57] One of the more thorough responses was from the factory inspector for several Rhineland districts, who rejected the claim that children working in glass manufactories were apprentices who should not be subject to factory laws, but concurred that production conditions unique to glassmaking—particularly the irregular duration of the melting process—made it impossible to forgo night work or institute a normal daily shift schedule. He therefore recommended a complicated shift system that would have allowed children between fourteen and sixteen to work nights in the glass manufactories, but only once every three weeks. His recommendation amounted to an endorsement of the idea that the factory rules should actually be relaxed for those industries in which their implementation proved onerous. By 1876, this notion had been embraced by the top Prussian officials, including Lohmann, involved in deliberations around the revision of the Industrial Code.[58] It was also unanimously endorsed by the rest of the Prussian factory inspectors at the conference organized for them by Lohmann in 1876.[59]

Why would Lohmann endorse exceptions to child labor rules for industries such as glassmaking? His position is understandable only if we concede that protecting children was not his primary motivation. Rather, his goal was to use state institutions to mediate between the needs of German industry and the interests of workers in a way that would reduce class conflict, promote social solidarity, and restore working-class domestic morality. Doing so would require recognizing not only the "legitimate" demands of workers but also the "legitimate" demands of employers. Workers deserved some protection, but only to the extent that these protections did not unduly burden German industry. To Lohmann as well as other upper-level Prussian bureaucrats and factory inspectors, the glassmakers had made a credible case.[60] Lohmann soon learned to use exceptions as a bargaining chip in his later negotiations with Bismarck.

In his 1876 Denkschrift, Lohmann justified exceptions to the child labor rules for specific industries by citing not only the glassmakers' petition but foreign policy precedents too: other countries, especially England, had established industry-specific regulations that adjusted the child labor rules to the industry's particular challenges and needs. In fact, compared to other countries, Germany's laws were the strictest in this respect. He again used an administrative efficacy frame to justify exceptions: because rigid, general child labor regulations could not be enforced, adjusting them in the interest of feasibility was necessary. Finally, he invoked an economic prosperity frame when he argued that relaxing the rules was in the "interest of industry": only if exceptions were granted would the affected employers be able to hire children and thereby secure for themselves a "sufficiently competent new generation of skilled workers."[61] Achenbach agreed with Lohmann's reasoning, reiterating many of Lohmann's frames by letter to Bismarck.[62]

Lohmann's Campaign for Revising the German Industrial Code

Beginning in June 1876, Lohmann transformed his problem definitions into a specific policy program. As he responded to political pressures and strove to overcome institutionalized barriers to reform, particularly Bismarck's veto power, Lohmann had to be flexible. Surmounting the chancellor's opposition required allies, and alliance building required Lohmann to agree to revisions to his program. Only through compromise and creativity could Lohmann hope to achieve his more controversial programmatic objectives: a mandatory Reich-wide factory inspectorate and restrictions on female employment in factories.

THE LOHMANN PROGRAM

In June 1876, Lohmann drafted a formal proposal for revisions to the Industrial Code; his boss, Achenbach, made minor revisions and submitted the proposal to Bismarck under his name.[63] With respect to child and youth labor, Lohmann proposed several key changes to the existing law. First, to close the oft-exploited loophole allowing children under twelve to work in factories under "extraordinary circumstances," he sought to bar them from factory employment without exception. Second, to help combat the specific dangers associated with the employment of teenage girls, he advocated that the daily ten-hour work limit for children between fourteen and sixteen be extended up to eighteen for females only. To give them time to attend to their household duties, all females—including grown women—would be barred from working at night as well as on Saturday afternoons and Sundays. To safeguard female morality, all effort should be made to keep the sexes segregated at work. Third, he suggested empowering the Bundesrat to ban children and women from physically and morally hazardous industries, yet enabling it to grant exceptions to the regulations on hours, breaks, and night work for those industries (such as glassmaking) in which regular work schedules were difficult to implement. Fourth, he proposed requiring children under fourteen to demonstrate a certain level of educational attainment—standards to be determined by the Bundesrat—before working, and proposed empowering local governments to require boys under sixteen and girls under eighteen to attend continuation schools. Finally, the proposal's most important feature was its call for the mandatory, Reich-wide employment of specialized factory inspectors to oversee as well as enforce the regulations on child and female labor and workplace safety.

These civil servants would be granted most police powers and authorized to inspect factories without notice at any time.[64]

To justify these proposals, he drew on the familiar litany of frames: health, education, and morality; administrative efficacy; economic prosperity; and gender roles. Citations included many insiders—particularly the responses to the 1874–75 Bundestag survey as well as factory inspectors' reports—but also foreign policy precedents, both as models for emulation and proof that the German law was in some respects too rigid.

Overall, the proposal was decidedly moderate. Its introduction openly considered some of the stronger regulations suggested by local governments in their responses to the Bundesrat survey—for example, barring children under fourteen from factories altogether, and requiring children to obtain a doctor's permission before working—before dismissing them. Moreover, the proposal did not heed calls from Social Democrats and labor advocates for a ten-hour normal day for all workers. By considering stronger measures before rejecting them, Lohmann and Achenbach tried to portray the proposal as a modest compromise measure to appeal to the chancellor, whose priority at this point was economic recovery, not worker protection.

Despite these efforts, Bismarck reacted negatively. Industrial interests were more politically powerful at this point than they had been in the 1830s, and Bismarck was probably influenced by a group of Alsatian industrialists that had been invited to comment on Lohmann's proposal and roundly rejected it as damaging to industry.[65] In Bismarck's comments in the proposal's margins, he accused it of being an "inappropriate intervention into [the] individual freedom" of female workers and a "restriction on [their] earning capacity."[66] The proposal did not meet with his approval because it was paternalist, unfeasible, and untimely—especially given the deepening economic crisis. The previously poor enforcement of child labor regulations, he contended, should not be dealt with by enacting yet more unenforceable rules. The restrictions on female employment would likely not have their intended effects; indeed, reducing the amount of time that girls were allowed to work would only undermine their ability to feed themselves and lead to even poorer health among them. In short, Bismarck rejected nearly all of Lohmann's proposals. The only part he liked was the suggestion that rules be waived for certain industries.[67]

Notwithstanding opposition from the man who was both his highest boss and the most powerful person in Germany, Lohmann proceeded undeterred. Rather than exercise creative flexibility, however, he dug in. He did so with only tepid support from Achenbach, lamenting in a private letter to a friend, "If only our boss had more hair on his teeth, we would be in a better position!"[68] Lohmann wrote a new memo in which he defended the proposed changes and particularly the creation of a mandatory system of factory inspection. His new citations and frames tried more explicitly than before to appeal directly to Bismarck's priorities. He reminded the chancellor that the proposed legislation was part of the state's positive response—initially recommended by Wagener and endorsed by Bismarck himself—to the legitimate demands of the socialist movement. He cited the 1871 Prussian-Austrian conference and extensive investigations that had ensued from it. He went on to invoke economic prosperity frames, contending that his proposed regulations would benefit workers and not harm industry. He argued that the benefits of the factory inspection system could be plainly seen where inspectors were already working; those provinces would suffer an unfair competitive disadvantage if the rest of Germany were allowed to continue not enforcing factory laws. In his closing comments, Lohmann slyly cited the chancellor himself, reminding Bismarck that he had called for an expansion of the factory inspectorate in 1874.[69] Bismarck, though, remained unswayed; exercising his veto power as Prussian minister president, he blocked any forward movement, and Lohmann's policy program stalled.

A NEW ALLIANCE: COMPROMISE AND PROGRESS

In late 1876, a new voice for child labor reform emerged, and gave Lohmann the possibility of a valuable alliance and new pathway to policy change. Arnold Nieberding was a high-ranking official in the Reich Chancellery, which was newly under Karl von Hofmann's leadership. In December, Nieberding wrote Hofmann expressing cautious support for a revision of the Industrial Code along the lines that Lohmann had suggested. "Our factory laws suffer from many deficiencies," Nieberding argued. They "do not sufficiently align with the needs of big industry and they have therefore often not been carried out." At the same time, the inadequate implementation of the existing factory rules served as fodder for socialist agitators and fueled workers' distrust of government.[70] With Hofmann's blessing, Nieberding soon formulated a proposal in which he adopted many of the provisions that Lohmann had suggested in 1876, including mandatory factory inspection, while softening some of them. For instance, the plan merely allowed districts to appoint factory inspectors, rather than requiring them to do so.[71]

Lohmann was given a copy of Nieberding's plan for review; in the margins, he critiqued its failure to propose tougher education requirements or special regulations for female workers as well as its lack of obligatory, Reich-wide factory inspection.[72] But Lohmann was willing to compromise in order to win a valuable alliance with the Reich Chancellery. A second draft of the proposal incorporated many, though not all, of Lohmann's suggestions. It lacked his desired provisions for educational attainment and continuation schools, but stipulated stronger regulations on female labor and made factory inspection obligatory throughout the Reich.[73] With this compromise, Lohmann and

Nieberding—and by extension, their bosses, the commerce minister and Chancellery president—became allies. The bill was modified slightly by a committee that included Lohmann and Nieberding, and was then prepared for distribution to the governments of the member states for comment.[74] Bismarck's authority was being challenged from below on two fronts: both the Prussian and imperial administrations had joined forces against him.

REICHSTAG RUMBLINGS

In the meantime, legislative developments were taking place in the Reichstag that seemed to lend energy, if not direct support, to Lohmann and Nieberding's joint efforts. These developments created the potential for yet another new alliance for Lohmann, though he did not seize on this potential right away. In spring 1877, many (by one count, 107) petitions were submitted to the Reichstag calling for revisions to the Industrial Code.[75] The petitions touched on many aspects of the Industrial Code, including the apprenticeship system, industrial courts, and regulations on the hospitality industry and sale of alcohol. In response, five of the six major political parties drafted motions to revise the code. Only two of these motions focused their attention on worker protection. The first was drafted by Catholic Center Party member Ferdinand von Galen (a nephew of Bishop Ketteler) and colleagues. Galen's motion was sweeping in its indictment of free market liberalism, but short on specific policy recommendations. It called for protecting the religious and moral rectitude of the "entire working population" by prohibiting work on Sundays, and also advocated stronger worker protections, including banning children under age fourteen from factory employment and placing unspecified restrictions on female workers. As motivation, the motion stressed the "sad economic condition of the working population" resulting from the prevailing "faulty [liberal] economic policy," the erroneousness of which was made clear by the economic crisis. A new course was needed to restore work, "the source of all prosperity," to its proper place of honor, and to protect the sanctity of the family and welfare of the next generation.[76]

A second motion, along with a detailed policy proposal, was submitted by Socialist Workers' Party members August Bebel, Friedrich Wilhelm Fritzsche, and others. It called for a prohibition on Sunday work, establishment of a normal working day of ten hours for adult males along with eight hours for youths and women, prohibition of child labor in factories, mandatory continuation schools for teenage workers, and the mandatory employment of factory inspectors.[77] It represented, as one party member stated, an effort by the socialists to seize responsibility for worker protection and stop waiting on "palliative" measures handed down from the state. It was also seen by some as a political tool that the party could use to rally its base and lure support away from the Center Party.[78]

The Reichstag debated the five proposals on April 16, 1877. The issues of child labor and factory inspection received some but not much attention; the assembly was more interested in issues pertaining to apprenticeship and industrial courts. Before the debate even began, Eduard Lasker of the National Liberal Party accused Galen's motion of being an illiberal "vote of no confidence" against the policies of the government and Reichstag. Galen retorted that he and his party were there to defend the laws of God. Free trade had unleashed a storm of egotism in German society, he said, which was attacking the basis of the Christian world order—namely marriage and the family. The following statement from Galen aptly summarizes his thoughts:

> The factory worker . . . has completely become a commodity subject to the laws of supply and demand. Through uninhibited freedom of movement, released from all organic relationships, he wanders around in the world, looking for the place where he can sell his labor power for the highest price, and still the price of labor does not, for the most part, rise above the subsistence level. Gentlemen, this picture can be compared with the heaving of the sea, on which the human eye can find no focal point, and yet in this estate too the core of organic creation can be found and this core is the Christian family. This is the question of all questions for the estate of factory workers: How can the family of the factory worker be protected? And we would therefore like to see the survey [of child and female factory labor] expanded to hear from the workers themselves, what sort of protection they need for their families. This examination will reveal that [we] should strive through every means to prevent the recruitment of married women into factory work, because where the mother is missing, there is no domesticity, no family anymore, but where the mother, where the woman is, there the children have their care and their education and the man his domesticity. Furthermore, from the Christian family arises automatically the right to stop bringing children into the factories, so that their moral-religious and their physical education no longer suffer any harm.

Galen's goals were ultimately the same as Lohmann's: to solve the social question by "returning" social relationships to a more wholesome, traditional state—in other words, to uphold the patriarchal Christian family, and restore a sense of mutual regard and responsibility to the employer-employee relationship. Unlike Lohmann, however, he attacked fundamental economic freedoms, such as freedom of movement and married women's right to work. In the words of Chancellery president Hofmann, who was present representing the position of the imperial government, Galen's proposal represented "a serious attack on the economic policy" of the state. His speech was ridiculed as an impractical wish to turn back the clock and revert to the Middle Ages. In a striking exchange in which the basically incompatible worldviews of the conservative and liberal factions of the parliament were made evident, a National Liberal Party member exclaimed that he and Galen "stand apart from one another like two different worlds, and cannot understand one another!" To this, Center Party members called out (perhaps sarcastically), "Yes, quite right! You are modern and we aren't!"[79]

The Socialist proposal, though recommending similar policy changes, did not deploy language broadly attacking liberal economic policy and was treated with greater consideration. Hofmann offered this praise: "I just want to express my satisfaction that the [Socialist] gentlemen have with this motion for the first time in this House, I think, embarked on a path of practical social policy; that they have finally for once come forward with proposals that we can actually debate. I think that if they stay on this path, they will be of much greater use to the working classes than through agitations, which only result in inciting class hatred." When Fritzsche rose to defend the Socialist proposal, he began by accusing the Industrial Code of protecting the freedom of capitalists but not of labor. The code needed to be revised to better represent the interests and liberty of workers. Fritzsche stressed the moral and educational benefits of worker protection. Workers—especially women and young people—needed a day of rest on Sundays, not for religious reasons, but because after six days of "soulless" labor, everyone required a day to physically and mentally revive themselves as well as enjoy family life. A normal ten-hour day would not only save workers from physical exhaustion and an early grave but also give them time to better themselves. Finally, the minimum employment age should be raised to fourteen because children often heard things at work that were morally inappropriate—even ruinous—for their impressionable natures. This, oddly, was the only justification that Fritzsche gave for raising the minimum age of factory employment. He did not discuss the proposed implementation of mandatory factory inspection in his speech.[80]

Rather than voting directly on the five motions, the Reichstag referred them to a multipartisan committee of twenty-one members. When the committee met later in April, it summarily rejected the Center Party motion on the grounds that it represented an attack on free trade and therewith the basis of the entire Industrial Code. Lacking the time to forge a coherent policy proposal out of the remaining motions, it simply forwarded all of them, including the Social Democratic one, to the Bundesrat chair, Bismarck.[81]

CREATIVE PROBLEM-SOLVING

While these legislative developments were taking place, two antagonistic encounters—the first between Bismarck and a factory inspector, and the second between Bismarck and Hofmann—threw the future of mandatory factory inspection into serious doubt. Bismarck was spending time at his estate in

Pomerania. During his stay, factory inspector Robert Hertel visited Bismarck's nearby paper mill, and finding safety standards there wanting, ordered certain changes be made. Bismarck responded to the inspector's warnings with "incivilities" and told him to mind his own business.[82] Less than two weeks later, Bismarck received a letter from Hofmann outlining recent work on the factory law. Bismarck, who until that moment did not know that legislative proposals had been circulating in the Chancellery and Commerce Ministry, was outraged. The proposal had been produced without his knowledge or consent even though he had expressed unequivocal opposition to any new factory legislation. The margins of Hofmann's letter are peppered with the chancellor's exclamation points and incensed remarks ("Who did this?" "Who authorized this?" "All without my knowledge!"). Bismarck immediately telegraphed Hofmann to demand that he be shown the bill before it circulated among the governments of the empire's member states.[83]

When he received the bill several days later, Bismarck tore into it with gusto. Many of his comments reflected his anger over the encounter with Hertel and centered on his newfound distaste for factory inspectors. Unlike the English inspectors, whom he respected for their reputed competence, Bismarck complained that Germany's inspectors had already shown themselves to be petty dictators (*Beamtenbefehlerle*) who had neither technical expertise nor the trust of the business community. Bismarck repeatedly asserted that empowering these inspectors to enforce new safety standards and child labor regulations would only amplify their power to make arbitrary decisions as well as open them up to bribery. Moreover, he pointed out, factory workers wanted more pay, not more protection. Their tendency was already to ignore safety measures and violate child labor rules. The proposed regulations were therefore dangerous and unnecessary.[84] Exercising his veto power—this time, as imperial chancellor—Bismarck ordered Hofmann to immediately halt all work on the new factory law.[85]

But Hofmann evidently had more "hair on his teeth" than Achenbach did. The value of Lohmann's alliance with Nieberding must have seemed vindicated when Hofmann, uncowed, replied to Bismarck with a letter in which he forcefully justified the proposed regulations. Hofmann argued that Lohmann and Nieberding's proposal resulted from a long line of administrative and legislative proceedings, including the Bundesrat survey on women and children in factories, the recent Reichstag debates, and official actions of the Prussian Ministry of Commerce and Reich Chancellery.[86] He thereby sought to employ institutional procedures as a defense against Bismarck's attack. In the early years of the Reich, rules were still somewhat ambiguous, and Hofmann, in an exercise of goal-directed creativity, tried to take advantage of this by interpreting the rules in a way that justified his actions.

The strategy did not work. Instead, Bismarck accused the proposal of being unconstitutional on the grounds that any new federal legislation required either his explicit approval, or a Reichstag or Bundesrat resolution to be pursued:

> In my view the related proceedings in the Reich Chancellery conformed neither with our constitutional provisions nor with administrative rules and requirements. This far-reaching proposal was developed in the Reich Chancellery without ascertaining the opinion of the Prussian Ministry of State [Bismarck, as Prussian prime minister], and without a resolution from the Bundesrat [Bismarck, as Bundesrat chair and leader of Prussia's powerful Bundesrat delegation] or Reichstag, without a decree from the Imperial Chancellor [Bismarck] . . . and, on distribution to the various governments of the member states [*Bundesregierungen*], would have become publici juris if I had not coincidentally—and, apparently, against your expectations—demanded to see its text before it was made public.[87]

Three of the four sources of legitimate legislative authority that Bismarck named could be reduced to his personal will. The exception was the Reichstag. In listing the three offices through which his power flowed, Bismarck sought to cloak his idiosyncratic opposition to factory inspection in institutional procedure. By referencing the rules regulating the legislative process and emphasizing procedures that privileged his personal authority, he matched and bested Hofmann's attempt to creatively exploit procedural rules.

Hofmann had made a credible case, but as chancellor, Bismarck had the final word. He ordered Hofmann to follow what he saw as the proper channels and submit the new proposal to the Prussian Ministry of State—which he led—for consideration. At the same time, however, he reiterated to both Hofmann and Achenbach his vehement opposition to any part of the bill that would enhance the discretionary powers of factory inspectors.[88] Mentioning again his run-in with Hertel, he wrote to Achenbach, "I think the factory inspectorate, the way it is currently organized, is dubious in its legality, damaging to industry in practice, and politically precarious in its broader repercussions for the [imperial] government's reputation and status in the country."[89] He was particularly worried that "meddlesome," technically unqualified factory inspectors would turn rural capitalists—people similar to himself—against the imperial government. The future of mandatory factory inspection in Germany remained dim. As Lohmann lamented to his family in a private letter, "[Now that] it has suddenly occurred to Bismarck that he should interfere in the factory legislation, everything, which had previously been accomplished, is once again thrown into doubt."[90]

Hofmann made one last, brave attempt to defend his actions and reputation. He wrote Bismarck another letter, this time arguing that the proposal was a necessary response to the petitions presented to the Reichstag by the Center Catholic and Socialist Parties.[91] Invoking the will of the Reichstag was Hofmann's last resort. It was the only organ that Bismarck recognized as having legislative authority independent of his own. Bismarck responded that this was still not enough and again upbraided Hofmann for his "unconstitutional" actions.[92] Hofmann was forced to back down. On September 24, 1877, he issued a statement in which he formally abandoned work on the proposed factory law on the grounds that the chancellor opposed it.[93] He shifted to working on a revision of the Industrial Code that included no significant new child labor or factory inspection regulations.[94] In fact, the new proposal weakened existing labor law considerably; at Bismarck's insistence, the proposal offered broad new exceptions to the existing rules.[95] Bismarck had apparently succeeded in preventing any real improvement to labor protection in Germany. Lohmann's second pathway to influence—the Reich Chancellery—had been blocked again by Bismarck wielding his veto power.

Although his promising alliance with Hofmann and Nieberding had proved fruitless, Lohmann did not give up on his abiding quest for mandatory factory inspection. In the midst of this problematic situation, he concluded that the last remaining path to influence lay with the Reichstag.[96] Lohmann knew that Hofmann's new, watered-down plan would soon be up for debate in the Reichstag and decided to do what he could to influence the members' opinions. He shifted tactics away from his hitherto behind-the-scenes campaign within the Commerce Ministry, and began—albeit anonymously and through other people—making a public case for factory inspection and special regulations for females. With these moves, Lohmann's advocacy went outside of the "proper" institutional channels available to him as a member of the Prussian upper civil service. Florian Tennstedt (1994, 551) has argued that Lohmann acted "at the outer limits of bureaucratic loyalty and discipline." Accordingly, his actions were carried out in secret since open lobbying against the official government position would surely have cost him his job. Lohmann's subversive tactics are evidence of his goal-directed creativity in the face of seemingly insurmountable opposition from Germany's most formidable veto player.

First, Lohmann asked his friend Rudolf Friedrichs, a midlevel East Prussian government official, to write an editorial for various newspapers praising Prussian factory inspectors and speak up in support of a mandatory factory inspectorate in conversations with Conservative Party members.[97] Furthermore, rushing to finish in time for meetings of a Reichstag commission assembled to discuss the government's bill, he wrote a series of eight anonymous articles for the *Deutsche Reichs-Post* in which he directly exhorted the Reichstag to mandate factory inspection: "If the bill is to enable factory legislation to take on a form that can be implemented without doing harm to industry, then one must assume that it truly will be implemented; yet the only means of securing implementation, namely the obligatory introduction of the institution of factory inspectors, is not applied. Here the Reichstag must in any case achieve modifications, if it does not want to be rightfully accused of not taking the whole of factory legislation seriously." In making this argument he used the economic prosperity frame, contending that factory inspection would be beneficial to industry: inspectors would not only enforce the rules, but they would identify industries and circumstances in which exceptions to the rules were needed to further industrial interests.[98] Lohmann also used the articles as an opportunity to criticize the lack of a protected Sunday as well as the absence of special regulations for women and girls working in factories.[99] Exhibiting a willingness to compromise with opponents such as Bismarck, he retreated from the educational provisions and other child labor regulations he had advocated in his earlier writings. Tougher age or hours restrictions were unwise too, he maintained, because they would be damaging to industry and working-class families' finances.[100] In short, emphasis should now be placed on enforcing existing rules rather than instituting new ones.

Finally and most consequentially, Lohmann met privately with one of the Reichstag commission's members—Catholic Center Party leader Georg von Hertling—and pressed him to support factory inspection and stronger regulations. In a private letter, he boasted that he was "buying Baron von Hertling" to try to "set something up with him."[101] With this meeting, Lohmann was pursuing the alliance-building strategy of piggybacking: he hoped the influential legislator would fight to reattach his favored programs—regulations on female employment and factory inspection—to the broader set of revisions to the Industrial Code already poised for passage. Hertling's own remembrance of the episode corroborates Lohmann's claims; the baron wrote in his memoirs that he had "repeatedly received expert suggestions pertaining to important specific issues" from Lohmann "as well as fully formulated proposals, which we then brought before the commission and advocated" (cited in Lohmann and Machtan 1995, 485; see also Tennstedt 1994).

In the end, Lohmann's creative circumvention of normal institutional procedures seems to have worked. The Reichstag commission amended Hofmann's plan considerably and largely along the lines that Lohmann wanted. First, representing the broad consensus among Social Democrats, Conservatives, and Catholics, it recommended prohibiting all factory and construction workers (not just women) from working on Sundays and holidays to allow workers time to rest and cultivate a wholesome family life. Second, in addition to prohibiting new mothers from working during the three weeks following delivery, the commission restored Lohmann's earlier suggestion that the Bundesrat be empowered to ban adult women and children from hazardous occupations. Last but not least, it resurrected Lohmann's plan for mandatory factory inspection. "Experience has shown," the report read, "that factory regulations, without oversight officials who are not only required but also empowered to carry out them out, remain a dead letter."[102] Supporters of this measure were odd bedfellows indeed; they included Center and Democratic Socialist Party members, but also representatives from the Conservative Party and Reichspartei.[103]

Historians have argued that Lohmann's influence "is very clearly discernable" in the commission's amendments and accompanying report (Machtan 1995, 485; see also Zitt 1997). Beyond the language in these documents, the timing of the Catholic Center Party's sudden embrace of factory inspection indicates that Lohmann's influence was significant. Recall that of the five bills for revisions to the Industrial Code introduced by Reichstag parties in 1877, only one—the Socialist proposal—included factory inspection. The Catholic Center plan made no mention of it. In 1878, however, after Lohmann had made his contacts, Catholic Center Party leaders suddenly became the leading advocates for inspection on the commission. In Lohmann's view, it was Hertling and the other Center Party members who "performed the most resolutely and skillfully" in defense of factory inspection during the commission meetings. Moreover, Conservatives whom Lohmann's friend and ally Friedrichs had lobbied supported the inspection measure even though the party was strongly aligned with Bismarck. In fact, Lohmann himself attributed Conservatives' about-face to Friedrichs's lobbying: "That the Conservatives supported the factory inspectors, despite Bismarck's well-known stance [against inspectors], was, I believe, brought about by [Conservative Party representative] Mahlzahn-Gülz, who himself was enlightened about the significance of the issue by Friedrichs."[104]

The Reichstag voted on the new proposal on May 24, 1878. Led by liberals objecting to "attacks" on freedom of contract, it narrowly rejected the prohibition against work on Sundays and holidays for adult workers.[105] Thus an important piece of Lohmann's program to restore gendered domesticity to working-class life was defeated. Yet the Reichstag approved the other regulations on female and youth employment, and crucially, mandated the introduction of factory inspectors with police powers throughout the Reich.

Bismarck's officials scrambled to minimize the blow without directly thwarting the Reichstag (Machtan 1995; Lohmann and Machtan 1995, 493–94n1–2). As leader of the Bundestag's Prussian delegation, Bismarck could have pushed the chamber to reject the Reichstag's bill, but apparently wanted to avoid such a fiasco. Moreover, Bismarck liked parts of the bill, such as the provisions empowering the Bundesrat to grant exceptions to industrial regulations. The solution to the dilemma lay in the fact that it was the Bundesrat, not the Reichstag, that controlled the administrative protocols stipulating how imperial legislation was to be practically carried out. Hofmann assured Bismarck that the factory inspectors could be reined in by restricting their tasks to inspection and consultation—not enforcement.[106] The new Prussian commerce minister, Bismarck's crony Albert Maybach, agreed, stating that the new inspectors should "in no way operate as police agents"; instead, they could "be restricted to inspection, mediating and advising roles."[107]

With these assurances, Bismarck relented and instructed the Prussian Bundesrat delegation to vote for the Reichstag bill.[108] It approved the measure on July 4, 1878, recommending that the police powers of factory inspectors be subject to "uniform standards"—administrative protocols requiring Bundesrat (but not Reichstag) approval.[109]

The new law was enacted on July 17, 1878, and applied to factories, construction sites, dockyards, and workshops in which steam power was routinely used. In regard to child labor, female labor, and factory inspection, it contained five new and noteworthy provisions. First, children under age twelve were barred from factory employment without exception. Second, mothers were not allowed to work during the three weeks following delivery. Third, the Bundesrat could grant exceptions to the rules regarding young workers' daily working hours so long as children under fourteen did not exceed thirty-six working hours per week and youths under sixteen did not exceed sixty working hours per week (sixty-six in spinning mills). Fourth, the Bundesrat was empowered to ban women, children, and youths from morally and physically hazardous industries. Finally, member states were required to employ an unspecified number of factory inspectors to carry out the regulations on women's and children's labor as well as those on workplace safety and sanitation. These inspectors were to have "all official powers of the local police authorities"—a provision that would soon be neutralized by administrative protocols.[110]

WRANGLING OVER THE ADMINISTRATIVE PROTOCOLS

Lohmann himself was charged with drafting the protocols for the Bundesrat. He stressed conciliation and mediation strongly in his first draft:

> The civil servants [inspectors] who are to be employed are not to replace the police department in their assigned districts; rather they will assist and augment the latter's duties, and by providing expert advice to the senior administration they will ensure appropriate and evenhanded execution of the Industrial Code. . . . Acting in that capacity, they must principally pursue benign supervisory, advisory and mediating activities to ensure not only for the workers the benefits of the law but also to tactfully support the employers in fulfilling the requirements of the law . . . [and] on the basis of their technical knowledge and professional experience they must justly mediate between the interests of the industrialists, on the one hand, and

the workers and the public, on the other. . . . [They must] earn the trust of both the workers and the employers, which will put them in the position to help initiate and preserve good relations between them.

Still, Lohmann was reluctant to cede *all* of the inspectors' enforcement powers. In his initial draft of the guidelines, he attempted to retain their authority to issue mandates in extreme cases:

> According to §139 paragraph 1 of the Industrial Code, the civil servants to be employed are entitled to the same powers as the local police authorities. To the extent that these powers entail the right to impose fines or the right to issue mandatory directives, however, [the inspectors] may not exercise the former in any case, and may only exercise the latter if necessary to prevent *immediate* threats to the life and health [of workers].[111]

Lohmann failed in this attempt when Bismarck himself replaced this clause with:

> According to §139 paragraph 1 of the Industrial Code, the civil servants to be employed are entitled to the same powers as the local police authorities. To the extent that these powers entail the right to impose fines or the right to issue mandatory directives, however, [the inspectors] may not exercise these rights.[112]

Well into the twentieth century, then, German factory inspectors had to contend with the fact that they had no autonomous coercive authority (Price 1914, 523; Simons 1984). When they encountered violations, they were supposed to make friendly suggestions for improvements. If these went ignored, they had no recourse but to appeal to the local police (Simons 1984, 41–42).

This deficit should not overshadow Lohmann's remarkable accomplishment. Against Bismarck's opposition and in spite of his superiors' acquiescence to the chancellor, he had, with the help of key Reichstag allies, succeeded in his quest to mandate factory inspection for the entire German Empire. It was a partial victory, but one that nonetheless manifested Lohmann's central definition of the labor problem. The protocols denied inspectors police powers, but the inspectors would still be able to act as expert advisers and beneficent mediators between labor and capital, helping—or so he hoped—mend the frayed social solidarity and class-based hostility that ailed industrial capitalist society.

Creativity and the Circumvention of Veto Power

As established in part I, policy entrepreneurs are creative actors—agents who flexibly negotiate emergent political situations, but who also pursue relatively stable, long-term policy goals in accordance with their problem definitions.

Their agency is seen in the distinctive (culturally embedded yet not culturally determined) ways they define problems, formulate programs to address them, and recruit allies using strategies such as framing, citation, and compromise. Their "creativity of action" (Joas 1996) is revealed in their willingness to flout institutionalized conventions when routine policy-making practices prove inadequate in the face of roadblocks. At the same time, their goal directed-ness is reflected in their stable commitment to the problem definitions that motivate them and constitute the heart of their policy agenda, but do not determine every detail.

Lohmann's field position at the overlap of the evangelical Protestant religious and policy fields gave him access to diverse discursive streams that he combined into a hybrid definition of the labor problem. His view melded Inner Mission theology, political conservatism, and secular historical materialism. It joined the Inner Mission idea that society's ills were primarily moral and required a spontaneous change in values with Stein's exposure of the underlying material causes of class conflict as well as Wagener's outline for a practical state response to socialism's "legitimate" grievances. The solution, he concluded, lay in building state institutions to promote self-help, class reconciliation, and working-class domesticity. He thus arrived at his chief programmatic goals: an advisory conciliation model of factory inspection along with limitations on girls' and women's employment.

To see these programmatic ideas through to enactment, Lohmann had to build political alliances. Using frames and citations that fit with the economic liberalism that dominated in the 1870s, he won the support of key members of the Prussian and imperial administrations. By 1873, Commerce Minister Achenbach, Finance Minister Camphausen, and Reich Chancellery president Delbrück had all lined up behind his labor reform program, including factory inspection. The problem was Bismarck. Each time Lohmann and his allies pressed for legislation, Bismarck invoked a new institutional basis of authority to veto their efforts. In reaction, Lohmann looked for alternative pathways to institutional change and new allies to help him get there.

His first alliance, with his immediate boss, Commerce Minister Achenbach, came easily, but proved useless when Achenbach caved before Bismarck's veto power as Prussian prime minister. Lohmann's second key alliance was initiated by the Reich Chancellery, which had recently come under new leadership. This alliance came unexpectedly when Nieberding proposed his own plan for new labor regulations. Instead of treating this alternative plan as a rival to his own, though (as Altenstein had done to Bodelschwingh in 1835), Lohmann compromised. He surrendered some of his education programs in exchange for stronger regulations on female labor as well as mandatory factory inspection. The resulting alliance with Nieberding and his boss, Chancellery president Hofmann, got Lohmann further down a second path to change, yet was ultimately blocked when Bismarck again exercised his veto power—this time as imperial chancellor.

In the face of this problematic situation, Lohmann refused to give up; he determined that one last route to reform remained open—the Reichstag. To form alliances with Reichstag members, he would need to get creative, bending protocol and stepping outside the institutional channels deemed proper for a bureaucratic official. This he did seemingly without hesitation, pressing his friend Friedrichs to exercise his influence with Conservative Party members, penning anonymous articles, and meeting secretly with Catholic Center Party leaders. The resulting new alliances, particularly with Hertling, were instrumental in enabling factory inspection to survive Bismarck's third source of veto power as leader of the Prussian delegation to the Bundesrat.

Lohmann was the prime mover behind the adoption of mandatory factory inspection in the German Reich. Economic depression and the rise of democratic socialism created a political opening for doing something about the social question, but given Bismarck's hostility to labor regulation, significant reform was unlikely. Socialists had called for inspectors, but they lacked the power resources to accomplish this reform on their own. The Catholic Center Party was more powerful, but it had to be convinced by Lohmann to piggyback factory inspection onto broader reforms to the Industrial Code. In short, without Lohmann, factory inspection would not have risen to the top of the labor reform agenda during Bismarck's tenure and would not have survived the Iron Chancellor's veto power. As in 1839, the lead author of this second major chapter in the history of the German regulatory welfare state was a Prussian state bureacrat exercising skillful and creative policy entrepreneurship.

6

Appeasing Labor, Protecting Capital

CONCILIATORY FACTORY INSPECTION IN MASSACHUSETTS

In summer 1874, Massachusetts labor reformers had cause to celebrate. After decades of disappointing defeats, the state legislature had finally yielded to the labor movement's demand for a normal working day for women. The law restricted the daily working hours of women and minors to ten; exceptions were allowed in the event of mechanical disruption, but the workweek could never exceed sixty hours. At least on paper, Massachusetts was now on par with the United Kingdom, where the ten-hour day for women and children had been on the books since 1847. The law's supporters soon faced a sobering reality, however. They knew from studying the history of labor legislation in England as well as their own state that labor laws were often ignored in the absence of strong enforcement mechanisms. Thus, although they continued to set their sights on the regulated working day for all workers, Massachusetts labor reformers now made factory inspection a top policy priority.

In August 1874, Edwin Chamberlin, one of the leaders of the Massachusetts labor movement, addressed a convention of labor reformers assembled at the dancing pavilion of the Harmony Grove in Framingham. Noting that English labor laws had been routinely evaded before a factory inspectorate was established there in 1833, he urged those assembled to turn their attentions to the issue of enforcement. He read aloud a draft bill calling on the governor to appoint four factory inspectors. The bill would have granted independent, professional inspectors full power to enter manufacturing establishments at will, question witnesses under oath, prosecute violators, and issue orders deemed necessary for the execution of the labor laws.[1] Clearly modeled on the British factory inspection system, it was the best law that Massachusetts labor reformers could imagine at the time—the ideal measure that they would strive toward over the next three years.

By the last quarter of the nineteenth century, labor reforms had become possible in Massachusetts without middle-class policy entrepreneurship. The rules governing the Massachusetts policy field had not changed, but new actors had altered the field's dynamics in significant ways. Foremost among these actors was semiorganized labor. Unlike the child labor laws of the 1830s and 1840s, the reforms described in this chapter were the result of fervent grassroots mobilization. Massachusetts workers were vocal and energized, and lawmakers were forced to concede that something needed to be done to appease them. But although labor was a political force to be reckoned with, it was still unable to achieve the full measure of influence it aimed for. It was hampered by infighting, and rapid turnover in administrative and legislative offices undermined its ability to get a firm hold on power. Manufacturing interests were well represented at the statehouse, and legislators were loath to appropriate significant funds to labor protection in the midst of a depression. The hegemonic Republican Party therefore adopted a strategy of throwing bones to working-class voters without truly responding to their demands (Montgomery 1967).

The factory inspection act of 1877 was one of those bones. One after another, five policy entrepreneurs tried to push the state to appoint an independent agency of professional factory inspectors. The fifth, James Mellen, managed only a partial success. Mellen was a working-class state legislator with a long history of labor movement activism. In spite of his best efforts, he and his allies were forced to accept a factory inspectorate put under the auspices of the state police, a young and weak institution that had recently been radically downsized. The police were already saddled with many competing responsibilities, including crime detection and liquor law enforcement. Now they were charged with inspecting factories and public buildings too, and labor reformers doubted they would be capable of doing so alongside their other duties.

A second factor that makes this period different from earlier in the century is the emergence of another new kind of political actor in the policy field: the self-styled expert administrative entrepreneur. On the leading edge of US political development, Massachusetts made major advances in public welfare administration in the last third of the nineteenth century.[2] Following a brief and unstable period of institutional ferment in which activists were appointed to newly minted but often short-lived administrative offices, Massachusetts settled into a phase of incremental administrative capacity building that lasted from the 1870s well into the twentieth century. Activists were replaced by politically moderate professionals who grew their agencies' bureaucratic autonomy (Carpenter 2001) by cultivating a reputation for impartial expertise and winning the support of diverse constituencies (Brock [1984] 2009). The bureaucratic agencies that these professionals built transformed how states engaged with the social question; they opened new governmental channels through which social regulation and policy making could become more routinized, less contentious, and less reliant on extraordinary feats of entrepreneurial reformism.

Rufus Wade exemplified this new type. Despite the police force's inauspicious beginnings, over the course of his twenty-five-year tenure as chief of police and chief factory inspector, Wade was able to transform it into one of the state's most respected public agencies. In time, Massachusetts lawmakers came to depend on him for information on industrial working conditions and incremental policy recommendations to further existing administrative mandates. The force's success hinged on its adoption of a conciliatory policing model of factory inspection. Seeking to balance the interests of labor and capital—protecting both while harming neither—Wade's conciliatory approach was an attempt to use compromise to build alliances with both sides. This strategy was essential to building the force's bureaucratic autonomy, but as eventually became clear to Massachusetts labor leaders, it came at the expense of truly protecting child and female workers.

Party Politics and the Labor Movement

In the decades leading up to the Civil War, Massachusetts had been a hotbed of labor activity. The war temporarily quelled this ferment, and replaced class consciousness with a general commitment to preserving the union and ending slavery, but toward the end of the war, the labor movement began to reassert itself in the Massachusetts policy field (Dawley [1976] 2000). In 1864, the machinist Ira Steward founded the Boston Labor Reform Association and went on to lead a campaign for an eight-hour legal working day. Together with fellow labor organizer George McNeill, he created the Boston Eight Hour League, which sustained its political advocacy into the 1870s (Zonderman 2011), but was increasingly overshadowed by the ten-hour campaign (Boston Eight Hour League 1872). Mill town activists, many of whom were English immigrants who brought their advocacy experience across the Atlantic, formed local Short Time Committees to agitate for the ten-hour day. Now joined by the eight-hour people, they carried out massive petition drives and rallied voters behind supportive candidates. In the 1873 election, opponents of the measure were voted out of the Massachusetts Senate and the long sought-after ten-hour law was passed the following year (Blewett 2000, 132).

Unions proliferated during this time as well, but most were small and short lived—"constantly organizing, failing, and re-organizing."[3] The state's largest union in the 1860s and early 1870s, the shoemakers' Knights of St. Crispin, even spawned a new political party, the Labor Reform Party, in 1869. This party too was short lived, surviving only until 1872; the Crispins soon dissolved as well after a failed strike in 1874. Strikes against wage cuts and other injustices proliferated, though the vast majority were unsuccessful in the face of employers' iron unwillingness to yield on any issue (Blewett 2000). The labor movement, then, cannot be characterized as powerful or unified, but it was vocal, energetic, and impossible for the state's politicians to ignore completely.

Ongoing labor activism for the regulated working day helped push the state's mainstream political parties toward a rhetorical and at times practical embrace of labor issues (Blewett 2000, 132). The Republican Party, successor to Carter and Mann's now-defunct Whig Party, was Massachusetts's indisputably dominant party. Patriotic fervor and an abhorrence of slavery cut across class lines, uniting the majority in Massachusetts behind the party of Abraham Lincoln during and immediately following the war. Over time, the party's hegemony weakened, though it was not until 1948 that it lost its majority in both houses of the legislature simultaneously (Dubin 2007, 94). Working-class voters were increasingly split between the Republican and Democrat camps (Baum 1984). Encouraged by the party's willingness to cover the two dollar poll tax, the growing population of naturalized Irish American citizens voted overwhelmingly Democratic. By 1875, 20 percent of Boston voters were Irish born (Miller 2009, 348). Despite continued Republican Party dominance, then, the allegiance of the state's working-class voters was increasingly up for grabs.

The absence of a strong opposition party allowed Republicans to avoid developing a clear and unified labor agenda. The party's constituency was diverse, and so it propped up its big tent with a broad and vague platform as well as by distributing patronage spoils (Abbott 1976; Bensel 2000, 144–45; Skocpol 1992, 77–81). As a result, individual Republican legislators were all over the map on labor issues. In the postwar years, many Radical Republicans— those who had strongly supported abolition and Reconstruction—embraced labor demands like the ten-hour day, and Governors John Andrew and Alexander Bullock both appointed commissions to investigate labor issues and expressed openness to moderate labor reforms. As Radical Republican dominance waned in the 1870s, the party fractured, particularly over issues of patronage and civil service reform. Many of the new Republican elites were closely aligned with industrial interests and opposed labor protections for adults (Abbott 1976, Baum 164–65). These affiliations, however, should not be overdrawn. The point is that individual Republican legislators, including those with ties to industry, could be found on all sides of the labor issue.

The most powerful prolabor politician of the time was the iconoclastic Radical Republican—and later Democrat—Benjamin Butler. Brash, ambitious, and unembarrassed to court votes wherever he could get them, Butler was a real thorn in the side of the Republican establishment, largely because he was a Greenbacker, but also because they regarded him as a dangerous populist demagogue. Butler was no true labor reformer (Montgomery 1967, 367), but his prolabor rhetoric garnered him working-class votes and even the endorsement of prominent labor activists like Wendell Phillips, a former abolitionist leader (Bergeson-Lockwood 2016, 183–85). Butler's popularity withstood the hostility of his colleagues, and thanks to support from Irish voters, he served five terms in the US House of Representatives in the 1860s and 1870s, and was elected governor for a one-year term in 1883 (Harmond 1968).

Massachusetts Democrats enjoyed a period of electoral strength beginning in 1873. That year, seventy Democrats were elected to the Massachusetts House of Representatives and eleven to the Massachusetts Senate, or 29 and 27.5 percent of each body, respectively (Dubin 2007, 93). Republican hegemony was challenged in the face of a financial panic and global depression that shuttered local factories and businesses, disgruntlement over the state's strict Republican-imposed liquor laws, and national corruption scandals plaguing the Grant administration. The last had helped fuel a brief split between the Radical Republicans, who supported Grant, and so-called Liberal Republicans, predecessors to the Mugwumps, whose primary objective was civil service reform. But Republican dominance was challenged by organized labor too; in the 1873 election, eight-hour movement leaders Steward, McNeill, and Chamberlain organized working-class voters to kick ten antilabor incumbents out of the state Senate (Blewett 2000, 128, 132). These developments helped Democrats make significant electoral gains—a change that had the potential to benefit labor. Massachusetts Democrats were more vocal and unified than Republicans in their support for northern white labor (Abbott 1976; Montgomery 1967). Still, both parties lacked the programmatic unity that they exhibit today; individual Democrats as well as Republicans could be found on all sides of the labor issue.

Third parties also put pressure on the Republican Party. The Labor Reform Party was created in 1869 on the initiative of the Knights of St. Crispin. It was a small minority party, but it managed to seat some representatives in the state legislature in 1869 and 1870 (Baum 1984, 152–53). In 1870, the party nominated Phillips for governor. Phillips ran a spirited campaign and managed to win 13 percent of the vote. The party fizzled out by 1872, but its brief success along with the growing power of the Democrats and "Butlerism" all demonstrated to Republicans that they would need to do more to forestall the defection of working-class voters (Baum 1984, 214–16; Montgomery 1967; Bergeson-Lockwood 2016; Harmond 1968).

Still, most Republicans were willing to do only so much. A repeated strategy was to concede to labor's wishes, but only in superficial ways. Factory inspection was an example of this. After the 1874 ten-hour law was enacted, Massachusetts labor leaders started to tackle its ongoing nonenforcement. Looking to England for inspiration, they demanded that Massachusetts erect an independent, professional factory inspectorate along similar lines. Chamberlin's proposed bill was the beginning of a coordinated three-year fight, but one that would prove only partially successful. Labor could occasionally force politicians to address its concerns, but not in the way it wanted. Instead of an English-style inspectorate staffed by experts, factory inspection was simply grafted onto an existing law enforcement agency and a conciliatory policing model of factory inspection was institutionalized.

Industrialization, Immigration, and Child Labor

Chapter 3 broke off the story of labor regulation in Massachusetts in 1842, when the state's industrial expansion was already well underway. Industrial and demographic transformation continued unabated over the following decades. Between 1845 and 1885, the Bay State's urban population ballooned from about 40 to nearly 75 percent of all residents (Siracusa 1979, 46). Agriculture, unable to compete with cheap imports from the Midwest, continued to decline, reaching a mere 12 percent of the workforce by 1880, as gains were made in white-collar, transportation, commercial, and domestic service sectors (Siracusa 1979, 34, 38). Most of all, Massachusetts was a manufacturing state. The state's nonindependent manufacturing workers made up 43 percent of the total labor force in 1880, up from 34 percent in 1845 (Siracusa 1979, 34). Textiles and leather (primarily shoes and boots) continued to be the largest industrial sectors, but ready-to-wear clothing, metal, and metalworking occupied a growing share.

As the state's manufacturing sector boomed, so did its population. Overall population growth peaked at 35 percent between 1840 and 1850, but still grew by 22 percent between 1870 and 1880. Most of this growth was due to massive immigration; whereas in 1840 a mere 5 percent of Massachussetts residents were foreign born, 25 percent were in the 1870s and 1880s (Siracusa 1979, 29). By the 1860s, the vast majority of mill workers were foreign born (Persons 1971, 92). Many were Irish, but by the late 1800s, factory labor came to be closely associated with the French Canadians that had been streaming into the state since the Civil War. Immigrants also continued to come from England; having spent their youth in the mills of Lancashire and Yorkshire, many took up work in the textile factories of the new world. They came looking for a better life, yet some reported that US conditions were worse than at home, where they worked fewer hours while enjoying a lower cost of living, more educational opportunities, and more freedom to participate in labor politics.[4]

Immigrants from everywhere flocked to the manufacturing towns that mushroomed along the Merrimack and Connecticut Rivers. Between 1840 and 1870, Lowell's population almost doubled, Lynn's tripled, and Fall River's nearly quintupled. Planned mill towns sprang up seemingly overnight. Lawrence, the site of a number of large woolen and cotton mills ten miles downriver from Lowell, grew from a few hundred residents in the 1840s to nearly twenty-nine thousand by 1870, making it the fifth-largest city in the state.[5] As vital as these newcomers were to industrial prosperity, they were regarded with apprehension and disdain by the native born, even those who might be considered progressive. Henry Oliver—one of the state's leading labor reformers—portrayed them as an encroaching menace: "The grand old class of educated American operatives, male and female . . . has almost wholly retired before the swelling wave of an untaught, degraded class, imported . . . [and] fast spreading."[6] Compared with the much-romanticized Lowell mill girls of the 1830s, immigrant factory workers were seen as uneducated, unskilled, and hostile. As a minister in a factory town observed, "Formerly, when the American element of school-taught girls was the operative class, we heard of their marrying clergymen, teachers and men of means. Is it so now? By no means, for [class] antagonism is now the rule."[7]

Nineteenth-century child labor statistics are flawed, but the data that exist suggest that like in Germany, child labor was already on the decline in Massachusetts (though not in the rest of the country) by midcentury. According to the 1870 US Census, 4.5 percent of the state's manufacturing, mechanical, and mining workforce was between ten and fifteen—much higher than the national average of 2.8 percent. This amounted to more than thirteen thousand children, or nearly eight thousand boys and more than five thousand girls. Economists Claudia Goldin and Kenneth Sokoloff (1982, 748) provide a similar estimate: in 1870, 5.1 percent of Massachusetts workers employed specifically in manufacturing were "children" (boys age sixteen and younger, and girls age fifteen and younger). This was a substantial decrease from forty years prior, when 9.3 percent of manufacturing workers were boys and an unknown percentage were girls. Still, in the state's mill towns, children continued to make up a significant part of the workforce. An 1867 inquiry found that 37.5 percent of factory operatives in a selected sample of larger mills in Lowell were between ten and fourteen; this figure was 36 percent in Fall River and 25.7 percent in Lawrence.[8] Child labor may have been on the decline in Massachusetts, but was still a vital part of the large-scale industrial economy and essential to the family finances of the state's industrial class.

Investigation, Legislation, and Enforcement

Over the 1860s and early 1870s, investigations repeatedly revealed an alarming truth: in Massachusetts, a state that had long prided itself on its public schools and commitment to education, thousands of children were growing up in ignorance. In 1852, Massachusetts had become the first state in the country to enact a compulsory schooling law; by 1865, workers under twelve were required to attend school for eighteen weeks per year, and those between the ages of twelve and fifteen for an eleven-week term. Despite these efforts, truancy and illiteracy were rampant in mill towns. Fall River and Lawrence reported illiteracy rates of 27 and 22 percent, respectively.[9] An estimated 10.5 percent of school-age children statewide were not attending school in 1870; in Boston, 20 percent were not.[10] This problem more than any other stoked the alarm of middle-class social reformers. Just as it had in the 1830s and 1840s, child labor discourse centered on the need to expose the children of the poor to the civilizing influence of the state's common schools.

Starting at the close of the Civil War, Radical Republican governors commissioned a series of three investigations into the labor question, including child labor. The investigations revealed widespread violations of the state's child labor and schooling laws. The 1866 commission lamented "frequent and gross" violations. Fall River, it reported, was home to "652 children, of both sexes, from eight to fourteen, working in the mills, most of them unable to read or write, all kept from school." When mills did not have enough "small help," factory overseers reportedly "raided" the local schools for children as young as seven.[11] Soon after the commission report was released, the state legislature enacted the state's first significant new child labor law since 1842. The law finally established a minimum working age of ten for manufacturing establishments.[12] It also increased the education requirements for working children under fourteen to six months of full-time schooling per year, and reduced their daily allowable working hours from ten to eight.[13]

In 1867, another commission found further evidence that child labor laws were being disregarded. The customary working day in textile mills was eleven hours; unsurprisingly, reports came in from all over the state of children working in mills at least eleven hours per day, sixty-six hours per week. Nonetheless, these commissioners recommended relaxing the child labor regulations enacted the previous year.[14] The legislature hastened to do so, raising children's allowable working hours to sixty per week, thereby effectively reinstating the old ten-hour day for minors. The schooling requirement was dropped as well, to three months per year. These changes were made not only in response to the commission's report but also at the behest of manufacturers that complained that requiring six months of schooling was dissuading migrant French Canadians from supplying the mills with cheap child labor (Persons 1971, 96–97).

Massachusetts industrialists had learned to exercise their political influence against child labor regulation.

The 1867 commission did push labor legislation forward in one important respect, calling for the appointment of a special inspector of labor, arguing that "no laws or regulations, however wise and humane, will afford protection to the laboring classes, unless they have an official friend, to whom they can appeal with confidence."[15] In response, the new child labor law required the constable of the Commonwealth, the head of the Massachusetts State Police, to assign one of his deputies to enforcing the law and prosecuting offenses.[16] Thus the state's earliest attempt at creating an inspection system to enforce its child labor laws placed this responsibility with the state police rather than in the hands of a new independent authority, as both the 1866 and 1867 labor commissions had recommended. Indeed, the latter alternative does not seem to have received any serious consideration from the legislature; the first draft of the bill, composed in direct response to the commission's report, put inspection under the purview of the constable.[17] None of the many subsequent drafts proposed otherwise.

This initial move was to have long-term consequences. The first state police force in the country, the Massachusetts State Police, was established in 1865 by Governor Andrew. Its primary responsibility was enforcing the state's liquor laws. This peculiar role only ended up making the force politically vulnerable because the liquor laws were unpopular, particularly among Democrats. The state police was repeatedly charged with corruption; its officers were accused of accepting bribes, and of personally consuming or selling the alcohol that they seized.[18] Hence, although the state police was the only existing state-level administrative entity that could have taken on the responsibility of enforcing the child labor laws, its ability to do so was undercut by an apparent lack of professionalism among at least some of its officers as well as frequent restructurings in the face of ongoing political attacks.

Oliver and the Beginning of Factory Inspection

The short-term consequence of placing factory inspection under the state police was that this initial experiment survived, at least in any meaningful form, for only two years. In 1867, the chief constable, in compliance with the new law, appointed Oliver, most recently a five-term state treasurer, to the task. The son of the pastor of Boston's famous North Church, he belonged to one of the leading families of the state and grew up in a middle-class Puritan household. After graduating from both Harvard and Dartmouth, Oliver started his career in 1819 as a popular common school teacher in Salem. In 1830, he founded a private academy, where he continued teaching until 1844, when he closed the school and was appointed adjutant general of the state. His military career lasted only until 1847, when he became superintendent of the Atlantic Cotton Mill in Lawrence. As director of this large mill, he gained a reputation for decency, establishing a free library and bathing facilities at the mill, and organizing lectures and wholesome entertainments for workers.[19] Oliver was eventually dismissed because he could not carry out a wage cut that the mill owners had ordered: "To cut down wages was about the hardest thing H.K.O. had to do, and he shrank from it, as from fire. To another it might be simply stopping so much money from flowing out of the treasury of the corporation. To him it was taking so much life-blood out of the operatives, for he saw that their wage was their *living*."[20]

Despite having served as a manager of capital, Oliver was already clearly inclined to be sympathetic toward workers. His new job only made him even more so. He poured all his energy into his new responsibilities, but soon found his efforts thwarted at every turn. The first problem was the impossibility of one man's investigating labor conditions in every factory in the state. Second, the 1867 act failed to grant Oliver the authority to properly carry out the law. He lacked the power to enter establishments at will and was sometimes flatly refused admittance into factories employing children. Many employers refused to answer his surveys, and he had no authority to compel them to do so. Records were nonexistent. The law did not require children to acquire certificates of school attendance, nor did it require factory owners to keep documents pertaining to the ages, school attendance, or duration of employment of their child workers.[21] Had Oliver had twenty people helping him, the law as written would still be practically unenforceable. Oliver wrote almost enviously in his reports of the British factory inspectors whose numbers and powers so vastly exceeded his own.[22]

In 1868, together with the secretary of the Board of Education, Oliver drafted a child labor bill at the request of the House Committee on Education.[23] The bill would have addressed many of the issues that he had confronted over the previous year. In addition to raising the minimum working age to twelve, it would have required working children to acquire a certificate from the local school committee verifying their age as well as their ability read, write, and compute. It would further have given the factory inspector the authority to inspect any establishment at will, and to demand information from employers, managers, and workers; those who failed to comply would have been fined.[24] This bill was evidently far too ambitious; after only thirty minutes of debate, it was voted down in the House. Oliver's first attempt at factory inspection policy entrepreneurship had ended in quick defeat.

In August 1869, having despite his best efforts failed to secure a single conviction, Governor Washburn appointed him chief of the newly established Bureau of Labor Statistics (BLS).[25] Oliver's old position was taken over by J. Waldo Denny, a deputy state policeman who lacked any of Oliver's professional qualifications or zeal for the job. Denny confessed to having limited experience with labor issues and having devoted little time to studying them. His reports reflected nowhere near the level of attention and effort that had characterized Oliver's; the first was merely three pages long, and the second even shorter.[26] In 1870, Denny received twenty complaints of child labor violations, but declined to seek prosecution for any of them.[27] In 1871, the state police, its corruption scandals mounting, came under the supervision of a special commission. No officer was any longer specially detailed to enforce the child labor law. Factory inspection, not having really got off the ground to begin with, had for the time being fizzled out.

The Massachusetts BLS

At least since 1866, calls had been circulating for the creation of a state statistical department to collect data on the working population and industrial conditions of the state. The 1866 and 1867 child labor commissions both recommended it.[28] Oliver had been pressing for better data on "the condition, moral and intellectual, of the operative classes, their wages and earnings, their homes, food, clothing and manner of life."[29] Steward's Eight Hour League formally petitioned the legislature for a labor bureau, and Governor William Claflin lent his support for the idea. But what made the BLS finally come to life was Republicans' need to appease organized labor after having denied the Knights of St. Crispin a corporation charter in 1869. The Knights retaliated by forming the independent Labor Reform Party; Republicans were afraid to lose votes to it at a time when the Democratic Party was also in ascendance. The BLS was the bone they threw to labor in an attempt to stave off working-class voter defections.[30]

As BLS chief, Oliver produced four annual reports. Although he avowed a sincere desire for cross-class harmony and was certainly no socialist, he made it increasingly clear that under the current conditions, his sympathies were with workers. Over and over, Oliver and his deputy George McNeill, the veteran labor organizer, used their reports as platforms to raise an alarm about the nonenforcement of the state's child labor law and need for a remedy:

> We have seen crowds of children, apparently not over ten or eleven years of age, working in mills, summer and winter, in over-heated rooms, amid cotton and woolen dust, amid unguarded cog-wheels and running belts, in danger at all moments from accidents. We have found them unable to read or write, pale in face, emaciated in body, and stunted in growth of body and brain;—and, proud of the noble history of our State, we have entreated for the strong arm of the law to interfere between the child and his employer, and his parents, to send him to school and to play; and so to educate him in good citizenship.[31]

Oliver's new position enabled him to continue publicizing his demands for labor reforms, including a ten-hour day for adult workers, a minimum working age of thirteen, statewide implementation of the half-time school system, and an independent factory inspectorate. His policy ideas modeled British legislative precedents, which Oliver followed closely and described in detail in his reports. In each report, he repeated his call for "a system of inspection, as in England," that entailed a "corps of Inspectors, with right to enter Mill or work establishment of any sort, to question owner, superintendent, or employer of any sort, who were *compelled* to give proper replies."[32]

As a result of Oliver and McNeill's strong labor advocacy, the BLS soon ran into political trouble. Employers and probusiness politicians accused it of painting an exaggerated picture. Its vocal support for a ten-hour day spurred a group of manufacturers to form an association to demand its abolition. The outrage directed at the bureau only grew when it investigated the state's savings banks—ostensibly there to encourage thrift among low-wage workers—and found that most of the value of the banks' deposits came from rich people using them as tax havens (Leiby 1960, 60).[33] After an exposé of the wretched conditions of Boston's tenement houses, landlords also went after Oliver and McNeill, demanding that the governor dismiss them.[34] It is not surprising that capitalists hated the bureau, but even some segments of the labor movement regarded it with distrust. The Crispins knew that its creation had been a mere appeasement tactic on the part of legislators who had refused them their charter; they treated the bureau as "an enemy in disguise," refusing to cooperate with its investigations.[35] Even Phillips, the Labor Reform Party's gubernatorial candidate, attacked the bureau because he felt that it represented only one side of the labor movement, that of Steward's Eight Hour League, and was thus biased against his faction.[36] In the context of infighting among labor activists and increasingly militant employers, the bureau found itself threatened from all sides.

It survived these attacks and went on to become a model of state administrative capacity building. But Oliver and McNeill took the blame for the controversy, and over the protest of 103 labor representatives, their contracts were not renewed.[37] Oliver continued to dabble in labor advocacy for a few years before going on to serve as mayor of Salem for four consecutive terms. In the end, he had been unable to use his institutional positions—first as factory inspector and then as labor statistician—to build a coalition of support around the factory inspection idea. On the spectrum between advocacy and objectivity (Furner 1975), Oliver fell too close to the advocacy pole for someone who was, after all, not a politician but rather a proto–social scientist and civil servant. His unequivocal support of labor over capital and particularly his vocal advocacy for the ten-hour day for all workers angered employers and alienated moderates who might otherwise have been open to the idea of factory inspection. Labor movement leaders were at the time still less interested in child labor law enforcement than in a normal working day. Oliver's repeated calls for a British-style system of factory inspection therefore fell largely on deaf ears.

Carroll D. Wright and Workplace Safety

Wright replaced Oliver as chief of the BLS. Cut from a different cloth than Oliver, despite their shared middle-class roots, he was not especially friendly to labor; in fact, as a state senator he had voted against a ten-hour bill for factory workers. Following the advice of Francis Amasa Walker, president of the American Statistical Association, Wright decided that the bureau should no longer take political sides and certainly not serve as an arm of the labor movement. Its purpose would now be limited to collecting "objective" statistics that political actors could use as they saw fit (Zonderman 2011, 155; Leiby 1960, 63). In short, Wright planned to build for the BLS a legitimating reputation for neutral social scientific expertise. His approach cooled capitalist opposition to the bureau, and in 1876 he reported that business had adopted a mostly friendly attitude toward it.[38]

Although Wright abandoned the fiery prolabor stance of his predecessor, he was not exactly hostile to labor either and regarded the (peaceful) labor movement as a vital part of the overall struggle for the improvement of the human condition (Leiby 1960, 67). Although he shied away from regulations to directly intervene in the relationship between adult male workers and employers, he did believe in the right of the state to intervene in working conditions in other ways. Despite his commitment to "objectivity," then, Wright did take stances on certain labor policy issues and more than once included legislative proposals in his reports, particularly in regard to workplace safety and child labor. Arguing that premature employment was "the greatest evil" of the factory system—one that not only harmed children intellectually and physically but also depressed adult wages—Wright advocated raising the minimum working age from ten to fifteen. He proposed safety and sanitary standards for factories as well as a factory inspection system along the lines of the British model. The beneficial effects of factory laws in England had only been achieved by means of "a strict and efficient system of government inspection," he contended; it was essential that Massachusetts follow suit.[39]

On September 19, 1874, a tragic focusing event added new reasons, beyond the need to enforce child labor laws, for the creation of a state factory inspectorate. The Granite Mill in Fall River caught fire; employees working on the upper floors were trapped, and twenty-three people perished. A BLS investigation found that many of the nineteen children who were killed or seriously injured were employed illegally—being under the legal working age, unschooled, or both. The bureau blamed the absence of adequate fire escapes and lack of water to douse the flames.[40] A subtext of its report, however, was that if child labor rules had been properly followed, fewer people would have died.

In March 1875, Wright proposed a factory act for Massachusetts. Primarily a workplace safety measure, it included specific regulations such as fencing off dangerous machinery and the provision of fire escapes as well as new sanitary regulations, among them adequate ventilation and clean toilets. It did not propose any new child labor regulations, but called on the governor to appoint a "chief inspector of factories" to enforce the existing child labor as well as the proposed health and safety rules. This should be a highly qualified "medical man" who possessed "practical knowledge of sanitary matters and of mechanics," and who would be aided by between three and seven deputies. The enactment of clear rules with competent and impartial professionals to enforce them would, Wright believed, be welcomed by factory owners and workers alike. Like Lohmann in Germany, Wright thought expert factory inspectors would garner respect and promote interclass harmony in place of the prevailing bitter antagonism.[41]

Wright's proposed act was not taken up. Like Oliver, he failed to build a coalition around the idea; indeed, there is no evidence that he ever tried to do so. Even though Wright did not completely stay out of politics, his professed commitment to objectivity precluded him from actively lobbying for his favored legislative reforms. Forming an alliance with labor in support of the act was out of the question for this committed centrist, and in any case, labor leaders had never forgiven him for his opposition to the ten-hour bill as a state legislator. Even though they had since the enactment of the ten-hour law turned their attentions to factory inspection, they had little interest in accomplishing this goal by working with the likes of Wright.

McNeill's Report

Since 1871, when the special commission was appointed to oversee the corruption-plagued state police, no officer had been expressly appointed to carry out the child labor laws. This changed in 1874, when the commission was disbanded and Lieutenant Governor Thomas Talbot appointed McNeill, who had just been dismissed from the BLS, to the position of deputy state constable (McNeill 1875). McNeill was a former mill worker and shoemaker who had begun working in the factories at age ten. Unlike his colleague Oliver, who was born into privilege and joined the cause of labor relatively late in life, McNeill had been active in the movement since age fifteen, when he participated in his first strike. He went on to write for various workingmen's newspapers and cofound, with Steward, the Massachusetts Eight Hour League.[42] He assumed his new office in the midst of the global depression instigated by the Panic of 1873.

McNeill's report came out in January 1875. On the basis of an analysis of the Board of Education's school returns, he concluded that sixty thousand school-age children—roughly a third of this population—were not attending school in Massachusetts (McNeill 1875, 11). In Fall River, this figure was nearly 50 percent (18). McNeill segued from his discussion of truancy to a discussion of factory child labor, assuming that the latter was a primary cause of the former. For him, the biggest problem with child labor was that it interfered with children's schooling. Citing education reformers such as Horace Mann, he framed the problem as a threat to the state's economic potential as well as its social stability, asserting that a "hundred thousand children growing up in ignorance are . . . a hundred thousand paupers in embryo" (67). He warned his readers that education was the only bulwark against extreme inequality and class conflict (72–73). But he also appealed to the legislators' morality. It was incumbent on a Christian nation to heed the pleas of the "little ones"— helpless slaves "robbed of the innocent sports of childhood, weighed down with care, grown prematurely old" (66). Children had rights—the right to "play and make merry; to be at school; to be *players*, not *workers*" (67)— that the state was bound to honor and protect. Drawing inspiration from the British Factory Acts, which he cited extensively, McNeill called for a child labor law that would significantly strengthen the existing rules, and require the governor to appoint a factory inspector and three deputies (75–76).[43]

McNeill's explosive report generated a great deal of public attention. Three thousand additional copies had to be printed.[44] Massachussetts residents were shocked to learn the alleged extent of the truancy problem and frequency with which child labor laws were being evaded. The *Boston Globe* ran an editorial in which it described McNeill's findings as "startling": "For years past, we have flattered ourselves that our educational system was as near perfection as circumstances would allow, and that, under the law, the children alike of the rich and the poor were able to secure its benefits. Instead, we are shown to have an army of illiterates growing up among us, each single member a possible future criminal or pauper."[45]

The Legislature Takes Action

On January 7, 1875, William Gaston became the first Democrat since the war to be elected governor of Massachusetts. Gaston was no special friend to labor, and he did not renew McNeill's appointment despite his being an avowed Democrat.[46] He did, though, include comments on the need for new labor legislation and the education of working-class children in his annual address to the General Court.[47] In response, the legislature formed a joint special committee. A day later, McNeill's explosive report was released.[48] The legislature could now no longer ignore the problem; McNeill's findings were too damning. Given these developments, policy entrepreneurship on behalf of a factory inspectorate shifted from the state's fledgling agencies to its legislature.

In February, Representative Stephen M. Allen, a Republican from Dux-bury, ordered the special committee to consider legislation to better enforce the law relating to the education and hours of labor of children employed in manufacturing and mechanical establishments.[49] Allen was responding to McNeill's report and Governor Gaston's message, but also to a petition from the Christian Labor Union, a group of labor reformers, McNeill among them, that had been founded in 1872. The union's petition cited McNeill's claim that one-third of the state's children were not attending school, and called for leg-islation to provide for the collection of reliable statistics, further limitations on children's working hours, and the appointment of inspectors to carry out the labor laws.[50]

The petition was signed by three men, including the union's president, Jesse H. Jones. Jones was a Harvard-trained Congregationalist minister from North Abington, a center of the shoemaking industry, and a leading figure in Massachusetts labor reform circles.[51] Although his Christian Labor Union did little to organize workers beyond holding monthly meetings and hosting a couple of sparsely attended conventions, it—and particularly Jones—helped inject Christian socialist ideas into Massachusetts labor reform discourse (Zon-derman 2011, 175–81). Jones, like McNeill, believed that the "wage system" was primarily to blame for workers' immiseration because it rendered workers totally dependent on unscrupulous employers and unstable markets. This perspective was shared by labor reformers across the country (Schneirov 1998). But Jones (1871, 280) went further than most of his contemporaries in advocating utopian Christian communal living as the best alternative to the wage system: "Pure communism is pure Christianity as applied to work life," he wrote. "Nothing else is."

Little came of Allen's order; a resolve and bill on better enforcement of the state's child labor laws were both defeated. Jones was undeterred, however; later that year he ran for the state House of Representatives as a Republican and won. During his single term in 1876, he mostly concerned himself with two issues: female suffrage (which he adamantly supported) and labor reform.[52] He took on the chairmanship of the Committee on the Bureau of Statistics, and one of his first acts as a state representative was to order the committee to consider legislation concerning "means of protection from accidents, and of escape from fire, in the factories of the Commonwealth; and also concerning the enforcement of the laws of the Commonwealth relating to the employment and schooling of children and minors, and to the hours of labor." In March, Jones's committee reported a bill "to establish a board of factory inspectors."[53]

Over the next several weeks, petitions arrived at the statehouse from work-ers pleading for the enactment of a factory inspection law.[54] One petition from more than five thousand male and female factory operatives in Fall River urged the appointment of a board of factory inspectors "whose duty it shall be to see to the enforcement of the 'Ten Hour Law' and 'The Law relating to the employment and schooling of Factory Children'; and also, to see to the proper providing of Fire-escapes and the necessary protection of the lives and limbs of the operatives from dangerous machinery."[55] A group of mule spinners from Fall River and New Bedford begged the House of Representatives to "grant us Factory Inspectors with power to enforce the Ten Hour law and the proper schooling of children."[56] Another petition from James Langford, leader of the Fall River mule spinners' association (Blewett 2000, 240), and six thousand others called for the appointment of an inspector of tenement houses, public buildings, and factories.[57] Workers were organizing and mobilizing in support of Jones's bill.

No sooner was the bill on the agenda, though, than machinations to weaken it began. First, the bill was amended to reduce the number of inspectors to one, and to include tenement houses and public buildings under his purview. The amendments also removed any mention of child labor laws. This draft was sent to the Senate, where it was further weakened by removing all references to a factory inspector, instead inserting the requirement that the chief of the state detective force detail between one and three deputies to examine tenements, workplaces, and public buildings as well as enforce hours of labor. Again children were not specifically mentioned. Further, the assignment was temporary and would end in the new year.[58] This was the bill enacted in April 1876.[59] With the exception of a provision formalizing inspectors' right to enter workplace premises, it was hardly an improvement over the 1867 law under which Oliver had been appointed—and complained bitterly about. Jones's brief career as a factory inspection policy entrepreneur had ended in disappointment. He was not reelected and returned to his ministry in North Abington.

In 1875, the embattled state police had been dissolved and replaced with a state detective force. Whereas the police had comprised more than one hundred officers, the new detective force was to include only thirty officers and one chief.[60] It fell to the state's first Democratic governor since the Civil War, Gaston, to appoint the inaugural cohort of detectives. Gaston had no interest in building up the power of the agency that had enforced the state's liquor laws—allegedly in abusive ways—and so angered the state's Democratic and particularly Irish American voters. Besides the chief, Gaston appointed only fifteen detectives, not the allotted thirty, a mix of Democrats and Republicans, to the force.[61] He tapped Luther Stephenson Jr., a fellow Democrat, as chief detective. The decision to place factory inspection with the detectives returned this function to a weak and politically vulnerable body. The temporary inspector was yet another meatless bone thrown to labor. The fight for a professional and independent factory inspectorate continued.

THE STATE POLICE RETAINS JURISDICTION

In 1877, organized labor again managed to seat one of its own in the state legislature. Representative Mellen of Worcester is the fifth and final—and the only semisuccessful—factory inspection policy entrepreneur profiled in this chapter. Mellen, an iron molder, had been active in unionizing that trade as a young man. This was his first year in office, but he would go on to serve nineteen terms—more than any other state legislator up to that time.[62] A proud Irish American and staunch Democrat, he was decried by his detractors as a "labor agitator and office seeker . . . [a] demagogue and sand-lot orator" who espoused "communistic ideas" (Rosenzweig 1983, 109). He continued labor organizing throughout the 1880s and eventually served as state chair of the Knights of Labor.[63]

The need to sustain factory inspection beyond the one-year position created in 1876 was made obvious when Chief Detective Stephenson released his annual report. Much of the report was devoted to detailing the inspection work to which he had assigned three deputies. On inspecting 1,287 factories over seven months, the detectives found 63 children younger than ten as well as 7,705 between ten and fourteen among the workers; in total, children under fourteen made up 4.7 percent of the labor force in these establishments. The detectives also discovered "numerous instances" of working children failing to attend school as required by law as well as many factories still not complying with the ten-hour working day for women and children. Further, the investigation revealed numerous health and safety hazards in factories and public buildings, including inward-swinging doors, inadequate fire escapes, unfenced machinery, old and dangerous steam boilers, and poor ventilation. Stephenson recommended that the state legislature enact a health and safety law for factories.[64]

In January 1877, Senator Byron Truell, a Republican, ordered the joint committee on labor and the decennial Census to consider legislation to create a State Board of Factory and Public Building Inspectors.[65] In March, Mellen reported a labor bill on behalf of the committee. It was primarily a safety measure, but also, unlike Truell's, retained the detective force's jurisdiction over factory inspection.[66] Mellen strongly favored an independent inspectorate, but had been unable to sway his fellow committee members, most of them Republicans. After the bill left the committee, five House members offered amendments, and on Mellen's motion it was sent back to the committee for further consideration.[67] This time the labor legislator came back to the full chamber victorious; the revised bill called for the governor to appoint independent factory inspectors with "practical knowledge of sanitary matters and of mechanics."[68] It seemed for the moment that Mellen had succeeded.

The success was fleeting. Further amendments were proposed—one of which moved factory inspection back into the hands of the state police. Mellen vehemently resisted, but to no avail. In a letter to the editor of the *Boston Globe*, McNeill described the outcome this way: "After a gallant fight by J.P. Mellen of Worcester a fatal amendment to the inspection bill was adopted against the united protest of the factory operatives. The inspection is to be made by—not men specially qualified or appointed for that work—but by men who were appointed to detect pickpockets, murderers, etc. Now does civil service suffer at the hands of its friends."[69] In McNeill's view, Liberal Republicans who had championed civil service reform were now hypocritically undermining their professed values by refusing to allow factory inspection to be carried out by independent professionals.

The Senate made one last push to establish an independent factory inspection department when Charles Theodore Russell, a long-serving Democrat, proposed an amendment reviving the idea of a "state board of factory inspectors."[70] Opposition to Russell's amendment was led by Senator Samuel Ginnodo, a Republican.[71] The amendment was defeated twelve (eleven Republicans and one Democrat) to nine (six Republicans and three Democrats) in a roll call vote. Aside from the fact that three out of four Democrats supported the amendment, there was no obvious pattern with regard to how the votes went; legislators with ties to manufacturing voted on both sides, as did senators from the western and eastern parts of the state. In any case, with Russell's amendment rejected, the option of an independent factory inspection department was now conclusively off the table.

The Act Relating to the Inspection of Factories and Public Buildings was signed into law by Governor Alexander Rice on May 11, 1877. It was primarily a workplace safety measure. The act required factories to guard machinery, secure elevators, construct fire escapes, and be kept ventilated and clean. It required public buildings to provide outward-swinging doors and egress in case of fire. It required the chief of the state detective force to appoint one or more deputies to enforce these safety provisions in addition to the laws regulating the employment of women and children. The act empowered the inspectors to enter manufacturing establishments and public buildings, carry out investigations, issue orders, and prosecute in any court of competent jurisdiction employers who failed to make the ordered changes within four weeks. Inspectors could not issue fines on the spot, but unlike the German inspectors, had limited policing power.[72]

Why were Mellen and Russell unable to secure the professional and independent factory inspectorate that labor reformers had long fought for? As Democrats from the perennial minority party, they were clearly at a political disadvantage. But at this time, party programs were weakly defined; individual

Republicans (Oliver, Wright, Jones, and Truell) as well as individual Democrats (Mellen, Russell, and McNeill) had all advocated for an independent board of inspectors at various points, and individual Republicans as well as Democrats had actively opposed it. Mellen's and Russell's failure therefore cannot be simply chalked up to party politics. It could be that opponents repeatedly pushed inspection back to the police because the agency had a poor reputation and they wanted to hobble inspection's potential effectiveness. But it is equally likely that legislators simply found it easier follow precedent. Factory inspection had been constructed as the responsibility of the state police ever since Oliver had been appointed to the constabulary in 1867. Sustaining the old policing model of inspection was a way to appease labor without setting up a new agency or appropriating additional funds. Although legislators were increasingly willing to enact new labor regulations, they were less keen on devoting resources to enforce them. This was particularly true during the depression of the 1870s, when the state's public revenue was shrinking dramatically.[73] Workers had grown politically powerful enough that they could not be ignored, but a show of responsiveness was possible without further straining the state's coffers or burdening employers. The 1877 factory inspection law was one way to do so.

CONSEQUENCES

The immediate result of the legislature's decision was that the child labor laws went unenforced for two more years. In his 1877 report, Chief Detective Stephenson lambasted the 1874 ten-hour law. In factories in which men's, women's, and children's labor was integrated—as it was in any textile mill—the law had necessarily reduced the workday of all operatives to ten hours. This, Stephenson claimed, "causes considerable complaint, not only from the mill owners, but from the operatives themselves, who object to a law which deprives them of the power of increasing their too scanty earnings, debarring them, as it does, from what they consider the right, of working more hours per day when they can find an opportunity." Because Stephenson personally disagreed with the ten-hour law, he felt free to ignore it: "I have made no effort to enforce this law," he wrote.[74] He also declined to prosecute cases against employers whose young workers were not attending school. Indeed, the only aspect of the child labor laws that Stephenson deigned to carry out was the minimum employment age.

The instability that had plagued the Massachusetts State Police since its inception continued. In 1879, Governor Talbot attacked the detective force in his annual address on the grounds that it undermined the local police; he suggested that it be abolished, and that factory inspection be transferred to "an authority which will command implicit confidence and respect"—the BLS.

Petitions calling for the retention of the force soon flooded the statehouse. These emphasized the detectives' criminal law enforcement role and did not mention factory inspection. Bills to kill the force entirely and move inspection to the BLS were defeated. Instead, the legislature opted once again to restructure, and the detective force was replaced by the Massachusetts District Police. The act required the governor to appoint two or more police officers as inspectors of factories and public buildings.

Conciliatory Policing and Bureaucratic Autonomy under Wade

Governor Talbot was forced to retain the state police, but did whittle it down to nine officers. He appointed Wade, a fellow Republican, as the chief, and made him and two other policemen responsible for factory inspection and labor law enforcement.[75] The force's other officers were assigned to crime detection and liquor law enforcement.

Like Stephenson, Wade was a patronage appointee. A middle-class product of the Boston public schools, he boasted a long history of Republican Party activism, but no experience with labor relations. The expertise he eventually acquired as the state's chief factory inspector was learned entirely on the job. This was typical for the time; it was an "age of amateurs"—of men (and soon women) claiming authority on the basis of practical experience, rather than formal training or academic credentials (Rodgers 1998, 26). Wade began his career in public service as an officer at the state prison and then turnkey at the house of corrections in East Cambridge, where he also served as secretary and treasurer of the local Republican committee. These positions taught him nothing about labor issues, but enabled him to forge connections with Republican Party leaders and cultivate a reputation for competence. In the 1860s and 1870s, his service to the party was rewarded with a string of federal appointments: railway mail service inspector, Boston customhouse clerk, and East Cambridge postmaster.[76] The appointment to the District Police in 1879 was the culmination of his career. Thus he came as close as possible, in the context of the fledgling US administrative state, to being a career civil servant akin to the men profiled in the German cases. The difference was that his positions were the result of party patronage as opposed to education, training, and experience. His field position placed him firmly within the state apparatus with no dual membership in any relevant overlapping social field.

Wade would go on to serve under eleven governors, including two Democrats, defying the norms of patronage politics at the time. The stability of Wade's tenure allowed him to build up the state police from a small body of just nine to a force of fifty-eight officers widely regarded as indispensable to the state's security and social welfare. As an administrative entrepreneur, he

FIGURE 6.1. Rufus R. Wade. *Source*: Massachusetts State Police Museum and Learning Center.

masterfully garnered a considerable measure of bureaucratic autonomy for the force. To review, bureaucratic autonomy refers to a government agency's ability to take sustained patterns of action in accordance with its own leaders' independently crafted goals versus at the behest of politicians or organized interests. Three conditions are required: organizational capacity to carry out their business efficiently, solve problems, and innovate; political legitimacy via positive reputations grounded in "an independent power base" of multiple and diverse networks; and political differentiation from other actors in terms of possessing distinct preferences and interests (Carpenter 2001, 14). Despite a focus on federal agencies, the theory elucidates the administrative development of state-level entities equally well. Under Wade's leadership, the District Police evolved to meet all three criteria. In addition, it incrementally expanded its jurisdiction to new areas of responsibility—a fourth indicator of growing bureaucratic autonomy.

Wade's ability to forge bureaucratic autonomy was supported by favorable institutional and political conditions. As a Republican, he enjoyed by default the support of the Republican-dominated legislature and Republican governors who never hesitated to reappoint him. Talbot's total housecleaning of the police force in 1879 meant that the most incompetent and dishonest officers were gone before Wade came on board. Furthermore, after 1884, civil service reform helped reduce the likelihood that political hacks would be appointed to serve under him (although he himself remained unprotected by these rules). Governors still made patronage appointments, but were constrained to name individuals who had passed a competitive exam. These factors helped pave the way for Wade's administrative entrepreneurship, but he must be credited with taking advantage of these conditions. He did so by steadily building the force's reputation for competence and disinterested expertise—qualities that were essential for attracting resources, shaping policy, and forging the alliances necessary to ward off political attack. Wade's commitment to moderation, however, eventually undermined the force's credibility among workers. Bureaucratic autonomy ultimately came at the expense of the vigorous protection of vulnerable child laborers.

ORGANIZATIONAL CAPACITY

Wade made it his mission to grow the force and its budget, and year by year, the legislature complied. After a decade, the force had grown from nine to thirty-three officers, with twenty assigned to factory and public building inspection. In 1903, the year before Wade's death, the number had reached fifty-eight, twenty-six of whom, including two women, were factory and building inspectors, and another ten of whom were boiler inspectors (see figure 6.2). As it expanded, the force's budget grew steadily, from just over $15,000 in 1879 to nearly $104,000 in 1903. With increased money and personnel came increased capacity. Whereas in 1879 inspectors visited 491 factories and other workplaces, in 1889 the number was 7,320, and in 1903 it reached nearly 9,000.

JURISDICTIONAL EXPANSION

Newspaper coverage of the District Police often noted the expanding variety of ways in which the force served the people of Massachusetts.

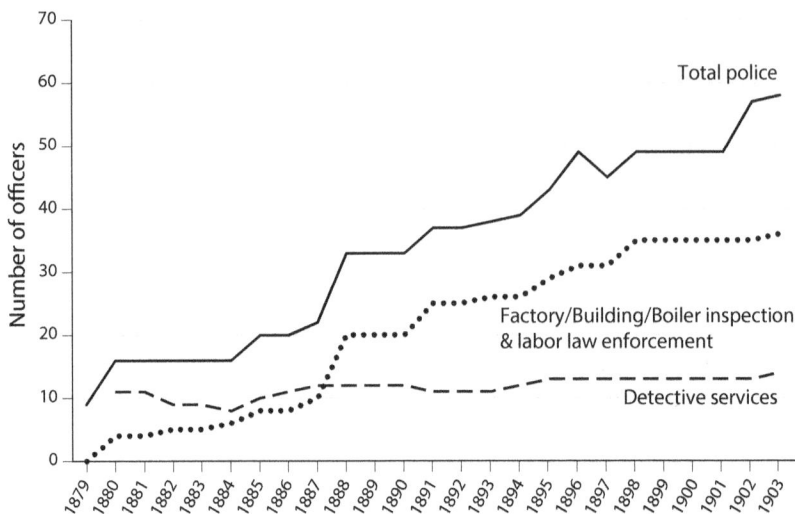

FIGURE 6.2. Massachusetts District Police personnel, 1879–1903. *Source*: Massachusetts District Police 1879–1903.

So strong was the regard of the members of the Legislature for [Wade's] opinion, and so highly was his integrity regarded, that, as the years went on and different branches were suggested for the enforcement of different kinds of laws, the suggestions usually ended [with] the proposed branch [being] attached to the district police, under the direction of Chief Wade. The district police now direct the fire marshall's department of the state, the examination of all public buildings except those in the city of Boston, the inspection of elevators, the enforcement of all labor laws, the enforcement of anti-sweating laws, the examination of firemen and engineers and the inspection of boilers, and the detective department. . . . In addition to all this, the chief is the official custodian of all liquors seized throughout the commonwealth.[77]

Some of these responsibilities, such as fire safety, had been foisted onto the force by the legislature.[78] Others—like elevator safety in public buildings, boiler inspection, and ventilation and sanitation in schools as well as other public buildings—were added as a result of Wade's lobbying for increased powers and responsibilities.[79] He was an active agent in expanding the department's sphere of jurisdiction.

One outcome of the force's jurisdictional expansion was that it progressively broadened its base of allies. Soon, the District Police served the interests of nearly everyone. Anyone who sent their children to public schools, attended performances at a public theater, or rode the elevator in a downtown department store depended on Wade's force to protect their health and safety.

Ironically, then, what most dismayed labor reformers in the 1870s—that the department was not devoted exclusively to factory inspection—likely ensured its survival in the near term and contributed to its accumulation of bureaucratic autonomy. No one could attack the District Police or undermine its functioning without also undermining the interests of thousands of voters from all walks of life. The flip side, however, was that the more the inspection department took on responsibilities aimed at protecting the general public from hazards such as elevator accidents and unclean air, the less time and resources were left for it to enforce the child and female labor laws.

POLITICAL LEGITIMACY

Bureaucratic autonomy depends on agencies' ability to build a broad-based reputation for "expertise, neutrality and public-spiritedness" (Carpenter 2001, 33). Wade achieved political legitimacy for the District Police by convincing diverse audiences of its competence and expertise.[80] He signaled expertise and competence in his annual reports, which were his primary method of communicating with lawmakers and the public, and accrued a loyal base of supporters within the legislature, state administration, and press as well as among the public.

First, Wade routinely claimed that thanks to his inspectors' hard work and professionalism, the labor laws were generally complied with. Second, in a manner later typical of self-styled Progressive era policy experts (Anderson 2008), Wade habitually maintained that his views were grounded in objective knowledge rather than ideological commitments or theoretical perspectives. His assertions of expertise were based mainly on his staff's technical knowledge of workplace and building safety. Wade described his inspectors as "experts in the knowledge of the construction and operation of mill and other machinery." For example, when explaining the decline in the number of industrial accidents, he credited new safety "statutes framed after careful investigation . . . by the District Police."[81] In regard to elevator safety, he noted that his inspectors' assessments were based on "strict and impartial tests."[82] Such statements presented Wade and his inspectors as holders of objective truth, and as specialists immune to the corrupting interference of interested parties.

Wade's expertise signaling contributed to the District Police's ability to build a diverse network of allies too. The media was one; news reports touted Wade's capabilities enthusiastically. Highlights from his widely distributed annual reports were covered under headlines such as "What Experts Say" and "An Able Public Document."[83] The statistics and findings that Wade reported were treated as undisputed fact, and his recommendations were regarded as wise and necessary. News reports also touted Wade and his force's professional competence.

In the following typical example, the *Boston Daily Globe* described the force's diligence in fulfilling its many responsibilities:

> Chief Wade and his little force are performing some of the heaviest police service, and doing some of the most difficult and meritorious detective work in the country. Outside the large cities they deal, in fact, with all the large crimes and criminals of the state. The prosecuting officers of the different counties testify to the fidelity and skill with which they cover this widely-extended field of duty. . . . The labor, factory and building inspection laws are all left to Chief Wade and his men to enforce, and it is something of a wonder that they contrive to do it all so well.[84]

Politicians and public officials of various stripes also uniformly supported the force. The repeated attacks suffered by the state police during the 1860s and 1870s ceased under Wade's tenure. Officials rallied behind the force because it helped them carry out their duties. Local police needed its help in solving tough criminal cases. The state's district attorneys valued its assistance in collecting evidence and helping prepare cases for trial. The governor and mayors needed it to keep the peace during mass strikes and other large gatherings.[85] The state Boards of Education and Health depended on it to monitor the sanitary conditions of school buildings as well as help enforce the compulsory schooling law.[86] Furthermore, the public needed it to fight crime, and ensure the safety and cleanliness of public buildings. Employers needed it to protect property and strikebreakers during periods of labor unrest. At the same time, labor needed it to protect workers from exploitative employers. This broad base of allies helped insulate the force from political attack.

An exceptional illustration proves the general rule. On one rare occasion when the District Police was severely criticized in the legislature—Representative Samuel W. George of Haverhill charged its criminal detectives with incompetence and drunkenness—Wade was able to mobilize a rebuttal from a key group of allies: the state's district attorneys.[87] In his annual report, he published seven of their letters, each testifying to the detectives' efficiency, integrity, thoroughness, and sound judgment.[88] George's attack was soon dismissed in the press as "not backed up by evidence" and quickly forgotten.[89] Thus Wade was able to draw on allies in the executive branch to ward off an assault coming from the state legislature and receive vindication in the media. By the late 1880s, the reputation of Wade and the District Police force seemed almost unassailable.

POLITICAL DIFFERENTIATION

Political differentiation refers to a state bureaucratic entity's political independence: its ability to form its own preferences and pursue its own goals

(Carpenter 2001, 25; Skocpol 1992, 42). No evidence—in either Wade's twenty-five annual reports, or hundreds of newspaper articles on him and his force—indicates that the District Police was in any direct way beholden to politicians. On the contrary, politicians deferred to Wade. As a law enforcement officer, Wade's primary responsibility was, of course, to carry out laws that legislators had made, but when he found those laws wanting, he discreetly and often successfully lobbied for their improvement. Lawmakers on Beacon Hill valued his opinion; they frequently invited him to provide expert testimony at legislative hearings and generally enacted the policy changes he recommended. Wade's reputation for disinterested expertise as well as his general reticence to comment on touchier policy questions bolstered the legitimacy of these recommendations while discouraging political meddling into the force's affairs.

A few representative examples demonstrate Wade's legislative influence. In 1879, he pointed out the inadequacy of ladderlike fire escapes; the legislature in 1880 required factories to replace the ladders with railed stairways.[90] In 1880, after a year of trying to catch violators of the ten-hour law by secretly staking out factories, Wade asked the legislature to facilitate enforcement by requiring factories to post written notices of women's and children's hours of employment. That way, if an inspector encountered a woman or child at work outside those stated hours, they would instantly know that a violation had occurred. This request was granted immediately by the legislature, and the *Boston Herald* rejoiced that the ten-hour law was at last actually enforceable.[91] In 1886, Wade recommended that employers be required to report workplace accidents to his office; the legislature quickly complied.[92] In 1888, he began a campaign to require clean air and better sanitation in school buildings; again the legislature immediately responded with new legislation, and a "great reformation in the old system of ventilation" ensued across the state's schoolhouses.[93] In 1892, he recommended that manufacturers of ready-made clothing operating out of private dwellings—so-called sweatshops—be required to obtain a license from the District Police.[94] This recommendation was adopted straightaway by the legislature too.[95] In each case, Wade offered experience-based fixes to better promote the realization of existing policy goals. In this way, state policy responses to at least some of the social problems of industrial capitalism became more routinized and less contentious.

There is also no evidence that Wade and the police were beholden, in any *direct* sense, to powerful interest groups. He and the other inspectors used their authority to issue orders to induce employers to undertake many, sometimes costly changes to their workplaces to make them safer for workers. These included installing new fire escapes and other means of egress from fire, fencing off machinery, improving ventilation and sanitation, and so on. He occasionally evinced positions that ran contrary to capitalist interests too. For instance, Wade was opposed to certain types of immigration, particularly

that of French Canadians.[96] In advocating reforms to make the state's population more "homogeneous," he contravened the interests of mill owners who
increasingly relied on French Canadian migrants, who worked for lower wages
than the native-born population would accept (Persons 1971). If the state police
had been mere agents of the employers they were supposed to regulate, Wade
would not have made these arguments.

COMPROMISE AND CONCILIATION

Why was Wade so successful in building the police force's bureaucratic autonomy? In addition to routinely *signaling competence and disinterested expertise*,
Wade adopted the role of *compromiser*. Compromise, as we have seen in previous chapters, is a hallmark of effective policy entrepreneurship. It is also a
mark of savvy administrative entrepreneurship, as it conveys that the agency
serves diverse interests equitably, thereby helping it win supporters from different segments of society. Wade approached factory inspection in a way that
ostensibly favored neither workers nor employers; instead, he believed that
their interests could and should be harmonized.[97] He advocated for stronger
labor laws, but enforced the laws in ways that avoided antagonizing capital.
He protected labor against abuses, but protected private property and "scabs"
against attacks from striking workers as well.[98] Wade was at times a stickler
in making sure that employers followed rules to the letter, but claimed to be
able to secure voluntary compliance in most cases, and he avoided prosecuting
violators if he could help it ("only when other means have failed to prove effective").[99] In these ways, he tried to act as an arbiter between labor and capital,
aiming to protect the interests of each without inflicting harm on the other.

Wade's conciliatory approach to factory inspection was grounded in a
definition of the labor problem that regarded the interests of employers and
workers as compatible; it was just that the two sides needed the help of the
state to come to this realization and act accordingly. "Educate the young toil-
ers," Wade wrote in his first annual report, "and they will . . . realize more
fully the mutual and harmonious relations which should exist between capital
and labor."[100] In his second report, he praised "mill-owners [who] show such
interest in their help as to provide reading-rooms, libraries and other privileges
of like character," because "they have laid the foundations of a mutual and
lasting respect." Any conflict between labor and capital, such as that on vivid
display in the mass strikes repeatedly occurring at Fall River, was due to an
incorrect mentality that distorted perceptions on both sides. Once employers
and workers recognized their mutual dependence, then employers would stop
abusing their workers, workers would stop making unreasonable demands of
employers, and harmony would prevail. It was the job of the public school
teacher to prepare poor children to accept this necessary and just inequality,

and likewise the job of the factory inspector to enlighten and "secure the co-operation of manufacturers and operatives."[101]

The notion that state regulation would ensure that the natural laws of the marketplace worked for the mutual benefit of all was mainstream among many social policy reformers on both sides of the Atlantic (Blewett 2000, 140; Persons 1971, 104–5; Rodgers 1998). In this view—neither socialist nor laissez-faire—labor laws were good and necessary, but they served as much of an *educational* purpose as a coercive one. They would teach labor and capital to view one another as partners rather than adversaries. Wade's perspective was thus strikingly similar to Lohmann's in Germany; both stressed the inspector's advisory and moral-pedagogical role, and both championed a conciliatory approach to the implementation of labor laws.

Wade emphasized his conciliatory policing approach to factory inspection in his annual reports: "It has been our policy to secure the co-operation of manufacturers and operatives; and, where the disposition to obey the laws has been manifest, prosecutions have been withheld."[102] Or "conciliatory, yet firm, [the inspector] must distinguish between those who defy the requirements of the statutes and those who are technical offenders only. These may be admonished, and in most cases such a course is sufficient."[103] Or "the best results are reached when zeal is guided by discretion."[104] Elsewhere, he underscored the need to keep violations out of the public record to deal with them more effectively.[105] Still, he signaled a willingness to use tougher methods when necessary: "But in no case where sufficient evidence has been secured to disclose intentional infringement of the law, has there been on our part remissness in the discharge of duty."[106] This approach—an administrative entrepreneur's version of compromise—won him and his inspectors a friendly relationship with employers, and according to Wade, their willing compliance with the laws. For instance, he was quoted as saying, "Whenever we have notified the Fall River agents that a violation of the law was being committed in their mills, they have acted as directed at once, and without complaint. . . . I have always understood that our representative there, [Inspector] J.F. Tierney, has been very well liked by the [mill] agents."[107]

In practice, Wade's commitment to conciliation amounted to a reluctance to make full use of the coercive powers with which the state of Massachusetts had endowed him. By requiring inspectors to give violators four weeks to clean up their act, the law did encourage them to use a soft touch, but Wade went further. The following example illustrates this. It was typical for the mills to get their machinery up to speed before the start of the workday so that they could fill the full ten hours with productive labor. Wade found that in so doing, mills were requiring women and children to start work between five to seventeen minutes early. Commenting on this practice, Wade wrote, "It is the duty of the mill authorities to provide that women and minors upon their premises shall be prevented from beginning work until the proper time. . . . This must be insisted upon, simply because it is the law, which no executive officer has the right to modify." Five of the offending mills were brought to court. Wade ended up dropping the charges against four of them, however, when their agents convinced him that the start-up times had been "materially reduced" enough to "conform substantially to the requirements of the statute."[108] Dropping the charges was Wade's decision rather than required by law.

An 1899 profile of Wade in the *Boston Herald* portrayed his apparent skill at winning the confidence of both labor and capital this way:

> He has worked with the tact of a diplomat and the sincerity of an honest man. He has not always traveled on the roads of macadam. Many a thorny path has he encountered. . . . On the one hand were irate manufacturers, angry at legislation which curtailed the hours of labor in their factories or mills, or in other ways interfered with their methods of doing business. On the other hand were dictatorial labor union representatives demanding the most radical enforcement of all laws. It was impossible to satisfy the extremists on either side, but among the moderate labor union men today there can be found hardly one who does not believe that in the chief of the Massachusetts district police he has a friend to whom he can always appeal . . . while among the warmest advocates of the labor laws affecting the employment of women and children are some of the manufacturers who most bitterly opposed them a few years ago.[109]

In sum, Wade's administrative entrepreneurship secured a high degree of organizational capacity, political legitimacy, jurisdictional breadth, and political differentiation for the District Police. He achieved this by cultivating a reputation for competence and disinterested expertise, but also by adopting a conciliatory policing model of inspection aimed at protecting the interests of workers and employers simultaneously. Wade tried to be responsive to workers' grievances without imposing penalties on employers. An administrative entrepreneur's version of compromise, this approach promised to win the District Police force allies from among capital as well as labor, thereby enhancing its independence from both factions. But how long could this compromise strategy be credibly sustained, and what were its consequences in the long run?

Disillusioned Labor

Despite Wade's conciliatory approach to labor relations, workers seem to have trusted him and his inspectors to intervene in as well as protect them against abusive labor practices—at least for a time. McNeill, now a venerated elder statesman of the labor reform movement, publicly supported Wade, noting in an 1898 speech that the chief "always had the leaders of the labor movement

APPEASING LABOR, PROTECTING CAPITAL 223

at his back."[110] Numerous accounts of workers appealing to Wade when they believed that labor laws were being violated are on record; evidently workers had faith that their complaints would be taken seriously.[111] Wade was skilled at making them feel heard. For example, when labor representatives met with him in 1900 to make him aware of certain violations of the hours law, they reportedly emerged "perfectly satisfied that, as a result of their conference with . . . [Wade], the labor laws relating to the employment of women and minors will be strictly enforced."[112]

From time to time, though, claims surfaced that child and other labor laws were actually going unobserved in Massachusetts. In 1887, a state senator revealed at a public hearing that he had received confidential letters from Lowell, Lawrence, and Fall River that children as young as eight were working in the mills. Employers avoided detection by hurrying the children out the back door when inspectors showed up.[113] In 1890, at the Central Labor Union's annual convention, delegates labeled Wade's enforcement of the laws pertaining to children in factories a "farce." The union resurrected the argument that criminal law enforcement and factory inspection should be separate; under the current structure Wade could not devote enough attention to the labor laws.[114] It repeated these charges at its convention in 1896, when many delegates maintained that the inspectors were allowing factories to work women and children for seventy to eighty hours a week.[115] Despite these few exceptions, the message that the press conveyed echoed what Wade asserted in his annual reports: child and other labor laws were being "cheerfully" complied with in Massachusetts.[116]

Near the end of Wade's career, the scene changed. In 1903, his twenty-fourth year of service, he was abruptly faced with a unified chorus of criticism from labor. That July, the state branch of the American Federation of Labor complained that children under fourteen (the minimum working age) were employed illegally in Lowell mills.[117] In September, mill worker Mary Freitas repeated the charges in a letter to the Lowell newspapers, alleging that children as young as ten were working in the mills for twelve and a half hours per day.[118] In the months that followed, the federation investigated conditions in multiple factory towns, including Fall River, Lowell, and Lawrence. At its October convention, delegates reiterated the charges, claiming that "many" underage children had been found at work in the mills and factories in these cities. Members denounced Wade, calling him laissez-faire and accusing him of taking the side of capital against labor. Some called for the reorganization of the state police force; others demanded its outright abolition.[119] The National Cotton Spinners' Association soon joined the chorus of complaints. At its annual convention in Lowell, local delegates repeated the allegation that underage children were at work in the mills. The spinners decided to send representatives to ask "why the law is applied one way in one city and another way in

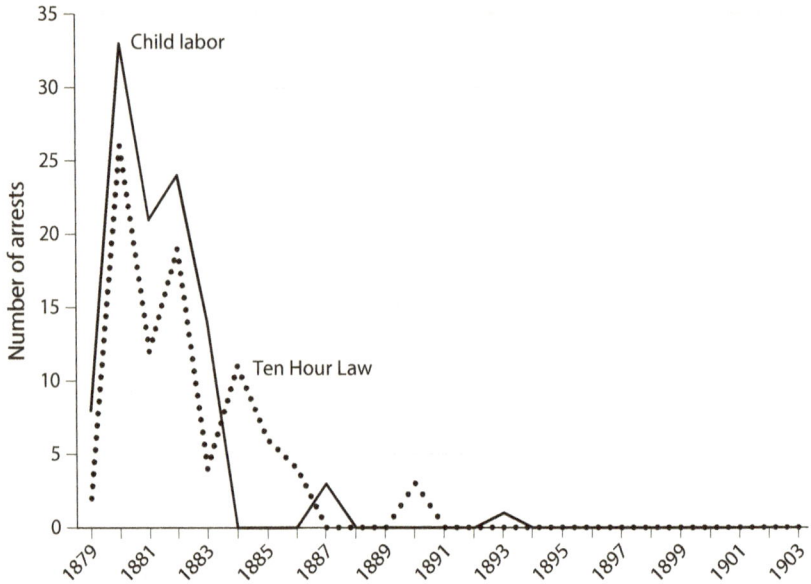

FIGURE 6.3. Massachusetts District Police, arrests for labor law violations, 1879–1903.
Source: Massachusetts District Police 1879–1903.
Note: The ten-hour law regulated the working hours of both women and children.

other cities."[120] The American Federation of Labor's secretary-treasurer, Dennis Driscoll, concluded that it was useless to expect the state police to enforce the labor laws; organized labor would have to work independently to discover and publicize violations.[121]

The statistics reported in Wade's annual reports lend credence to labor's accusations. The number of arrests for labor law violations peaked in 1880, Wade's second year on the job—twenty-six for the ten-hour law and thirty-three for child labor. The arrests, however, soon plummeted (see figure 6.3).

Likewise, the types of orders that inspectors issued shifted dramatically. Whereas the number of orders pertaining to safety and sanitation in buildings and factories ballooned after 1882, the number related to child and female labor violations remained relatively stable in the late 1880s and 1890s (see figure 6.4). Whereas in 1879, 60 percent of orders pertained to child labor, only 20 percent were related to women's and children's labor violations in 1900; over the same period, the proportion pertaining to health and safety rose from 40 to nearly 80 percent (see figure 6.5). Wade and the force were evidently shifting their energies away from child labor law enforcement, and toward building safety and sanitation.

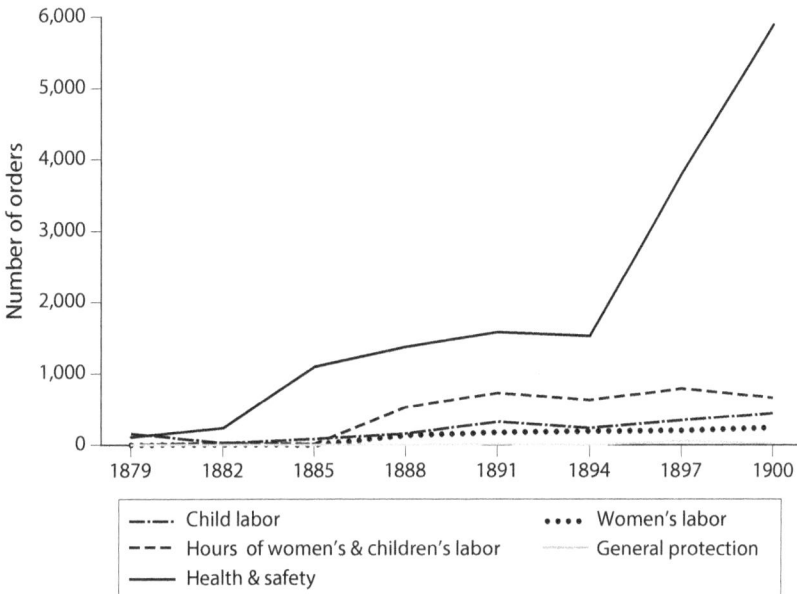

FIGURE 6.4. Massachusetts District Police orders, 1879–1900. *Source*: Massachusetts District Police 1879–1900.
Note: *Child labor* orders pertain to keeping schooling and age certificates on file, sending illiterate minors to night school, and discharging underage minors. *Hours of women's and children's labor* orders pertain to posting timetables and hours of labor, posting and enforcing the fifty-eight-hour law, and dismissing children after ten hours of work. *Health and safety* orders pertain to fire and elevator safety; guarding machinery, steam pipes, boilers, and ovens; sanitary arrangements; ventilation; lighting; unsafe building construction; separating shop and tenement areas; improving heating; repairing smoke flues; and repairing or replacing boilers. *Women's labor* orders pertain to providing seats for females and segregating wash closets. *General protection* orders pertain to paying workers weekly and posting prices as well as specifications.

Wade responded to labor's allegations by touring the factories in the western part of the state. Afterward, he sent the governor a special report: "Statements have been publicly made on more than one occasion that the provisions of the law relating to child labor are grossly violated in our manufacturing establishments throughout the state. . . . Without hesitation I pronounce the statements untrue, and would further add that while exceptional cases of violation do occur, the child labor law has never been better enforced and complied with than at the present time."[122] The problem with this declaration was that the cities in which the grossest violations were alleged—Fall River, Lawrence, and Lowell—were not in the western parts of the state. His denials were therefore not credible. Still, he repeated them in his annual (and final) report.[123]

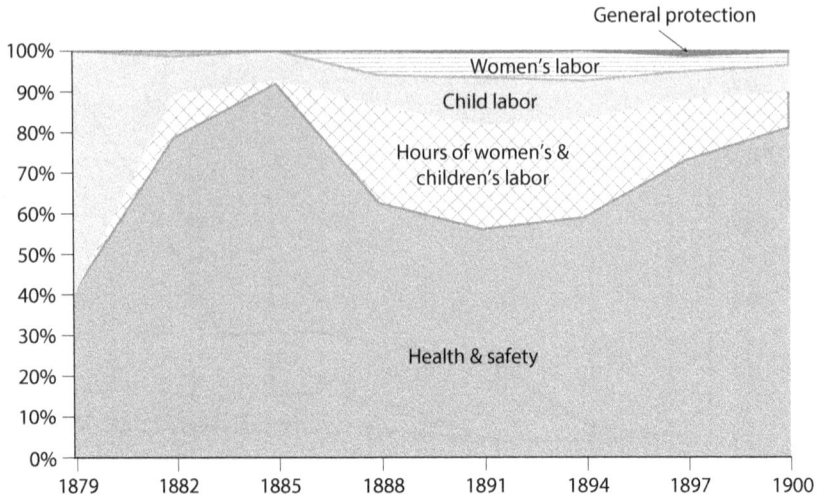

FIGURE 6.5. Massachusetts District Police orders pertaining to particular violations as a proportion of total orders, 1879–1900. *Source*: Massachusetts District Police 1879–1900.

These remarks betrayed a willful oversight: Wade and his inspectors had become reluctant to assess whether child labor laws were really being followed. He acknowledged this obliquely when he professed that his hands were tied, asserting that the inspectors "could not go behind the certificate of a child's age even in cases where they felt sure that the child working was under the legal age limit."[124] But if Wade suspected that children were presenting false age and schooling certificates, he instead could have pursued the matter with energetic police work. Not surprisingly, this tendency to look away allowed labor violations to proliferate. An in-depth academic report published eight years after Wade's death concluded that serious enforcement problems had been festering for years in Massachusetts. It stressed the lightness of fines and penalties, inadequacy of the inspectors' civil service exam, insufficient specialization among them, and scanty data collection. The authors were unable to quantify the extent of labor law violation, but cited multiple claims from labor leaders to make the case that violations were common (Reeves and Manning 1971, 223). According to historian Mary Blewett (2000, 337), Fall River mill agents violated labor laws routinely and with impunity. They fired workers who complained, creating a chilling effect against whistleblowers. In the rare instances that the mills were fined, they treated it as a cost of doing business and went on as before.

It is telling that when labor's accusations exploded in 1903, the employers, not the unions, rallied to Wade's defense. A representative of the Arkwright Club, an employers' interest group that lobbied the legislature against labor laws (Rosenberg 2013, 19), claimed that violations were "very few" because

Wade and his deputies had been "vigilant" in enforcing the law.[125] The Massachusetts Cotton Mill similarly denied the charges, urging Wade to offer a reward to anyone able to substantiate the "absurd" arraignment.[126] That it was employers who defended Wade suggests that his credibility among workers had finally dissipated. Another such indication is that when he announced his plans to retire in 1902, he received a "score of letters from business men from all parts of the state" paying "tribute" to his administration and urging him to stay on.[127] No such letters were reported to have come from labor.

In short, Wade's success in forging the bureaucratic autonomy of the Massachusetts District Police came at a steep price. That price was the rigorous execution of child and female labor laws. Wade increasingly betrayed labor's trust in him, presenting a sunny picture of near-universal child labor law compliance when the true situation was much darker. A more open acknowledgment of the ongoing challenges and stronger effort to enforce the laws, however, would likely have angered employers and probusiness politicians, jeopardizing Wade's position and the autonomy of the force.

Scope Condition 2: Weak Labor

This chapter has grappled with two questions. Why did Massachusetts place the enforcement of labor laws in the hands of the state police rather than an independent board of inspectors, as labor advocates had fought for? What were the implications of the conciliatory policing model of inspection for the force's bureaucratic autonomy and for labor law enforcement?

In answer to the first, the chapter presented profiles of five men who each took a brief stab at factory inspection policy entrepreneurship, but who each failed to exert the influence he had hoped for. These failures can be attributed to the institutional and political context as well as individual mistakes. Three of the most overtly labor-friendly reformers—Oliver, McNeill, and Jones—did not occupy field positions from which they could exert sustained policy influence. They lacked the long-term access to power required for goal-directed policy entrepreneurship. Although the labor movement occasionally managed to vault one of its own into the legislature or administration, these incursions were often fleeting. In part, this was because the institutions themselves were unstable: Oliver's and McNeill's deputy constable positions both lasted only a year or two. Legislative terms lasted only a year, and thus prolabor politicians were rarely in office long enough to build alliances and influence; this describes Jones's fate. Moreover, officials perceived as too "radical" or divisive could not last long. This liability applied to Oliver, whose policy influence was undercut by how he used his position as the state's chief labor statistician as a pulpit for the labor movement. Oliver failed to signal disinterested expertise in a way that might win him a broad spectrum of allies.

Jones's fellow labor reformer, first-term representative Mellen, was the policy entrepreneur who finally managed to make factory inspection permanent, but he was unable to secure the independent board that labor reformers wanted. The 1877 factory inspection act locked in the policing model of labor law enforcement in Massachusetts for the next thirty-six years. Given the lack of legislative transcripts, we cannot know precisely why Mellen was only partially successful. Certainly that he was a working-class Irish Democrat could not have helped in this Republican-dominated state, but in an era of fluid party positions on labor issues, this does not explain everything. More decisive was the institutional precedent set in 1867 with Oliver's appointment to the State Constabulatory as well as the general reluctance, in the depression of the 1870s, to make major new appropriations or place significant new burdens on employers.

Why, given the institutional and political weakness of its advocates, did the Republican legislature adopt any factory inspection at all? This can be attributed to labor activism. The fates of Oliver, McNeill, and Jones point to the challenges that labor along with its allies faced in maintaining a toehold on the rungs of power. Still, workers exercised influence via rank-and-file agitation. They had already proven their capacity to punish antilabor legislators in 1873, when they had organized to vote out ten state senators who opposed the ten-hour law and handed Democrats major victories in the polls. The petition campaign of 1876 drove home to Republicans that they would need to do more to appease labor or else face a new wave of working-class voter defections. Alongside the political opposition condition established in chapter 4, then, this chapter points to a second scope condition for the pragmatist field theory of middle-class policy entrepreneurship. Middle-class reformers, acting largely on their own initiative, are more likely to be necessary for regulatory welfare development when labor is weak. On the contrary, when workers are politically mobilized and politicians need to court labor's votes, then such reformers may not be required. Instead, organized labor's power resources take center stage in the causal explanation.

In this case, this still did not mean that Republicans needed to satisfy labor completely. Instead, they repeatedly deployed a bone-throwing strategy. They did so when they established the BLS to make up for denying the Crispins their charter. They did so for decades by enacting unenforced and unenforceable labor laws. They did so, too, by repeatedly creating temporary inspectorships that lacked enforcement power. And they did so again by assigning factory inspection to the embattled District Police. The 1877 factory act was ultimately a way to appease labor on the cheap, and in a manner that did not significantly threaten industrial interests. Employers had little to fear from a politically vulnerable agency that was ill equipped—in resources, expertise, political capital, and will—to carry out the new responsibilities.

This disappointing half measure was the result of a labor movement that was mobilized, but lacked sustained and direct access to power.

Nonetheless, Wade proved to be a remarkably effective administrative entrepreneur who steadily built the police force back up from near oblivion, transforming it into one of the state's most respected and influential public agencies. He grew its organizational capacity by lobbying the legislature for additional personnel and funds. He bolstered its political legitimacy by framing its activities as grounded in impartial expertise. Wade forged a diverse coalition of supporters, not only by signaling competence and expertise, but by expanding the force's jurisdiction to many new areas of vital concern to middle-class people in Massachusetts. Most important, he pursued political differentiation—autonomy from politicians and interest groups—by practicing a conciliatory approach to factory inspection that attempted to strike a compromise between the interests of labor and capital. For a time, the approach worked. Eventually, however, the trust of workers proved unsustainable, and the cooperation of employers proved illusory. Conciliatory policing and labor protection turned out to be deeply incompatible.

Conciliatory policing was essential to the survival and bureaucratic autonomy of the Massachusetts District Police; it insulated the force from backlash from powerful employers and attack by procapital legislators. Yet these successes came at the expense of vulnerable workers who were left unprotected. The next chapter addresses what happened to an administrative entrepreneur who took a different approach, pursuing a "feminist enforcement" model that constructed factory inspection as a weapon of labor in its ongoing struggle against exploitative capital.

7

Social Justice Feminism and Labor Law Enforcement in Illinois

In 1893, Illinois enacted the Workshop and Factories Act, establishing new regulations on the employment of women and children in manufacturing, and creating the state's first factory inspection system. The system was markedly different from those of Germany and Massachusetts: not only did it grant inspectors robust policing power, but it mandated that five of the state's twelve inspectors be women. This feminist enforcement model was the brainchild of lifelong child labor activist Florence Kelley. A newcomer to Illinois, Kelley made her way into the state's policy field by capitalizing on alliances and experiences gained through her affiliation with Jane Addams's Hull House in Chicago. From this position at the center of the state's nongovernmental social reform field, she seized professional opportunities that opened doors to the policy field; once inside those doors, she mobilized a diverse set of Hull House–affiliated allies to help her achieve her policy goals. These allies included social workers, public intellectuals, reform-minded elites, and—most important—organized labor.

Two political conditions facilitated Kelley's influence. First, she benefited from the unique window of opportunity created by the election of the progressive Democratic governor John Peter Altgeld and first Democratic majority in both houses of the state legislature since the Civil War (Dubin 2007). Second, she was helped by the state's exceptionally strong labor movement. Even more so than in Massachusetts, labor—and particularly laboring *women*—had become a political force to be reckoned with in Illinois. Women had always

been involved in the labor movement, but by the late 1880s, they were forming their own unions and joining forces with middle-class women to initiate campaigns for protective labor legislation as well as other kinds of social
reform. In the early 1890s, they took on the issue of female and child labor in
sweatshops, and Kelley, mobilizing her Hull House allies, piggybacked on this
antisweatshop movement to usher in one of the strongest factory inspection
laws in the country.

How did she do it? To answer this question, this chapter compares Kelley's
policy entrepreneurship with that of a rival reformer, Elizabeth Morgan. Before
Kelley's arrival in Illinois, Morgan was the state's leading female labor activist.
Between 1889 and 1892, she was at the forefront of the Illinois Woman's Alliance's efforts to raise public awareness of working conditions in sweatshops,
and to promote legislation strengthening child labor and compulsory education laws. After completing an investigation of the sweating system in Chicago,
Morgan briefly became the state's leading authority on the subject before losing
this position to Kelley, whose impact soon eclipsed hers.

Kelley's success and Morgan's failure can be explained neither by the ideas
that motivated them nor by how they framed their policy proposals. Both
drew on Marxist theory, new ideas about the role of women in society, and
the legacy of abolitionism. Both framed sweatshops as a public health issue.
Rather, Kelley's success can be attributed to two factors: first, a stronger and
more diverse alliance network that in turn hinged on her position at the heart
of the state's social reform field; and second, her superiority at signaling the
kind of competence and expertise increasingly expected of policy reformers
in the Progressive era (Rueschemeyer and Skocpol 1996; O'Connor 2001).
Her substantive knowledge, research experience, and advocacy know-how
placed Kelley among the country's first modern professional policy experts at
a time when "scientific" approaches to social policy development were gaining
credibility. Comparing Kelley with Morgan therefore points to the continued
importance of field position as well as the increasing importance of expertise
signaling in explaining policy entrepreneurs' alliance-building effectiveness
and likelihood of success.

After Governor Altgeld appointed her chief factory inspector in 1893, Kelley
seized the opportunity to put her vision of labor law enforcement into action.
Unlike Lohmann in Germany or Wade in Massachusetts, Kelley had no interest in mediation or conciliation between labor and capital. She understood
the industrial employer-worker relationship to be one of naked exploitation,
and viewed the factory inspector as a tool through which labor could harness
the power of the state to protect itself against capitalism's worst abuses. As a
factory inspector, Kelley embarked on an enforcement campaign in which
she and her staff zealously rooted out violations, and pursued prosecutions
aggressively.

Thus Kelley took on two political roles: policy and administrative entre-preneur. This was not uncommon when US administrative institutions were still in their infancy; advocates were often tapped to helm the very agencies that they had fought to bring into being. But it was also not uncommon for such advocate-administrators to soon be replaced by less polarizing moder-ates (Brock [1984] 2009). This is what happened to Oliver in Massachusetts and also Kelley in Illinois; her prolabor enforcement approach invited intense backlash from angry employers. When Altgeld lost his reelection campaign in 1896, Kelley was soon out of a job and replaced with a patronage appointee who served at the behest of the state's largest employer of child labor. If we compare Kelley's fate with Wade's, it suggests a trade-off between bureaucratic autonomy and rigorous labor law enforcement. At this point in the history of the US admin-istrative state, it was next to impossible to achieve both goals simultaneously for a sustained period of time.

Labor Movement and Politics during the Great Upheaval

In the last quarter of the nineteenth century, Chicago's population grew by 268 percent. By 1890, 40 percent of the city's residents were foreign born, and another 37 percent had foreign-born parents (Pierce 1957, 519). Cultural fragmentation was reflected in a patchwork of ethnic enclaves in which people retained their native languages and customs, and organized ethnic associations, newspapers, and celebrations. Germans and Irish, the two largest groups, were active in the civic life of the city, and exercised significant political power, whereas Italians, Bohemians, Poles, and Russian Jews were fewer in number, and among the poorest and most marginalized of the new arrivals (Pierce 1957; Miller 1996). Unabated migration alongside the development of the westward railway network fed rapid economic development. Chicago's great postwar industries famously included meatpacking as well as iron, boots and shoes, railcars, and furniture. The ready-to-wear garment trade, operating on the sweatshop system, got its start in the 1880s. By 1890, Illinois ranked third in the nation, after New York and Pennsylvania, in aggregate industrial output.[1]

Intense competition among Chicago's workers, fueled by a growing reserve army of the unemployed, shift to piecework, and increasing division of labor, steadily drove down wages while ramping up working hours. The result was seething class tension between workers and the "titans of industry" and "mer-chant princes" who employed them. Class conflict frequently manifested in strikes and occasionally exploded into violence. Unrest peaked in 1886, which saw 307 strikes, many aimed at achieving an eight-hour normal working day (Schneirov 1998, 252). On May 1, an estimated thirty-five thousand workers walked off their jobs, and thousands more joined in the following days. The tension culminated on May 4, when a mass meeting at Chicago's Haymar-ket Square, organized by socialists and anarchists to protest police brutality against strikers, was disrupted by a bomb thrown by an unknown assailant. Seven police officers and at least four civilians were killed; many others were wounded. In the public hysteria that followed, eight anarchists were arrested and tried, and though their connection to the bombing was never proved, seven were sentenced to death, and one to fifteen years' imprisonment.

Proletarization yielded not only conflict and violence but also the productive association of workers into labor unions. Between the formation of Chicago's first Trades Assembly in 1864 and the founding of the Chicago Federation of Labor in 1896, "the city's workers grew increasingly aware of themselves as a distinct class" (Schneirov 2004, 6). The nationwide railroad strike of 1877—the largest strike in the world up to that time—helped spur the rise of the Knights of Labor. The group reached its heyday in the mid-1880s; in Chicago alone, membership soared from two thousand to nearly twenty-two thousand between 1885 and 1886 (Pierce 1957, 264). The Knights of Labor's broad-based membership was a change from the craft unions of the past; under its banner, skilled and unskilled workers joined forces (Schneirov, Stromquist, and Salvatore 1999; Voss 1993). Women began organizing across trade lines as well. Chicago's first female non-trade-specific union, the Working Women's Union, was formed in 1878, and included both housewives and wage earners. In 1888, Chicago women formed a new mixed-trades union, the Ladies' Federal Labor Union, under the auspices of the newly formed American Federation of Labor (Tax 1980). After the repression that followed the Haymarket bombing, the Knights receded, but by 1890 the Chicago labor movement had fully recovered and actually exceeded its pre-Haymarket strength (Schneirov 1994), and the city was on its way to rivaling London as the "trade-union capital of the world" (Montgomery 1987, 269).

Despite some ambivalence toward partisan politics—labor leaders, like middle-class progressives, regarded it as hopelessly tainted by patronage— the labor movement of the 1880s and early 1890s was as politicized as ever, particularly at the local level. Labor unions and activists, including the Knights of Labor, wanted to recapture "government for the people," and rallied enthusiastically behind progressive policy interventions ranging from the regulated working day to the public ownership of utilities, to tax and election reform. They also founded short-lived labor parties (Fink 1983, 33; Schneirov 1994, 1998). Labor's retreat to "pure and simple" unionism—Samuel Gompers's rejection of political action in favor of collective bargaining directly with employers—was still in the future.

Organized labor was not the only source of progressive political activism. By the late 1880s, Chicago had produced a vibrant nongovernmental social reform field in which labor activists and middle-class progressives both participated. Several organizations anchored this field: the Chicago Ethical Club (later the Sunset Club) hosted conferences where Chicagoans of diverse backgrounds discussed social issues and ideas; muckraker Henry Demarest Lloyd turned his home into a salon, where middle- and working-class reform leaders met to debate the "social question" as well as rally to the cause of labor; and the Society for Christian Socialists brought together religiously inclined labor leaders and sympathetic clergy preaching the social gospel. The plight of laboring women and children received special attention from the cross-class Illinois Woman's Alliance along with the working- and middle-class social reformers centered around Addams's Hull House (Schneirov 1994, 1998). These alliances with "respectable" middle-class reform elements put organized labor in a stronger position to push for protective legislation than had been the case in 1870s Massachusetts.

In the midst of this ferment, Altgeld, a German-born progressive Democrat, was elected governor in 1892. Democrats also seized control of both houses of the state legislature for the first time since the Civil War. Notwithstanding a few short-lived attempts to establish third parties, the Democratic Party was essentially the labor party of Chicago in the 1880s and 1890s. Democratic administrations practiced a hands-off policy when it came to strikes, and a Democratic mayor established an eight-hour day and overtime pay for city workers in 1889. The *Chicago Tribune* estimated that 80 percent of the party's voters were workers (Schneirov 2004, 20). Democrats' statewide victory was secured by a remarkably well-organized campaign that successfully mobilized the immigrant and urban labor vote (Jensen 1971, 169).[2] Germans, who had until then split between the two major parties, rallied to support Altgeld, who charmed them by speaking in their native tongue on the campaign trail. George Schilling, a Knights of Labor organizer and reporter for the socialist *Arbeiter Zeitung*, campaigned tirelessly for Altgeld. Schilling was joined by Lloyd, and together they "worked like beavers" to get Altgeld elected (Barnard 1938, 161). The Democratic victory of 1892 was a crucial enabling condition for the passage of the Workshop and Factories Act the following year. Because prolabor politicians controlled both the executive and legislative branches, a critical window of opportunity for legislation to protect the state's laboring women and children was open.

Saving Chicago's Children

In *Pricing the Priceless Child*, Viviana Zelizer notes that the social valuation of children in the United States changed dramatically between 1870 and 1930, moving from a view of children as valuable producers and contributors to the family economy, to a view of them as economically worthless but emotionally priceless objects of parental love. For Zelizer, this change resulted not from economic or demographic developments but rather from changing cultural values, especially a new middle-class "sacralization" of children's lives first imposed on, yet later embraced by, working-class families. This sacralization was at the root of late nineteenth- and early twentieth-century child labor laws (Zelizer 1985, 56–112; for a similar argument applied to Europe, see Cunningham 2005, chapter 6).

Historical evidence of the rhetoric deployed by "child savers" and child labor reformers suggests that Zelizer's argument is incomplete. Certainly, these reformers believed that overwork and other forms of child abuse were indefensible violations of children's right to be free from suffering and even to childhood itself. But late nineteenth-century reformers rarely framed their aims exclusively in these terms. Instead, like their forebears in the 1830s and 1840s, they connected children's well-being and particularly education with the interests of the state. The children of the poor were not simply an end unto themselves but always also the key to the long-term peace and prosperity of the nation. As Elbridge Gerry (1883, 68), founder of the New York Society for the Prevention of Cruelty to Children, declared, "The future status of the nation will largely depend on the proper physical and intellectual training of [the nation's] children." Similarly, Jacob Riis (1902) opened his influential exposé of the condition of New York City's poor children by asserting that "the problem of the children is the problem of the State." Kelley (1905, 3) made the connection between the right to childhood and the state interest explicit, contending that the "right to childhood . . . follows from the existence of the Republic . . . which must perish if it should ever cease to be replenished by generations of patriots, who can be secured on no other terms than the full recognition of the need of long-cherished, carefully nurtured childhood for all the future citizens."

As discussed in the previous chapter, these concerns were particularly acute when applied to immigrants. Reformers worried about what they perceived to be the inadequate Americanization of first- and second-generation immigrant children who were failing to learn English along with the history, institutions, and values of the United States. This was especially so for Roman Catholics from Italy and eastern Europe, who were feared to be in the thrall of a "foreign potentate"—the Pope—a situation that undermined not only their own life chances but the stability of the US government too.[3] Partly as a result of this bias, anticruelty societies disproportionately targeted immigrants, sometimes breaking up families simply because foreign child-rearing practices seemed inappropriate to native middle-class eyes (Gordon 1985).

The late nineteenth-century "child savers," as they came to be called, focused their energy on segregating children from family and community environments they believed would not only damage them physically but also degrade them morally (Pearson 2011, 89–97). In Chicago, child savers concentrated particularly on shielding children from the vices of the street. According to one report, in the 1870s thousands of children could be found staggering drunk through Chicago's streets on a nightly basis. Thanks to the work of the Chicago Citizen's

League to compel the prosecution of saloon proprietors who sold liquor to minors, the scourge of public "infantile drunkenness" was brought largely under control by 1890.[4] But although children were less likely to be found intoxicated, juvenile street roaming, peddling, and begging were still prevalent in the 1880s and 1890s.[5] Italian orphans—many of them victims of an extensive human trafficking network—ground organs for pennies they handed over to the *padrones* who exploited them (Pierce 1957, 43–44). Children also swarmed the streets hawking newspapers, collecting cigarette butts, shining shoes, selling flowers, and picking pockets. Reformers feared that this constant exposure to drunkenness, prostitution, crime, and uncouth behavior in Chicago's streets, saloons, and dance halls would morally degrade children for life, and "form a dangerous element in the voting population of the country."[6]

Toward the end of the century, the child-saving movement expanded its focus by trying not only to remove poor children from dangerous environments but also to change the environment itself. Its efforts included establishing kindergartens and schools as well as parks and recreational facilities in poor neighborhoods. Kindergartens, invented in Germany in the late 1830s by the Pestalozzi acolyte Friedrich Fröbel, would take advantage of "the pliable period of early childhood" to eradicate "vicious tendencies" and develop "latent capacities for good." This would serve their interests as well as the state's; as one kindergarten reformer declared, "The foundations for national prosperity and perpetuity are to be laid deep down in our infant schools" (Cooper 1893, 90). By the 1880s, kindergartens were well established in Chicago, but older children's environment was more difficult to control. As the city's population grew by leaps and bounds, the number of public schools proved inadequate, and truancy soared. By the mid-1890s, as a result of pressure from various women's groups, new schools were being constructed en masse, and truant officers were sporadically being deployed to bring absenteeism under control. "By removing children from the vices and temptations of the city's streets, and placing them in properly designed and supervised environments," reformers believed, "children could be taught 'morals,' 'social consciousness,' and 'citizenship'" (Hogan 1985, 70).

Child Labor and Its Regulation in Illinois

Many poor children who were not abandoned to Chicago's streets could be found working in its sweatshops, factories, and retail stores. Poor families were still far more likely to rely on income from children than from mothers (Hogan 1985, 103), and after having declined significantly in the first half of the century, the number of children engaged in manufacturing began to creep up again.[7] According to the US Census, the nationwide percentage of the manufacturing labor force under the age of sixteen (boys) and fifteen (girls) rose from 5.6 to 6.7 percent between 1870 and 1880. Illinois's rates of child labor in manufacturing were not unusual relative to other industrialized states. According to the Census, children constituted just over 6 percent of the total manufacturing labor force in Illinois, placing it fifteenth among the thirty states for which data was reported.[8] A study conducted by the Illinois BLS in 1882 found that 20 percent of Chicago's working-class families depended on income from children, though not necessarily full time; many children combined work with school in some proportion.[9]

No issue concerned the child savers more than child labor. For them, "no reform could be accomplished with as little difficulty and friction. From no other would follow such immediate beneficial results, to employer, employé, and the community alike" (Willoughby 1890, 9). For middle-class reformers, ending child labor would do more than protect innocent children; it was central to safeguarding the future of the republic. For working-class reformers, on the other hand, ending child labor was essential to improving the economic and political standing of their class. In 1874, the fledgling Illinois Working-men's Party demanded that children under fourteen be barred from factory labor and called for compulsory education for all; over the next ten years, similar demands were made by the Chicago Labor League, Council of Trade and Labor Unions of Chicago, and Illinois State Federation of Labor. These demands reflected not only moral opposition to child labor and self-interested concern about its effect on adult wages but also the conviction that workers required education to participate fruitfully in a democracy (Hogan 1985, 97). As labor leader Tommy Morgan pled at a meeting of progressive Chicago citizens, "We are trying to lift ourselves. . . . We are trying to get more time to think. We are trying to be human beings fit for a republic. . . . We [therefore] ask that you take infancy out of the workshop and the store, and place it in the public schools."[10] Despite these expressions of support, workingmen's groups did little to actively pursue child labor legislation. The reform movement did not really take off in Illinois until working- and middle-class women took on the issue in the late 1880s.

Illinois had begun regulating child labor in the 1870s, but to little practical effect. The General Mining Code of 1872 prohibited females and boys under the age of fourteen from entering the mines, and an 1877 law barred children under fourteen from certain types of entertainments as well as employments dangerous to health, life, limb, and morals (Storment 1978, 46–47, 49–50). A compulsory education law enacted in 1883 required all children between eight and fourteen to attend school full time for three months per year. In 1889, the education law was amended to lower the mandatory school age to seven, increase the annual duration of school attendance to four months, and require localities to appoint truant officers. A law enacted in 1891 required children under thirteen to obtain a certificate attesting that they had attended school for eight weeks during the current academic year before being allowed to work in retail and manufacturing establishments (Storment 1978, 55–57)—a rule that contradicted the compulsory education law. A Chicago city ordinance also prohibited children younger than ten from engaging in remunerated employment unless required to do so to support a disabled adult relative, and barred children under fifteen from working more than eight hours per day or at night. Parents or guardians were required to apply for a permit to allow children under fifteen to work, and permits were to be issued only in cases of financial need.[11] Other municipal labor ordinances required that every working person have at least five hundred cubic feet of airspace, that all places in which women and children were employed be whitewashed once per year, and that separate rooms be furnished for males and females as places to dress and wash.

Because of inadequate or nonexistent municipal and state administrative structures, however, these ordinances and laws went unenforced. Many city agencies were corrupted by political machines or staffed by incompetents unwilling to uphold the law.[12] Moreover, many lacked the resources and/or jurisdiction to do so effectively.[13] Truant officers were not allowed to enter places of business. When Chicago truant officers reported high levels of absenteeism, the city Board of Education dismissed them, reportedly for fulfilling their duties with too much zeal and exposing a truancy problem bigger than the board cared to confront.[14] The city health department, which was charged with implementing municipal sanitary ordinances, was not authorized (or claimed not to be authorized) to implement the child labor measure. The Board of Education was only empowered to force children to attend school for four months per year; it had no jurisdiction over illegally employed children once they had satisfied their annual schooling requirement.[15] No factory inspection department existed.

As a result, many children in Chicago in the late 1880s worked far more than eight hours per day, and between 20 and 30 percent were reportedly not attending school at all.[16] Moreover, Chicago did not have enough public schools to absorb all of its children. In 1892, Kelley reported that in Chicago's nineteenth ward, where Hull House was located, only 2,579 school sittings were available for a total of about seven thousand school-age children—a situation "making possible child labor in most cruel forms."[17] These "cruel forms" increasingly took place in sweatshops, which now dominated the textile and garment industries.

The "Sweating System"

In both Germany and the United States, child labor laws passed in the second and third quarters of the nineteenth century did not extend their reach to wage labor carried out in tenements or private homes. This changed in the United

States in the 1890s, when—led once again by Massachusetts—the first states began to tackle the abuses of the sweating system. In 1901, labor economist John R. Commons (1901, 319–20) defined sweating this way:

> The term "sweating" or "sweating system," originally denoted a system of subcontract, wherein the work is let out to contractors ["sweaters"] to be done in small shops or homes. . . . The system to be contrasted with the sweating system is the "factory system," wherein the manufacturer employs his own workmen, under the management of his own foreman or super-intendent, in his own building. . . . In the factory system the workmen are congregated where they can be seen by the factory inspectors and where they can organize or develop a common understanding. In the sweating system they are isolated and unknown.

The sweating system was a "surviving remnant" of older forms of cottage industry and putting out that predated factories.[18] Using materials provided to them by manufacturers or their contractors, women workers had long pro-duced or finished commodities in their homes. But though rural women had traditionally used their earnings to supplement the family's farming income, urban women increasingly turned to subcontract labor as a primary source of earnings when men were either absent or unable to secure a living wage. Unlike their rural counterparts, who intermittently combined industrial home-work with other domestic and farm duties, homeworkers in cities such as New York, Boston, and Chicago experienced "grinding immiseration," often working from sunrise until late at night trying to balance low-paid work with their domestic and childcare responsibilities (Boris 1994, 12). In many of these families, children were required to contribute to the work as soon as they were old enough to pull basting threads from finished garments or wind thread around a card.

Chicago was the nation's second-largest center of ready-to-wear garment making, following New York City, with approximately thirteen thousand people employed in the trade (Boris 1994, 70). According to Kelley, who investigated the subject in 1892, the three types of garment manufacturing operations in cities such as Chicago and New York were "inside shops," those operated in factorylike spaces by the manufacturers themselves; "outside shops," those conducted by contractors (see figure 7.1); and "home shops" (see figures 7.2 and 7.3).[19] Only the latter two qualified as true sweatshops. Conditions in the inside shops tended to be comparatively good; they relied more on skilled labor, and because they were known to the municipal authori-ties, tended to comply with sanitary ordinances. The inside shops, though, had a symbiotic relationship with the others; for example, inside shop cutters cut the fabric, but sent it out for finishing. Moreover, clothing manufacturers in the 1880s increasingly did away with inside shops altogether.[20]

FIGURE 7.1. Boy pulls threads from coats, New York City sweatshop, c. 1890. *Source*: Jacob A. Riis / Museum of the City of New York.

Outside shops were run by sweaters—contractors who partnered with clothing manufacturers and wholesalers such as Marshall Field. The sweaters set up small workshops in tenements and any other structure "strong enough to sustain the jar of the machines." By 1890, clothing manufacture in Chicago was dominated entirely by these outside shops. Though it had been in existence for "scarcely a generation," the sweatshop system quickly superseded workshops and factories as a result of an oversupply of cheap immigrant labor. Because of their ethnic fragmentation and dispersion across many small workplaces, most of these workers were not unionized.[21] Competition between the outside shops was extremely fierce, so sweaters were forced to constantly underbid one another to obtain contracts. Consequently, their own profits and their employees' pay were extremely low, and getting ever lower. Whereas a skilled cloak maker could expect to be paid $3.25 for making a fine coat in 1885, for instance, this price was cut to $2.75 in 1887, $1.75 in 1889, and a paltry 90¢ by 1892.[22] But most sweatshop workers were not skilled; the minute division of labor that characterized the sweating system had produced rapid de-skilling, an increase in child labor, and a concomitant erosion of wages.[23]

Sweatshops were concentrated in the "lowest quarters" of the city where impoverished Russian Jews, Poles, and Italians predominated. The sweaters

FIGURE 7.2. Girls in industrial homework, New York City, c. 1890. *Source*: Jacob A. Riis / Museum of the City of New York.

found it easy to avoid paying rent and to evade health inspections by simply moving around from site to site. According to Kelley, "Such easy evasion of the authorities places the sweater almost beyond official control, and many of them overcrowd their shops, overwork their employees, hire small children, keep their shops unclean, and their sanitary arrangements [toilets] foul and inadequate." Frequently, she found, sweaters set up shop in their own apartments so that "cooking, sleeping, sewing and the nursing of the sick are going on simultaneously" in the same space.[24]

The worst conditions prevailed in such home shops: "Here the greatest squalor and filth abounds and the garments are of necessity exposed to it. . . . A single room frequently serves as kitchen, bed-room, living-room and working-room. In the Italian quarter four families were found occupying one four-room flat, using one cook stove, and all the women and children sewing in the bed-rooms."[25] This combination of living and working in the same space helped spur public opposition to sweating because it was widely believed that

FIGURE 7.3. Family making cigars in their tenement, New York City, c. 1890. *Source*: Jacob A. Riis / Museum of the City of New York.

it exposed garments to communicable diseases that were then transmitted to middle-class consumers in the city.

Democratic Socialism, Maternalist versus Social Justice Feminism, and Abolitionism

By the late 1880s, the sweatshop system, particularly its reliance on poorly paid child and female labor, generated public condemnation and campaigns for regulation. Outrage was grounded in the now broadly accepted child-saving creeds that children had a right to a childhood free from abusive overwork, and that the peace and prosperity of the republic depended on the education of its young. But three additional sets of interlocking discourses, each grounded in the discursive opportunity structure of late nineteenth-century progressivism, informed Morgan's and Kelley's definitions of the labor problem, especially as it pertained to child and female labor.

The first was democratic socialism. Whereas the effort to enact mandatory factory inspection in Germany was born of conservative antisocialist sentiment, child labor policy entrepreneurs in Illinois were socialists. In particular, the leading reformers, Morgan and Kelley, were moderate, democratic socialists—"English Fabian socialists"—who believed not in abrupt revolution but instead in incremental reforms that would gradually sweep away large-scale private property and give rise to a new socialist state. They saw the state as a potential ally of the working class, and directed their efforts to pressuring the government to pass laws and create institutions to advance the interests of workers, especially women and children. Democratic socialists like them also linked the reduction of economic inequality with the preservation of republican ideals. In particular, they thought that sending working-class children to school rather than to work would teach them to exercise their democratic rights in ways that would preserve as well as transform the state. Unlike Massachusetts reformers, who thought that educating the working class would safeguard the status quo, they hoped that education would enable workers to peacefully bring about a more just society through self-representation in unions and working-class political parties.

By the late 1880s, democratic socialists were no longer an exotic breed in Chicago; they belonged instead to a vibrant community of working-class labor leaders and middle-class intellectuals. German immigrants dominated Chicago's Socialist Labor Party and published German-language socialist newspapers. English-speaking socialists included Elizabeth's husband, Tommy Morgan, a leading figure in socialist politics and the union movement, along with Kelley's close associates, Mary Kenney of the Ladies' Federal Labor Union and Abraham Bisno of the Cloakmaker's Union. A leading member of the middle-class group was Kelley's close friend and longtime Hull House supporter, the muckraking journalist Lloyd. Although Lloyd declined the socialist label, he associated freely with them and promoted "industrial democracy," or public participation in the governance of industry. A vocal and at times melodramatic critic of capitalist exploitation, he nevertheless advocated arbitration to resolve strikes and other class conflicts (Feffer 1993, 104; Digby-Junger 1996). The leadership of such moderates helped change the general perception of socialism, which had turned severely negative after the Haymarket bombing. By 1891, the editor of the Knights of Labor newspaper remarked that Chicagoans had "ceased to regard socialists as wild animals" and "half" the city's ministers had become Christian Socialists (quoted in Schneirov 1998, 331). This estimate was certainly an exaggeration, but what was true was that socialism (at least in its more moderate forms) had come to be seen by many progressive

Chicagoans as a legitimate political viewpoint that deserved to be part of the respectable dialogue.

Second, both Morgan and Kelley were feminists, but in different ways. Despite her progressive political orientation, Morgan embraced a traditional view of women as possessing distinctly female weaknesses that warranted special protection as well as distinctly feminine virtues that qualified them to enter the public sphere. Like Lohmann in Germany, she favored special protections for laboring women because she believed that unremitting toil—especially when performed by young girls—not only undermined their health but "rob[bed] woman of her virtue" too.[26] At the same time, she promoted women's labor unions on the belief that they would make women more "self-reliant," and less likely to "marry worthless husbands for a home and the bare necessities of life" (quoted in Ritter 1971, 243). In this way, her thinking diverged sharply from Lohmann's conservative tolerance of women's labor force participation only in cases of economic necessity. Morgan's thinking drew on the maternalist ideology that pervaded middle-class women's reform rhetoric, and stressed particularly the thrift and diligence of "social housekeepers" (Koven and Michel 1990, 1993; Skocpol 1992; Miller 1996). Maternalism "exalted women's capacity to mother and extended to society as a whole the values of care, nurturance, and morality" (Koven and Michel 1990, 1079), and social housekeeping highlighted women's supposedly innate intolerance of material and moral filth, and their concomitant drive to clean up "dirt" in political and economic life. On this basis, Morgan justified her political activism, and advocated the appointment of women as health inspectors and truant officers.

Kelley, on the other hand, was committed to what historian Kathryn Kish Sklar has called "social justice feminism," which sought to create a more just society in general, but particularly sought justice—economic and social, not merely formal legal—for women and children (Sklar, Schüler, and Strasser 1998). More overtly feminist than maternalism and social housekeeping, it relied not on essentialist notions of woman's virtue but instead on the belief that men and women were intellectually as well as morally equal, but physically and socially different. In regard to wage labor, Kelley recognized that women were physically more vulnerable than men. To protect working women's physical well-being, especially their reproductive health, she, like Morgan, believed that they required special protection under the law. Kelley (1923) therefore made legislation to limit the working hours of laboring women a central pillar of her lifelong reform agenda. In regard to middle-class women, however, her policy platform was based on a conviction that men and women possessed equal intellectual capacity to contribute to society. At the same time, she believed that women offered a unique perspective, born out of their socially gendered experiences as women and mothers, that made their public contribution both distinctive and essential for the development of inclusive, just, and effective policies. This belief that the sexes were both equal and different informed Kelley's support of equal educational and professional opportunities for women. In the case of the 1893 Workshop and Factories Act, in fact, she went beyond equal opportunity to advocate reserving five factory inspector positions specifically for women (Kelley 1898, 1923).

Finally, both women, but especially Kelley, were influenced and motivated by the values of abolitionism, which they believed could be directly applied to white industrial workers. Kelley's family had long been committed to the abolitionist cause. Her father, the long-serving US representative William D. Kelley, spoke out against slavery and helped form the modern Republican Party after the repeal of the Missouri Compromise, and her great aunt was the Quaker abolitionist and suffragist Sarah Pugh. Like other labor reformers of the day, Morgan and Kelley compared the exploitation of industrial workers under capitalism with slavery, and even declared the former problem worse. As Kelley wrote to a friend in 1885, "The wrong to the working people, all the world over, is a question much graver than our slavery question was, as the working class is greater than the number of our slaves." Like the abolitionists, middle-class consumers were "bound," she thought, "to make restitution. . . . To act on this belief seems to me as imperative as the agitation for the freeing of the negroes seemed to the antislavery workers. And to ignore the question seems to me to be shirking the highest duty that our powers and education lay upon us."[27] By taking up the cause of labor reform, Kelley believed she was carrying her family's abolitionist torch into a new era.

Morgan and Kelley were not alone in viewing labor activism as the next phase of the abolitionist movement. The analogy to slavery, however insensitive to the depths of slavery's horrors, had more universal appeal than socialism or social justice feminism. The tropes of "slavery" and "white slavery" were frequently used as an invective against child labor and sweatshops during the post–Civil War era (and as a euphemism for prostitution). For example, in 1891, the social gospel minister Louis Albert Banks sermonized on the "White Slaves of the Boston 'Sweaters'" before crowds of working people in that city (Boris 1994, 49). An open letter to the Missouri state legislature from a group of citizens that same year excoriated lawmakers for "prating" over having liberated Black slaves while tolerating the "white slavery" of millions of poor children in mills and mines.[28] An 1890 symposium on child labor, published in the literary and political magazine the *Arena*, was titled "White Child Slavery."[29] This rhetoric infused social reform discourse and shaped both women's thinking.

In sum, Morgan and Kelley drew on the socialist, feminist, and abolitionist discourses to develop broadly similar definitions of the child and female labor problem. As democratic socialists, both saw women and children as victims of capitalist exploitation whose situation was little better than that of slaves. They both viewed state regulation, rather than class revolution, as the appropriate remedy, and believed that women should take the lead in promoting and implementing reforms—work they saw as a continuation of the abolitionist movement.

The Illinois Woman's Alliance

In 1888, a reporter writing under the pseudonym Nell Nelson published a series of articles titled "City Slave Girls" in the *Chicago Daily Times* in which she described in lurid prose the Chicago sweatshops, and the women and "girls of thirteen in rags and death-like pallor" who worked in them.[30] The series had an electrifying effect on the public conscience. Hundreds of letters poured into the *Times* calling for an end to the sweatshop system (Schneirov 1998, 271). Soon, the response became more coordinated, thanks to burgeoning public interest group activism and the extragovernmental institutional resources it had generated (Clemens 1997). In October 1888, seventy Chicago women representing twenty-six organizations met at the Palmer House Hotel and emerged united as the Illinois Woman's Alliance (IWA). The IWA was from its inception a cross-class alliance of women, but its leadership positions were initially dominated by working-class labor organizers, including Morgan and Corinne Brown of the Ladies' Federal Labor Union. Middle-class representatives of charitable organizations like the Ladies' Aid Society, members of neighborhood groups such as the Woodlawn Reading Club and South End Flower Mission, and political activists from the Cook County Suffrage Association also joined (Tax 1980).

The organization's stated purpose was "to prevent the moral, mental, and physical degeneration of women and children as wage-workers" by enforcing the municipal factory sanitation ordinance, municipal child labor laws, and Illinois compulsory education law. In a circular announcing its creation sent to an additional seventy women's organizations along with various churches and labor unions, the IWA expressed the following motivations: "[Nelson's] exposures show that the sanitary conditions surrounding our working girls are a blot upon the nineteenth century civilization, are destructive to womanly purity, are dwarfing the physique, starving the intellect, and weakening the morality of our children, thus sapping the very life-blood of our nation by destroying the many womanly virtues on which our country was founded."[31] These sentiments reflect the same trio of concerns that had driven child labor regulation since the 1830s: health, education, and morality. Like the German and US reformers that preceded them, the Chicago women framed abusive industrial working conditions as corrosive to young workers' morality and thereby a contributor to national decline. But unlike that of their predecessors, their rhetoric exalted the public as well as private contributions of women.

They proudly declared that the United States drew its strength not just from the male-dominated spheres of commerce and combat but from the "womanly virtues" on display in homes and communities too. These virtues, they argued, must be preserved in working-class families if the United States' international standing was to remain undiminished.

Over the next several years, the IWA mounted several campaigns to address issues affecting women and children. It joined forces with the Chicago Women's Club to secure the appointment of women to the school board (Flanagan 2002, 33) and successfully lobbied the city council for women health inspectors.[32] It was also the main force behind improvements to Chicago's municipal child labor ordinance. The ensuing changes required working children to obtain age and health certificates, and prohibited children under fifteen from working at night or in places where machinery was used.[33] This was followed in 1891 by another ordinance limiting the labor of children to eight hours per day. Nevertheless, the continued absence of factory inspection left these laws widely disregarded.

The Morgan Report

In 1890, on the heels of a Christmas shopping season in which reports of gross violations of the municipal child labor ordinance by Chicago-area merchants surfaced, the IWA began a piecemeal campaign for better enforcement of the city's child labor laws.[34] Nothing systematic was done, however, until the striking Cloakmakers' Union along with the Trade and Labor Assembly asked Morgan to investigate and report on sweatshops in Chicago. An IWA founding member, Morgan was a self-educated, English-born labor union activist. Like McNeill in Massachusetts, she knew from personal experience the suffering that many young workers endured. She herself had begun working long hours in a factory in her hometown of Birmingham at age thirteen. At nineteen, she immigrated to the United States with her husband, Thomas J. Morgan, a brass finisher and machinist. After settling in Chicago, she found work as a bookbinder. In the early years of their marriage, the Morgans were poor, experiencing severe deprivation when Thomas was left unemployed for fifteen weeks after the financial panic of 1873. This converted the pair to socialism, and they became active in the Chicago labor movement (Scharnau 1973b).

In 1880, Tommy cofounded the Chicago Trade and Labor Assembly, an umbrella labor union that united Chicago's many smaller trade-specific unions under one banner (Scharnau 1973a). When the organization was disrupted by radical anarchists in 1886, he reorganized it under the credo of "intelligence" not "dynamite" (Pierce 1957, 267). Also in 1886, he helped found a socialist political party, the United Labor Party of Chicago, which was backed by the Knights of Labor and achieved brief success in that year's state elections.

FIGURE 7.4. Elizabeth Morgan. *Source*: Illinois History and Lincoln Collection Library, University of Illinois at Urbana-Champaign.

An ideological purist, Morgan insisted on maintaining the party's political independence from the Democratic and Republican parties, and opposed patronage appointments for party members (Scharnau 1973b). These positions were controversial, and by the 1890s Morgan was known as a fomenter of discord and was "hated" by more conservative factions of the labor movement in Chicago.[35]

As both the wife of a prominent labor leader and well-known organizer in her own right, Morgan had to walk a fine line. A newspaper interview conducted with her in the mid-1890s offers a fascinating look at how she, like other female reformers of her generation, sought to create a public image that reconciled traditional femininity with activist political engagement. Morgan presented herself as a "model housekeeper" who kept her disorderly husband's office tidy and whose thrift made it possible for the Morgans to own a nice home. She lightly poked fun at her husband for his messy personal habits, inability to manage money, and tendency toward bloviating self-importance. In reference to his recent failure to collect the correct change at the post office, she proclaimed it was not safe for her husband "to be running at large without a guardian." Morgan then added, "Man and wife are one, you say. Yes, that's all right, but you see my husband is under the pleasing impression that *he* is the *one*. Do I ever try to set him right? Oh no! What's the use? 'It pleases him and it don't hurt me!,' and besides, everyone who is acquainted with us knows better, you see, so I just let him go on." Such statements were not meant to cast doubt on Tommy's dominant position in the Illinois labor movement or the Morgan household. Rather, they sought to highlight Elizabeth's inherent feminine qualities—cleanliness, thrift, modesty, and diligence—and convince readers that women had special talents to contribute to the public sphere. Further, political engagement would not defeminize women or upend their subordination to their husbands. Any readers left doubting could be reassured by the article's final paragraph, in which Elizabeth, on being asked whether she planned to follow her husband and son in their ambition to join the legal profession, replied, "Not a bit of it. We shall have lawyers enough in one family without that, and it takes all my time to look after them."[36]

Though she publicly described her primary occupation as housekeeping, Morgan was no mere helpmeet to her more famous husband. She was a major figure in Chicago's nongovernmental social reform field. By the 1880s, she was taking on leadership roles in the women's movement that was beginning to grow in the shadow of the male-dominated labor movement. In 1881, she was one of the first women to obtain membership in the Knights of Labor, which later elevated her to the position of Master Workman. In 1888, she organized the Ladies' Federal Labor Union, a mixed-trades union that included dress-makers, confectioners, typists, bookbinders, and other wage-earning women. Morgan served as this body's secretary as well as its delegate to both the Trade and Labor Assembly and IWA.[37] Her early work with the IWA included report-ing on bad conditions in Chicago-area prisons and leading its campaign for free public bathhouses in Chicago.[38] In 1890, she was made chair of the IWA committee on child labor. By 1891, she had become third vice president. Thus Morgan was, for a time, positioned at the top of the women's social reform field in Illinois.

In April 1891, in response to requests from the cloakmakers and the Trade and Labor Assembly, Morgan began her investigation of Chicago sweatshops. Guided by members of the Cloakmakers' Union, and accompanied by Trade and Labor Assembly representatives, a city health inspector, and members of the press, Morgan visited about thirty sweatshops where coats, clothing, and cigars were being made or finished.[39] Her ensuing report, titled "The New Slavery" in keeping with the prevailing neoabolitionist discourse on the issue, combined moral outrage with graphic descriptions of conditions in sweating "dens." Bracketed at both ends by references to Morgan's native England, the report aimed to demonstrate that "the English 'sweating system' is in full operation in this World's Fair city."[40] It did not cite Marx, but advanced a simple historical materialist explanation for the origin of sweating, tracing it to the changing modes and means of production associated with the mechanization of textile manufacturing and particularly the invention of the sewing machine. Laborsaving machinery encouraged the replacement of men by women and women by children; child labor deprived adults of work and drove down their wages. In a sort of press release sent to Chicago newspapers, Morgan condemned the "merchant princes" who profited from sweatshop child labor and used their ill-gotten wealth to destroy the "political equality of a true republic."[41]

The bulk of Morgan's report consisted of brief portraits of twenty-six sweatshops, including information on the number of workers and their sex, daily working hours, and daily or weekly wages. The data were presented ad hoc, and the descriptions inconsistently included additional information such as workroom dimensions or the number of windows. Data were not summarized or analyzed in the report in any methodical way. The following snapshot of child labor, however, can be gleaned from the depictions: of the twenty-six shops, fifteen had employees described as "girls," and nine had employees described as "children," all of whom were female.[42] The children tended to work between ten and twelve hours per day, and typically earned about $1 per week, in comparison with between $2 and $5 for girls and adult women, and between $4 and $10 for adult men.

In the report, Morgan most often used the health frame: workshops were "overcrowded and filthy, with no regard for sanitary conditions." Her notes included frequent mentions of "sickening" odors, "horrible" air, and "foul" toilets. Sweatshop workers were being "slowly murdered" by toiling in, on average, only one-tenth of the airspace required by municipal law. The morality frame also appeared: "the sexes are commingled to an extent to shock and outrage decency."[43]

Building on these simple frames, Morgan used three fundamental frames through which she connected working conditions in sweatshops to the broader interests of the state and elites as well as to core social values. First, she used a public health frame: sweating endangered the physical well-being of the workers, no doubt, but it threatened the health of the wider public too: "That long hours in ill-ventilated dens produce disease none will dispute. This is communicated to the product there turned out. This in turn is spread to the community at large, and finally the family of the workingman and the well-to-do middle class, who wear ninety-nine per cent of this output, is liable to contract a case of diphtheria, scarlet fever, or some other contagious disease from the germs developed in the pestilence breeding sweat-holes of this city."[44] Similarly, in an editorial to publicize her findings, she wrote, "Many of the dainty ladies and boys whose home life is far removed from poverty and squalor are wearing clothing that have [sic] been trodden under the naked feet, handled by the fevered hands and infected with the spatter of the consumptive or otherwise diseased workers . . . bearing disease and death into the homes of the better classes."[45] Morgan thus appealed not only to middle-class readers' pity but also to their self-interest. It was this self-interest, she later surmised, that underlay the public outcry against sweatshops that contributed to the passage of the 1893 Workshop and Factories Act.[46]

Second, she portrayed the sweating system as akin to and even worse than slavery. Unlike slave owners, manufacturers who subcontracted with sweaters had no stake in workers' physical survival. As a result, "the physical, mental and moral conditions of these workers are matters which neither interest nor concern their employers, who indignantly deny all connection and responsibility."[47] Morgan's references to slavery strategically likened Chicago's child labor problem to a productive system whose immorality most readers already took for granted.

Finally, Morgan used a nativist social order frame to portray immigrant sweatshop laborers as dangerous to the American way of life. Russian Jews, in particular, were "demoralizing and breaking down" the local labor market as well as undermining the "institutions of government" with their passivity, bred by "centuries of mistreatment and tyranny of the Old World." This framing portrayed sweatshops as sources of extreme, "Old World" inequality that was incompatible with democracy, and inimical to US institutions and values. If the sweating system were to be allowed to continue expanding, Morgan warned, the complete "degradation" of the entire working class would be the inevitable result. Civilization itself was at stake.[48]

Although it neglected to propose a coherent policy program, Morgan's report concluded with several general policy recommendations. These included the establishment of a separate Bureau of Sanitation to enforce the municipal health codes (presumably under the auspices of the Chicago Health Department, which was already charged with enforcing these rules) and the distribution of materials to educate the public about the "inhumanity" of sweatshop conditions as well as the health risks they posed to consumers. State factory inspectors were not on Morgan's reform agenda; her attention was local and focused on sweatshops, not factories.

Morgan was soon given the opportunity to share her findings with a prestigious audience. By early 1892, a "fever heat" of national public interest in the
sweatshop system had arisen.[49] Massachusetts enacted a sweatshop law in 1891
(Whittelsey 1901, 23), and New York followed suit in 1892—developments that
were noted in the Chicago papers. The attention was stoked by a US House
of Representatives committee investigation led by Massachusetts representative Sherman Hoar. Hoar came to Chicago as part of his "travelling about the
country poking into the dens at night and unattended."[50] Morgan was asked
to testify at a hearing chaired by Hoar, offering her a chance to enter and
exert influence in the policy field. In her testimony, Morgan revealed herself
to be not as knowledgeable about local labor market conditions as perhaps she
should have been; for example, she did not know whether sweatshop wages
were increasing or decreasing, whether the labor supply was increasing or
decreasing, or if any particular immigrant group's numbers had been increasing. She was unable to give precise answers to many of the questions asked
of her, such as the number of the thirty sweatshops she visited that employed
children, average number of workers they employed, or number of shops in
which people lived and worked in the same space.[51] Her report and testimony
reveal that she did not see the need to compile her findings into a statistical
summary, or to situate her findings in broader empirical context. She remained
a concerned amateur observer who could provide well-informed but still only
impressionistic descriptions of the child labor problem in Chicago sweatshops.

Although Morgan remained active in the antisweatshop campaign as well
as efforts to strengthen legislation regulating child and female labor, her leading position in the women's labor reform field eroded after 1891 as a result of
conflicts within the IWA and the Trade and Labor Assembly. There had always
been some tension between some of the IWA's middle-class members, who
were more comfortable limiting their activities to charitable endeavors, and
its working-class members, who favored direct confrontations with employers and legislative reform. In 1891, the debate was intense within the organization over whether to support a group of female shoemakers who were on
strike. President Brown, supported by Morgan, who was directly involved in
organizing the shoemakers, managed to push through a resolution expressing
support for the strikers.[52] Opponents, though, felt that it was "an endorsement
of strikes generally and hence contrary to the spirit of the Alliance" (quoted
in Tax 1980, 85). Brown soon stepped down, and Morgan resigned from the
board (Tax 1980, 85). Evidently, she no longer enjoyed the unified support of
the group that she had helped found. This conflict foreshadowed further class-
based splintering within the IWA and its eventual demise (Flanagan 2002).[53]

Morgan's influence was also seriously undermined by her inability to
cooperate with Hull House. This tension was the side effect of a battle within
the Trade and Labor Assembly over whether members should be allowed

to hold public office. Tommy strenuously opposed office holding because he feared, with good reason, that it would weaken the assembly's capacity to wield political pressure and lead to co-optation by political machines. Ever the loyal wife, Morgan endorsed her husband's view. The rule against office holding was controversial and generated much opposition from other assembly leaders, especially the president of the waiters' union, W. C. Pomeroy, who had joined the Democratic political machine. At an assembly meeting in 1892, the tension came to a head when Mary Kenney, a Hull House–based labor organizer, accused Morgan of blackballing a group of shirtmakers from her Ladies' Federal Labor Union because they supported Pomeroy. Kenney publicly questioned Morgan's credentials, and—much to the delight of the reporters present—an ugly scene between Kenney, Morgan, and numerous young shirtmakers unfolded.[54] This altercation problematized subsequent cooperation between Morgan and Hull House representatives—a situation that disadvantaged Morgan and got in the way of her continued leadership of the child labor reform movement in Illinois.[55] These conflicts suggest that Morgan was not someone particularly adept at reaching compromises in order to form pragmatic alliances with people she partially disagreed with. Indeed, scholar Ellen Ritter (1971, 243) characterizes Morgan's style as "vituperative." As a result, she grew increasingly isolated and less influential.

Kelley and Child Labor

By 1892, the mantle of child labor reform leadership in Illinois had passed to a newcomer to Chicago, Florence Kelley. One of the most famous and influential reformers of the Progressive era, Kelley made a lifelong career of crusading against the abuse of industrial workers. Child labor was the issue she cared about most. Her fight began in earnest in Illinois in 1892. Having fled her physically abusive husband with her three young children, Kelley had arrived in Chicago the previous Christmas with little more than two trunks of clothes and a contact at the Women's Christian Temperance Union. The contact directed her to Hull House, a settlement house on Chicago's near South Side presided over by Jane Addams, and staffed by a community of activist social workers, physicians, researchers, and labor reformers, most of whom were unmarried women. Addams swept Kelley in off the snowy Chicago streets and into a new life as a settlement house reformer (Kelley and Sklar 1986, 77). Her tenure at Hull House lasted seven years, and focused squarely on the problem of child labor in sweatshops and factories.

In contrast to Morgan, whose influence was undermined by her husband's embroilment in controversy, the newly divorced Kelley was an independent woman unconstrained by any man's political views or ambitions. Also in contrast to Morgan, who came from poverty and had little formal education,

FIGURE 7.5. Florence Kelley. *Source*: National Women Suffrage Association Collection, Library of Congress, Rare Book and Special Collections Division.

Kelley was among the first generation of college-educated women in the United States. She was born into a prominent middle-class Pennsylvania family with a distinguished history of progressive activism. Her abolitionist Unitarian father, William "Pig Iron" Kelley, served in the House of Representatives for twenty-nine years. Florence's childhood was privileged yet hard; she was nurtured by her conscientious and erudite parents, but she suffered prolonged illnesses, and five of her younger sisters died of disease. According to her biographer, Kathryn Kish Sklar (1995, 27), this childhood heartbreak was transformed into an "adult capacity for rage and . . . helped her wage war against public policies that tolerated the loss of human life."

Before arriving in Chicago, Kelley had already spent two decades developing a sophisticated intellectual and moral view of the exploitation of labor under industrial capitalism. Much of her thinking was shaped by close relationships with two powerful mentors: first, her father, and later, when she was a young woman studying in Europe, none other than Friedrich Engels.

When Kelley was a young girl, her father made a national reputation for himself fighting in Congress for protective tariffs that he believed would protect the wages and job security of US workers (Gordon 1977). In 1871, he left the Republican Party that he had helped found because he thought its "cruel" policies would "concentrate in the hands of a few people all the property in the United States" (quoted in Sklar 1995, 43). He became an active supporter of the Greenback-Labor movement, and advocated for "fair American wages" and an eight-hour day. Although he supported and was fascinated by industrial progress, William introduced his daughter to its harsh underbelly at a young age. When she was seven, he taught her to read using a "terrible little book" that contained illustrations of physically stunted children working in English brickyards (Kelley and Sklar 1986, 26). When Florence was twelve, he took her to see the new Bessemer process at an Allegheny steel mill, where she saw "boys smaller than myself . . . carrying heavy pails of water and tin dippers, from which the men drank eagerly. The attention of all present was so concentrated on this industrial novelty that the little boys were no more important than so many grains of sand in the molds. For me, however, they were a living horror, and so remained" (quoted in Sklar 1995, 45–46). On the same trip, Florence and her father visited a glass factory where even more children were employed. Her observation of the dangerous work that young glassmakers' assistants performed gave her an "impression of the utter unimportance of children compared with products" (46). William later told his daughter that whereas his generation's responsibility had been to ensure that the United States developed its productive capacities and national wealth, her generation's task was to ensure that the fruits of this progress were distributed equitably (46).

Kelley's abolitionist father and aunt had instilled in her a social conscience along with a belief in the ameliorative power of the state. Her postgraduate exposure to socialist theory provided her with an intellectual framework within which to imagine more far-reaching remedies. When Kelley enrolled at the University of Zurich to pursue a master's degree in government, she joined the transnational exchange of ideas that fertilized progressive movements on both sides of the Atlantic (Rodgers 1998). There she began attending lectures on Marxist theory and meetings of exiled members of the German Democratic Socialist Party. She also initiated perhaps her most important intellectual relationship when she approached Engels with a proposal to translate his *Condition of the Working Class in England* into English. This work and her communications with its author effectively ended for Kelley any belief that workers and employers had mutual interests and joint stakes in the progress of industrial capitalism (Sklar 1995, 104). In light of the increasing strength of the labor movement and volatility brought on by the business cycle, she grew convinced of the inevitability of capitalism's impending downfall. She saw herself as fulfilling the role of an intellectual revolutionary leader by introducing American socialists and workers to Engels's rigorous historical analysis as well as his "scientific" approach, which she considered far superior to the output of left-leaning intellectuals in the United States.[56]

In the late 1880s, Kelley began publishing essays on the child labor problem. Although the arguments she outlined in these writings would guide her child labor reform advocacy for the next four decades, her rhetoric was initially more strident and provocative than it would later become. In an essay published in the *Christian Union* in 1887, she laid out the social justice feminism that motivated her reform activism, attempting to use it to convince other privileged women to take up the mantle of socialist activism. She excoriated middle-class progressive women for "fritter[ing] away the days of [their] youth" on social work and charity. The palliative measures they pursued served not to achieve social justice, she charged, but rather merely to lessen the revolutionary danger posed by the "dependent and defective classes," and thereby prop up and preserve an unjust system. It was time for women reformers to abandon "bourgeois philanthropy," embrace Marxist theory, and join the workers' movement (Kelley 1887, 12). Defending herself later against the criticism that this article provoked, she again compared her ideas with those of the abolitionists, whom she said were similarly tarred as fanatics before being vindicated by the Fourteenth Amendment (Sklar 1995, 133–35).

Kelley soon started to back away from radical Marxism, however, finding ways to reconcile her family's faith in incremental state intervention with socialist theory. Even the 1887 essay pointed in this direction in that it treated legislation to shorten the working day and regulate child labor not as bourgeois palliative measures but instead as "heavy blows at the production of surplus value" (Kelley 1887, 12). She came to see herself as a proponent of English Fabian socialism, or "the realization of socialism step by step" through state-sponsored regulations and social provisions (Bisno 1967, 116). This softening made it easier for her to form productive alliances with other progressive women; her willingness to conform to contemporary progressive urban US political culture—the "acceptable and legitimate ways of doing politics" (Ray 1999, 7)—made it possible for her to participate in the mainstream policy field.

In an essay titled "Our Toiling Children" published in 1889, Kelley was still relying on Marxist analysis, but tempered it by taking pains to link child labor with issues of concern to middle-class readers. The bulk of the essay relied on direct citations of long passages from state factory inspectors' reports to construct three simple frames: "child slavery" threatened children's physical health and safety, morals, and education. Reminding her readers of the Granite Mills disaster in Massachusetts, her discussion of physical safety reflected the growing awareness of the hazards posed by fire as well as steam boiler explosions and unguarded machinery, which could all too easily injure a careless child: "Heedlessness and folly belong to childhood, and to place a child in a position in which a natural quality of childhood becomes a source of mutilation and death is a crime premeditated" (Kelley 1889, 15). Her discussion of morality focused on inspectors' appalled revelations that young girls worked alongside "almost nude" adults in excessively hot tenement workshops and risked being lured into "wickedness" (27). Finally, she drew readers' attention to working children's lack of education, pointing out that the problem was not only that working children did not attend school but also that the number of schools had not kept apace with population growth (32–33). These simple frames fit well with the discursive opportunity structure in that they reiterated arguments that child labor reformers had been making for decades; Kelley could safely assume that her audience would recognize them as inherently valid. Moreover, her extensive citation of inspectors' reports conveyed that her analysis was based on impartial facts gathered by professional insiders, not on radical ideology imported from abroad. Kelley was already building a reputation for herself for fact-based, objective expertise.

Kelley also used two fundamental frames that linked child labor with the interests of middle-class readers and the state. Like Morgan in "The New Slavery," Kelley (1889, 22) briefly used a public health frame, citing testimony from inspectors' reports that products being made in disease-ridden tenement sweatshops were likely spreading infection to consumers. Further, she used a social disorder frame that linked child labor with adult unemployment and the resulting danger of social unrest. Capitalists' increasing reliance on cheap child labor arose from fierce competition among them; the result was reduced adult wages, increased adult unemployment, and weakened labor unions. The "blind movement of industrial development" threatened to usher in a time of "utter social chaos," Kelley warned (39). Social change was inevitable, but the transition "may excel the horrors of the French Revolution, or be ushered in as calmly as the dawning of the day." Which it would be depended on the "insight of the workers and the women of the nation," and particularly their ability to put the children of the working class into schools (39–40).

By the late 1880s, Kelley had transitioned from scholarship into political activism. In 1889, she joined forces with Leonora Barry, head of the women's division of the Knights of Labor, to found the Philadelphia Working Women's Society, a cross-class organization of women that focused on issues pertaining to female wage earners. Together with middle-class women from the Century Club, Kelley and Barry's organization successfully lobbied for a Pennsylvania law requiring that the state employ factory inspectors, two of whom had to be women. Later that year, Kelley helped create a similar organization in New York that initiated a successful push for women factory inspectors in that state too (Sklar 1995, 140–42).

These efforts reveal Kelley's growing conviction that labor regulations combined with forceful factory inspection, especially if carried out by women, were the key ways the state could protect workers and children. Two points bear emphasis here. First, Kelley's view that women should be factory inspectors bore no trace of an essentialist veneration of women's "natural" virtues. Unlike Morgan, who believed that women's entry into the public sphere was justified by their inherent feminine qualities, Kelley argued that the professions should be open to all who wanted to pursue them. Although nothing about their biological sex made women better factory inspectors than men, the special value of appointing them to these positions was grounded in their social position. For one thing, their disenfranchisement shielded them from political corruption and made them less dependent on party leaders. Women inspectors were therefore not by nature less corruptible; their exclusion from politics made them so. Furthermore, the existence of women factory inspectors was valuable because it stimulated other women's interest in the social condition of workers and the need for factory legislation. Women's participation in the profession was justified by their equal capacity to do the job, but its desirability was bolstered by their social position as political outsiders and motivators of other women (Kelley 1898).

Second, Kelley saw the factory inspector unequivocally as an enforcer of labor laws for the benefit of workers. In 1890, she wrote in a labor newspaper, "The factory inspector of to-day . . . is the child of the struggle of labor against capital. The factory inspector enforces the law for the worker against the capitalist . . . [and helps] check the devastation of childhood, which Capitalism unbridled is working upon the rising generation" (quoted in Sklar 1995, 155). Later, she noted with approval that the existence of working-class inspectors drove home for employers the realization that inspectors had "been forced upon them by the workers in their interest, not the interest of the whole society" (Kelley 1898, 136). Clearly, this perspective differed markedly from Lohmann and Wade's shared conviction that the inspector should serve as a friendly mediator between labor and capital. For Kelley, capitalists and laborers had no interests in common, and the inspector was a way for the workers to harness the power of the state in their struggle against capital. During her upcoming residency at Hull House, she would get the chance to put this view into practice as Illinois's first chief factory inspector.

Hull House Work and the Kelley Report

Hull House was not Kelley's first opportunity to engage with the social question, but it was the first time she found a hospitable institutional home in which she could share ideas and apply her research skills. Hull House residents were diverse. The most famous were unmarried, middle-class, college-educated women, but working-class women affiliated with the labor movement were active there as well. Kenney, a bookbinder with a fourth-grade education, used Hull House as a base to organize unions for female bookbinders, cloakmakers, and shirtmakers. Alzina Stevens was a Knights of Labor organizer and editor of a labor newspaper. By joining Hull House, Kelley was given immediate access to a well-connected set of potential allies from both the middle and working classes.

Kelley's influence on Hull House was profound. As Addams later recalled, Kelley "galvanized us all into [a] more intelligent interest in the industrial conditions around us" (Knight 2005, 230). Addams learned from Kelley how women could work around their disenfranchisement to become political advocates (243). The nature of Addams's influence on Kelley is less clear, but the more moderate socialist stance that Kelley developed in the early 1890s can only have been reinforced at Hull House. Addams and other leading residents were progressives who felt great compassion for the poor, promoted public policies to help the working class, and supported unions, collective bargaining, and arbitration, but certainly stopped short of advocating the public ownership of the means of production.

When Kelley joined Hull House, she secured a field position at the heart of Chicago's progressive social reform field, gaining access not only to diverse middle- and working-class allies but also new professional resources and opportunities. In particular, she was given two prestigious research assignments that allowed her to begin making inroads into the policy field. The first involved heading up the Chicago portion of a federal investigation led by Carroll Wright—now the federal commissioner of labor statistics—on urban slums in the United States. Funded by federal dollars and with four "schedule men" working under her supervision, Kelley canvased a square mile of the immigrant

Italian neighborhood surrounding Hull House. Through this work, she became aware of the large numbers of women and children engaged in industrial home-work in the area. "From the age of eighteen months few children able to sit in high-chairs at tables were safe from being required to pull basting threads" from garments that their mothers finished at home (Kelley and Sklar 1986, 80). Kelley and her collaborators used the data they gathered through house-to-house questionnaires to create color-coded social ecology maps. Similar to research conducted by social reformer Charles Booth in London, these maps depicted graphically the relationship between ethnicity and income, demon-strating that poverty was a trait of communities, not of individuals. Published in 1895 as part of the *Hull House Maps and Papers*, Kelley's work was a model for the young male academics at the University of Chicago who developed the Chicago school of urban sociology (Deegan 1988).

The second project allowed her to investigate child and female industrial homework more directly. Secured through Addams's "wire-pulling"—another example of her Hull House alliances opening professional doors—Kelley was commissioned by the Illinois BLS to study the sweating system in Chicago (Kelley, Sklar, and Palmer 2009, 60–62). She and several assistants conducted a systematic house-to-house canvas to gather and record data. The ensuing report described 666 shops, including garment factories, workshops, and home-based workplaces, with a total of nearly eleven thousand workers.[57] It included detailed statistical tables on the types of garments manufactured in the shops, their geographic locations, the dimensions of the work spaces, and information about the workers' gender, nationalities, wages, and working hours. For example, three-quarters of the workers in these shops were women and girls. Tables and statistics such as these strikingly distinguished Kelley's report from Morgan's earlier, far less comprehensive one. Morgan had neither Kelley's state-sponsored resources nor Kelley's social scientific training, and her work still fell within the boundaries of compassionate, if well-informed, amateurism. Kelley's was professional, systematic, and more restrained in tone.

Kelley's report combined facts and statistics with economic theory, norma-tive evaluation, and appeals to the self-interest of readers. She placed sweating firmly within the context of modern capitalism, arguing that it was "the cul-mination and final fruit of the competitive system in industry." The occasional Marxist turn of phrase ("reserve army of labor") was the only hint of Kelley's ideological leanings. She framed sweating as a system of extreme exploita-tion; it was an "evil" resulting from "extortion practiced upon people whose environment prevents their escape from it . . . a deliberate preying upon the necessities of the poor." This frame was the dominant one in the report, but Kelley also linked sweating with matters of interest to the broader society. Sweatshops frayed the social fabric: they took women away from their domes-tic and parenting responsibilities, and relied on children whose work caused injury to themselves, adult wages, and the state. Finally, a section titled "Disease and Infection" directly linked the "moral evil" of sweating with the spread of communicable illnesses: "Two children, with a loathsome skin disease, were sewing buttons on knee-pants. The mother, to show how bad the case was, passed her hand over their faces, brushing the scales upon the clothing."[58] Highlighting the threat to public health with vivid descriptions like this helped attract the attention of legislators and middle-class consumers by appealing to their fear of contagion.

The report concluded with policy recommendations. These included requiring all sweatshops to be licensed; prohibiting the manufacture of clothing in tenements; defining the age at which children were allowed to work as well as limiting children's and women's working hours; requiring all garments made by contract labor to be labeled; and extending the powers of the municipal health inspectors to include licensing, inspecting, and enforcing both sanitary and labor laws in sweatshops and factories. Measures such as these, Kelley hoped, would serve as a significant check on the "evils" of sweating.[59]

There are similarities between Kelley's report and the earlier one by Morgan. Both Kelley and Morgan used the health frame, arguing that sweating undermined the physical well-being of women and child workers. Both used a public health frame that connected sweating with the interests of middle-class consumers and the general public. Both characterized sweating as the inevitable outgrowth of unregulated capitalism, but both proposed moderate solutions to the problem. Morgan used the slavery frame in a way that Kelley did not, but Kelley had also used it in other contexts. The main difference between the two reports was in how the authors tried to establish their credibility and authority. The scope of Kelley's report was far greater, the language was more restrained, and the facts were presented in a more organized and systematic way. Kelley's report included twelve statistical tables, and Morgan's none. In their place, Morgan inserted snippets of poetry, and indulged liberally in emotive language and lurid details. Finally, Kelley's recommendations were more specific and feasible than Morgan's. In short, whereas Morgan sought to establish credibility by signaling passion and outrage, Kelley did so by signaling expertise.

The Legislative Investigation

The campaign against the sweatshop, spearheaded by organized labor and the Illinois Woman's Alliance, had been ongoing since Nelson's 1888 exposés. Kelley's investigation helped inject it with new energy and spurred Hull House, including Addams, to a more active participation in the reform effort. After Kelley's report was released, Kenney began organizing mass meetings to denounce the system and rally public opinion, and the Socialist Labor Party and the Trade and Labor Assembly followed suit with "indignation meetings" of their own.[60] Lloyd, who had been an ally of Hull House since its founding, began a series of speaking engagements on the issue, and various progressive clubs and churches discussed it as well. The antisweatshop campaign took on the quality of a tightly organized and focused grassroots social movement. The meetings brought together a diverse coalition of men and women from organized labor—Kenney, Stevens, Bisno, and the Morgans—as well as liberal churches, women's clubs, socialists, and progressive civil society. Kelley gave speeches that the press described as "sensational" (Sklar 1995, 217).[61] The newspapers presented her as a person "who has made a study of the child-labor problem," and had "spent many days and nights in looking up the subject"—in other words, as someone whose credibility was grounded in her objective knowledge.[62] Kelley's expertise served to bolster the legitimacy of labor's grievances as well as sharpen the focus on the need for specific remedial legislation.

The campaign received a major boost when the Illinois legislature, responding to the agitation coming from Hull House and Bisno's Cloakmakers' Union, appointed a joint investigative committee to hold hearings directly in response to issues raised in Kelley's sweatshop report (Boris 1994, 75). This was a turning point. Thanks to research opportunities opened by her affiliation with Hull House, Kelley now fully occupied a dual membership position at the intersection of Illinois's social reform and policy fields. The legislative investigation was inspired less by concern for the exploitation of sweatshop labor than by fears of the spread of infectious disease through contaminated clothing—a problem that Morgan's and Kelley's reports had vividly exposed.[63] The committee turned to the two women for further information. Recognizing the opportunity to educate the legislators, Kelley insisted on introducing them to the human realities of sweating. Putting aside their differences, she and Morgan personally guided committee members and newspaper reporters through some of the most squalid sweatshops on Chicago's near South and Northwest Sides.[64] In Kelley's recollection, "We could and did show the commissioners sights that few legislators had then beheld" (Kelley and Sklar 1986, 81).

The investigation garnered substantial public attention. While hearings—which included testimony from sweaters, workers, labor union representatives, physicians, Health Department officials, Morgan, and Kelley—were still underway, Bisno, Morgan, and Kenney organized a mass meeting to publicize the investigation. Every seat of the Central Music Hall was filled. Together with her middle- and working-class reform allies, Kelley sat on the stage as speaker after speaker rose to denounce the evils of the sweatshop system. She must have been pleased when Lloyd was repeatedly interrupted by cheers as he read aloud a long list of resolutions declaring sweatshops a "covenant with death."[65] In her own speech, Kelley discussed the findings from her investigation and "details of legislation needed," including factory inspection.[66] Kelley, along with Lloyd, Morgan, Kenney, Addams, fellow Hull House resident Ellen Gates Starr, and twenty others, was named to a special committee, later dubbed the Chicago Anti-Sweat Shop League, to promote remedial legislation.

Press coverage of the investigation and Central Music Hall meeting was extensive. Reporters dwelled on the bad working conditions and low pay, unscrupulousness of sweaters and greed of the "merchant princes" who employed them, child labor and the systematic evasion of the municipal child labor ordinance, and threat of contagious disease. Such muckraking not only aroused public sympathy for the garment workers but also stoked fears of the infiltration of the foreign-born "other's" germs into the homes of the middle class.[67] Above all, it rallied public opinion in favor of legislative reform. The target of the public's outrage was unequivocally the sweatshop. Yet Kelley would soon ride this powerful wave of antisweatshop sentiment—a wave that she and her allies had helped create—to put forward a bill that was as much a factory inspection measure as it was a bid to regulate the sweating system.

The Factory Inspection Bill

When the legislative committee solicited policy proposals, it received two: one from Morgan and one from Kelley. Despite having together led the committee on its sweatshop tour and serving together on the Anti-Sweatshop League, the two women did not seize the opportunity to cooperatively craft a legislative response. As discussed, part of the reason was the tension between Morgan and Hull House. After the altercation with Kenney, Morgan did not want to associate with Hull House any more than she had to (Sklar 1995, 278). Moreover, Kelley did not especially like Morgan and her husband. In her view, orthodox socialists like the Morgans were regarded as "bores, nuisances and professional promoters of discord" by the laboring public, "and certainly the local Socialist agitators, Morgan and the Germans, faithfully earn the dislike with which they are regarded."[68] Kelley later characterized Morgan as "irascible" (Sklar 1995, 278).

Kelley may also have thought that Morgan was not much of a political asset. First, as mentioned, Morgan no longer enjoyed the unified support of the IWA, and her position in the social reform field was slipping. Second, Morgan's skills as a policy entrepreneur were limited, as evidenced by her uncertain performance before the Hoar commission and again in her testimony before the joint legislative committee. In comparison to Kelley, Morgan's testimony before the latter was again weak. In keeping with the committee's primary interest, both women framed sweating as a public health issue and provided examples of garments being made in disease-filled tenement rooms. Their similarities ended there. Whereas Morgan characterized her occupation as "housekeeping," Kelley confidently introduced herself as an "expert" and representative of the

BLS. Whereas Morgan tended to answer questions briefly, Kelley spoke in long, well-organized, informative monologues. On two occasions, Morgan voluntary confessed that she had "forgotten" details from her investigation and was unable to answer several of the questions directed at her. In contrast, Kelley never admitted to not knowing something; she protected herself against such exposure by taking charge of her testimony, which meant that she was only asked four questions, compared with Morgan, who was asked forty-three by the same questioner. Finally, whereas Morgan's legislative proposal was simply a list of broad and in some cases overambitious recommendations, Kelley's was a comprehensive and feasible plan presented in the form of a proper bill.[69] Despite the by-now universal recognition that labor laws do not enforce themselves, Morgan's plan, unlike Kelley's, contained no inspection provisions. In short, Kelley convincingly presented herself as an expert with clear solutions, whereas Morgan came off as an amateur.

Piggybacking on the antisweatshop sentiment that had swept Chicago and the nation, Kelley's plan applied not only to sweatshops but also to factories and all other manufacturing establishments. It included six provisions: prohibiting children under fourteen from working in manufacturing establishments, factories, and workshops; limiting the daily working hours of women and minors to eight per day; prohibiting women (not men) and minors from manufacturing apparel in dwellings; requiring fourteen- and fifteen-year-olds to demonstrate literacy before being allowed to work; demanding parents of young workers obtain an affidavit of proof of age; and requiring a state department of factory inspection to enforce the rules and prosecute violators.[70] Kelley had attached factory inspection as well as new child and female labor regulations to the sweatshop legislation that the public was demanding. Notably, her bill contained no special public health measures—clear evidence that the public health argument she had repeatedly used was for her a strategic frame, not a motivating problem definition. Kelley was more interested in protecting workers than middle-class consumers.

According to Bisno, the leader of the Cloakmakers' Union, Kelley's bill was written by Kelley with advice from himself, Lloyd, and several attorneys, including the celebrated labor lawyer and Hull House supporter Clarence Darrow.[71] Yet Kelley was reluctant to take public credit for it. Instead, she presented it as the work of the Cloakmakers' Union—an attribution soon taken up by the press.[72] Characterizing it thus may have been a move to rally the support of other unions, whose members might be more likely to endorse a bill that they thought had been conceived by members of their own class. It may also have simply been a way for Kelley to assuage her own discomfort with being an elite woman speaking for and about labor.

Kelley's inroads into the Illinois policy field met with success; her expert performance won her an alliance with the sweatshop committee. At the conclusion of the hearings, the committee produced a bill that incorporated nearly all her main proposals. The bill also strengthened existing sanitary measures, which Kelley had not done in her proposal. Further, it prohibited not only women and children but also men from manufacturing apparel and other consumer goods in dwellings, while adding the caveat that such home-based production would be allowed in cases where all the producers were members of the same immediate family. This measure dealt a serious blow to the "outside" sweatshops, but did not threaten the family-run "home" shops—a failure that was undoubtedly disappointing to Kelley, who had long charged that conditions in the home shops, where women and their children slaved unceasingly to finish garments, were the worst of all. It also did nothing to eliminate shops in which no one lived. But the bill retained Kelley's most important proposal, namely the creation of an office of factory inspection composed of one chief factory inspector and eleven deputies, five of whom were to be women.[73]

Legislative Victory

Despite the bill's shortcomings, which Kelley openly acknowledged, she and her allies from Hull House, foremost among them Addams, Kenney, and Lloyd, advocated tirelessly for it at trade union meetings, benefit societies, church groups, and social clubs "literally every evening for three months" (Addams 1912, 201).[74] Their willingness to lobby for an imperfect bill is evidence of their ability to compromise—an essential quality of effective policy entrepreneurship. According to Addams, "The most energetic help as well as intelligent understanding" came from the labor unions. Kenney and Bisno (1967, 122), through their membership in the Trade and Labor Assembly, helped rally unions behind the measure. The final push in the state capital of Springfield was orchestrated by Kelley and Addams, and included representatives from Hull House, labor unions, and several "well-known Chicago women," such as Ellen Martin Henrotin, the future chair of the General Federation of Women's Clubs. Addams considered the active support of society women like Henrotin to be indispensable (Addams 1912, 202). In June 1893, the Workshop and Factories Act passed the legislature with a landslide vote of 108 to 6 in the House, and 40 to 0 in the Senate (Gordon 1977, 239). Soon after, the governor signed it into law.

The law's major provisions were all traceable to Kelley's bill. The factory inspectors it stipulated were empowered to inspect all factories and workshops at will, issue orders, and prosecute violators. Unlike the Massachusetts law, no grace period was set for correcting violations; it was up to the discretion of the inspectors to decide when to prosecute. The inspectors were also empowered to destroy contaminated clothing at their discretion and to require children to be pronounced healthy by a physician before being allowed to work. The law thus granted Illinois inspectors greater enforcement powers than their counterparts in either Massachusetts or Germany.[75]

The ease of the bill's passage was due as much to the energetic and well-organized movement behind it as to the window of political opportunity opened by the one of the most progressive legislatures and executive administrations in Illinois history. The bill faced almost no opposition in the legislature and was enthusiastically endorsed by the governor. Best remembered for having pardoned, for lack of evidence, the three surviving anarchists convicted of the Haymarket bombing—an act of courage that later cost him his political career—Altgeld had been a longtime supporter of protective labor legislation. Following Nelson's "City Slave Girls" series, he had written a letter to the editor of the *Chicago Tribune* calling for regulations on sweatshops and repeated this call in his inaugural address (Gordon 1977, 230; Harmon 1981, 166). Bisno (1967, 145) later described Altgeld: "He was a liberal, rather a radical, very sympathetic to the cause of the labor movement and a man independent in character, powerful in will, and a great and intense student of the social problem."

The bill's passage was also facilitated by an anemic reaction to it from its natural enemies, the big clothing wholesalers and retailers. At first, they denied that sweating was as bad as reformers claimed it was. For example, in April 1892, Marshall Field maintained that child labor and sweatshops were New York problems that did not affect Chicago very much.[76] Two months later, Kelley met with Field to try to convince him of the merits of the law that she had planned, but he remained steadfast in his refusal to "deprive worthy widows of the chance of working at home with their children."[77] After the publicity generated by Kelley's report, the national- and state-level legislative investigations, and Central Music Hall meeting, however, it became much more difficult to brush off sweating as a socially beneficial form of family employment. Moreover, public panic about disease-ridden sweatshop clothing had reached a fever pitch. To avoid losing customers, the wholesalers and big retailers had little choice but to express unanimous opposition to sweating.

Although they claimed to oppose the very system from which they profited, wholesalers and retailers denied any personal responsibility for it. Instead, they blamed the Chicago Health Department and sweaters themselves. "We are decidedly opposed to the sweat system," a Marshall Field company representative avowed. "No good of ours are made by them." This, of course, was a bald lie; the Field company contracted directly with sweaters.[78] "I am very much opposed to having any of my clothing made in these shops," said A. L. Singer of Singer and Co., a uniform wholesaler. "But what can I do? These tailors come from the old country and never were used to clean quarters. . . . I can't go personally to investigate the shops. That is the business of the health department and they pay no attention to the matter."[79] Although aspersions cast on the health department had merit, the wholesalers' claims of innocence were disingenuous.[80] They were the ones who always contracted with the lowest bidding garment maker, and the lowest bidder was always by necessity a sweater. Moreover, many were probably quite happy about the health department's incompetence and assumed that the new law would remain largely unenforced too (Kelley and Sklar 1986, 85). Bisno (1967, 148) surmised that most employers of the time thought labor legislation was basically a "joke." Thus a combination of public pressure and underestimation of the likely practical effect of the new law underlay the weakness of capital's response to it.

Implementation and Aftermath

What the garment wholesalers and other large employers of women and children did not contend with was that Governor Altgeld would appoint Kelley chief factory inspector, and that she would enforce the law with unflagging zeal. Kelley's appointment was lucky; the governor—no stranger to patronage, despite his progressivism—actually initially tapped his campaign booster Lloyd for the job, but Lloyd declined and suggested Kelley instead (Kelley and Sklar 1986, 83). This outcome was consequential. Kelley's view of society as divided into warring classes with no common interests distinguished her from Lloyd and shaped her understanding of how she should approach her new job. As noted, Kelley placed no stock in arbitration or reconciliation between labor and capital. Her focus was entirely on exposing wrongdoers and prosecuting them to the fullest extent of the law. She had been willing to compromise on the content of the Workshops and Factories Act, but not on enforcement. Had Lloyd been appointed chief factory inspector, it is quite likely that the office would have been carried out in a less forceful way.

With her appointment, Kelley transitioned from policy entrepreneur to administrative entrepreneur. It was now up to her to build the capacity, reputation, and bureaucratic autonomy of the factory inspection department. Working with three deputies—Kenney, Stevens, and Bisno—and eight assistants, Kelley initially poured most of her energies into rooting out illegal child labor in large manufacturing establishments.[81] The problem that had mobilized broad middle-class support for the bill—the potential spread of disease in sweatshops—received relatively less attention. In their first five months in office, Kelley and her deputies canvased 2,452 workplaces. Fourteen- to sixteen-year-olds made up 9.7 percent of the workforce in these establishments.[82] Illegally employed children under fourteen numbered in the "hundreds." The first report is a litany of specific examples of unfortunate children, physically stunted, diseased, and illiterate, and forced to work in factories and workshops contrary to the law. It uses none of the conciliatory language that Wade so often did, and no suggestion that violations were the result of

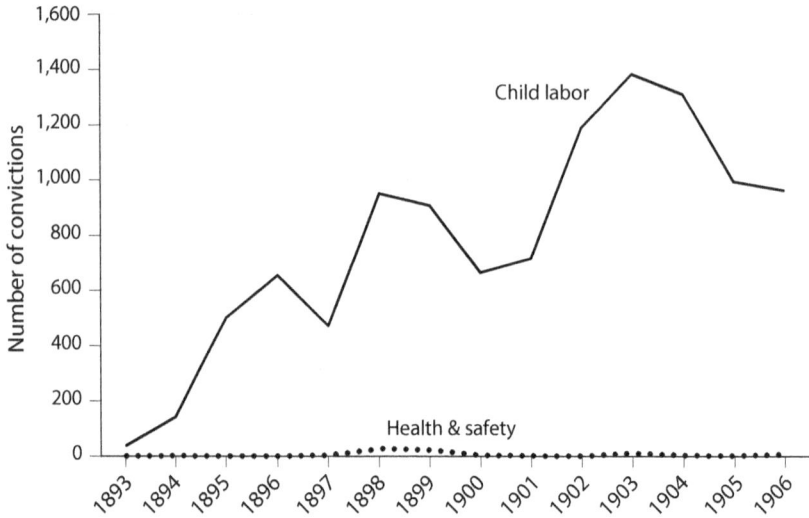

FIGURE 7.6. Convictions for child labor and health/safety violations in Illinois, 1893–1906.
Source: Illinois, Office of Inspectors of Factories and Workshops 1893–1906.
Note: Child labor violations included: employing children under fourteen; employing children under sixteen: without an affidavit, without wall postings about the hours of labor, without keeping a register, at dangerous occupations, between the hours of 7 p.m. and 7 a.m., in places of amusement where intoxicating liquors are sold, for more than ten hours in one day, for more than eight hours in one day, or without age, school, or health certificates. Health and safety violations included: filthy shop, failure to provide fans or blowers, and failure to guard metal-polishing wheels.

ignorance or accident on the part of well-meaning employers. Accordingly, Kelley brought "suit in every case of violations for which evidence can be obtained."[83]

Kelley and her inspectors spent their four years in office enforcing the law with the utmost energy. They discharged "large numbers" of working children under fourteen, weeded out frail older children by arranging medical examinations—carried out for free by Hull House affiliates—to declare them unfit for work, and demanded age affidavits for fourteen- and fifteen-year-olds, thereby causing many parents to withdraw their underage children rather than forswear themselves. They vigorously pursued prosecutions against employers. Bisno (1967, 148) later recalled that both he and Kelley were "fanatical almost to the point of blindness with regard to the law." This is evident in the statistics of convictions, which far exceeded those for Wade's department. Whereas Wade's arrests for child labor violations peaked at 33 in 1880, Kelley's force secured 656 convictions in 1896. Meanwhile, the number of convictions for health and safety violations remained negligible in Illinois (see figure 7.6).

As chief factory inspector, Kelley did not restrict herself to enforcing the law. Like Lohmann and Wade, she used her bureaucratic authority and access to push for further reforms. First, in her reports, her critiques of the existing law's shortcomings were always followed by well-reasoned and feasible recommendations for amendments. She often referred to Massachusetts statutes as models that Illinois should emulate. Second, soon after taking office she secured a ruling from the state attorney general to confirm that the law's child labor and hours provisions could be applied to every factory and workshop in the state, not just sweatshops.[84] This ruling extended her sphere of jurisdiction in a way that provoked the ire of Illinois manufacturers, particularly glassmakers, who believed themselves beyond the reach of the law. Finally, she and several members of her staff continued to be involved in union organizing while in office, making it clear that their sympathies were with labor. Reacting to this mingling of official bureaucratic and unofficial reformist activity, the conservative *Chicago Tribune* complained that "most of the inspectors are trying everywhere to organize unions among employés. . . . [W]hen they turn themselves into labor organizers they go beyond all bounds. . . . [I]t is not the business of any employé of the state to neglect his legitimate duty for the purpose of preaching 'organization.'"[85]

Capitalists Unite

As in Germany, employers' recalcitrance was most pronounced in the glass industry, where young children were viewed as indispensable (Addams 1912, 205–6). By far the largest single employer of children in the state was the Illinois Glass Works in the southern town of Alton; it employed more than six hundred workers between age fourteen and sixteen as well as many under fourteen, some as young as seven. According to Kelley, kidnappers had made a practice of rounding up children from orphanages and poorhouses near Alton. Claiming to be their guardians, these kidnappers produced false affidavits testifying that orphaned seven- and eight-year-olds were the legal working age of fourteen. They then proceeded to live off the children's earnings. Kelley also charged that various municipalities had adopted the practice of sending indigent and dependent families to Alton, where their sons were required to work in the glassworks for the families to qualify for public outdoor relief. The entire city of Alton, from the mayor down, seems to have been in the pocket of the glass company (Kelley 1905, 43–52).[86]

Kelley went after the glassworks with a vengeance (Sklar 1995, 280–81). In 1894, she prosecuted the company for employing 200 boys under fourteen and 400 under sixteen who lacked the required age affidavit. In response, the company protested that it could not carry on and would be forced to shut down furnaces.[87] After a hearing at which Governor Altgeld personally ordered the glassworks to clean up its act and dismiss its underage employees, the company did in fact shut down a furnace, putting 325 people out of work.[88] By the end of 1894, it was back to illegally employing children. On November 8, Bisno issued eleven warrants for the arrest of the Illinois Glass Works' superintendent on charges of employing boys under fourteen.[89] The next day, the company vowed to challenge the constitutionality of the Workshop and Factories Act in court.[90]

This soon proved unnecessary, however. The law's main sticking point with most employers was not its child labor regulations but rather its limit on the working hours of women. In 1893, a group of manufacturers responded to the hours measure by forming the Illinois Manufacturers' Association (IMA). Organized capital of this type was one of the great threats to the US labor movement, and one of the key reasons that the American Federation of Labor retreated to a more conservative "pure and simple unionism" in the mid-1890s (Voss 1993). According to its newly elected secretary, the IMA felt that "the law is a good one and would meet with no opposition if it were a national law," but as it stood, it would make it impossible for Illinois manufacturers to compete with those in other states where female labor was not regulated.[91] By the beginning of 1894, the IMA had one thousand members. Though the IMA's chief goal was to test the constitutionality of the women's hours provision, and it pledged not to challenge the sections regarding child labor or workplace sanitation, it did deploy its considerable resources to defend members against prosecution for violations of the child labor regulations.[92] In January 1894, for example, Kelley's office lost five child labor cases against a paper box manufacturer that retained the IMA's secretary as its defense attorney (Sklar 1995, 255).

In the first five months of 1894, the state prosecuted nine violations of the section on hours of female employment; on conviction, all nine defendants, represented by the IMA's lawyer, appealed.[93] The Illinois Supreme Court heard *Ritchie v. People of Illinois* in May. In March 1895, the court unanimously struck down the law's eight-hour rule for women on the grounds that women had just as much right to freedom of contract as men. To deprive any individual of her right to make contracts would be to deprive her of property in violation of Section 2, Article 2 of the Constitution, the court concluded. "It sprang from the needs of paternalism and socialism, neither of which has any place in this country," the exultant IMA attorney declared. "The law in question was contrary in principle to American ideas of freedom and independence. . . . [W]oman is equal to man before the law and . . . her right to her labor, which constitutes her property, is sacred and impregnable."[94] The sections of the law pertaining to child labor as well as sanitation and factory inspection were never brought into question. Kelley was still free to enforce these aspects of the law.

This freedom lasted only a few more months, though. Democrats had already lost their fleeting majority in the General Assembly in 1894; they would not win it back until 1932 (Dubin 2007). In 1896, Governor Altgeld, having been smeared relentlessly for pardoning the three surviving Haymarket anarchists, lost his reelection campaign. Although his successor had pledged to keep Kelley in office, he soon went back on his word and allowed none other than the state senator from Alton to choose her replacement. Not surprisingly, the new chief factory inspector, Louis Arrington, turned out to be a former manager of the glassworks who enjoyed the full support of the Illinois Glass Works' board. Its insider status secured, the company no longer needed to challenge child labor regulations in court; it had instead captured the agency that was supposed to regulate it.[95] All prosecutions of the glass manufacturer ceased during the seven years that Arrington was in office.[96]

The glass company was now free to exploit child labor with impunity, but overall the enforcement approach to factory inspection continued in Illinois. Convictions actually ballooned under Arrington's leadership (see figure 7.6). Several factors explain this. First, thanks to Kelley's advocacy, the law had been amended in 1897 to dramatically expand the types of establishments under its purview from factories, workshops, and sweatshops, to "almost every trade and occupation," including retail and services.[97] This naturally led to an increase in prosecutions and convictions. Second, although Arrington protected the Illinois Glass Works in Alton, he was quite willing to go after other employers. The factory inspection department had been captured by the glass company, not by capital as a whole. Third, Arrington seems to have steered the department toward prosecuting small employers against which it was easier to secure convictions.[98] He bitterly criticized the IMA—"they seem to think more of a thousand dollars than they do of a thousand human lives"—and bemoaned how difficult it was to win convictions against its members.[99] Small employers, on the other hand, would have had fewer resources to defend themselves in court and not have had the advantage of the IMA's legal counsel.

Arrington's child labor convictions peaked in 1902. That year, he was abruptly replaced with Edgar T. Davies, who resumed prosecuting child labor violations at the Alton glass company and lasted in the position until 1913. Illinois continued to follow a punitive model of factory inspection into the 1920s, when "wearing badges and issuing tickets," Illinois inspectors were still rooting out as well as prosecuting child and female labor violations by the hundreds (Rogers 2009, 146). Kelley's enforcement model was enduring, even if it proved vulnerable to regulatory capture by some, if not all, capitalist class interests.

Working-Class Mobilization, Middle-Class Policy Entrepreneurship

The Illinois Workshop and Factories Act of 1893 was made possible by a rare window of political opportunity that opened when prolabor Democrats took over Springfield, but it was the joint accomplishment of organized labor and middle-class reformers. The campaign against sweatshops took on the form of a tightly focused, energetic, cross-class social movement. Labor's central role in this movement reflected its increasing prominence in public affairs since the Civil War. As we have seen, organized labor in this period was actively pushing for legislative reforms, not just pure and simple unionism. What made the Chicago labor movement different from Massachusetts twenty years earlier was not only its size and strength but also its inclusion of women in leadership positions and in partnership with progressive middle-class women. These alliances directed attention toward issues of particular interest to working women, foremost among them child and female labor in the sweatshop-based garment industry.

Among the middle-class contingent, Kelley played the essential role of lead policy entrepreneur. She could not have accomplished what she did without labor's active support, but without her, Illinois's 1893 law would not have created a factory inspection department. Why did Kelley supersede Morgan to become Illinois's leading child and female labor reformer? How did their alliance-building skills and respective field positions contribute to this outcome? The answer has little to do with the two women's framing or citation strategies since these were similar. Instead, Kelley's success and Morgan's failure hinged on two other differences between them.

First, Kelley was able to build alliances with lawmakers by signaling expertise at a time when disinterested, objective knowledge was increasingly valued. With her advanced education along with her experience conducting federal- and state-commissioned studies, Kelley fit the image of a modern policy expert perfectly. Her official reports were grounded in systematic data collection, replete with statistics presented in tabular form and largely devoid of inflammatory polemics. Kelley was able to present testimony and answer questions before legislative commissions in a clear, confident, and informative manner. She consulted with lawyers and presented her draft legislation in a format that conformed with a proper bill, and hence could easily be translated into law. In short, Kelley's expertise signaling resonated with the discursive opportunity structure of the Progressive era. In contrast, Morgan's reports were ad hoc and emotional, and her public testimony was tentative. Her policy plan was presented as a simple list of recommendations that would have required substantial revision to be turned into law. She continued to present herself publicly as a housekeeper, not as a professional policy expert, as though this domestic experience naturally qualified her to engage in policy entrepreneurship. Morgan's attempts to establish credibility by signaling passion and traditional femininity were less suited to the progressive political moment.

Just as important as Kelley's ability to signal expertise was the advantageous field position bestowed on her by her affiliation with Hull House. Hull House was at the heart of Chicago's late nineteenth-century progressive social reform field, and joining it gave Kelley direct access to both professional opportunities and potential allies. It was thanks to her connection to Addams and Hull House that Kelley secured assignments with both the federal and Illinois BLSs; this work, in turn, enabled her to make inroads into the Illinois policy field as an expert witness and policy entrepreneur. The cross-class reform coalition that she helped build was composed largely of Hull House affiliates. The men who assisted her in drafting the bill—labor organizer Bisno and progressive attorney Darrow—were both known to her through Hull House, and those who helped her mobilize the final advocacy effort—Addams, Kenney, and Lloyd—were as well. In contrast, just as Kelley's leadership position at the intersection of the social reform and policy fields was solidifying, Morgan's position in the labor reform field was eroding. By 1893, the IWA had succumbed to infighting between working- and middle-class members, and Morgan had resigned from its board; the Morgans' status within the Trade and Labor Assembly had also declined. Morgan could have joined forces with Kelley—they could have presented a joint bill, for example—but personal animosity between herself and Hull House seems to have precluded her from compromising. This road not taken was a missed opportunity for Morgan. As a result, whereas Kelley's plan was backed by a cross-class coalition of socially prominent Chicagoans, settlement house workers, and labor organizers, Morgan stood alone. Weak in allies and unable to convincingly signal the expertise increasingly expected of Progressive era policy reformers, her tenure as Chicago's leading child labor activist came to an abrupt end.

Thus it was a middle-class reformer, Kelley, who was primarily responsible for the enactment and implementation of an enforcement model of factory inspection in Illinois. It was she who drafted the winning bill, piggybacking on antisweatshop sentiment to turn it into a factory inspection measure. It was she who secured crucial allies for it by signaling expertise in her legislative testimonies and reports. It was she, alongside her Hull House allies, who led the final lobbying effort on its behalf. The outcome was a strong feminist enforcement factory inspection law—one that empowered women to serve as inspectors, and included neither the loopholes that weakened the Massachusetts law nor the German law's restraints on inspectors' authority. Without Kelley, Illinois probably would still have enacted sweatshop legislation in 1893, but it would have been a weaker measure. It likely would have kept enforcement under the jurisdiction of existing local agencies, such as the incompetent, patronage-plagued Chicago Health Department, instead of creating a new (and relatively large and powerful) state office of factory inspection. In short, this case shows that the burgeoning political power of labor did not render middle-class reformers superfluous for late nineteenth-century regulatory welfare development; indeed, many of the social policy accomplishments of the Progressive era would have been unthinkable without these kinds of political actors. It suggests instead that middle-class reformers now had a different role to play: as labor's partners rather than as its paternalistic (or maternalistic) saviors.

Conclusion to Part II

Imperial Germany, Massachusetts, and Illinois all built factory inspection systems in the last quarter of the nineteenth century. These enabled the state to take a direct and proactive role, not only in unearthing labor violations and implementing labor laws, but in identifying problems requiring further legislative attention. The state's response to the social question of the nineteenth century thereby became more routinized and in some ways less contentious. The countermovement against laissez-faire liberalism was on its way to becoming institutionalized and bureaucratized.

Middle-class policy and administrative entrepreneurs continued to play a pivotal role in this administrative state building, but organized labor became increasingly important. In Germany, labor's growing power was bolstered by institutional changes: the legalization of unions, introduction of universal manhood suffrage, birth of party politics, and resulting rise of the Socialist Workers' Party. In the United States, government institutions had not changed fundamentally since the 1830s, but increasing electoral competition forced politicians to make concessions to win working-class votes. Elites came to recognize that something needed to be done to appease the politically mobilized working class, though this did not necessarily entail acceding to its most fundamental demands.

A second impetus was the failure of child labor laws. Data proved what labor advocates had long alleged: the laws did not enforce themselves, and evasions were rampant. The need for some sort of enforcement mechanism became manifestly apparent thanks to the systematic collection of social statistics. Yet the models of inspection adopted in each state—advisory conciliation, conciliatory policing, or feminist enforcement—differed in significant ways. This variation can be explained by the different problem definitions motivating reformers in each case, the institutions that governed their policy fields and their positions within those fields, and the historically contingent political opportunities and barriers they faced.

Advisory versus Police Authority

Granting inspectors some police powers was the default approach; otherwise, how were they to enforce the laws? That the German inspectors lacked this power cannot be attributed to Lohmann's ideas or strategies; he and his allies in the administration and legislature had all assumed that factory inspectors would be able to issue orders when necessary. Instead, the inspectors' purely advisory authority was a product of the imperial government's institutional structure and Bismarck's policy priorities. The chancellor wielded the executive power to override legislative prerogative in a way that US presidents or governors did not: in addition to occupying multiple veto positions, Bismarck could selectively change the parts of laws he did not like by dictating administrative protocols through the Bundesrat. Bismarck opposed factory inspection in general, but especially hated the prospect of inspectors being able to boss industrialists around. He could have vetoed the Reichstag's factory inspection bill, and likely would have, had his subordinates not assured him that the inspectors' enforcement authority could simply be removed from the administrative protocols and replaced with an advisory role. Inspectors' authority would have to be exercised through expert advice rather than coercion. Thus the advisory model adopted in Germany was the only one possible given the institutional structure and political dynamics of the country's policy field.

Conciliation versus Enforcement

Despite vast differences between the two states, a conciliatory model of factory inspection was put place in both Germany and Massachusetts in the 1870s. This outcome is attributable, in part, to lead reformers' definitions of the labor problem. Lohmann and Wade both defined it as the result of workers' and employers' failure to recognize their common interests, and a resulting lack of social solidarity. They both conceptualized factory inspectors as third parties, men aligned with the state rather than with a particular social class, whose job was to educate labor and capital toward reconciliation and cooperation. Nevertheless, the fact that conciliation-oriented conservatives were able to shape these administrative outcomes in both Germany and Massachusetts was no accident. Institutional and political conditions in both states made it difficult for more progressive labor advocates, let alone socialists, to gain field positions in the inner sanctum where the details of policy were worked out. Given Bismarck's socially conservative yet economically liberal policy priorities as well as his near-absolute control over who rose to the top of the Prussian administration, only a policy entrepreneur who promoted a conciliatory approach to labor relations could have ascended to Lohmann's high-level position in the German policy field. In contrast, potential advocates of a more robust enforcement model had less direct access to policy making. Socialists could exert legislative influence through the Reichstag, but they were still a small minority and excluded from the administration by a chancellor who literally saw them as enemies of the state. Their ability to shape the details of policy—particularly administrative protocols—was therefore constrained. As a result, the factory inspection model that emerged embodied Lohmann's vision of class conciliation, but was also the only one possible given Bismarck's priorities and power.

Conciliation was not a forgone conclusion in Massachusetts, but there too was encouraged by the institutional and political context. New labor laws—a ten-hour law along with a factory inspectorate to enforce it—were made possible by labor's growing power resources, manifested most clearly in petition campaigns with many thousands of signatures and labor's ability to punish legislators who had opposed the ten-hour bill in the 1873 election. Still, labor lacked sustained access to field positions from which it could stipulate the precise terms of these concessions. Its influence was undermined by rapid turnover in the legislature stemming from yearly elections as well as an unstable fledgling administrative bureaucracy in which offices created in the interest of labor were often vulnerable, temporary, and staffed by patronage appointees. The result of labor's marginalization was watered-down legislation, the placement of factory inspection under the auspices of the embattled state police, and personnel appointments that the state's industrialists would tolerate. Wade, a party loyalist with a reputation for competence but no experience with labor issues, was a safe choice. Once he was installed as chief factory inspector, a strongly prolabor enforcement approach was off the table in Massachusetts.

Ideas, politics, and institutions combined to produce a different outcome in Illinois: an enforcement model of inspection in which violations were met with punishment, not advice. Kelley scoffed at the notion that labor and capital had mutual interests; trained in Marxist analysis, she defined the labor problem as the bitter fruit of ruthless exploitation that could only be mitigated by a strong state working on labor's behalf. The factory inspector's job was to enforce the law in the interests of workers—not to promote reconciliation between them and their abusers.

The deeper question, of course, is how a person with such ideas could secure the policy influence needed to transform them into reality. What conditions enabled Kelley's policy and administrative entrepreneurship? First, Progressive era appreciation for policy expertise and investment in social research, including the major research studies that Kelley ran for both the state of Illinois and federal government, opened the door for her to achieve dual membership in the state's social reform and policy fields. Once there, she could easily import allies from the former into the latter. Second, the labor movement with which Kelley allied was stronger, and cooperation between workers and middle-class reformers more fully developed, than in Massachusetts in the 1870s. Third, Illinois politics created a rare opening for a far-reaching new labor law and unabashedly prolabor inspector to enforce it. The state's Democratic Party had evolved into a labor party, and when Democrats won a majority in both houses of the legislature as well as the governorship in 1892, labor and its allies achieved a measure of influence rarely seen in US history. These favorable political conditions made the enforcement model and Kelley's history-making appointment possible, though they did not predetermine these outcomes. Had Kelley not been in the picture, or had she not managed to secure political allies, Illinois likely would have enacted a weaker sweatshop law that lacked an enforcement mechanism. Had she not achieved prominence and been on the market for a job, moreover, someone with a more conciliatory, arbitration-oriented approach to labor relations—someone like Lloyd—would likely have been appointed chief inspector.

Women as Factory Inspectors

Given the requirement that five of the state's twelve inspectors be female, the Illinois model of factory inspection qualifies as feminist. Although Massachu-setts and other states began employing female inspectors in the early 1890s, they did not assign them to leadership positions. The first woman inspector in Germany was not appointed until 1899, and she and others who followed were relegated to lower-paid assistant positions with little autonomy.[1] Why did the Illinois factory inspection system include women both as assistants and in leadership roles? The simple answer is that Kelley was a social justice feminist who believed that it was the special responsibility of middle-class women to better the condition of their less fortunate sisters and their children. The feminist enforcement model of inspection embodied in her bill and later put into practice by her as an administrative entrepreneur is the one that best realized her principles.

But again, it was only because of the state's political and institutional land-scape that a social justice feminist like Kelley was able to shape policy out-comes in accordance with her ideals. Despite not being able to vote, women were far more politically empowered in the United States than in Germany in the late nineteenth century (Sklar, Schüler, and Strasser 1998; Koven and Michel 1990). No women were in the German bureaucracies where policy was crafted, and in Saxony and Prussia, women's activism was curtailed by laws that barred them from participating in political associations or attending political meetings (Anderson 2000, 297–98). Women's voices were therefore largely absent from politics. Moreover, the conservative bureaucrats who were empowered to design social policy did not think it appropriate for women to work outside the home; in Lohmann's view, women's labor force participation weakened families and was only to be tolerated in cases of extreme economic necessity. The advisory approach that defined German factory inspection also depended on the appointment of highly educated, skilled, experienced, and well-paid inspectors who would be able to command the respect as well as cooperation of large employers. Appointing women to such prestigious posts would have seemed ludicrous to these policy makers.

In 1880s and 1890s Illinois, however, a vibrant women's political culture created many opportunities for maternalists like Morgan and social justice feminists like Kelley to directly lobby government. The ideologies of maternalism and social housekeeping provided them with discursive resources to frame women's political activism, while also justifying their employment as factory and health inspectors. It was widely thought that working women and children were more likely to confide in female inspectors, and that women had a natural ability to root out filth and disease given their keener eyesight as well as better sense of smell. Kelley's agenda benefited from these assumptions although she did not buy into them. Furthermore, the precedent of hiring female factory inspectors had already been set in Massachusetes in 1891.[2] Some states, including Pennsylvania and New York, even required that a certain number of inspectors be women. Chicago had already hired female health inspectors. Kelley's call for the mandatory appointment of five women factory inspectors thus fit with progressive discourses and policy precedents, and consequently met no significant resistance from progressive Illinois lawmakers.

In sum, the model of factory inspection adopted in each of the three states resulted from an interplay between (1) reformers' ideas, (2) the political and institutional conditions of their respective policy fields, (3) the opportunities afforded by their field positions, and (4) their alliance-building and problem-solving strategies. Factory inspection models embodied the problem definitions of the reformers who championed them, but the processes leading to these outcomes were politically and institutionally mediated. Policy-making institutions determined whether and how reformers in certain field positions could exercise policy influence. Lohmann, Kelley, and Wade all occupied positions—high-ranking civil servant, government-commissioned policy expert, and administrative agency chief—in which they were institutionally empowered in one way or another to shape policy. Yet field-specific institutions structured *how* and *to what extent* they could exert influence. For instance, Lohmann, as a civil servant bound to comply with the Bundesrat's mandates, could not dictate the contents of the administrative protocols governing factory inspectors' powers and responsibilities. Additionally, political dynamics conditioned whether a reformer with a certain set of ideas could achieve an influential field position. Whereas it was (briefly) possible for a socialist feminist to be appointed chief factory inspector in Illinois, for example, such a thing was unlikely in 1870s Massachusetts and impossible in 1870s Germany. At the same time, favorable political conditions did not *guarantee* well-positioned reformers' ability to shape policy outcomes in accordance with their ideas; this hinged on whether they used field-appropriate alliance-building and creative problem-solving strategies.

Bureaucratic Autonomy and Regulatory Capture

Comparing Massachusetts and Illinois exposes the catch-22 that well-meaning US factory inspectors—those for whom the office was not simply pork—perennially faced. Bureaucratic autonomy was difficult and achieving it came at a cost. If, like Kelley, inspectors chose a strong enforcement approach in the interest of labor, they stood a good chance of backlash, removal, and agency capture by politically connected capitalists.[3] Most turn-of-the-century factory inspectors were not agents of employer interests to the same obvious degree as Arrington, who declined to regulate the state's largest employer of child labor because he had personal ties to Alton and the glass company there. Given their incompetence and indifference, though, they may as well have been. "There are few blacker chapters in the history of this republic," Kelley (1907, 52) lamented, "than the ever-recurring story of removal of efficient officers because they have attempted to enforce child labor laws in communities which were willing to have those laws on the statute books [only] so long as they were not enforced."

The Massachusetts case, however, suggests that inspectors risked a more insidious form of capture even when they adopted a less punitive approach. By all indications, Wade had good intentions and truly believed in the value of conciliation. He was not a direct pawn of capital and was effective in getting employers to make certain kinds of changes, such as fencing off machinery or installing fire escapes. Such changes were not only easier to enforce but also were in employers' financial interest because they reduced the likelihood of expensive workplace injury lawsuits (for a similar point, see Mares 2003, 64–71). But when it came to the more difficult task of enforcing the child and female labor laws—a move that would have imposed greater costs on employers and required constant surveillance by inspectors—conciliation did not work. In practice, then, conciliation ended up looking a lot like concession. Concession was likely necessary if inspectors were to protect themselves against employer backlash, but it was essentially a soft form of capture—an apparently self-imposed blindness that only increased over time as the rewards for not seeing accumulated.

These rewards included not only job security but also bureaucratic autonomy. By continuously signaling competence and expertise while avoiding angering employers, Wade's reputation grew even as his enforcement of the child and female labor laws waned. This reputation was critical to the state police's administrative capacity building; because of it, politicians granted the agency an ever-increasing budget and personnel, leeway to carry out its job as it saw fit, expanded jurisdiction, and direct influence over policy. Employers, likewise, do not seem to have tried to meddle directly in the force's affairs. They didn't need to. A paradoxical scenario thus evolved in which bureaucratic autonomy and soft regulatory capture coexisted and fed on one another.

8

Conclusion

The modern welfare state began in the 1830s, not the 1880s, and started with child labor regulation, not social insurance. Child labor laws were important, less because of their practical impact, which remains debatable (see Moehling 1999; Feldenkirchen 1981), than because of the principle they established. They legitimized the notion that the state has the right and responsibility to intervene in private market relationships to shield workers from exploitation. In doing so, child labor laws built the foundation for ever more interventionist reforms: regulations on women's employment, occupational health and safety standards, and new administrative institutions—factory inspectorates—to routinize the implementation of these measures. These developments opened the door to the kinds of interventions typically associated with the welfare state, such as mandates requiring employers to contribute to their employees' health or accident insurance premiums, or to give workers paid time off to recover from illness or care for family members. By striking the first blow on behalf of labor against laissez-faire, regulatory welfare made welfare as we know it possible.

This book demonstrates that elite and middle-class reformers are the main characters in regulatory welfare's origin story. Across political and institutional contexts as varied as absolutist Prussia, July Monarchy France, Imperial Germany, and Progressive era Illinois, upper- and middle-class policy entrepreneurs played a pivotal role in shaping worker protection policy outcomes. They took the initiative, and the laws enacted reflected their ideas and priorities. Granted, toward the end of the nineteenth century, middle-class reformers' influence was shared with, or even eclipsed by, a mobilized and institutionally empowered working class. At other times, such as 1830s–40s Massachusetts, reformers' individual impact is difficult to distinguish from a more diffuse cultural consensus. But when opposition to reform was strong and the power resources of labor were weak, middle-class policy entrepreneurs took up the mantle of labor protection and pushed legislation through to enactment. Even when labor was strong, such as in 1890s Illinois, middle-class reformers made significant contributions by acting as policy designers and social movement organizers. Moreover, middle-class administrative entrepreneurs shouldered the task of regulatory institution building when the first factory inspection systems were forged.

Reformers never accomplished these tasks alone, of course; political influence requires allies. What distinguished effective policy and administrative entrepreneurs was their ability to recruit these allies using various relational strategies, and to overcome obstacles via creative problem-solving. Not everyone displayed the kind of framing and citation skill that Dupin showed when he rallied the French parliament to replace the government's weak enabling bill with a proper child labor law. Not everyone exhibited Bodelschwingh's flexible willingness to compromise, Lohmann's creative bending of institutionalized rules of procedure, or Kelley's ability to signal expertise in public settings. These qualities were properties of individuals—made possible, to be sure, by their occupation of certain class and field positions in a given social and political setting, but not reducible to these factors either. Moreover, each reformer brought a different definition of the child labor problem to the policy drawing board, shaping the content of legislation in meaningful ways. These definitions were culturally constituted, but they also embodied reformers' distinctive recombinations of discursive elements, developed in response to idiosyncratic personal experiences and relationships. Explanations of institutional change should take into account such individual-level ideas and skills, simply because they really can matter for the outcomes under analysis.

Theoretical Implications

These findings point to the need for social scientists to pay more systematic, theoretically informed attention to the impact of the individual on institutional change: the conditions under which individual actors matter most as well as the potentially generalizable processes through which individuals exert influence. It is not that individuals never feature in social scientific accounts of institutional change; the issue, rather, is that individual influence needs to be folded into theoretical accounts of such change. This entails treating individual influence as neither residual nor as reducible to more fundamental structural forces and conditions. I address this by advancing a pragmatist field theoretical approach to explaining institutional change. This approach directs the researcher to uncover the culturally embedded ideas (problem definitions) that motivate actors to pursue change, to trace the alliance-building strategies they use to forge coalitions, to identify the creative problem-solving efforts through which they overcome obstacles, and to specify the scope conditions under which these processes might yield the sought-for change. It involves situating all this in a social field that dictates what types of actors will be best positioned to become change agents, what types of allies these actors need to accrue, what types of institutions they need to navigate, and what types of barriers they need to surmount. Because field dynamics are not isolated from the broader society, it further requires situating the field as a whole in socioeconomic, cultural, and political contexts. This pragmatist field theoretical approach does not propose a sweeping, generalizable causal theory of change along the lines of historical materialism or modernization theory; instead, it draws attention to individual actors and provides guidelines for analyzing their impact on social outcomes.

What types of actors and institutional change is this approach best suited for? First, actors are assumed to be goal oriented. Their action is creative in the pragmatist sense because they are flexible about modifying their goals and altering their strategies in the face of problematic situations. Still, within this flexibility, actors are assumed to know in a general sense what their goals are, stay broadly true to these goals, and pursue them strategically. It is a model, therefore, that is most appropriate for analyzing actors engaged in conscious, deliberate acts of intended transformation with fairly clear desired outcomes. In addition to policy and administrative entrepreneurs, it is potentially applicable to social movement organizers and organizational leaders. Furthermore, it is more appropriate for explaining clear cases of fairly rapid, clear-cut change, and less appropriate for analyzing slow, incremental change that is the accumulated effect of inputs generated by many different actors and untraceable to any unique influence. Finally, because it treats political actors as initiators of change, it is more appropriate for analyzing institutional transformation that occurs as a result of endogenous processes as opposed to exogenous shocks.

Implications for Welfare State Studies

The analyses presented in this book have multiple implications for welfare state studies. Here I highlight three. First, they contribute to our understanding of the role of middle-class actors as drivers of social policy development. Second, they demonstrate the need to conceptualize the welfare state broadly. Third, they support the argument that religious commitments and church-state relations may promote or hinder welfare state development in significant ways.

As much as capitalists and proletarians, the middle class owes its existence to modern capitalism. Yet it is uniquely positioned relative to the system as a whole: it has a less obvious stake in either preserving or transforming the status quo; at the same time, its members have resources—education and credentials, social and cultural capital, and time—that situate them well to effect change. Moreover, the position of the middle class relative to the other classes is variable. In this book's case studies, middle-class actors' position vis-à-vis workers ranged from paternalism to partnership; many imposed their values and ideas on workers with little regard for their preferences, whereas others served as true partners to labor in its battle for emancipation. Likewise, middle-class reformers ran the gamut of political ideology. They included social conservatives like Lohmann, who thought worker protection would dampen the appeal of socialism and restore traditional gender roles; free market liberals like Dupin, who thought it would enhance economic productivity and national security; and democratic socialists like Kelley, who thought it would serve as a weapon for workers in their ongoing struggle against capital. The cases also include middle-class actors who opposed labor protections because they feared regulation would tank the national economy.

Thus middle-class actors' class position may facilitate their ability to effect institutional change, but does not neatly predict how they will use that ability, and to what ends. This accords with other research demonstrating that middle-class voter preferences regarding welfare and redistribution depend heavily on context. When their risk profiles are similar, factions of the middle class have sometimes acted in solidarity with workers; at other times they have not (Baldwin 1990). Middle-class women have sometimes joined forces with working-class women to promote family policies when they benefit both groups (Hobson and Lindholm 1997; Koven and Michel 1993; Morgan 2006). State institutions may also influence cross-class alliance patterns. For example, multiparty systems may encourage cross-class coalitions by granting the middle class greater bargaining power than other classes (Iversen and Soskice 2006).[1] This may promote universalistic policies more likely to gain the long-term support of middle-class voters (Korpi and Palme 1998). But universalistic policies do not always gain middle-class support, and middle-class reformers sometimes promote policies from which they do not stand to directly benefit. Further research is needed to explain when and why middle-class actors might promote or support regulatory welfare in particular. Existing research and the case studies in this book warn against answering this question in sweeping terms; political and institutional context, factions within the middle class, and ideological variation among middle-class actors all need to be taken into account.

A second major implication is that the welfare state can and should be conceptualized more broadly than it currently is. Most fundamentally, scholars should incorporate labor regulation into their analyses and classifications of welfare state regimes. Worker protection was the great accomplishment of the nineteenth- and early twentieth-century welfare state, and continues to play a vital role in workers' lives. Its relative absence from the contemporary literature is perplexing, especially given that it fits with the field's dominant conceptualization of welfare: it decommodifies labor by reducing the extent to which workers' quality of life depends on market forces alone (Esping-Andersen 1990, 37).[2] Regulatory welfare imposes various restraints on the market: limiting working hours to shield employees from the physical consequences of overwork; carving out time for rest, leisure, and family; protecting workers against occupational hazards; guaranteeing workers the right to take time off to recover from illness or care for dependents; and mandating a minimum wage in excess of the market wage. These restraints prevent labor power from being treated like any other commodity; they are decommodifying even if they do not allow for a complete exit from the market (just as social insurance too is often contingent on employment and also precludes complete market exit). Regulatory welfare mitigates risk, not by pooling risks among workers in the way that social insurance typically does, but by imposing costs on employers. Age, hours, wage and safety regulations increase production costs while reducing workers' risk of illness, injury, ignorance, exhaustion, family breakdown, and misery.

Bridges can be built between analyses of regulatory welfare and social provision. One avenue worth exploring is how each contributed to the other's historical evolution. For example, did workplace safety laws pave the way for accident insurance? Did child labor laws stimulate investment in public education? Did health insurance presuppose sick leave? Furthermore, the possibility of historical or contemporary elective affinities between models of labor protection (such as conciliatory versus enforcement) and social provision regimes deserves attention. These questions are beyond the scope of this analysis, but that corporatist Germany adopted the most fully articulated model of conciliatory factory inspection is suggestive. Corporatism and conciliation have in common the underlying logic that workers and employers are "social partners" who can cooperate for their mutual benefit, with the state playing a mediating or coordinating role (Bonoli and Palier 1998). In corporatist welfare regimes, "social insurance schemes are less an arena of industrial conflict than an instrument of social partnership designed to address the issue of the social and political integration of industrial workers . . . and a guarantee of social peace" (Palier 2010, 604). The mediation model of factory inspection that Lohmann designed fits this characterization perfectly. It stands to reason that conciliatory inspection helped pave the way for the tripartite consultation and bargaining institutions that are the hallmark of the continental Bismarckian welfare state (Ebbinghaus 2001, 2010), but further research is needed to confirm this.

The case studies presented here suggest not only that education should receive more attention from welfare state scholars (Busemeyer and Nikolai 2010) but also that the relationship between education and welfare is more nuanced than generally assumed. Education is, of course, a buttress to com-modification because it prepares workers for the labor market, which is how it is conceptualized in most of the literature (see Allmendinger and Leibfried 2003; Iversen and Stephens 2008; Busemeyer 2014). Moreover, education systems reproduce inequality more than they reduce it and do not serve as a corrective to market forces in most cases. But schooling can be *decommodify-ing* too when it serves as an *alternative* to labor force participation. For child labor reformers, getting children out of factories and putting them into schools were inseparable twin goals. Often, schooling was conceived in the typical, commodifying way: it would enhance economic growth by turning out crops of more intelligent, disciplined, skilled, and productive workers. But for pro-gressive reformers and possibly for children themselves, mandatory schooling was an opportunity to temporarily escape the exploitation of the market, and potentially, to cultivate civic and human capacities beyond those of direct instrumental use to future employers. Education is a social right of citizenship not wholly reducible to the human capital needs of employers or the state (Marshall 1964, 81–82). Child labor regulation was part and parcel of securing that right for the lower working classes.

Chapter 3 points to another way in which education and regulatory welfare history intersect. In Belgium, conflict between the secular state and Catho-lic church over the role of religion in schools contributed to a decades-long delay in the enactment of child labor legislation. That the same thing did not happen in France, where such conflict existed as well, indicates a need for the systematic investigation of the effect of church-state relations on trajecto-ries of regulatory welfare development. More generally, greater attention is needed on how religion shapes regulatory welfare advocacy and outcomes. The policy entrepreneurs featured in this book were frequently (though not always) motivated by religiously informed definitions of the labor problem. Many of Massachusetts's child labor reformers were Unitarians deeply com-mitted to the idea that working children must be educated to become virtuous and rational citizens. From Bodelschwingh's Lutheran perspective, securing a religious and moral education for the children of the poor would help secure a stable social order in which everyone was reconciled with their God-given call-ing, no matter how humble. For Ducpétiaux, child labor laws were an essential aspect of social Catholicism's commitment to preserving human dignity and social solidarity. For Lohmann, conciliatory factory inspection and regula-tions on female employment were practical manifestations of his Inner Mission theology. His Reichstag allies, the social Catholic leaders of the Center Party, agreed that labor laws were in accordance with divine will, helping to restore social solidarity as well as traditional gender norms and family values. It was the Center Party's support for Lohmann's program that made it politically possible—a finding in keeping welfare state scholars' discovery that Christian

Democracy has been at least as important as Social Democracy in furthering social policy progress (Castles 1982; Kersbergen 1995). Whether regulatory welfare schemes follow more general religiously derived patterns—as social provision regimes have been shown to do (Gorski 2003, 163; Kahl 2005; Morgan 2006; Kersbergen and Manow 2010)—remains to be seen. But clearly the role of religion in stimulating (or impeding) regulatory welfare development and shaping the content of regulatory welfare policy merits further analysis.

Implications for Contemporary US Social Politics

The US regulatory welfare state has been neglected and attacked in recent decades. One major issue is the weakness and neglect of the regulatory bodies that have replaced the state factory inspection departments of the nineteenth century. After the passage of the 1938 Fair Labor Standards Act, labor law enforcement was taken over by the US Department of Labor's Wage and Hour Division. In 1970, Congress created the Occupational Safety and Health Administration to enforce federal workplace health and safety standards. Many state-level departments of labor also created divisions to coordinate with the Department of Labor and enforce state-specific labor laws. Whereas factory inspection departments of the past sought to root out labor violations by proactive inspection, these entities today rely largely on complaints to bring violations to light (Meyer and Greenleaf 2011, 26). This approach is likely to be ineffective when it comes to protecting the most vulnerable workers, who may be too afraid of employer retribution to register grievances. Moreover, federal and state enforcement agencies have experienced significant personnel attrition in recent years. Under the Bush administration, the Wage and Hour Division saw sharp decreases in personnel along with a dramatic decline in agency enforcement actions (Government Accountability Office 2008); these trends were only partially reversed under Barack Obama (Meyer and Greenleaf 2011, 6). Under the Trump administration, the Occupational Safety and Health Administration's inspectors reached their lowest number since 1975, and 42 percent of its leadership positions remained unfilled; consequently, the agency conducted five thousand fewer health and safety inspections annually than under the previous two administrations (National Employment Law Project 2000). Regulatory agency attrition is a problem at the state level too; a 2011 study found that most states had reduced the number of full-time equivalents, or had instituted furloughs among staff dedicated to wage and hours enforcement (Meyer and Greenleaf 2011, 20). These trends have dangerous and at times deadly consequences; for example, they directly undermined state and federal capacity to mitigate the impact of COVID-19 on frontline workers.[3]

Defunding and attrition have been accompanied by more direct assaults on regulatory welfare rights and protections. US states have repealed, restricted, or stagnated their minimum wages; stripped workers of overtime pay rights; and limited workers' right to take sick leave (Lafer 2013, 25–26). They have reined in workers' collective bargaining capacity with a proliferation of "right to work" laws, which are now in force in twenty-seven states (Leon 2015). The rise of the "gig economy," epitomized by ride-sharing companies such as Uber, has left millions of workers unprotected by the rights and benefits afforded regular employees—a situation that industry lobbyists have strongly and in most cases successfully fought to maintain (Collier, Dubal, and Carter 2018, 925). Even seemingly sacrosanct child labor laws are being questioned and scaled back. In 2011, former House speaker Newt Gingrich, a Republican, notoriously characterized child labor laws as "truly stupid," and proposed that schools fire their unionized janitors and hire poor children to clean the schools instead.[4] Tea Partiers challenged the validity of child labor standards, branding federal regulations unconstitutional and calling for a lower legal working age.[5] These attacks have induced some states to weaken their child labor laws; for instance, whereas Idaho reduced its minimum age of employment to twelve, Wisconsin, Michigan, and Maine have increased the number of hours that high school students may work while school is in session (Fliter 2018, 231–39; Lafer 2013, 32–33). At the same time, Democrats' attempts to strengthen child labor legislation have faltered. When the Obama administration tried to partially remedy the Fair Labor Standards Act's failure to regulate agricultural child labor by issuing a proposal to bar farmworkers under sixteen from certain dangerous tasks, the plan came under heavy fire from Republican lawmakers and farmers. Facing an election, the administration withdrew it.[6]

Organized labor has largely been unable to prevent this assault on regulatory welfare; it simply no longer has the political clout and organizational strength needed to do so. In labor's current weakened state, it needs allies—not only progressive civil society actors, but more important, politically influential government insiders. Indeed, one persuasive argument holds that US policy change mainly stems not from public opinion or bottom-up activism but rather from coalitions and compromises among small networks of powerful political elites: presidents and their staffs, long-serving congressional leaders, major interest group lobbyists, and prominent policy entrepreneurs (Grossmann 2014). A rich literature on contemporary policy entrepreneurship indicates that even in today's ostensibly more open and inclusive political-institutional landscape, these relatively elite actors are no less relevant now than they were 180 years ago, and their influence still hinges on their capacity to forge coalitions with dominant policy makers (indeed, many *are* dominant policy makers).[7] In fact, one of the most consequential regulatory policy achievements in recent memory came out of precisely such an elite alliance, with Harvard law professor and future senator Elizabeth Warren acting as the policy entrepreneur who rallied political power players—Senator Ted Kennedy, House

Finance Committee chair Barney Frank, and key Obama administration officials—around her proposal for a Consumer Financial Protection Bureau. Consumer groups and labor unions did play a significant role, focusing public opinion and pressuring lawmakers, but the legislation ultimately came out of negotiations among a core group of political insiders and policy experts—Warren foremost among them (Kastner 2017). In a division of labor akin to that between Kelley and organized labor in 1890s Illinois, a well-connected policy entrepreneur accomplished more than grassroots groups could on their own.

What might advocates working to forge such strategic alliances and strengthen regulatory welfare in the twenty-first century learn from the policy entrepreneurs profiled in this book? Most crucial among the strategies distinguishing effective nineteenth-century labor reformers was a willingness to compromise: whereas ideological purists who rigidly insisted on ideal legislation failed to make headway, eager compromisers built the coalitions needed to push regulatory welfare forward. The result of these compromises was typically less than ideal legislation, but the historical record proves that imperfect laws are not only better than nothing but can also serve as institutional stepping-stones for stronger measures in the longer term. Evidence from Prussia and Saxony indicates that child labor regulation did at least reduce factory employment among the very youngest children. Weak child labor laws were progressively strengthened, and laid the groundwork for protections for adult workers and new administrative structures through which the state could proactively as well as routinely regulate working conditions. Likewise, regulatory capture did undermine factory inspectors' ability to rein in child labor, but even as inspectors used a soft touch on major employers like the Fall River mills and Alton glassworks, they pursued easier-to-fix building safety violations and punished less powerful labor law offenders. On the whole, workers were made better off by child labor laws and factory inspectorates, despite their flaws.

In today's hyperpolarized political climate, it is worth asking whether compromise and incrementalism are still worthwhile. I think they are, simply because, if history is any guide, the alternative is typically no progress at all. The best policy and smart politics are often not the same thing; a narrowly divided Congress and right-wing obstructionism will require twenty-first-century labor advocates to secure allies wherever they can find them. Given Republican extremism, bipartisan coalitions are largely off the table, but within today's ideologically heterogeneous Democratic Party, progressives and moderates must work together. The imperative to compromise goes both ways, of course; just as progressives should avoid rhetoric and demands likely to alienate moderates, moderates must recognize the contributions of progressives and embrace working with them too. After all, it is thanks to progressive advocacy that many regulatory policies that once seemed unthinkable are politically mainstream today.

The value of compromise applies to contemporary regulatory implementation as well; as economist Michael Piore and sociologist Andrew Schrank (2018) argue, regulators are more likely to actually improve working conditions on the ground when they seek holistic solutions mindful of diverse stakeholder perspectives, including those of employers. For example, requiring employers to address safety violations by replacing outdated machinery, as opposed to levying fines, can benefit workers while increasing productive efficiency. As seen in the case study of late nineteenth-century Massachusetts, a conciliatory approach is more likely to ward off the kind of employer backlash that threatens regulators' bureaucratic autonomy and agency survival. Piore and Shrank's research suggests, moreover, that conciliatory approaches do not have to come at the expense of soft regulatory capture and workers' welfare if inspectors are granted the discretion as well as resources they need to address what these scholars call the "root causes" of violations.

Finally, when it comes to bringing influential political insiders on board a twenty-first-century labor reform agenda, framing proposals in ways that resonate with dominant discursive opportunity structures will be most effective. This will require today's labor policy entrepreneurs to connect regulatory welfare with the concerns of elites and the state. In the nineteenth century, successful child labor reformers did not stake their claims on children's rights or social justice—at least not exclusively. Instead, they drew a straight line from industrial child labor to elites' fear of the nascent proletariat's destabilizing potential as well as to elite hopes for an economically and militarily competitive nation. If popular pressure, such as a rising socialist movement or spirited antisweatshop campaign, lent credibility and urgency to these claims, so much the better. But with or without the support of such grassroots mobilizations, labor policy entrepreneurs should project a similar logic today. Workers have a social right to regulatory welfare, but their welfare must also be (re)conceptualized as a matter of order, security, and prosperity.

Chapter 1. Introduction

1. In England, the 1563 Statute of Artificers set wage scales for craftspeople, agricultural work-ers, and all other laborers, servants, and workers; required all craftspeople to undergo a seven-year apprenticeship; protected servants and apprentices against arbitrary or abrupt dismissal (as well as disallowing resignation without three-months notice); protected apprentices against "mis-use" and "evil" treatment; and limited working hours. Regulations were at least as much geared toward social control as labor protection. Poor people could not refuse employment, quit their jobs without cause, or travel without permission (Hargreaves 2009; Scott 1913, 445–46; Hay 2004, 64). Protections were meager; for example, in summer, the legal workweek exceeded one hundred hours (Ayers 2014, 45), and wage scales were intended to keep wages below market rates because a demographic crisis had resulted in an undersupply of labor (Woodward 1980; Hunt and Lautzenheiser 2011, 27). In practice, regulatory maxima often simply fixed the official rates at the level of market wages, or were worked out via compromise between masters and journeymen (Lis and Soly 1994, 38). Workers could and did bring suit under the law against employers for failure to pay and other forms of mistreatment, and wages were to be adjusted upward by local authorities as prices rose (Hay 2004, 69, 80).

In eighteenth-century Prussia, King Frederick II fixed wages for laborers and craftspeople (Biernacki 1995, 262), and a 1776 law exempted coal miners from taxation and military service, and restricted their workday to eight hours while guaranteeing fixed income, the right to work, and sickness and accident insurance; state-run supervisory offices ensured these regulations were upheld (Tampke 1981, 72). In other German states, authorities prohibited abrupt changes to piece rates and protected homeworkers from dismissal (Biernacki 1995, 262). In France, pre-nineteenth-century regulations on "free labor" were largely repressive in nature. The right to quit was restricted, and certificates of leave, aimed at restricting workers' mobility and preventing them from switching jobs, became mandatory in 1749 (Kaplan 1979, 58). State-imposed labor protec-tions were few, but in the seventeenth century the French government issued various decrees prohibiting night work (Coornaert 1941, 261–62).

The major source of labor regulation in the ancien régimes was of course not the state but rather the guilds. In England, France, Germany, Flanders, and elsewhere, guilds restricted entry into the trades (which as Adam Smith famously complained in *The Wealth of Nations* [1976, 132–45], restricted competition, and raised the price of labor and its produce), regulated who could become a master and who could take on apprentices, required masters to provide appren-tices with adequate training, settled disputes and enforced labor contracts (sometimes in their own courts, and sometimes with the help of the public courts), imposed minimum ages of apprentice-ship and determined the number of apprentices a master might take on, set apprentices' length of service, and fixed working hours (which were often long) and sometimes wages. Masters' ability to dismiss apprentices without cause as well as apprentices' right to leave service were likewise restricted (Nicholas 1995; Epstein 1998, 691; Lis and Soly 1994). A master accused of paying his journeymen unfair wages could be forced to submit to arbitration, and his workshop could be blacklisted (Coornaert 1941, 275).

2. The apprenticeship clauses of the Statute of Artificers were repealed in 1814 (Hay 2004, 65). Guilds were abolished in 1791 in France and in 1835 in England (Epstein 1998, 706). Napoléon's Code Civil of 1803 established freedom of contract, treating employers and employees as formally equal parties requiring no special protection or restraint on either side (Kaplan 1979, 26). Guilds were not abolished in Germany until 1869, but their power was greatly weakened in Prussia in 1811 when freedom of contract and the freedom to practice a trade were established; only in mining were some of the older regulations—wage scales, hours regulations, and restrictions on hiring and firing—retained (Zycha 1937, 305).

3. Many European states passed laws specifically regulating the industrial labor of children in the nineteenth century. These included Great Britain (1802, 1819, and 1833), Prussia (1839), Bavaria (1840), Baden (1840), France (1841), Italy (1843), Austria (1859), Saxony (1861), Württemberg (1862), Denmark (1873), Switzerland (1873); the Netherlands (1872), Sweden (1881), Russia (1882), Belgium (1889), and Finland (1889). The United States did not regulate child labor at the federal level until 1938 with the passage of the Fair Labor Standards Act. Many US states adopted their own child labor regulations, however, beginning with Massachusetts in 1836 (Meyer 1894; Trattner 1970; Rahikainen 2004; Hindman 2009).

4. This lacuna in the welfare states scholarship does have some notable exceptions. One is Theda Skocpol's (1992) *Protecting Soldiers and Mothers*, which includes a chapter on protective legislation for women workers as well as some discussion of child labor laws in the early twentieth-century United States. Another is work-family policies (such as parental leave), which have received substantial attention from scholars interested in gender and the welfare state (see O'Connor, Orloff, and Shaver 1999; Morgan 2006). Such policies fall at the border between regulatory welfare and social provision, because they both grant workers the right to take time off from work (a regulatory measure) and frequently provide partial income replacement (an insurance measure). A third exception is Jacob Hacker's concept of predistribution, which includes worker protections aimed at making markets work for the middle class (Hacker 2011, 2013). A fourth is policies regulating hiring and firing, which have received substantial attention in the varieties of capitalism literature (see, e.g., Hall and Soskice 2001). Economist Michael Piore and sociologist Andrew Shrank (2018) compare worker protection regimes across the United States, Europe, and Latin America, but do not couch their study in the welfare states literature.

5. Regulatory welfare is also sometimes conceptualized to include policies that protect consumers and the public (see, for example, Novak 1996; Prasad 2012; Levi-Faur 2014; Haber 2017). Monica Prasad (2012) argues that the US welfare state, while weak in social provision, has historically been stronger than Europe with regard to consumer protection and antitrust regulations, but the same cannot be said for worker protection, except in the area of antidiscrimination.

6. The exception is the United Kingdom, where the 1833 Factory Act was the outcome of a massive grassroots labor movement.

7. For example, Hugh Heclo (2010) highlights the essential contribution of certain welfare policy entrepreneurs like William Beveridge.

8. Following Douglass North (1990), institutions are typically defined in this literature as intersubjectively agreed-on rules, and their associated infrastructures and practices, both formal and codified as well as informal and customary.

9. For example, a classic work of labor history in the historical institutionalist tradition is Kathleen Thelen's (2004) *How Institutions Evolve*. In her examination of the evolution of vocational training regimes in the United States, Germany, Britain, and Japan, Thelen demonstrates how organized interests struggled over control of worker training, producing small changes that yielded major transformations in some areas while preserving continuity in others. Thelen (2004, 286)

argues that both continuity and change depend on the actions of historical agents, not on agentless selection or adaptation processes. However, her analysis concentrates on collective actors—large firms, labor unions, and employers' associations—pursuing straightforward material interests, and does not bring specific individuals with potentially more complex motives to the fore. There are exceptions to this general tendency in the historical institutionalist literature. Bo Rothstein (1992), for instance, stresses the causal impact of Sweden's Social Democratic minister of social affairs, Gustav Möller, on the country's adoption of a Ghent system of unemployment insurance.

10. For example, James Mahoney and Kathleen Thelen's (2010) emphasis on how battles over resource allocation drive institutional creation as well as change conceptualizes change agents as self-interested actors pursuing interests derived more or less directly from their social, institutional, and economic locations.

11. Sociologists have extended Joseph Schumpeter's theory of capitalist entrepreneurship (Schumpeter and Swedberg 1991) to not only build a sociology of business entrepreneurship (Thornton 1999; Swedberg 2000) but also describe other types of social leaders. Scholars have theorized moral entrepreneurship (Becker 1963), reputational entrepreneurship (Fine 2001), cultural entrepreneurship (DiMaggio 1982), and most helpfully for the current analysis, institutional entrepreneurship (DiMaggio 1988; Beckert 1999; Fligstein 2001; Fligstein and McAdam 2012) and policy/political entrepreneurship (Mintrom 1997, 2000; Mintrom and Norman 2009; Dahl 2005; Kingdon 1984; Sheingate 2003, 2007; Baumgartner and Jones 1993; Pettinicchio 2013; Béland and Cox 2016).

12. For one thing, I do not attempt a full mapping of the policy field or any other. Second, I do not use the concept of the habitus simply because data limitations do not allow me to observe the habitus of my research subjects. Instead I focus on explicitly articulated ideas—that is, problem definitions and programs. Third, I reject Pierre Bourdieu's contention that "objective," patterned social relations are the basic units of social life (Bourdieu and Wacquant 1992, 97; Bourdieu 1983, 311). Like Max Weber, I believe that individuals are the basic units of social life, and patterned relations become visible by studying individuals and their social interactions with other individuals. Focusing on individuals—following them as they move through situations and time—does not preclude thinking relationally. Further, social life does not always occur in the context of patterned social relations, and situations in which patterned relations do not exist or break down can be important openings for social change. Fourth, I am less interested in actors' attempts to improve their positions within a field (such as their political careers) than in their attempts to affect field-level (policy) outcomes; the two are not unrelated, but Bourdieu would seem to be interested mainly in the former. Fifth, I stress cooperation more than Bourdieu, who often "evokes a quasi-Hobbesian world of struggle for competitive advantage" (Steinmetz 1999, 28). Finally, I agree with Bourdieu's critics that his emphasis on the correspondence between social position, habitus, and action (Bourdieu and Wacquant 1992, 128–37) goes too far toward structural determinism. I therefore prefer the pragmatist distinction between routine action (largely determined by habitus perhaps) versus creative and deliberative action in the face of problem situations—which occur more frequently than Bourdieu seems to think (Bourdieu and Wacquant 1992, 131). Both types of action are "agency" (Emirbayer and Mische 1998).

13. For a similar critique of institutionalist theory applied to politics, see Clemens and Cook 1999, 442; the coauthors, though, argue that institutionalist theory is equipped to resolve this tension itself.

14. Bruno Latour traces how scientists promote their ideas by joining forces with human and nonhuman allies through the practice of translation. This involves, among other things, interest alignment. It usually also entails the partial transformation of the idea being promoted as allies mold it to suit their projects. The power of scientific ideas is derived from the strength of the alliance network that supports them.

15. Borrowing is similar to what William Sewell (1992) refers to as the transposition of schemata from one context to another, but whereas Sewell conceptualizes resources as "actual" (i.e., nonvirtual), and thus as distinct from schemata and ideas (10–11), I treat ideas as a type of resource.

16. Both types of action—routine and creative—are "agency" (Emirbayer and Mische 1998).

17. Thank you to Chas Camic for helping me formulate this idea.

18. Fligstein and McAdam do not expressly situate themselves within the pragmatist tradition, but there are many parallels between pragmatist theory and their discussion of skilled social action within strategic action fields.

19. In addition, the Swiss cantons of Argovia (Aargau) and Zurich regulated child labor before 1840 (Horner 1840, 105), though the federal government followed suit only in 1877.

20. At first glance, the genetic approach may seem identical to process tracing. Unlike process tracing, however, it emphasizes uncovering actors' *subjective motives and understandings* to build causal explanations for their action as well as its consequences. Also unlike process tracing, it explicitly avoids a variable-based explanatory logic for several reasons: variables are atemporal, reify human action by seeming to take on autonomous causal agency, and are vulnerable to a host of biases, including retrospective and selection biases (Ermakoff 2019). My case selection logic allows me to rule out deterministic independent variables, but the genetic analysis replaces them with processual narratives, not with alternative causal variables.

21. For Prussia, see Anton 1953; Kastner 2004. For France, see Heywood 1988; Lynch 1988; Weissbach 1989. For Imperial Germany, see Boentert 2007; Tennstedt 1994. For Illinois, see Sklar 1995; Harmon 1981; Tax 1980.

22. See Gubin and Lefèvre 1985; Hilden 1993; Loriaux 2000; Scholliers 2009.

23. Prussian archival sources were transcribed from the old German script—some by me, and some by a professional transcriber. All quotations of German-language sources that appear in the book are my own translations. French-language sources were either summarized in English by a native French-speaking research assistant or translated into English by a professional translator.

Introduction to Part I

1. Agricultural child labor was generally deemed wholesome and unproblematic, and was not the target of reformers' efforts until the twentieth century.

2. In addition to textiles, metalworking, and glass, children could be found in large numbers in paper mills, tanneries, brickyards, potteries, canneries, ironworks, and stamping mills.

3. The technical improvement alluded to here was the installment of railways to facilitate the hauling of coal wagons.

4. One way to distinguish between the two types of frames is to think in terms of nested whys. Why is child labor reform necessary? To protect children's health (simple frame). Yes, but why should we care about protecting children's health? Because otherwise, we will be unable to recruit enough strong soldiers and could lose the next war (fundamental frame).

Chapter 2. Securing the Social Order: The Politics of Child Labor Regulation in Prussia

1. This chapter is a revised and expanded version of Anderson 2013.

2. The district governments could also bypass the Oberpräsident and communicate directly with the ministries in Berlin.

3. Frederick William III to Altenstein and Schuckmann, May 12, 1828, GstA, Berlin, I. HA Rep. 120, BB VII 3.1, 85a. See also GstA, Berlin, I. HA Rep. 120, BB VII 1.4, 1:38.

4. Letter from Hardenberg to Merckel in Breslau, von Heydebreck in Berlin, von Bülow in Magdeburg, von Vincke in Münster, and Count Solms-Laubach in Köln and Minister von Ingersleben in Koblenz, September 5, 1817, transcribed in Hoppe, Kuczynski, and Waldmann 1960, 23–26.

5. Regulative on the Employment of Young Workers in Factories, GstA, Berlin, I. HA Rep. 120, BB VII 3.1, 83a. For the full text of the law, see Kastner 2004, 177–78.

6. Bülter (1953, 8) makes this argument. But the beginnings of a semiorganized labor movement in Prussia date to the 1848 revolutionary period (Dowe 1970; Tenfelde 1987, 48–59).

7. An exception to this was the Allgemeiner Deutscher Handels- und Gewerbeverein (General German Association of Commerce and Industry), founded in 1819 by Friedrich List to advocate for tariff reforms. This association did not get involved in the policy debates surrounding child labor.

8. *Allgemeines Landrecht für die Preussischen Staaten,* 1794, Zweiter Theil, Achter Titel, Dritter Abschnitt, von Handwerkern und Zünften: §292–94, 298–99, 301.

9. *Allgemeines Landrecht für die Preussischen Staaten in Verbindung mit den dasselbe ergänzenden, abändernden und erläuternden Gesetzen, Königlichen Verordnungen and Justiz-Ministerial-Rescripten. Zweiter Theil, Zweiter Band. Vierter Band, enthaltend Theil II. Tit. 8 und 9,* 1837, Achter Titel, Abschuss 3–5: Verhältnisse der Gewerbe, Edict v. 2, November 1810, über die Einführung einer allgemeinen Gewerbesteuer und der Gewerbefreiheit, 121–26.

10. *Allgemeines Landrecht für die Preussischen Staaten in Verbindung mit den dasselbe ergänzenden, abändernden und erläuternden Gesetzen, Königlichen Verordnungen and Justiz-Ministerial-Rescripten,* Edict v. 7, September 1811, über die polizeilichen Verhältnisse der Gewerbe, §6–13, 130.

11. *Allgemeines Landrecht für die Preussischen Staaten,* Zweiter Theil, Achter Titel, Vierter Abschnitt, von Künstlern und Fabrikanten, §417–23.

12. *Allgemeines Landrecht für die Preussischen Staaten,* Zweiter Theil, Zwölfter Titel, von niedern und höhern Schulen, §43, §46.

13. *Allgemeines Landrecht für die Preussischen Staaten,* Zweiter Theil, Zwölfter Titel, von niedern und höhern Schulen, §2–6, 9, 12–16, 24–25, 29, 34. Householders were only required to financially support the schools if no private endowment for that purpose existed.

14. Stein's "Political Testament" was drafted by Theodor von Schön and signed by Stein on December 5, 1808.

15. At least one of these articles, published 1826 in *Jahrbucher des Preussischen Volks-Schul-Wesens,* was noticed and publicly acknowledged by a high-ranking government official, who took the opportunity, in an article of his own in the same journal, to assure Diesterweg and the reading public that the state had already investigated the child labor problem, and had begun to develop child labor legislation (Beckedorff 1827a).

16. *Allgemeines Landrecht für die Preussischen Staaten,* Zweiter Theil, Zwölfter Titel, von niedern und höhern Schulen, §45.

17. Zirkularreskript des Kultusministers, April 27, 1827, reprinted in Anton 1953, 190–92; Altenstein to Schuckmann, July 4, 1828, GstA, Berlin, I. HA Rep. 120, BB VII 1.4, 1:30b.

18. Hardenberg to Merckel in Breslau, von Heydebreck in Berlin, von Bülow in Magdeburg, von Vincke in Münster, and Count Solms-Laubach in Cologne and Minister von Ingersleben in Koblenz, September 5, 1817, transcribed in Kuczynski and Hoppe 1958, 70–74; see also Hoppe, Kuczynski, and Waldmann 1960, 23–26.

19. Hoppe, Kuczynski, and Waldmann 1960, 23–24.

20. See, for example, Solms-Laubach to Hardenberg, June 25, 1818, and Ingersleben to Hardenberg, August 7, 1818, in Hoppe, Kuczynski, and Waldmann 1960, 30–49.

21. Zirkularreskript des Kultusministers, June 26, 1824, transcribed in Anton 1953, 18–190. See also GstA, Berlin, I. HA Rep. 120, BB VII 1.4, 1:19–20.

22. The local governments' responses to Altenstein's survey are transcribed in Beckedorff 1827a.

23. Beckedorff 1827a, 229–30, 231–32.

24. Altenstein to Schuckmann, November 8, 1825, GstA, Berlin, I. HA Rep. 120, BB VII 1.4, 1:17a–b.

25. Johannes Schulze, GstA, Rep. 92, Altenstein, A. Via, Nr. 36, transcribed in Müsebeck 1918, 293–307.

26. Schuckmann to Altenstein, November 24, 1825, GstA, Berlin, I. HA Rep. 120, BB VII 1.4, 1:21–22.

27. Altenstein to Schuckmann, December 28, 1825, GstA, Berlin, I. HA Rep. 120, BB VII 1.4, 1:23; Schuckmann to Altenstein, April 13, 1826, GstA, Berlin, I. HA Rep. 120, BB VII 1.4, 1:24. The 1819 British child labor act established nine as the minimum working age, limited working hours to twelve a day, and prohibited night work for children. The law had little practical impact, however, because its inspection and enforcement mechanism was weak. Nonetheless, it was an important advance on the 1802 Apprentices Act—which applied only to apprentices—in that it represented the first modern attempt at state regulation of the free labor market (Thomas 1948).

28. Frederick William III to Altenstein and Schuckmann, May 12, 1828, GstA, Berlin, I. HA Rep. 120, BB VII 3.1, 85a. See also GstA, Berlin, I. HA Rep. 120, BB VII 1.4, 1:38.

29. Altenstein to Schuckmann, July 4, 1828, GstA, Berlin, I. HA Rep. 120, BB VII 1.4, 1:30a–36a.

30. Schuckmann to Altenstein, January 16, 1829, GstA, Berlin, I. HA Rep. 120, BB VII 1.4, 1:39–46.

31. His only use of a fundamental frame was a brief, passing mention of Lieutenant General Horn's report.

32. Altenstein to Schuckmann, October 28, 1929, GstA, Berlin, I. HA Rep 120, BB VII 1.4, 1:58.

33. For example, he abolished serfdom and made all individual subjects equal under the law (Palmer, Colton, and Kramer 1984, 398–404; Kocka 1990, 16). He increased the political power of the bourgeoisie by opening the civil service and city councils (*Stadträte*) to nonnobles, and allowing the creation of chambers of commerce (*Handelskammern*) and industrial courts (*Handelsgerichte*). He enhanced their economic power by lifting tariffs and trade regulations, and allowing members of all classes to buy up the newly secularized church lands. This latter move created an elite class of landowning capitalists, who retained their status even after Napoléon was defeated and the Rhineland was annexed by Prussia (Boch 1991, 36–37).

34. Solms-Laubach to Hardenberg, June 25, 1818, transcribed in Hoppe, Kuczynski, and Waldmann 1960, 31.

35. Report of Privy Councilor Keller, February 1, 1834, in Hoppe 1958, 75–81. Hoppe's collection of documents was compiled by Marxist historians in the former East Germany and is quite biased. Keller's report is not reproduced in full, and selections seem to have been chosen to make the child labor situation seem as bad as possible, with a tendency to leave out accounts that portray employers in a positive light. I have relied on Dieter Kastner's (2004, 81–96) discussion of Keller's investigation to cover the segments that Hoppe left out.

36. Report of Privy Counsilor Keller, 75, 80.

37. Report of Privy Counsilor Keller, 76–77, 79.

38. Bodelschwingh to A. D. Fallenstein, March 30, 1848, reprinted in Diest 1898, 14–27.

39. Bodelschwingh to the district governments of Düsseldorf, Aachen, and Cologne, March 31, 1835, LHA, Koblenz, Best. 403, Nr. 8082, 1–2.

40. The plan that Bodelschwingh submitted to Altenstein would have required children to have three years of schooling before working and limited the daily working hours of children under age twelve to seven. The requirement that children attend school while working had been dropped in favor of a measure prohibiting them from working while religious instruction was taking place. This shift suggests that Bodelschwingh's primary concern was children's religious

and moral education, not their overall intellectual development. Bodelschwingh to Altenstein, LHA, Koblenz, Best. 403, Nr. 8082, 49–61; see also Bodelschwingh to Altenstein, November 20, 1835, GstA, Berlin, I. HA Rep. 120, BB VII 1.4, 1:62–73.

41. District government of Aachen to Bodelschwingh, September 6, 1835, LHA, Koblenz, Best. 403, Nr. 8082, 25–29; Aachen Handelskammer to Aachen district government, June 16, 1835, LHA, Koblenz, Best. 403, Nr. 8082, 31; Eupen Handelskammer to Aachen district government, July 3, 1835, LHA, Koblenz, Best. 403, Nr. 8082, 33–34.

42. District government of Aachen to Bodelschwingh, September 6, 1835, LHA, Koblenz, Best. 403, Nr. 8082, 25–29; Aachen chamber of commerce to Aachen district government, June 16, 1835, LHA, Koblenz, Best. 403, Nr. 8082, 31.

43. Eupen chamber of commerce to Aachen district government, July 3, 1835, LHA, Koblenz, Best. 403, Nr. 8082, 33–34.

44. Bodelschwingh to Altenstein, November 20, 1835, GstA, Berlin, I. HA Rep. 120, BB VII 1.4, 1:65b–66a.

45. District government of Cologne to Bodelschwingh, November 9, 1835, LHA, Koblenz, Best. 403, Nr. 8082, 43–44.

46. Bodelschwingh to Altenstein and Rother, n.d., LHA, Koblenz, Best. 403, Nr. 8082, 68; Bodelschwingh to Altenstein, n.d., LHA, Koblenz, Best. 403, Nr. 8082, 79.

47. "Aus Barmen," *Der Sprecher* or *Rheinisch-Westphalischer Anzieger*, no. 25, March 29, 1837, LHA, Koblenz, Best. 403, Nr. 8082, 71–74.

48. Bodelschwingh to Altenstein, LHA, Koblenz, Best. 403, Nr. 8082, 79, 81.

49. Minutes of the proceedings of the Fifth Landtag of the Rhineland Province, July 6, 1837, Archiv des Landschaftverbandes Rheinland, Pulheim, Best. Archiv der Provinzialstände, Nr. 278, 486–501; see also Kastner 2004, 124–27. Schuchard's bill included the following provisions: it set the minimum employment age at nine, limited the working hours of children under eighteen to ten per day, granted children ninety minutes of break time in fresh air per day, required them to attend four hours of school per week, and barred them from working at night.

50. This can be gleaned from the Landtag debate transcript, which on page 486 mentions that the committee chair brought a number of documents shared with him by Bodelschwingh to the debate. Furthermore, the committee's proposal combined elements from both Schuchard's and Bodelschwingh's bills, which only could have happened if it had access to Bodelschwingh's law proposal.

51. The Landtag committee's bill would have set the minimum employment age at nine, limited the working hours of children to ten per day, required them to obtain three years of schooling before commencing a job, granted them two hours of break time in fresh air per day, and required them to attend seven hours of schooling per week. It would have also required the state to appoint factory inspectors to carry out the law.

52. Minutes of the proceedings of the Fifth Landtag of the Rhineland Province, 486–501.

53. Minutes of the proceedings of the Fifth Landtag of the Rhineland Province, 486–501; Landtagmarschall to Friedrich Wilhelm III, July 20, 1837, GstA, Berlin, I. HA Rep. 120, BB VII 1.4, 1:112–13. Petition transcribed in Kastner 2004, 285–86.

54. Gutachten of the Landtagskommisar [Bodelschwingh], August 14, 1837, GstA, Berlin, I. HA Rep. 120, BB VII 1.4, 1:113–18.

55. Altenstein to Bodelschwingh, August 20, 1837, LHA, Koblenz, Best. 403, Nr. 8082, 124.

56. Altenstein to Alvensleben, July 5, 1837, GstA, Berlin, I. HA Rep. 120, BB VII 1.4, 1:94–100.

57. Beuth to Altenstein, September 19, 1837, GstA, Berlin, I. HA Rep. 120, BB VII 3.1, 1:101–11; unauthored and undated notes, GstA, Berlin, I. HA Rep. 120, BB VII 3.1, 1:119.

58. Bodelschwingh to the Ministers of Education and the Interior, August 1, 1838, LHA, Koblenz, Best. 403, Nr. 8082, 129–30.

59. In 1837, Rochow enraged liberals when he wrote that critics of the dismissal of seven pro-gressive professors—including the Brothers Grimm—from the University of Göttingen possessed "limited understanding" (*beschränkter Untertanenverstand*) and should refrain from "offering, with ignorant presumptuousness and limited insight, a public opinion about the legitimacy of the decisions of their superiors" (Wipperman 1893, 734).

60. Rochow to Kottwitz, August or September 1838, GstA, Berlin, I. HA Rep. 120, BB VII 3.1, 1:26.

61. Rochow to Altenstein, September 13, 1838, GstA, Berlin, I. HA Rep. 120, BB VII 3.1, 24; Rochow to Altenstein, January 6, 1839, GstA, Berlin, I. HA Rep. 120, BB VII 1.4, 1:134–35. In these missives, Rochow tells Altenstein that the proposed legislation falls primarily under Rochow's jurisdiction and only "secondarily" under Altenstein's, and that Rochow was therefore justified in taking over the initiative.

62. Ministry of the Interior to Bodelschwingh, November 20, 1838, GstA, Berlin, I. HA Rep. 120, BB VII 1.4, 1:119; Rochow to Altenstein, September 13, 1838, GstA, Berlin, I. HA Rep. 120, BB VII 3.1, 24; Rochow to Altenstein, January 6, 1839, GstA, Berlin, I. HA Rep. 120, BB VII 1.4, 1:134–35; Gustav von Rochow, "Reasons for the Law for Regulating the Employment of Young Operative in Manufactures, Contained in the Official Gazette of the Laws for the King-dom of Prussia, No. 2005. Dated the 9th of March, 1839," April 14, 1840, translated in Horner 1840, 98–104.

63. Bodelschwingh to Altenstein, LHA, Koblenz, Best. 403, Nr. 8082, 139–42.

64. For instance, it included the minimum age contained in the Landtag's 1837 petition, borrowed Schuchard's proposal that working children be granted daily outdoor breaks, and incor-porated various provisions that had been recommended by local officials in 1835.

65. Bodelschwingh had proposed granting exceptions to the minimum age and three-year schooling requirements to those children working in factories that had an on-site school. The committee accepted that children working in factories with such a school should not have to attend school for three years before working, but it rejected exceptions to the minimum age because of its health benefits. Hesse, meeting minutes, December 21, 1838, LHA, Koblenz, Best. 403, Nr. 8082, 160.

66. Hesse, meeting minutes, December 21, 1838, LHA, Koblenz, Best. 403, Nr. 8082, 151–72.

67. Altenstein to Rochow, January 15, 1839, GstA, Berlin, I. HA Rep. 120, BB VII 3.1, 58a, 59.

68. Rochow to Altenstein, January 27, 1839, GstA, Berlin, I. HA Rep. 120, BB VII 3.1, 61a; Alvensleben to Rochow, January 25, 1839, GstA, Berlin, I. HA Rep. 120, BB VII 3.1, 62a. See also Rochow to Altenstein, September 13, 1838, GstA, Berlin, I. HA Rep. 120, BB VII 3.1; cabinet meeting minutes, February 5, 1839, GstA, Berlin, I. HA Rep. 120, BB VII 3.1, 69a.

69. At the cabinet meeting to finalize the law, Privy Councillor Keller of the Interior Ministry raised Altenstein's concerns, but the cabinet decided not to address them directly in the law, preferring to include a clause authorizing the ministries to later issue ordinances pertaining to sanitation and public morality if necessary. Cabinet meeting minutes, February 5, 1839, GstA, Berlin, I. HA Rep. 120, BB VII 3.1, 67a–68a, 69b–70a.

70. Cabinet meeting minutes, February 5, 1839, GstA, Berlin, I. HA Rep. 120, BB VII 3.1, 64–71.

71. Rochow to Frederick William III, GstA, Berlin, I. HA Rep. 120, BB VII 3.1, 72–80. See also an English translation of this document in Horner 1840, 98–104.

72. Rochow to Frederick William III, GstA, Berlin, I. HA Rep. 120, BB VII 3.1, 72–77.

73. Germany, Reichskanzler-Amt 1877; Brentano, 1873, 14–15.

74. Altenstein to Schuckmann, July 4, 1828, GstA, Berlin, I. HA Rep. 12, BB VII 1.4, 1:30a–36a; Bodelschwingh to the district governments of Düsseldorf, Aachen, and Cologne, March 31, 1935, LHA, Koblenz, Best. 403, Nr. 8082, 1–2; see also Kastner 2004, 154.

Chapter 3. A Tale of Two Reformers: Success in France, Failure in Belgium

1. This chapter is a revised and updated version of Anderson 2018.

2. Universal male suffrage was introduced in France after the revolution of 1848.

3. Bruno 2010, *Code Administratif de Belgique V2 (1842)*, 314–20.

4. France enacted compulsory schooling in 1882; Belgium did not do so until 1919.

5. The monitorial or Lancastrian system, in which large numbers of pupils were instructed by a single teacher assisted by a small army of student monitors, was viewed as efficient. It relied heavily on recitation, rote learning, highly structured routines, uniformity of expectations, and strict discipline. Though its factorylike approach came under criticism, its proponents believed it would enhance children's life chances in the new industrial economy and contribute to the general social welfare.

6. Belgium, Ministère de l'Intérieur 1848, vol. 1.

7. The sources differ significantly in regard to gender patterns. Although both agree that more than three-quarters of the total workforce was male, the youngest workers were much more likely to be male in the 1848 *Enquête* and more likely to be female in the 1846 Census. This is because the *Enquête* did not capture data on the small craft industry, particularly cottage linen production, which was the sector where young girls were most heavily employed.

8. The 1846 Census found that 2 percent of Belgium's industrial workforce was under age nine, 4.7 percent was nine to eleven years old, and 14.4 percent was twelve to fifteen years old. Calculated from Belgium, Ministère de l'Intérieur 1851, x.

9. Statistics from other sources confirm the large proportion of children and teenagers working in the textile industry. A government survey conducted in Ghent in 1817 found that 277 children under seventeen worked in spinning mills, or some 25 percent of the labor force (de Herdt 2011, 178). Claude Desama (1985, 112) estimates that 19.2 percent of all girls between twelve and fourteen living in Verviers worked in the district's woollen mills.

10. Excerpt from Alban de Villaneuve-Bargemont, *L'Économie politique chrétienne ou recherches sur la nature et les causes du paupérisme en France et en Europe et sur les moyens de le soulager et de le prévenir* (1834), 228–29, in Moody 1953.

11. Villermé 1837; Petition no. 209 from La Société pour l'encouragement de l'Instruction Primaire parnu des Protestant de France a la Chambre des Députés, Chambre des Députés Session de 1839, Archives Nationales, F12–4704, folder "Petitions . . . 1837–1840."

12. Lee Shai Weissbach (1989, 45) characterizes the chambers' attitudes more negatively. According to him, nine chambers were ambivalent toward child labor legislation, ten opposed it, and five supported it. A closer look, however, indicates that many did support more specific regulations of some kind.

13. *Pétition adressé aux deux Chambres et aux Ministres de L'Intérieur, du Commerce et de L'Instruction Publique* from the Société Industrielle de Mulhouse; Petition no. 209 from La Société pour l'encouragement de l'Instruction Primaire parnu des Protestant de France a la Chambre des Députés, Chambre des Députés Session de 1839, Archives Nationales, F12–4704, folder "Petitions . . . 1837–1840."

14. *Annales du Parlement Français, Chambre des Pairs* 1840d, 128–31.

15. *Annales du Parlement Français* 1840a. For an English translation of Dupin's report, see Horner 1840, 42–61. The two Académie des Sciences members were the economist Pellegrino Rossi and the philosopher Cousin. A third committee member, Adrien de Gasparin, was not a member of a learned academy, but had published numerous agriculturist studies.

16. *Annales du Parlement Français* 1840a, 87.

17. *Annales du Parlement Français* 1840a, 80.

18. *Annales du Parlement Français* 1840a, 82–83, 88–89.

19. *Annales du Parlement Français* 1840c, 94.

20. *Annales du Parlement Français* 1840d, 128–31

21. *Annales du Parlement Français* 1840a, 86.

22. *Annales du Parlement Français* 1840c, 90; *Annales du Parlement Français* 1840b, 99.

23. *Annales du Parlement Français* 1840c, 95.

24. *Annales du Parlement Français* 1840c.

25. *Annales du Parlement Français* 1840b,128.

26. *Moniteur Universel*, June 1840, 1292.

27. *Moniteur Universel*, June 1840, 1293.

28. *Moniteur Universel*, June 1840, 1292.

29. *Moniteur Universel*, June 1840, 1294–95.

30. *Moniteur Universel*, June 1840, 1293.

31. *Moniteur Universel*, June 1840, 1294.

32. Ministère de l'Agriculture et de Commerce, June 10, 1840, Circular No. 14, Archives Nationales, F12–4706.

33. *Proces-verbaux des seances de la chambre des deputes 1840,* 331–471.

34. For an English translation of the 1841 child labor law, see Weissbach 1989, 231–34.

35. Belgium, Ministère de l'Intérieur 1848, vol. 1, i–cxcii.

36. Belgium, Ministère de l'Intérieur 1848, ix.

37. Fonds Ducpétiaux, Inventaire definitive, L'Académie royale de Belgique.

38. Fonds Ducpétiaux, Inventaire definitive, L'Académie royale de Belgique.

39. Later, Ducpétiaux explicitly acknowledged Fourier's influence. After the book was published, he sent a copy to Fourier's disciple, Considerant, who had been giving a series of lectures in Brussels. In the attached letter, he credited the Fourierist École Sociétere for his reformist ideas: "I have sown here and there a few views of the future, a few aspirations toward an entirely new order of things. These views and aspirations I owe to the *Ecole Sociétere*. My plan of reform is thus, properly speaking, only a transitional project. Unable to gain acceptance for the heroic remedy, I have had to limit myself to proposing palliatives. . . . But I have never lost sight of the final goal toward which, like you, I am aiming" (quoted in Beecher 2001, 115).

40. Fonds Ducpétiaux, Inventaire definitive, L'Académie royale de Belgique. These included the aforementioned Villaneuve-Bargemont as well as the theologian and political theorist La Mennais.

41. Belgium, Ministère de l'Intérieur 1848, cxcii–cci.

42. Ducpétiaux and Visschers were the commission's recorders. Visschers was, second only to Ducpétiaux, Belgium's leading social welfare policy expert and reformer. His particular interests were in criminal justice and penitentiary reform (including abolition of the death penalty), public education, and pacifism (Lubelski-Bernard 1985).

43. Belgium, Ministère de l'Intérieur 1848, cxviii.

44. Belgium, Ministère de l'Intérieur 1848, cxxii.

45. Belgium, Ministère de l'Intérieur 1848, cxcii–cxcv.

46. Archives Générales du Royaume-Algemeen Rijksarchief (AGR-ARA), Liège, Archives de la Chambre de Commerce de Verviers, O.1/2, 4, Procès verbaux des séances de la Chambre, 1848–50.

47. For the Ostende chamber, see AGR-ARA, Bruges, Archief Kamer van Koophandel Oostende, TBO 116, 151: Register van de processen verbaal der zittingen van de Kamer van 14 september 1840 tot 14 Juli 1851. For the Aalst chamber, see AGR-ARA, Ghent, Archief Kamer van Koophandel Aalst, B47, 1: Registre des procès verbaux des séances 1842–71, Séance du 31 septembre 1849. For the Dendermonde chamber, see AGR-ARA, Ghent, Archief Kamer van Koophandel Dendermonde, B48, 17: Registre de correspondance 1849, nr. 74, 12 octobre 1849, Police des manufactures, fabriques, usines et travail des enfants. For the Brussels chamber, see

AGR-ARA, Brussels, 2 Joseph Cuvelier, T563, 6: Registre aux procès-verbaux du 15 septembre 1840 au 31 décembre 1851, Assemblée du 3 novembre 1849. For the Ieper and Diksmuide chambers, see AGR-ARA, Bruges, Archief Kamer van Koophandel Ieper and Diksmuide, TBO 116, 211: Register van processen verbaal van kamervergaderingen van 3 januari 1847 tot 19 december 1852. For the Kortrijk chamber, see AGR-ARA, Kortrijk, Archief Kamer van Koophandel Kortrijk, 205, 6: Registre aux procès-verbaux et autres documents à l'appui du 24 août 1845 au 10 septembre 1851. For the Leuven chamber, see AGR-ARA, Leuven, Archief Kamer van Koophandel Leuven, 355, 4: register met de processen verbaal van 1847 tot en met 1851, AGR-ARA Leuven, Archief Kamer van Koophandel Leuven, 355, 59: register met de kopies van de correspondentie 1848–1850. For the Tournai chamber, see AGR-ARA Tournai, Archives de la Chambre de Commerce de Tournai, 04/01, 838: Registre aux procès-verbaux de la Chambre du 13 mai 1848 au 15 mars 1858. For the Bruges chamber, see AGR-ARA, Bruges, Archief Kamer van Koophandel Brugge, TBO 116, 88: Register met briefwisseling van 1844 tot 1852. For the Verviers chamber, see AGR-ARA, Liège, Archives de la Chambre de Commerce de Verviers, O 1/2, 4. Procès verbaux des séances de la Chambre, 1848–1850. For the Liège chamber, see Liège Chamber of Commerce. 1849. *Avis de la Chambre de Commerce de Liège sur le projet de loi relatif à la condition des classes ouvrières et le travail des enfants.* In: Liège Chamber of Commerce 1860.

48. With the exception of the Liège chamber's response, these responses were all found after the publication of Anderson 2018. They reveal that the chambers were not actually unanimous in their opposition, as previously reported in Gubin and Lefèvre 1985; Loriaux 2000.

49. A law that Ducpétiaux drafted, mandating the cellular system for all Belgian prisons, was passed in 1870 shortly after his death.

50. This fatal conflation of child labor regulation with infringements on religious freedom was avoided in Catholic France, where religion was freely taught in both congregational and lay schools (with a parental option to opt out in the latter), and in Prussia, where Protestant and Catholic children were educated separately, and religion was taught in the public schools. Church-state conflict in Belgium was eventually resolved in the church's favor; to this day, primary schooling is handled mainly by the church, but includes generous funding from the state (Busemeyer and Nikolai 2010).

51. Programma en statuten van de Belgische Werkerspartij, August 15–16, 1885, accessed June 5, 2017, https://www.marxists.org/nederlands/documenten/1886/1886program_bwp.htm.

Chapter 4. Defending Democracy: Cultural Consensus and Child Labor Reform in Massachusetts

1. Massachusetts Board of Education 1838–39, 302. The returns do not indicate whether this figure includes private school enrollment.

2. Massachusetts Board of Education 1838–39, 50, 244, vii.

3. Pestalozzi (1746–1827) was a Swiss pedagogue who pioneered a child-centered, individualized teaching method that stressed active learning along with the integration of intellectual, physical, and moral training. Lancaster (1778–1838) was an English public education reformer. His Lancastrian system, in which large classes were taught by a single teacher with the help of student monitors, was modeled on the factory system and was widely adopted in England in the early nineteenth century. It relied heavily on recitation, rote learning, highly structured routines, uniformity of expectations, and strict discipline.

4. Massachusetts, Constable of the Commonwealth 1868, 23.

5. Massachusetts Board of Education 1838–39, 50.

6. No official child labor statistics for Massachusetts for this period exist. The figures that do are rough and inconsistent. According to the New England Association of Farmers, Mechanics, and Other Workingmen, two-fifths of the workers in manufactories in Massachusetts, New Hampshire,

and Rhode Island were under sixteen in 1832 (Commons et al. 1910, 195–96). Other counts present a less dire picture. Economists Claudia Goldin and Kenneth Sokoloff (1982) estimate that in 1832, 9.3 percent of industrial workers in Massachusetts were "boys" of unspecified age. According to a contemporary observer, about 10 percent of the workers at the cotton and woolen mills of Fall River (at that time, Troy) were under fifteen in 1827 (White [1836] 2010, 128). In other places, such as Waltham, children under fourteen were reportedly not hired at all (Persons 1971, 6)

7. House of Representatives Education Committee report, March 17, 1836, passed acts, Acts of 1836, c. 245, Act to Provide for the Better Instruction of Youth Employed in Manufacturing Establishments, approved April 16, 1836, SC1/series 229, Massachusetts State Archives.

8. House of Representatives Education Committee report.

9. House of Representatives Education Committee report.

10. Legislative draft, April 13, 1836, passed acts, Acts of 1836, c. 245, Act to Provide for the Better Instruction of Youth Employed in Manufacturing Establishments, approved April 16, 1836, SC1/series 229, Massachusetts State Archives; *Massachusetts House Journal*, April 14, 1836, Massachusetts State Archives; *Massachusetts Senate Journal*, April 14, 1836, Massachusetts State Archives.

11. Act to Provide for the Better Instruction of Youth Employed in Manufacturing Establishments, approved April 16, 1836, Massachusetts Acts and Resolves, 1836, c. 245, 950–51.

12. "Deaths," *British Friend* 16, no. 2 (February 1, 1858): 52–53.

13. *Massachusetts House Journal*, 1869, 457, 539.

14. Petition of Battelle, Wilbur, and Gunn, January 19, 1842, passed acts, Acts of 1842, c. 60, Act concerning the Employment of Children in Manufacturing Establishments, approved March 3, 1842, SC1/series 229, Massachusetts State Archives.

15. Petition of Battelle, Wilbur, and Gunn.

16. Act concerning the Employment of Children in Manufacturing Establishments, approved March 3, 1842, Massachusetts Acts and Resolves, 1842, c. 60, Massachusetts State Archives, 517–18.

17. I could find no newspaper coverage of either bill, with the exception of a few newspapers that simply reported the contents of the acts once passed.

Chapter 5. Restoring Solidarity and Domesticity: Conciliatory Factory Inspection in Imperial Germany

1. *Gewerbeordnung für den Norddeutschen Bund* 1869, §128. The major difference between the North German Gewerbeordnung and the earlier Prussian child labor law was that it no longer required a certain amount of education before children could begin a job.

2. The notion that childhood ended at age fourteen was historically specific and culturally constructed. In the *Allgemeines Landrecht für die Preussischen Staaten* (1794), childhood was defined as the period from birth to age seven. The conceptual duration of childhood began to expand after compulsory schooling was introduced in Prussia (Quandt 1978).

3. *Gewerbeordnung für den Norddeutschen Bund* 1869, §129, §133.

4. *Gewerbeordnung für den Norddeutschen Bund* 1869, §134, §107. The law left the specification of safety measures up to the local authorities. Since the 1850s, local governments had been issuing various safety requirements on an uncoordinated and ad hoc basis. See Ayass 1996, 213–17.

5. His personal power was further consolidated in 1877 and 1878, when he reorganized the Reich administration to reduce communication across departments (Lerman 2004, 163–65).

6. For a pithy overview of the parties and their basic platforms, see Craig 1978, 62–64. For a more comprehensive discussion, see Ritter 1973.

7. Deutsches Historisches Institut, n.d.

8. Deutsches Historisches Institut, n.d.

9. Deutsches Historisches Institut, n.d.

10. Deutsches Historisches Institut, n.d.

11. In 1877, for example, Arnold Lohren, a mill owner and cofounder of the Association of German Industrialists, published a widely read pamphlet in which he attacked worker protections, the factory inspectorate, and the Ministry of Commerce (Machtan 1995, 480). On the subject of praise, see petition from the Mönchengladbach Handelskammer to the Prussian minister of commerce Dr. Heinrich Achenbach, January 31, 1874, transcribed in Ayass 1996, 199.

12. In 1872, for example, the Hörder Mining and Iron Works Association petitioned the Prussian interior minister for a repeal of the prohibition on night work for teenage workers. Similarly, the Mönchengladbach Handelskammer petitioned the Prussian commerce minister for a repeal of *all* restrictions on teenage workers. See petition from the Hoerder Mining and Iron Works Association to the Prussian minister of the interior Friedrich von Eulenburg, November 30, 1872, transcribed in Ayass 1996, 146–47; petition from the Mönchengladbach Handelskammer to the Prussian minister of commerce Dr. Heinrich Achenbach, January 31, 1874, transcribed in Ayass 1996, 199.

13. Marx was a qualified supporter of child labor in factories. In his 1866 instructions to the delegates to the International Workingmen's Association congress, he wrote, "We view the tendency of modern industry to include children and young people of both sexes in social production to be progressive, beneficial and lawful, even though the way and means through which this tendency is realized under capitalism is abominable." Every child age nine and older should work, Marx (2019, 1023–43) argued, but only for a few hours a day, and only in tasks that were intellectually, physically, and technically educational.

14. Program of the Social Democratic Workers' Party, August 9, 1869, transcribed in Ayass 1996, 50–51.

15. Program of the German Socialist Workers' Party, May 25, 1875, transcribed in Ayass 1996, 283–84.

16. Protocol of the fourth Association of German Labor Unions, October 7, 1867, transcribed in Ayass 1996, 13.

17. Call of the chairman of the German Tobacco Workers' Union, Friedrich Wilhelm Fritzsche, with a proposed worker protection law, December 13, 1873, transcribed in Ayass 1996, 190–94.

18. Wilhelm Emmanuel von Ketteler, excerpt from "Die Arbeiterbewegung und ihr Streben im Verhaeltnis zur Religion und Sittlichkeit" (speech delivered before several thousand workers in the Liebfrauenheide near Offenbach, July 25, 1869), transcribed in Heitzer 1991, 30–34.

19. The International Workingmen's Association (1864–76), also known as the First International, was an international organization aimed at uniting a variety of socialist, communist, and anarchist political groups and trade unions. Despite—or perhaps because of—the strong economy, socialist agitation and protest activity had intensified dramatically in 1869 and 1870 (Tilly 1980, 156–57). Strikes were also becoming more common—with a total of twenty-two strikes and more than ten thousand participants in the month of October 1871 alone (Ayass 1996, 80n5). In 1873, this activity was suppressed by a law against breach of contract that punished workers for participating in strikes.

20. Petition of Pastor Ernst Muehe to the Reichstag, October 31, 1871, transcribed in Ayass 1996, 80–82.

21. Ayass 1996, 82n1.

22. Petition from Pastor Wilhelm Quistorp to the Reichstag, February 20, 1872, transcribed in Ayass 1996, 82–84.

23. Memo from the Prussian foreign minister and German chancellor Otto von Bismarck to the Prussian commerce minister Heinrich Graf von Itzenplitz, November 17, 1871, transcribed in Ayass 1996, 250.

24. Memorandum re: the Prussian-Austrian conference on the social question, December 15, 1872, transcribed in Ayass 1996, 380–431.

25. Memorandum re: the Prussian-Austrian Conference on the social question, 383–85, 413, 417.

26. Memorandum re: the Prussian-Austrian conference on the social question, 97n1.

27. Report of the Berlin chief of police Willibald Wolf von Wolffsburg to the Prussian minister of commerce Heinrich Graf von Itzenpliz, August 28, 1872, transcribed in Ayass 1996, 119.

28. Denkschrift of Theodor Lohmann for the Prussian minister of commerce Heinrich Graf von Itzenplitz, January 2, 1873, transcribed in Ayass 1996, 151–62.

29. Communication of the president of the Reich Chancellery Rudolf Delbrück to the Bundesrat, July 5, 1873, transcribed in Ayass 1996, 180–83.

30. Germany, Reichskanzler-Amt 1877, 123, 170–75.

31. Germany, Reichskanzler-Amt 1877, 123, 170–75.

32. 1866 annual report of Factory Inspector Heinrich Adolf Junkermann to the Düsseldorf government, February 10, 1867, transcribed in Ayass 1996, 1; 1867 annual report of Factory Inspector Heinrich Adolf Junkermann to the Düsseldorf government, February 10, 1867, transcribed in Ayass 1996, 27.

33. Report of the Düsseldorf government to the Prussian minister of commerce Dr. Heinrich Achenbach, January 25, 1875, transcribed in Ayass 1996, 271.

34. See, for example, petition from the Mönchengladbach Handelskammer to the Prussian minister of commerce Dr. Heinrich Achenbach, 199–200.

35. See, for example, Brentano 1873, 14–15. In his report, Brentano noted that several Saxon Handelskammern had called for the regulation of child labor in smaller workshops and homes because they wanted to put an end to these businesses' competitive advantage over factories. See also *Votum* of the Prussian Minister of Commerce Heinrich Graf von Itzenplitz for the Prussian Ministry of State, March 12, 1873, transcribed in Ayass 1996, 163–69. In this document, Itzenplitz recommended extending child labor regulations to all paid work not being carried out in the children's homes. This suggestion was dismissed by Reich Chancellery president Rudolf Delbrück as "totally dubious," and did not come up again in official discussions of the child labor issue in the 1870s.

36. Germany, Reichskanzler-Amt 1877.

37. Letter from Theodor Lohmann to the Lohmann/Winkel family, January 28, 1877, transcribed in Lohmann and Machtan 1995, 464–65.

38. Letter from Theodor Lohmann to Ernst Wyneken, October 28, 1877, transcribed in Lohmann and Machtan 1995, 476.

39. Letter from Theodor Lohmann to the Lohmann/Winkel family, March 12, 1873, transcribed in Lohmann and Machtan 1995, 362–63.

40. Letter from Theodor Lohmann to Ernst Wyneken, May 19, 1872, transcribed in Lohmann and Machtan 1995, 337.

41. Letter from Theodor Lohmann to the Lohmann/Winkel family, February 25, 1877, transcribed in Lohmann and Machtan 1995, 465–66; Deutsches Historisches Institut, n.d.

42. Düsseldorf and Aachen (both in the Rhineland), and Arnsberg (Westphalia).

43. Letter from the Badenese minister of commerce Ludwig Turban to the government of Düsseldorf, December 17, 1872, transcribed in Ayass 1996, 148.

44. Protocol of a conference of Prussian factory inspectors, October 20, 1876, transcribed in Ayass 1996, 377–84.

45. Letter from the Prussian commerce minister Dr. Heinrich Achenbach to Imperial Chancellor Otto von Bismarck, transcribed in Ayass 1996, 220–22.

46. Letter from Theodor Lohmann to Rudolf Friedrichs, April 6, 1874, transcribed in Lohmann and Machtan 1995, 396.

47. Denkschrift of Theodor Lohmann for the Prussian minister of commerce Heinrich Graf von Itzenplitz, January 2, 1873, transcribed in Ayass 1996, 151–62.

48. Votum of the Prussian commerce minister Count Heinrich von Itzenplitz for the Prussian Ministry of State, March 12, 1873, transcribed in Ayass 1996, 163–73; Votum of the Prussian finance minister Otto Camphausen for the Prussian Ministry of State, April 9, 1873, transcribed in Ayass 1996, 163–73; communication of the president of the Reich Chancellery Rudolf Delbrück to the Prussian Ministry of State, April 22, 1873, transcribed in Ayass 1996, 163–73.

49. Denkschrift of Theodor Lohmann for the Prussian minister of commerce Dr. Heinrich Achenbach, March 10, 1876, transcribed in Ayass 1996, 299–310.

50. Actually, he characterized Delbrück's support as the imperial chancellor's, on the assumption that as Bismarck's agent, Delbrück acted with the latter's blessing. Bismarck himself expressed support for the employment of additional inspectors along the lines of the British model in 1868. See Communication of the Prussian prime minister Count Otto von Bismarck to the Prussian minister of commerce Count Heinrich von Itzenplitz, February 2, 1868, transcribed in Ayass 1996, 31–33.

51. Denkschrift of Theodor Lohmann for the Prussian minister of commerce Dr. Heinrich Achenbach, March 10, 1876, transcribed in Ayass 1996, 309.

52. Directive from the Prussian minister of commerce Heinrich Graf von Itzenplitz to the district governments, landdrosts, and Berlin chief of police, April 27, 1872, transcribed in Ayass 1996, 86–88.

53. Report of the government of Düsseldorf to the Prussian minister of commerce Heinrich Graf von Itzenplitz, August 19, 1872, transcribed in Ayass 1996, 102–13. For a similar line of argument, see the report from the mayor of Barmen, August Bredt, to the government of Düsseldorf, July 18, 1872, transcribed in Ayass 1996, 93–97.

54. Report of the government of Aachen to the Prussian minister of commerce Heinrich Graf von Itzenplitz, August 25, 1872, transcribed in Ayass 1996, 114–19. For a similar line of argument, see report of the Barmen chamber of commerce to the mayor of Barmen, August Bredt, May 30, 1872, cited in Ayass 1996, 89–91. See also report of the Berlin police chief Guido von Madai to the Prussian minister of commerce Heinrich Graf von Itzenplitz, August 8, 1872, transcribed in Ayass 1996, 100–101.

55. Denkschrift of Theodor Lohmann for the Prussian minister of commerce Heinrich Graf von Itzenplitz, January 2, 1873, transcribed in Ayass 1996, 151–62.

56. Petition of the German Association of Glass Industrialists to the Bundesrat, November 5, 1874, transcribed in Ayass 1996, 240–48.

57. Circular directive of the Prussian minister of commerce Dr. Heinrich Achenbach to the governments in Danzig, Marienwerder, Koeslin, Potsdam, Frankfurt/O, Breslau, Liegnitz, Oppeln, Posen, Schleswig, Kassel, Minden, Arnsberg, Aachen, Cologne, Trier, Hannover, Hildesheim, and Stade, April 23, 1875, transcribed in Ayass 1996, 281–83.

58. Denkschrift of Theodor Lohmann for the Prussian minister of commerce Dr. Heinrich Achenbach, March 10, 1876, transcribed in Ayass 1996, 299–310.

59. Protocol of a conference of Prussian factory inspectors, October 20, 1876, transcribed in Ayass 1996, 378.

60. Denkschrift of Theodor Lohmann for the Prussian minister of commerce Dr. Heinrich Achenbach, March 10, 1876, transcribed in Ayass 1996, 299–310.

61. Denkschrift of Theodor Lohmann for the Prussian minister of commerce Dr. Heinrich Achenbach, March 10, 1876, transcribed in Ayass 1996, 304, 306.

62. Letter from the Prussian minister of commerce Dr. Heinrich Achenbach to the Imperial Chancellor Otto von Bismarck, April 21, 1876, transcribed in Ayass 1996, 315–29.

63. Votum from Prussian minister of commerce Dr. Heinrich Achenbach for the Ministry of State with Denkschrift and legislative proposal, June 30, 1876, transcribed in Ayass 1996, 333–60.

64. These powers included requiring that work spaces, machines, and equipment be maintained in such a way as to protect the health and safety of workers; that workplaces contain enough light and clean air; and that employers report injury-causing accidents to the local authorities.

65. Protocol of a conference of Alsace-Lorraine Industrialists, September 22, 1876, transcribed in Ayass 1996, 363–73.

66. Votum from Prussian minister of commerce Dr. Heinrich Achenbach for the Ministry of State with Denkschrift and legislative proposal, June 30, 1876, transcribed in Ayass 1996, 340–41.

67. Letter from Legation Secretary Herbert Graf von Bismarck to the privy government councillor in the Prussian Ministry of State, Christoph Teidemann, September 15, 1876, transcribed in Ayass 1996, 360–61; Votum of Prussian prime minister Otto von Bismarck for the Ministry of State, September 30, 1876, transcribed in Ayass 1996, 373–76.

68. Letter from Theodor Lohmann to Ernst Wyneken, November 5, 1876, transcribed in Lohmann and Machtan 1995, 459.

69. Votum of the Prussian minister of commerce Dr. Heinrich Achenbach for the Ministry of State, November 24, 1876, transcribed in Ayass 1996, 395–407. This memo was written by Lohmann, and edited and signed by Achenbach.

70. Proposal of Privy Councilor Arnold Nieberding for a Votum of Reich Chancellery president Karl Hofmann for the Prussian Ministry of State, December 18, 1876, transcribed in Ayass 1996, 407–10.

71. Like Lohmann's bill, Nieberding's proposed regulations applied to factories, mines, and quarries—but also to smaller workshops using steam power. Other similarities included a minimum employment age of twelve without exceptions; a limitation of six daily working hours for children between twelve and fourteen, and ten for those between fourteen and sixteen; and provisions for factory inspection. In addition, it empowered the Bundesrat to ban children from certain dangerous workplaces or occupations altogether, and grant exceptions to the rules for certain industries where necessary. Unlike the Lohmann plan, however, Nieberding's bill did not require districts to appoint factory inspectors. It also did not require children to demonstrate a certain level of educational attainment before working and made no mention of continuation schools. It also did not include any special new regulations for girls or women. Finally, it went so far as to ban factory work on Sundays and holidays for all workers—not just women and girls, as Lohmann had suggested. First draft of a proposal for a factory law, April 30, 1877, transcribed in Ayass 1996, 425–30.

72. First draft of a proposal for a factory law; see also notes of Privy Councilor Theodor Lohmann regarding directives of the Prussian commerce minister Dr. Heinrich Achenbach, May 2, 1877, transcribed in Ayass 1996, 431–32.

73. Second draft of a proposal for a factory law, June 1, 1877, transcribed in Ayass 1996, 439–47.

74. Letter from Reich Chancellery president Karl Hofmann to Government Assessor Friedrich von Kurowski, transcribed in Ayass 1996, 453.

75. Germany, Reichstag 1877, 22 Session, April 16, 3rd Legislative Period, 1st Session.

76. Proposal of Reichstag deputy Count Ferdinand von Galen and colleagues to the Reichstag, transcribed in Ayass 1996, 411–13.

77. Proposal of Reichstag deputies August Bebel, Friedrich Wilhelm Fritzche, and colleagues to the Reichstag, with bill, transcribed in Ayass 1996, 414–19.

78. Germany, Reichstag 1877, 533.

79. Germany, Reichstag 1877, 496, 501–4, 510.

80. Germany, Reichstag 1877, 511–17.

81. Protocol of the second session of the IX. Reichstag Commission, April 24, 1877, transcribed in Ayass 1996, 420–22.

82. Protocol of the second session of the IX. Reichstag Commission, 450n1.

83. Letter from Reich Chancellery president Karl Hofmann to Friedrich von Kurowski, July 24, 1877, transcribed in Ayass 1996, 452–53, 453n12. Kurowski was a close friend and adviser of Bismarck's, and was with him in Pomerania at the time.

84. See marginalia in letter from Reich Chancellery president Karl Hofmann to Government Assessor Friedrich von Kurowski with three legislative proposals and two Denkschriften, July 30, 1877, transcribed in Ayass 1996, 455–72.

85. Letter from Friedrich von Kurowski to Reich Chancellery president Karl Hofmann, August 1, 1877, transcribed in Ayass 1996, 473–74.

86. Letter from Reich Chancellery president Karl Hofmann to Government Assessor Friedrich von Kurowski, with Denkschrift, August 3, 1877, transcribed in Ayass 1996, 474–78.

87. Decree of Imperial Chancellor Otto von Bismarck to the president of the Reich Chancellery, Karl Hofmann, August 5, 1877, transcribed in Ayass 1996, 479.

88. Decree of Imperial Chancellor Otto von Bismarck to Reich Chancellery president Karl Hofmann, 482.

89. Letter from Prussian prime minister Otto von Bismarck to Minister of Commerce Dr. Heinrich Achenbach, August 10, 1877, transcribed in Ayass 1996, 485.

90. Letter from Theodor Lohmann to the Lohmann/Winkel family, August 26, 1877, transcribed in Lohmann and Machtan 1995, 471.

91. Report from Reich Chancellery president Karl Hofmann to Imperial Chancellor Otto von Bismarck, August 27, 1877, transcribed in Ayass 1996, 499–510.

92. Draft of a decree of Imperial Chancellor Otto von Bismarck to Reich Chancellery president Karl Hofmann, September 14, 1877, transcribed in Ayass 1996, 510–11.

93. Statement from Reich Chancellery president Karl Hofmann, September 24, 1877, transcribed in Ayass 1996, 512–13.

94. Votum of Reich Chancellery president Karl Hofmann for the Prussian Ministry of State with legislative proposal, October 20, 1877, transcribed in Ayass 1996, 539–44; Votum of Reich Chancellery president Karl Hofmann for the Prussian Ministry of State, November 20, 1877, transcribed in Ayass 1996, 555–58.

95. Votum of Prussian minister of commerce Dr. Heinrich Achenbach for the Ministry of State, November 4, 1877, transcribed in Ayass 1996, 548–50; letter from Privy Councilor Christoph Tiedemann to Reich Chancellery president Karl Hofmann, November 20, 1877, transcribed in Ayass 1996, 554–55; session protocol of the Prussian Ministry of State, November 29, 1877, transcribed in Ayass 1996, 558–61.

96. Letter from Theodor Lohmann to Rudolf Friedrichs, December 3, 1877, transcribed in Lohmann and Machtan 1995, 479.

97. Letter from Theodor Lohmann to Rudolf Friedrichs.

98. Theodor Lohmann, "Noch Einmal die Gewerbe-Ornungs-Vorlage," *Deutsche Reichs-Post*, no. 64, March 16, 1878, transcribed in Lohmann and Machtan 1995, 668–69.

99. Theodor Lohmann, *Deutsche Reichs-Post*, no. 61, March 13, 1878, transcribed in Lohmann and Machtan 1995, 664.

100. Theodor Lohmann, *Deutsche Reichs-Post*, no. 63, March 14, 1878, transcribed in Lohmann and Machtan 1995, 667.

101. Letter from Theodor Lohmann to Ernst Wyneken, March 6, 1878, transcribed in Lohmann and Machtan 1995, 485–86. Presumably, Lohmann meant this as a joke and was not actually planning to bribe Hertling.

102. Report of the IX. Commission of the Reichstag, April 11, 1878, transcribed in Ayass 1996, 576.

103. Letter from Theodor Lohmann to Ernst Wyneken, April 14, 1878, transcribed in Lohmann and Machtan 1995, 487; report of the IX. Commission of the Reichstag, transcribed in Ayass 1996, 579, 600n8.

104. Letter from Theodor Lohmann to Ernst Wyneken, April 14, 1878, transcribed in Lohmann and Machtan 1995, 486–89.

105. "Die dritte Beratung der Gewerbeordnungsnovelle," *Der Gewerkverein*, no. 21, May 24, 1878, transcribed in Ayass 1996, 594.

106. Report of the president of the Imperial Chancellery, Karl Hofmann, to the Imperial Chancellor, Otto von Bismarck, May 27, 1878, transcribed in Ayass 1996, 595–96.

107. Letter from Prussian commerce minister Albert Maybach to the president of the Reich Chancellery, Karl Hofmann, June 4, 1878, transcribed in Ayass 1996, 598.

108. Letter of the president of the Reich Chancellery, Karl Hofmann, to the Privy Counselor Christoph Tiedemann, June 28, 1878, transcribed in Ayass 1996, 603.

109. Proceedings of the Bundesrat, July 4, 1878, transcribed in Ayass 1996, 604.

110. Law pertaining to revisions to the Gewerbeordung, July 17, 1878, transcribed in Ayass 1996, 610. For all the new provisions pertaining to child and female labor and to factory inspection, see Ayass 1996, 605–11.

111. Letter from the Prussian commerce minister Albert Maybach to the vice president of the Ministry of State Count Otto zu Stolberg-Wernigerode, September 11, 1878, transcribed in Ayass 1996, 621–22.

112. Votum of the Prussian commerce minister Albert Maybach for the Ministry of State, transcribed in Ayass 1996, 634; letter from Privy Councilor Christoph Tiedemann to Reich Chancellery president Karl Hofmann, November 18, 1878, transcribed in Ayass 1996, 645–46.

Chapter 6. Appeasing Labor, Protecting Capital: Conciliatory Factory Inspection in Massachusetts

1. "The Report in Detail," *Boston Daily Globe*, August 13, 1874, 1.

2. Not only was Massachusetts the first state in the country to institute a factory inspectorate. In 1863, it was the first to create a state board of charity; in 1869, the first to establish a state Bureau of Labor Statistics; and the first, also in 1869, to appoint a board of health. It was the second, after New York, to enact a civil service law to tackle political patronage, promote merit-based appointments, and protect incumbents from politically motivated dismissal (Miller 2009).

3. Massachusetts, Bureau of Statistics of Labor 1873, 251.

4. Massachusetts, Bureau of Statistics of Labor 1870, 111–15; Massachusetts, Bureau of Statistics of Labor 1871, 477–78, 480.

5. US Census 1998.

6. Massachusetts, Constable of the Commonwealth 1868, 0.

7. Massachusetts, Bureau of Statistics of Labor 1871, 474.

8. Massachusetts, Constable of the Commonwealth 1868, 18–19.

9. Massachusetts, Bureau of Statistics of Labor 1873, 386.

10. Massachusetts, Bureau of Statistics of Labor 1872, 468.

11. Massachusetts, Special Commission on the Hours of Labor 1866, 5–7.

12. This age minimum was not raised until 1888, when it was changed to thirteen.

13. An Act in Relation to the Employment of Children in Manufacturing Establishments, Massachusetts Acts and Resolves, Acts of 1866, c. 273, 253–54.

14. Massachusetts, Special Commission on the Hours of Labor 1867.

15. Massachusetts, Special Commission on the Hours of Labor 1867, 6.

16. An Act in Relation to the Schooling and Hours of Labor of Children Employed in Manufacturing and Mechanical Establishments, Massachusetts Acts and Resolves, Acts of 1867, c. 285, 683–84.

17. An Act in Relation to the Employment of Persons under Eighteen Years of Age in Manufacturing Establishments, House Document No. 162, 1867.

18. An Act to Establish a Better System of Police, House Document No. 442, 1871; An Act for the Repeal of the State Police, House Document No. 442, 1871.

19. Newspaper Clippings, vol. 2, Henry Kemble Oliver Papers; Jesse H. Jones, "Henry Kemble Oliver," transcribed in Bureau of Statistics of Labor 1866.

20. "Statement of the Steps Taken by Which Gen. H.K. Oliver Was Forced Out of His Place as Superintendent of the Atlantic Cotton Mill, Lawrence, as Related to Me by the Mr. C.K. Pillsbury," Memoirs, 1861–86, vol. 4, Henry Kemble Oliver Papers.

21. Massachusetts, Constable of the Commonwealth 1869, 14–15.

22. Massachusetts, Constable of the Commonwealth 1868, 37–38.

23. Massachusetts, Constable of the Commonwealth 1869, 26.

24. An Act Concerning the Employment of Children in Manufacturing and Mechanical Establishments. Massachusetts House Document No. 295, 1868.

25. Massachusetts, Special Commission on the Hours of Labor 1866, 49. The bureau was created under Chapter 102, Resolves of 1869.

26. Massachusetts, Constable of the Commonwealth 1870; Massachusetts, Constable of the Commonwealth 1871, 42–44.

27. Massachusetts, Constable of the Commonwealth 1871, 42.

28. Massachusetts, Special Commission on the Hours of Labor 1867, 21.

29. Massachusetts, Constable of the Commonwealth 1869, 13.

30. Massachusetts, Bureau of Statistics of Labor 1873, 7–9.

31. Massachusetts, Bureau of Statistics of Labor 1873, 500.

32. Massachusetts, Bureau of Statistics of Labor 1871, 136, 197, 458–59.

33. Newspaper Clippings, Henry Kemble Oliver Papers, 2:24.

34. Newspaper Clippings, Henry Kemble Oliver Papers, 1:136, 1:159.

35. Massachusetts, Bureau of Statistics of Labor 1873, 8–17.

36. Massachusetts, Bureau of Statistics of Labor 1873; Newspaper Clippings, Henry Kemble Oliver Papers, 2:22–23.

37. Newspaper Clippings, Henry Kemble Oliver Papers, 1:136.

38. Massachusetts, Bureau of Statistics of Labor 1877, vi–vii.

39. Massachusetts, Bureau of Statistics of Labor 1875, part III, 180; part I, 61–63; part III, 141.

40. Massachusetts, Bureau of Statistics of Labor 1875, part III, 145.

41. Massachusetts, Bureau of Statistics of Labor 1875, part III, 186–87, 185.

42. "George E. McNeill, Friend of Labor," *Cambridge Chronicle*, May 26, 1906, 10.

43. McNeill's (1875, 74–75) proposal called for a vast expansion of these types of regulated employments, raising the minimum working age to twelve, requiring school attendance for young people up to the age of fifteen (eighteen if they had failed to graduate grammar school), and reducing the hours of labor for persons under eighteen to eight per day. It also called for the widespread adoption of the half-time system.

44. *Massachusetts Senate Journal*, 1875, 31.

45. "Our Factory Children," *Boston Daily Globe*, January 13, 1875, 4.

46. "The Report in Detail," *Boston Daily Globe*, August 13, 1874, 1.

47. *Address of His Excellency William Gaston, to the Two Branches of the Legislature of Massachusetts, January 7, 1875*, Massachusetts Senate Document No. 1, 1875.

48. *Massachusetts House Journal*, 1875, 14, 21.

49. *Massachusetts House Journal*, 1875, 129–30.

50. Petition of the Christian Labor Union, Jesse H. Jones, president, n.d., Senate unpassed legislation, 1875 miscellaneous, bill relating to the employment of children and regulations concerning them, SC1/series 231, Massachusetts State Archives.

51. "Boston Eight Hour League," *Boston Daily Advertiser*, June 1, 1876, 4.

52. *Massachusetts House Journal*, 1876, 23, 29, 37, 108, 198, 281.

53. Report of the Committee on the Bureau of Statistics, n.d., passed acts, Acts of 1876, c. 216, Act in Relation to the Inspection of Factories and Public Buildings, and for Other Purposes, approved April 28, 1876, SC1/series 229, Massachusetts State Archives.

54. Miscellaneous petitions, passed acts, Acts of 1876, c. 216, Act in Relation to the Inspection of Factories and Public Buildings, and for Other Purposes, approved April 28, 1876, SC1/series 229, Massachusetts State Archives.

55. Petition of Philip Murry and others, n.d., passed acts, Acts of 1876, c. 216, Act in Relation to the Inspection of Factories and Public Buildings, and for Other Purposes, approved April 28, 1876, SC1/series 229, Massachusetts State Archives.

56. Petition of citizens of Fall River and New Bedford, April 4, 1876, passed acts, Acts of 1876, c. 216, Act in Relation to the Inspection of Factories and Public Buildings, and for Other Purposes, approved April 28, 1876, SC1/series 229, Massachusetts State Archives.

57. *Massachusetts Senate Journal*, 1876, 241.

58. Legislative draft, n.d., passed acts, Acts of 1876, c. 216, Act in Relation to the Inspection of Factories and Public Buildings, and for Other Purposes, approved April 28, 1876, SC1/series 229, Massachusetts State Archives.

59. An Act in Relation to the Inspection of Factories and Public Buildings, and for Other Purposes, Massachusetts Acts and Resolves, 1876–77, c. 216, Acts of 1876, 215.

60. Massachusetts State Police 1874.

61. This conclusion is based on an analysis of various newspaper articles. See, for example, "The General Court," *Boston Daily Advertiser*, February 27, 1875, 4.

62. "Rep. James H. Mellen Dies," *Boston Daily Globe*, June 17, 1910, 16.

63. "The Butler Labor Party," *Worcester Daily Spy*, August 28, 1884, 1; "Mellen's Mark," *Boston Journal*, October 18, 1897.

64. *Massachusetts State Detective Force*, 1877.

65. Order of Sen. Byron Truell Relative to Factory Inspectors, January 11, 1877, passed acts, Acts of 1877, c. 214, Act Relating to the Inspection of Factories and Public Buildings, approved May 11, 1877, SC1/series 229, Massachusetts State Archives.

66. An Act Relating to the Inspection of Factories and Public Buildings, and for Other Purposes, Massachusetts House Document No. 193, 1877.

67. *Massachusetts House Journal*, 1877, 372.

68. An Act Relating to the Inspection of Factories and Public Buildings, Massachusetts House Document No. 337, 1877.

69. George E. McNeill, "Protection and Inspection: A Criticism of the Legislature's Doings," *Boston Daily Globe*, May 3, 1877, 5.

70. "In Ripe Old Age: Death of Hon. Charles Theodore Russell Last Evening," *Boston Daily Advertiser*, January 17 1896, 1; *Massachusetts Senate Journal*, 1877, 338.

71. "The Senate Session," *Boston Daily Globe*, May 5, 1877, 2.

72. An Act Relating to the Inspection of Factories and Public Buildings, Massachusetts Acts and Resolves, 1876–1877, c. 214, Acts of 1877, 599–601.

73. *Address of His Excellency Alexander H. Rice to the Two Branches of the Legislature of Massachusetts, January 4, 1877*, Massachusetts Senate Document No. 1, 1877, 9–12.

74. Massachusetts State Detective Force 1877, 20–21.

75. Massachusetts District Police 1880, 6–7.

76. "Boston and Vicinity," *Boston Journal*, July 8, 1869; "A Good Appointment," *Boston Traveler*, July 8, 1869, 3; *New England Postal Record*, July 17, 1869, 2; "The City and Departments," *Daily National Republican*, June 22, 1871, 1.

77. "Death of Chief Wade," *Springfield Republican*, February 11, 1904, 10.

78. "Chief Wade's Men Are Astir: Taft's Bill to Make Fire Aids Detectives Worries Them," *Boston Daily Globe*, January 31, 1903, 14.

79. Massachusetts District Police 1882, 23–24; Massachusetts District Police 1883, 6, 19–21; Massachusetts District Police 1894, 13–14, 27; Massachusetts District Police 1895, 61–71; Massachusetts District Police 1888, 25–26; Massachusetts District Police 1889, 6, 17–18; "Chief Wade in Earnest," *Boston Herald*, July 28, 1889, 11.

80. "Again Chief Wade," *Boston Journal*, April 21, 1894, 1; "Wade to Be Reappointed," *Boston Daily Globe*, April 22, 1894, 3.

81. Massachusetts District Police 1887, 7.

82. Massachusetts District Police 1884, 22.

83. "What Experts Say," *Boston Herald*, January 7, 1882, 5; "An Able Public Document," *Boston Herald*, January 14, 1892, 8.

84. "It Ought to Pass," *Boston Daily Globe*, March 14, 1887, 4.

85. Massachusetts District Police 1880, 3; *Boston Herald*, August 25, 1889, 13; "Passing Bay State Topics," *Springfield Republican*, August 14, 1892, 4; "Almost a Riot," *Worcester Daily Spy*, February 21, 1894, 1; "State Police: Gov. Wolcott Is Asked for Their Aid," *Boston Journal*, April 15, 1898, 1; "Fifty Police," *Boston Daily Advertiser*, January 2, 1899, 8.

86. "Dangerous Schoolrooms," *Boston Herald*, March 12, 1888, 3.

87. "State Police under Fire," *Boston Herald*, April 4, 1894, 10.

88. Massachusetts District Police 1885, 6–9.

89. "District Policemen's Work," *Boston Daily Globe*, December 10, 1894, 8.

90. "Fire Escapes," *Boston Herald*, January 24, 1882, 5.

91. "An Enforced Ten-Hour Law," *Boston Herald*, January 31, 1881, 2.

92. "The Legislature: Reporting Accidents in Factories," *Boston Herald*, April 13, 1886, 3.

93. Massachusetts District Police 1888; "Dangerous Schoolrooms," *Boston Herald*, March 12, 1888, 3; "Schoolhouse Sanitation," *Boston Herald*, January 4, 1889, 5; "Chief Wade in Earnest," *Boston Herald*, July 28, 1889, 11.

94. Massachusetts District Police 1892, 48.

95. Massachusetts District Police 1893, 22.

96. Massachusetts District Police 1888, 21.

97. Massachusetts District Police 1881, 17; Massachusetts District Police 1886, 23–24.

98. Massachusetts District Police 1880, 4; "The Cape Cod Canal: No Outbreak of Laborers Yet," *Springfield Republican*, October 21, 1880, 5; "The Millville Strike," *Worcester Daily Spy*, September 15, 1885, 4; "Strikers and Police," *Boston Daily Globe*, September 16, 1885; "Peabody and Salem Secure," *Boston Herald*, August 11, 1886, 2.

99. "Why Mr. Cummings Is Angry: He Objects to Interference of the State Police," *Boston Herald*, July 3, 1888, 8; *Boston Herald*, July 4, 1888, 4; "Important, If Good Law," *Boston Daily Globe*, January 11, 1891, 6; "No More Overtime Work: Practice in the Fall River Mills Must Stop," *Boston Herald*, December 26, 1899, 8; *Boston Herald*, January 5, 1884, 2; "Regulating Children's Work: Chief Wade Thinks That Employers Generally Respect the Law," *Boston Herald*, August 20, 1889, 2; Massachusetts District Police 1881, 13; "No Overtime Work," *Boston Herald*, December 28, 1899, 3.

100. Massachusetts District Police 1880, 12.

101. Massachusetts District Police 1881, 17.

102. Massachusetts District Police 1881, 17.

103. Massachusetts District Police 1888, 6.

104. Massachusetts District Police 1890, 9.

105. "An Able Public Document," *Boston Herald*, January 14, 1892, 8.

106. Massachusetts District Police 1885, 19.

107. "Wade Resents It," *Boston Daily Advertiser*, December 29, 1899, 1.

108. Massachusetts District Police 1883; "The District Police," *Boston Herald*, January 6, 1883, 1.

109. "Work of Chief Wade," *Boston Herald*, May 14, 1899, 34.

110. "Great Advance in the Improvement of Labor Conditions Reported," *Boston Daily Advertiser*, September 8, 1898, 2.

111. *Boston Herald*, June 24, 1881, 2; "Constitution of the C.L.U.," *Boston Herald*, March 13, 1893, 8; "Violation of Law Reported," *Boston Herald*, May 22, 1893, 6; "Will Appeal to Chief Wade," *Boston Herald*, June 12, 1893, 5; "Has Neither Authority or Time," *Boston Herald*, August 24, 1894, 5; "New England," *Boston Herald*, August 27, 1894, 3; "Weekly Payment Law," *Boston Daily Globe*, May 17, 1896, 17; "Will Do What He Can," *Boston Herald*, December 20, 1899, 7; "Labor Men to See Chief Wade," *Boston Herald*, January 27, 1900, 4; "Shirtmakers' Grievances," *Boston Herald*, October 25, 1900, 1.

112. "Obstacles in Their Path," *Boston Daily Globe*, February 3, 1900, 4.

113. "The Work Children," *Boston Daily Advertiser*, July 27, 1887, 8.

114. "Child Labor in Factories," *Boston Herald*, March 10, 1890, 2.

115. "Factory Laws: Gross Violation Alleged at Meeting of C.L.U.," *Boston Daily Globe*, December 7, 1896, 4.

116. "Labor Laws Effective: Chief Wade Finds Much to Commend," *Boston Daily Globe*, January 3, 1890, 2; "The State Police," *Boston Journal*, January 7, 1893, 4; "Children in Mills," *Boston Daily Advertiser*, October 20, 1893, 4; "Work of District Police," *Springfield Republican*, January 5, 1895, 9; "Good Labor Laws," *Boston Daily Globe*, January 5, 1898, 4.

117. "Fights Child Labor: Federation Asks Police to Enforce the Law," *Boston Herald*, July 13, 1903, 10.

118. "Makes Answer to Mrs. Freitas," *Boston Herald*, September 24, 1903, 7.

119. "Labor Men Arraign the State Police Force," *Worcester Daily Spy*, October 8, 1903, 1.

120. *Boston Herald*, October 8, 1903, 7; "Wade Finds No Violations," *Springfield Republican*, October 13, 1903, 7.

121. "Local Unions Must Do Supplementary Work," *Worcester Daily Spy*, October 9, 1903, 1.

122. "Finds No Violations," *Boston Herald*, October 18, 1903, 19.

123. "Chief Wade's Report," *Springfield Republican*, January 6, 1904, 1; Massachusetts District Police 1904, 12–13.

124. *Boston Journal*, October 6, 1903, 1; Massachusetts District Police 1904, 11–12.

125. "Both Sides' Ideas on Labor Laws," *Boston Herald*, September 9, 1903, 5.

126. "Makes Answer to Mrs. Freitas," *Boston Herald*, September 24, 1903, 7.

127. "Chief Wade's Men Are Astir," *Boston Daily Globe*, January 31, 1903, 14.

Chapter 7. Social Justice Feminism and Labor Law Enforcement in Illinois

1. Illinois, Office of Inspectors of Factories and Workshops 1895.

2. Immigrants—particularly Catholics and Germans—also defected from the Republican Party in 1890 and 1892 because of the Edwards education law, enacted 1889, which made schooling compulsory and required that basic subjects be taught in English (Campbell 1980, 28).

3. "Why Compulsory Education Is Attacked," unsourced newspaper clipping, hand dated March 1890, Thomas Morgan and Elizabeth Chambers Morgan Papers, Illinois History and Lincoln Collections, University of Illinois at Urbana-Champaign [Morgan Papers], Morgan Family Scrapbook, 2:45.

4. "After the Beggars," unsourced newspaper clipping, hand dated March 1892, Morgan Papers, Morgan Family Scrapbook, 2:42.

5. "The League, the Police, the Saloons," unsourced newspaper clipping, hand dated May 1890, Morgan Papers, Morgan Family Scrapbook, 2:52.

6. "Why the Compulsory Law Was Enacted," unsourced and undated newspaper clipping, Morgan Papers, Morgan Family Scrapbook, 2:43; "Compulsory Education in Chicago," unsourced newspaper clipping, hand dated May 1890, Morgan Papers, Morgan Family Scrapbook, 2:51.

7. This upward trend has been called into question by economists Susan Carter and Richard Sutch (1995), who argue that the 1880 Census figures were deliberately cooked by Francis Amasa Walker, superintendent of the tenth Census, to make the rates of child, female, and elderly male employment seem lower than they actually were. They also call into question the 1870 figures, maintaining that the actual rate was higher than reported in the official Census publications. If their indictment is correct, then child labor may have actually been declining over the final three decades of the century. Contemporary child labor reformers and critics relied on the official Census data, however, and believed the rates were rising.

8. US Census Bureau 1895.

9. Children's tendency to work only intermittently (such as only during the holidays or to make up for a temporary shortfall in paternal earnings) and combine work with school was probably common, but was largely ignored by reformers, who painted child labor in the direst terms possible. The notion that children and families might strategically use child employment in ways not necessarily damaging to the child did not square with reformers' conviction that industrial child labor was uniformly destructive and abusive.

10. Minutes of the forty-second meeting of the Sunset Club, February 4, 1892, Morgan Papers, folder 46.

11. "In Favor of Many Reforms," *Chicago Herald*, hand dated April 4, 1891, Morgan Papers, Morgan Family Scrapbook, 2:59.

12. Unsourced newspaper clipping, hand dated October 24, 1888, Morgan Papers, Morgan Family Scrapbook, 2:1.

13. "Testimony of David McDonald, Chicago Health Department Inspector," cited in Illinois, Joint Committee to Investigate the "Sweat Shop" System 1893, 133.

14. "Report of the Delegates to the Women's Alliance," unsourced clipping, hand dated July 4, 1889, Morgan Papers, Morgan Family Scrapbook, 2:28.

15. "Little Ones at Work," unsourced newspaper clipping, hand dated February 2, 1892, Morgan Papers, book #6, 24.

16. Unsourced newspaper clipping, hand dated December 17, 1888, Morgan Papers, Morgan Family Scrapbook, 2:5; unsourced newspaper clipping, hand dated December 18, 1888, Morgan Papers, Morgan Family Scrapbook, 2:6; "The Law a Dead Letter," unsourced newspaper clipping, hand dated April 18, 1892, Morgan Papers, book #6, 26.

17. Letter from Florence Kelley to Friedrich Engels, May 27, 1892, reprinted in Kelley, Sklar, and Palmer 2009, 58–59.

18. Illinois, Bureau of Labor Statistics 1893, 357.

19. "The Sweating System in Chicago," in Illinois, Bureau of Labor Statistics 1893, 355–43.

20. Illinois, Bureau of Labor Statistics 1893, 364.

21. Illinois, Bureau of Labor Statistics 1893, 364, 398.

22. These figures were on display alongside examples of the clothing in question at a mass meeting to rally public opposition to sweating held in Chicago on February 19, 1892 ("Like Priest and Levite," *Chicago Times*, newspaper clipping, hand dated February 20, 1892, Hull House Collection, Scrapbook vol. 1, Special Collections and University Archives, University of Illinois at Chicago). The general trend of precipitously declining wages for sweatshop workers was verified in numerous reports and testimonies; see, for example, Illinois, Joint Committee to Investigate the "Sweat Shop" System 1893.

23. Illinois, Bureau of Labor Statistics 1893, 362.

24. Illinois, Bureau of Labor Statistics 1893, 362, 365.

25. Illinois, Bureau of Labor Statistics 1893, 365.

26. Elizabeth Morgan, "Committee on Child's Labor," unsourced clipping of newspaper editorial, hand dated November 1891, Morgan Papers, Morgan Family Scrapbook, vol. 2.

27. Elizabeth Morgan, "Committee on Child's Labor," unsourced clipping of newspaper editorial, hand dated November 1891, Morgan Papers, Morgan Family Scrapbook, vol. 2.

28. "Is 3,000,000 Prisoners of Poverty: An Open Letter to the Missouri Legislature," unsourced newspaper clipping, Morgan Papers, book #6.

29. "White Child Slavery: A Symposium," *Arena* 1, no. 5 (April 1890): 589.

30. Nell Nelson, "City Slave Girls: Startling Experiences of 'The Times' Lady Reporter in the Factory of Julius Stein & Co.," *Chicago Times*, August 1, 1888, 1.

31. Unsourced newspaper clipping, hand dated October 24, 1888, Morgan Papers, Morgan Family Scrapbook, vol. 2.

32. Unsourced newspaper clipping, hand dated October 24, 1888, Morgan Papers, Morgan Family Scrapbook, vol. 2.

33. "Regulating Child Labor," unsourced newspaper clippings, hand dated June 8, 1890, Morgan Papers, book #6; "The Child-Labor Ordinance," n.d., Morgan Papers, book #6; Child's Labor Law, enacted by the City Council, June 26, 1890, Morgan Papers, book #6.

34. *Trade Assembly*, hand dated January 19, 1890, Morgan Papers, Morgan Family Scrapbook, 2:39.

35. "Eva Writes of Tommy Morgan," *Minneapolis Tribune*, hand dated September 25, 1891, Morgan Papers, book #6, 53.

36. "Mrs. T.J. Morgan," [*Chicago*] *Times*, Morgan Papers, Morgan Family Scrapbook, vol. 2; see also Scharnau 1973b.

37. "Testimony of Elizabeth Morgan," Illinois, Joint Committee to Investigate the "Sweat Shop" System 1893, 144.

38. "Replacing the Booths," *Chicago Tribune* clipping, hand dated September 16, 1889, Morgan Papers, Morgan Family Scrapbook, 2:26; *Trade Assembly* clipping, hand dated September 15, 1889, Morgan Papers, Morgan Family Scrapbook, 2:26.

39. "Testimony of Elizabeth Morgan, April 4, 1892," US Congress, House of Representatives, Committee on Manufactures 1893, 71. The investigation was covered in the newspapers. See "'Sweating' Out Lives: Sewing Pants for Six Cents a Dozen on the West Side," *Chicago Daily Tribune*, August 21, 1891, 9; "In Filth and Disease: How the Employees of Chicago 'Sweaters' Shops Live," *Chicago Daily Tribune*, September 7, 1891, 3.

40. Chicago Trade and Labor Assembly 1891, 7–8.

41. Elizabeth Morgan, "Committee on Child's Labor," unsourced clipping of newspaper editorial, hand dated November 1891, Morgan Papers, Morgan Family Scrapbook, vol. 2.

42. "Testimony of Elizabeth Morgan."

43. Chicago Trade and Labor Assembly 1891, 10, 16.

44. Chicago Trade and Labor Assembly 1891, 20.

45. Elizabeth Morgan, "Committee on Child's Labor," unsourced clipping of newspaper editorial, hand dated November 1891, Morgan Papers, Morgan Family Scrapbook, vol. 2.

46. "Mrs. T.J. Morgan," [*Chicago*] *Times*, Morgan Papers, Morgan Family Scrapbook, vol. 2.

47. Chicago Trade and Labor Assembly 1891, 5.

48. Chicago Trade and Labor Assembly 1891, 8–9, 20, 24. In contrast, Kelley regarded Russian Jewish immigrants as the "most open minded" of them all (Sklar 1995, 204).

49. Letter from Florence Kelley to Friedrich Engels, April 7, 1892, reprinted in Kelley, Sklar, and Palmer 2009, 57–58.

50. "Will Destroy the Sweating System: Gov. Flower Signs the New Factory Inspection Bill— Its Provisions," *Chicago Daily Tribune*, May 22, 1892, 47; "Sweat-Shops by Gaslight: Messrs. Hoar

and Warner Pursue Their Investigation by Night," *Chicago Daily Tribune*, April 5, 1892, 1; "Work amid Disease: Deplorable State of Affairs at the Sweating-Shops," *Chicago Daily Tribune*, April 6, 1892, 9.

51. "Testimony of Elizabeth Morgan," 71–74.

52. Letter from Samuel Gompers to Elizabeth Morgan, March 11, 1892, Morgan Papers, folder 46.

53. "Going to Pieces: Illinois Woman's Alliance Has Fallen from Grace," unsourced newspaper clipping, hand dated 1894, Morgan Papers, Morgan Family Scrapbook, vol. 2.

54. "War of Words between Women," unsourced newspaper clipping, hand dated January 18, 1892, Morgan Papers, book #6; see also Sklar 1995, 215.

55. Letter from Samuel Gompers to Elizabeth Morgan, November 25, 1892, Morgan Papers, folder 46.

56. Letter from Florence Kelley to Mary Thorne Lewis, March 19, 1885. For example, she considered labor economist Richard Ely a "false prophet" and disdained US Christian socialism (Kelley, Sklar, and Palmer 2009, 21–25).

57. "The Sweating System in Chicago," Illinois, Bureau of Labor Statistics 1893, 355–443.

58. "The Sweating System in Chicago," Illinois, Bureau of Labor Statistics 1893, 358, 401, 380. The affliction described may have been scabies, which is contagious and can be spread through clothing.

59. "The Sweating System in Chicago," Illinois, Bureau of Labor Statistics 1893, 401–2.

60. "To Protest against 'Sweat-Shops': The Socialists to Hold an Indignation Meeting," *Chicago Daily Tribune*, April 11, 1892, 2; "To Abolish Sweating: Jewish Branch of the Socialistic Labor Party Protests," *Chicago Daily Tribune*, April 18, 1892, 10; "Scored by Speakers: Chicago's Sweating System Bitterly Denounced," *Chicago Daily Tribune*, May 9, 1892, 6.

61. Florence Kelley to Henry D. Lloyd, November 28, 1892, Kelley, Sklar, and Palmer 2009, 65–66.

62. "War on the System: Stirring Speeches Made against Sweat Shops," *Daily Inter-Ocean*, April 18, 1892; "To Stop the System: Mrs. Kelley's Suggestion regarding the Sweaters," *Chicago Daily Tribune*, September 26, 1892, 7.

63. Illinois, Joint Committee to Investigate the "Sweat Shop" System 1893, 8.

64. "'Sweating' Must Go: Disease-Breeding Dens Examined by Legislators," *Chicago Daily Tribune*, February 11, 1893, 8; "The Sweating Committee Investigation," *Chicago Daily Tribune*, February 12, 1893, 28; "After 'Sweaters': The Legislative Committee Continues Its Investigation," *Chicago Daily Tribune*, February 12, 1893, 6.

65. "Protest of Labor: Mass-Meeting Held to Denounce the Sweat Shops," *Chicago Daily Tribune*, February 20, 1893, 1.

66. "Mass-Meeting on the Sweating System," *Chicago Daily Tribune*, February 18, 1893, 8; "Suggestions for Legislation: Mrs. Florence Kelly [*sic*] Speaks of Points That Should Be Covered in Future Laws," *Chicago Daily Tribune*, February 20, 1893, 2.

67. See, for example, "Modern Slave Dens: Tour of the Legislative Committee to Sweat Shops: Disease and Sewer Gas: Children Under Age Found Slaving on Clothing and Earning a Pittance," *Daily Inter-Ocean*, hand dated February 12, 1893, Hull House Scrapbook, vol. 1, Hull House Collection; "They Must Lie to Live: Shops Where Disease Is Stitched into the Clothes We Wear," *Chicago Times*, hand dated February 12, 1893, Hull House Scrapbook, vol. 1, Hull House Collection; "Protest of Labor: Mass-Meeting Held to Denounce the Sweat Shops," *Chicago Daily Tribune*, February 20, 1893, 1; "Mass-Meeting on the Sweating System," *Chicago Daily Tribune*, February 18, 1893, 8; "Suggestions for Legislation: Mrs. Florence Kelly [*sic*] Speaks of Points That Should Be Covered in Future Laws," *Chicago Daily Tribune*, February 20, 1893, 2.

68. Letter from Florence Kelley to Friedrich Engels, November 27, 1892, Kelley, Sklar, and Palmer 2009, 63–64.

69. Illinois, Joint Committee to Investigate the "Sweat Shop" System 1893, 135–40 (Kelley's testimony), 144–48 (Morgan's testimony). Morgan recommended a prohibition on manufacture in buildings erected for dwellings; the application of sanitary laws to all buildings used for manufacturing purposes; state licenses for all manufacturers, not just in Illinois, but in all states; mandatory reporting by manufacturers on the composition of their workforce, hours, and wages, not just in Illinois, but in all states; the labeling of manufactured goods in all states; a minimum working age of fourteen in any sort of workplace; and pensions to poor families to make up for children's lost earnings.

70. Illinois, Joint Committee to Investigate the "Sweat Shop" System 1893, 139–40.

71. "Testimony of Abraham Bisno," in Illinois, Joint Committee to Investigate the "Sweat Shop" System 1893, 239; Bisno 1967, 144.

72. "Suggestions for Legislation: Mrs. Florence Kelly [*sic*] Speaks of Points That Should Be Covered in Future Laws," *Chicago Daily Tribune*, February 20, 1893, 2; "Cloakmakers Frame a Labor Bill: They Want the Employment of Women and Children," *Chicago Daily Tribune*, February 26, 1893, 6.

73. "Report on the Evils of Sweat-Shops: Legislative Committee Declares Them Productive of Wretchedness," *Chicago Daily Tribune*, March 2, 1893, 4.

74. "Cloakmakers Frame a Labor Bill: They Want the Employment of Women and Children," *Chicago Daily Tribune*, February 26, 1893, 6.

75. For the full text of the act, see *Laws of the State of Illinois, Passed by the Thirty-Eighth General Assembly* (Springfield, IL: H. W. Rokker, 1893), 99–102.

76. "Millionaires Deny It: Do Not Violate Child Labor Laws," unsourced newspaper clipping, hand dated April 16, 1892, Morgan Papers, book #6.

77. Letter from Florence Kelley to Henry Demarest Lloyd, June 30, 1892, reprinted in Kelley, Sklar, and Palmer 2009, 61.

78. "Testimony of Jacob Lasky, Cloak Manufacturer," in Illinois, Joint Committee to Investigate the "Sweat Shop" System 1893, 55, 59–60. This man, a sweater, would go directly to the coat department at Marshall Field and Co. to get his orders and raw materials from the manager there. See also "Millionaires Deny It: Do Not Violate Child Labor Laws," unsourced newspaper clipping, hand dated April 16, 1892, Morgan Papers, book #6.

79. "All against the Shops," unsourced clipping, Hull House Scrapbook, Hull House Collection, 1:38.

80. City health department officials were patronage appointees who served only as long as the mayor who appointed them. They were regarded as incompetent and corrupt ("Work amid Disease: Deplorable State of Affairs at the Sweating-Shops," *Chicago Daily Tribune*, April 6, 1892, 9).

81. As she stated in her introduction to her first annual report, "The inspectors devot[ed] themselves principally to places employing children." The bulk of her first and second report is devoted to child labor. Illinois, Office of Inspectors of Factories and Workshops 1894; Illinois, Office of Inspectors of Factories and Workshops 1895.

82. Illinois, Office of Inspectors of Factories and Workshops 1895.

83. Illinois, Office of Inspectors of Factories and Workshops 1896, 94.

84. Letter from M.T. Moloney to Florence Kelley, August 7, 1893, in Illinois, Office of Inspectors of Factories and Workshops 1894, 7.

85. "Altgeld's Factory Inspectors," *Chicago Daily Tribune*, July 31, 1893, 4.

86. Illinois, Office of Inspectors of Factories and Workshops 1896, 14–18.

87. *Outlook* 57, no. 3 (September 18, 1897): 151.

88. "Miss Kelley Upheld: Gov. Altgeld Sides with Factory Inspector," unsourced newspaper clipping, Hull House Scrapbook, Hull House Collection, 1:46½; "Sparks from the Wires," *Chicago Daily Tribune*, January 31, 1895, 1.

89. "For Violating Child Labor Law: Alton Glass Manufacturer Arrested on Eleven Separate Warrants," *Chicago Daily Tribune*, November 9, 1895, 3.

90. "Will Attack Child Labor Law: Illinois Glass Works Proposes to Appeal to the State Supreme Court," *Chicago Daily Tribune*, November 10, 1895, 11.

91. "Illinois Manufacturers Organize: They Will Protect Their Interests in the Female Labor Law," *Chicago Daily Tribune*, September, 30, 1893, 4.

92. "Attacking the Law: Manufacturers Test the Eight-Hour Labor Statute," *Chicago Daily Tribune*, January 31, 1894, 5; "More Time to Work: Movement to Abolish the Eight-Hour Law," *Chicago Daily Tribune*, February 1, 1894, 8; "Manufacturers Indorse the Law: Association Declares for Sanitary Features," *Chicago Daily Tribune*, March 22, 1895, 8.

93. Illinois, Office of Inspectors of Factories and Workshops 1895.

94. "Flaws in the Law: Supreme Court Punctures the Eight-Hour Act," *Chicago Daily Tribune*, March 15, 1895, 1.

95. *Outlook* 57, no. 3 (September 18, 1897): 152. The politicization of factory inspection was a universal phenomenon across all states, Kelley noted with exasperation in 1898. Writing for a German journal, she informed her audience that US factory inspectors secured their positions through patronage, and not on the basis of skills and experience. Many were therefore incompetent, indifferent, or physically unfit to carry out their duties. This was a situation that disadvantaged politically disempowered women, and it was the reason why the number of women inspectors lagged behind the number of male ones. Kelley (1898) hoped that civil service reform would reverse this trend and open up more opportunities for women in government.

96. "Factory Inspection," *Charities*, May 16, 1903, 493–94; Illinois, Office of Inspectors of Factories and Workshops, 1897–1902.

97. Illinois, Office of Inspectors of Factories and Workshops 1898, 1.

98. "Hunt for Child Labor: State Factory Inspectors Making a Thorough Canvass," *Chicago Daily Tribune*, February 24, 1900, 16.

99. Illinois, Office of Inspectors of Factories and Workshops 1899, 7.

Conclusion to Part II

1. "Wie hat sich die weibliche Fabrikinspektion in der Praxis bewährt?," *Volksstimme* Nr. 238, December 1, 1901, reprinted in Ayass 2005, 551–54.

2. "Named by the Governor: Two Women to Serve as State Factory Inspectors," *Boston Daily Globe*, May 9, 1891, 4.

3. Regulatory capture refers to a situation in which a regulatory body is directly or indirectly controlled by the industry or group that it is supposed to regulate, rendering it functionally toothless.

Chapter 8. Conclusion

1. Political scientists Torben Iversen and David Soskice (2006) argue that middle-class voters will more often support center-left, pro-welfare parties in multiparty systems than in majoritarian ones. They contend that in majoritarian systems, middle-class voters more frequently vote center-right because they fear that the left-wing party will tax them without rewarding them with benefits (all benefits will go to the poor); in multiparty systems, the middle-class party can join forces with the working-class party to "soak the rich" and share the spoils.

2. An exception is policies regulating hiring and firing, which have received substantial attention in the varieties of capitalism literature (see, e.g., Hall and Soskice 2001). Another is family leave policies, which feature prominently in studies of gender and the welfare state (e.g., O'Connor et al. 1999).

3. Noam Scheiber, "Protecting Workers from Coronavirus: OSHA Leaves It to Employers," *New York Times*, April 20, 2020, https://www.nytimes.com/2020/04/22/bsusiness/economy/coronavirus-osha-workers.html; Eyel Press, "Safety Last," *New Yorker*, October 26, 2020, 16–24.

4. Jordan Weissmann, "Newt Gingrich Thinks School Children Should Work as Janitors," *Atlantic*, November 21, 2011, https://www.theatlantic.com/business/archive/2011/11/newt-gingrich-thinks-school-children-should-work-as-janitors/248837.

5. Since 1938, child labor has been regulated not only at the state level but also at the federal level by the Fair Labor Standards Act. Ian Millhiser, "Sen. Mike Lee Calls Child Labor Laws Unconstitutional," *Think Progress,* January 11, 2011, https://thinkprogress.org/sen-mike-lee-calls-child-labor-laws-unconstitutional-d13870345c3f; Niraj Chokshi, "Maine's Governor Wants to Make It Easier for Children to Work," *Washington Post*, January 8, 2014, https://www.washingtonpost.com/blogs/govbeat/wp/2014/01/08/maines-governor-wants-to-make-it-easier-for-children-to-work; Lauren McCauley, "LePage Advocates for Weaker Child Labor Laws to Reduce 'Pressure to Raise Wages,'" *Maine Beacon*, April 27, 2018, http://mainebeacon.com/lepage-advocates-for-weaker-child-labor-laws-to-reduce-pressure-to-raise-wages.

6. Associated Press, "Obama Criticized in Reversal on Child Farm Labor Regulations," *Washington Post*, April 29, 2012, https://www.washingtonpost.com/politics/obama-criticized-in-reversal-on-child-farm-labor-regulations/2012/04/29/gIQAZvEDqT_story.html.

7. For a comprehensive overview of the policy/political entrepreneurship literature, see Sheingate 2003; Mintrom and Norman 2009.

Archival Collections, with Abbreviations

BELGIUM

Archives Générales du Royaume-Algemeen Rijksarchief (AGR-ARA), Bruges
  Archief Kamer van Koophandel Ieper and Diksmuide, TBO 116, 211: Register van processen verbaal van kamervergaderingen van 3 januari 1847 tot 19 december 1852
  Archief Kamer van Koophandel Brugge, TBO 116, 88: Register met briefwisseling van 1844 tot 1852
Archives Générales du Royaume-Algemeen Rijksarchief (AGR-ARA), Brussels
  2 Joseph Cuvelier, T563, 6: Registre aux procès-verbaux du 15 septembre 1840 au 31 décembre 1851
Archives Générales du Royaume-Algemeen Rijksarchief (AGR-ARA), Ghent
  Archief Kamer van Koophandel Aalst, B47, 1: Registre des procès verbaux des séances 1842–71
  Archief Kamer van Koophandel Dendermonde, B48, 17: Registre de correspondance 1849
Archives Générales du Royaume-Algemeen Rijksarchief (AGR-ARA), Kortrijk
  Archief Kamer van Koophandel Kortrijk, 205, 6: Registre aux procès-verbaux et autres documents à l'appui du 24 août 1845 au 10 septembre 1851
Archives Générales du Royaume-Algemeen Rijksarchief (AGR-ARA), Leuven
  Archief Kamer van Koophandel Leuven, 355, 4: register met de processen verbaal van 1847 tot en met 1851
  Archief Kamer van Koophandel Leuven, 355, 59: register met de kopies van de correspondentie 1848–50
Archives Générales du Royaume-Algemeen Rijksarchief (AGR-ARA), Liège
  Archives de la Chambre de Commerce de Verviers, O.1/2, 4/. Procès verbaux des séances de la Chambre, 1848–50
Archives Générales du Royaume-Algemeen Rijksarchief (AGR-ARA), Tournai
  Archives de la Cambre de Commerce de Tournai, 04/01, 838 : Registre aux procès-verbaux de la Chambre du 13 mai 1848 au 15 mars 1858
Fonds Ducpétiaux, L'Académie royale de Belgique

FRANCE

Archives Nationales de France
  Commerce et Industrie, Travail des enfants dans les manufactures (F12–4704, F12–4705, F12–4706)

GERMANY

Archiv des Landschaftverbandes Rheinland, Pulheim
  Best. Archiv der Provinzialstände, Nr. 278

Geheimes Staatsarchiv Preußischer Kulturbesitz (GstA), Berlin
    I. HA Rep. 120 (Handelsamt), BB VII 1.4
    I. HA Rep. 120 (Handelsamt), BB VII 3.1
    VI. HA, N1 Altenstein, A VI b
Landeshauptarchiv (LHA), Koblenz
    Best. 403 (Oberpräsidium der Rheinprovinz), Nr. 8082

ILLINOIS

Illinois History and Lincoln Collections, University of Illinois at Urbana-Champaign
    Thomas Morgan and Elizabeth Chambers Morgan Papers
Special Collections and University Archives, University of Illinois at Chicago
    Hull House Collection

MASSACHUSETTS

Massachusetts State Archives, Boston
    Passed acts
    Senate unpassed legislation
Peabody Essex Museum, Phillips Library, Salem, MA
    Henry Kemble Oliver Papers

REFERENCES

Abbott, Grace. 1947. *The Child and the State: Selected Documents.* Chicago: University of Chicago Press.

Abbott, Richard H. 1976. "Massachusetts: Maintaining Hegemony." In *Radical Republicans in the North: State Politics during Reconstruction,* edited by James C. Mohr, 1–25. Baltimore: Johns Hopkins University Press.

Académie Royale des sciences, des lettres et des beauxarts de Belgique. 1848. "Liste des Membres, des Correspondants et des Associés de L'Académie." In *Annuaire de l'Académie des sciences, des lettres et des beaux-arts de Belgique* 14:102–15.

Adams, Julia, Elizabeth Stephanie Clemens, and Ann Shola Orloff. 2005. *Remaking Modernity: Politics, History, and Sociology.* Durham, NC: Duke University Press.

Addams, Jane. 1902. *Democracy and Social Ethics.* New York: Macmillan.

———. 1912. *Twenty Years at Hull-House: With Autobiographical Notes.* New York: Macmillan.

Adolphs, Lotte. 1972. *Industrielle Kinderarbeit im 19. Jahrhundert unter Berücksichtigung des Duisburger Raumes: Ein Beigtrag zur Geschichte der Wirstschafts- und Sozialpädagogic.* Duisburg, Germany: Walter Braun Verlag.

Allgemeines Landrecht für die Preussischen Staaten. 1794. Accessed October 1, 2020. https://opinioiuris.de/quelle/1623.

Allgemeines Landrecht für die Preussischen Staaten in Verbindung mit den dasselbe ergänzenden, abändernden und erläuternden Gesetzen, Königlichen Verordnungen and Justiz-Ministerial-Rescripten. Zweiter Theil, Zweiter Band. Vierter Band, enthaltend Theil II. Tit. 8 und 9. 1837. Berlin: Nauckschen Buchhandlung.

Allmendinger, Jutta, and Stephan Leibfried. 2003. "Education and the Welfare State: The Four Worlds of Competence Production." *Journal of European Social Policy* 13:63–81.

Altenstein, Karl von. 1931. "Denkschrift über die Leitung des Preußischen Staats an S. des Herrn Staatsministers Freiherrn von Hardenberg Exzellenz." In *Die Reorganisation des preussischen Staates unter Stein und Hardenberg. Erster Teil: Allgemeine Verwaltungs- und Behördernreform,*

Band I: Vom Beginn des Kampfes gegen die Kabinettsregierung bis zum Wiedereintritt des Ministers vom Stein, edited by Georg Winter, 364–566. Leipzig: Hirzel.

Anceau, Éric. 2009. "Charles Dupin et la question sociale: Trois éclairages parlementaires (1840–1848, 1848–1849, 1864–1868)." In *Charles Dupin (1784–1873): ingénieur, savant, économiste, pédagogue et parlementaire du Premier au Second Empire*, edited by Carole Christen and François Vatin, 253–70. Rennes: Presses universitaires de Rennes.

Anderson, Elisabeth. 2008. "Experts, Ideas, and Policy Change: The Russell Sage Foundation and Small Loan Reform, 1909–1941." *Theory and Society* 37 (3): 271–310.

———. 2013. "Ideas in Action: The Politics of Prussian Child Labor Reform, 1817–1839." *Theory and Society* 42:81–119.

———. 2018. "Policy Entrepreneurs and the Origins of the Regulatory Welfare State: Child Labor Reform in Nineteenth-Century Europe." *American Sociological Review* 83:173–211.

Anderson, Eugene N. 1970. "The Prussian Volksschule in the Nineteenth Century." In *Entstehung und Wandel der modernen Gesellschaft: Festschrift für Hans Rosenberg zum 65. Geburtstag*, edited by Gerhard A. Ritter, 221–60. Berlin: De Gruyter.

Anderson, Margaret Lavinia. 2000. *Practicing Democracy: Elections and Political Culture in Imperial Germany*. Princeton, NJ: Princeton University Press.

Annales du Parlement Français, Vol. 2, Part II: Chambre des Pairs. 1840a. "Rapport par M. Le Baron Ch. Dupin," February 22, 77–90. Paris: Chez Fleury, Ponce Lebas et Compagnie, Éditeurs.

———. 1840b. "Travail des Enfans—Discussion des Articles," March 5–10, 97–128. Paris: Chez Fleury, Ponce Lebas et Compagnie, Éditeurs.

———. 1840c. "Travail des Enfans—Discussion Générale," March 4–5, 90–97. Paris: Chez Fleury, Ponce Lebas et Compagnie, Éditeurs.

———. 1840d. "Travail des Enfans—Projet de Loi," 128–31. Paris: Chez Fleury, Ponce Lebas et Compagnie, Éditeurs.

Anonymous. 1827. "Review of Essays upon Popular Education, by James G. Carter." *U.S. Review and Literary Gazette* 1:346–68.

Anton, Günther Kurt. 1953. *Geschichte der preussischen Fabrikgesetzgebung bis zu ihrer Aufnahme durch die Reichsgewerbeordnung*. Berlin: Rütten und Loening.

Aubert, Roger. 1964. "Édouard Ducpétiaux." In *Biographie nationale de Belgique*, 32:154–75. Brussels: Académie Royale des sciences, des lettres et des beaux-arts de Belgique.

Ayass, Wolfgang, ed. 1996. *Arbeiterschutz: Quellensammlung zur Geschichte der deutschen Sozialpolitik. Von der Reichsgründerzeit bis zur Kaiserlichen Sozialbotschaft (1867–1881). Part I, vol. 3*. Stuttgart: Gustav Fischer Verlag.

———, ed. 2005. *Arbeiterschutz: Quellensammlung zur Geschichte der deutschen Sozialpolitik. Ausbau und Differenzierung der Sozialpolitik seit Beginn des neuen Kurses (1890—1904). Part III, vol. 3*. Darmstadt: WBG.

Ayers, James. 2014. *Art, Artisans and Apprentices: Apprentice Painters and Sculptors in the Early Modern British Tradition*. Oxford: Oxbow Books.

Bahne, Siegfried. 1996. "Ernst von Bodelschwingh—ein preußischer Staatsmann und Politiker aus Westfalen in der Zeit der Restauration, Revolution und Reaktion." *Westfälische Zeitschrift* 146:173–89.

Bairoch, Paul. 1982. "International Industrialization Levels from 1750 to 1980." *Journal of European Economic History* 11 (2): 269–334.

Baldwin, Peter. 1990. *The Politics of Social Solidarity: Class Bases of the European Welfare State, 1875–1975*. Cambridge: Cambridge University Press.

Barkin, Kenneth. 1983. "Social Control and the Volksschule in Vormärz Prussia." *Central European History* 16:31–52.

Barnard, Harry. 1938. *Eagle Forgotten: The Life of John Peter Altgeld*. New York: Duell, Sloan and Pearce.

Barnard, Henry. 1851. *Normal Schools and Other Institutions*. Applewood Education Series. Carlisle, MA: Applewood Books.

———. 1858. *Biographical Sketch of James G. Carter*. Hartford, CT: F. C. Brownell.

Bass, Hans H. 1991. *Hungerkrisen in Preussen während der ersten Hälfte des 19. Jahrhunderts*. Sankt Katharinen, Germany: Scripta Mercaturae.

Baum, Dale. 1984. *The Civil War Party System: The Case of Massachusetts, 1848–1876*. Chapel Hill: University of North Carolina Press.

Baumgartner, Frank R., and Bryan D. Jones. 1993. *Agendas and Instability in American Politics*. Chicago: University of Chicago Press.

Bazillion, Richard J. 1985. "Urban Violence and the Modernization Process in Pre-March Saxony, 1830–1831 and 1845." *Historical Reflections* 12 (2): 279–303.

Beck, Hermann. 1992. "The Social Policies of Prussian Officials: The Bureaucracy in a New Light." *Journal of Modern History* 62 (2): 263–98.

———. 1995. *The Origins of the Authoritarian Welfare State in Prussia: Conservatives, Bureaucracy, and the Social Question, 1815–70*. Ann Arbor: University of Michigan Press.

Beckedorff, Ludolph. 1827a. "Gebrauch der Kinder zu Fabrik-Arbeiten (Part I)." *Jahrbücher des Preußischen Volks-Schul-Wesens* (June): 222–48.

———. 1827b. "Gebrauch der Kinder zu Fabrik-Arbeiten (Part II)." *Jahrbücher des Preußischen Volks-Schul-Wesens* (August): 161–82.

Becker, Howard S. 1963. *Outsiders: Studies in the Sociology of Deviance*. New York: Free Press.

Beckert, Jens. 1999. "Agency, Entrepreneurs, and Institutional Change: The Role of Strategic Choice and Institutionalized Practices in Organizations." *Organization Studies* 20 (5): 777–99.

Beecher, Jonathan. 2001. *Victor Considerant and the Rise and Fall of French Romanticism*. Berkeley: University of California Press.

Béland, Daniel, and Robert Henry Cox. 2016. "Ideas as Coalition Magnets: Coalition Building, Policy Entrepreneurs, and Power Relations." *European Journal of Public Policy* 23 (3): 428–45.

Belgium, Ministère de l'Intérieur. 1848. *Enquête sur la condition des classes ouvrières*. Vols. 1–2. Brussels: Imprimerie de Th. Lesigne.

———. 1851. *Industrie: recensement générale 1846. Statistique de la Belgique*. Brussels: Imprimerie de Th. Lesigne.

Bensel, Richard Franklin. 2000. *The Political Economy of American Industrialization, 1877–1900*. Cambridge: Cambridge University Press.

Bergeson-Lockwood, Millington W. 2016. "The People Coming to Power! Wendell Phillips, Benjamin F. Butler, and the Politics of Labor Reform." In *Wendell Phillips, Social Justice, and the Power of the Past*, edited by A. J. Aiséirithe and Donald Yacovone, 181–207. Baton Rouge: Louisiana State University Press.

Bergmann, Jürgen. 1980. "Das Zunftwesen nach der Einführung der Gewerbefreiheit." In *Preußische Reformen, 1807–1820*, edited by Barbara Vogel, 150–65. Königstein Germany: Verlagsgruppe Athenäum, Hain, Scriptor, Hanstein.

Beuth, Peter. 1826. "Ueber Kammgarn-Maschinenspinnerei: Nachtrag." *Verhandlungen des Vereins zur Beförderung des Gewerbfleißes in Preußen* 5:173–91.

Biernacki, Richard. 1995. *The Fabrication of Labor: Germany and Britain, 1640–1914*. Berkeley: University of California Press.

Bishop, James Leander, Edwin Troxell Freedley, and Edward Young. 1864. *A History of American Manufactures from 1608 to 1860*. Philadelphia: Edward Young and Co.

Bisno, Abraham. 1967. *Abraham Bisno, Union Pioneer; an Autobiographical Account of Bisno's Early Life and the Beginnings of Unionism in the Women's Garment Industry*. Madison: University of Wisconsin Press.

Blasius, Dirk. 1971a. "Lorenz von Stein und Preußen." *Historische Zeitschrift* 212 (2): 339–62.

———. 1971b. "Lorenz von Steins Lehre vom Königtum der sozialen Reform und ihre verfassungspolitischen Grundlagen." *Der Staat* 10 (1): 33–51.

Blewett, Mary H. 2000. *Constant Turmoil: The Politics of Industrial Life in Nineteenth-Century New England*. Amherst: University of Massachusetts Press.

Block, James E. 2012. *The Crucible of Consent: American Child Rearing and the Forging of Liberal Society*. Cambridge, MA: Harvard University Press.

Blyth, Mark. 2002. *Great Transformations: Economic Ideas and Institutional Change in the Twentieth Century*. Cambridge: Cambridge University Press.

Boch, Rudolf. 1991. *Grenzenloses Wachstum? Das rheinische Wirtschaftsbürgertum und seine Industrialisierungsdebatte 1814–1857*. Göttingen: Vandenhoeck und Ruprecht.

Boentert, Annika. 2007. *Kinderarbeit im Kaiserreich 1871–1914*. Paderborn, Germany: Ferdinand Schoningh.

Bonoli, Giuliano, and Bruno Palier. 1998. "Changing the Politics of Social Programmes: Innovative Change in British and French Welfare Reforms." *Journal of European Social Policy* 8 (4): 317–30.

Borden, Alanson. 1899. *Our County and Its People: A Descriptive and Biographical Record of Bristol County Massachusetts*. Boston: Boston History Company.

Boris, Eileen. 1994. *Home to Work: Motherhood and the Politics of Industrial Homework in the United States*. New York: Cambridge University Press.

Boston Eight Hour League. 1872. *Boston Eight Hour League, Its Objects and Work*. Boston: Boston Eight Hour League.

Bourcart, Jean-Jacques. 1828. "Proposition sur la nécessité de fixer l'âge et de réduire les heures de travail des ouvriers des filatures." *Bulletin de la Société industrielle de Mulhouse* 5:325–28.

Bourdieu, Pierre. 1983. "The Field of Cultural Production, or: The Economic World Reversed." *Poetics* 12:311–56.

———. 1988. *Homo Academicus*. Stanford, CA: Stanford University Press.

Bourdieu, Pierre, and Loic Wacquant. 1992. *An Invitation to Reflexive Sociology*. Chicago: University of Chicago Press.

Bowles, Samuel, and Herbert Gintis. (1976) 2011. *Schooling in Capitalist America: Educational Reform and the Contradictions of Economic Life*. Chicago: Haymarket Books.

Bradley, Margaret. 2012. *Charles Dupin (1784–1873) and His Influence on France: The Contributions of a Mathematician, Educator, Engineer, and Statesman*. Amherst, NY: Cambria Press.

Bradley, Margaret, and Fernand Perrin. 1991. "Charles Dupin's Study Visits to the British Isles, 1816–1824." *Technology and Culture* 32 (1): 47–68.

Brakelmann, Günther. 1994. "Theodor Lohmann: Ein protestantischer Sozialpolitiker aus der Inneren Mission." In *Zwischen Widerstand und Mitverantwortung: Vier Studien zum Protestantismus in sozialen Konflikten*. Bochum, Germany: SWI Verlag.

Breger, Monika. 1982. *Die Haltung der industriellen Unternehmer zur staatlichen Sozialpolitik in den Jahren 1878–1891*. Frankfurt: Haag und Herchen Verlag.

Bremner, Robert Hamlett. 1970. *Children and Youth in America: A Documentary History*. Cambridge, MA: Harvard University Press.

Brentano, Lujo. 1873. "Fabrikgesetzgebung." In *Verhandlungen der eisenacher Versammlung zur Besprechung der socialen Frage am 6. und 7. Oktober 1872*, edited by Heinrich Roller, 8–28. Leipzig: Duncker und Humblot.

Brepoels, Jaak. 2015. *Wat zoudt gij zonder 't werkvolk zijn?: de geschiedenis van de belgische arbeidersbeweging 1830–2015*. Antwerp: Van Halewyck.

Brock, William R. (1984) 2009. *Investigation and Responsibility: Public Responsibility in the United States, 1865–1900*. Cambridge: Cambridge University Press.

Bron, Jean. 1968. *Histoire du mouvement ouvrier français. Tome 1: Le droit à l'existance. du début de XIXe siècle à 1884*. Paris: Les éditions ouvrières.

Brophy, James M. 2007. *Popular Culture and the Public Sphere in the Rhineland, 1800–1850*. Cambridge: Cambridge University Press.

Brose, Eric Dorn. 1993. *The Politics of Technological Change in Prussia: Out of the Shadow of Antiquity, 1809–1848*. Princeton, NJ: Princeton University Press.

Brown, Richard D., and Jack Tager. 2000. *Massachusetts: A Concise History*. Amherst: University of Massachusetts Press.

Bruno, Alexandre. 2010. *Code Administratif de Belgique V2 (1842)*. Whitefish, MT: Kessinger Publishing.

Bucher, Peter. 1983. "Kinderarbeit im 19. Jahrhundert: die Anwendung des Regulativs vom 9. März 1839 im Regierungsbezirk Koblenz." *Jahrbuch für westdeutsche Landesgeschichte* 9:221–67.

Buck-Heilig, Lydia. 1989. *Die Gewerbeaufsicht: Enstehung und Entwickelung*. Opladen, Germany: Westdeutscher Verlag.

Bülter, Horst. 1953. "Einführung." In *Geschichte der preussischen Fabrikgesetzgebung bis zu ihrer Aufnahme durch die Reichsgewerbeordnung* by Günther K. Anton. Berlin: Rütten und Löning.

Busemeyer, Marius R. 2014. *Skills and Inequality: Partisan Politics and the Political Economy of Education Reforms in Western Welfare States*. Cambridge: Cambridge University Press.

Busemeyer, Marius R., and Rita Nikolai. 2010. "Education." In *The Oxford Handbook of the Welfare State*, edited by Francis G. Castles, Stephan Leibfried, Jane Lewis, Herbert Obinger, and Christopher Pierson, 494–510. Oxford: Oxford University Press.

Cameron, Rondo, and Charles E. Freedeman. 1983. "French Economic Growth: A Radical Revision." *Social Science History* 7 (1): 3–30.

Campbell, Ballard C. 1980. *Representative Democracy: Public Policy and Midwestern Legislatures in the Late Nineteenth Century*. Cambridge, MA: Harvard University Press.

Campbell, John L. 2004. *Institutional Change and Globalization*. Princeton, NJ: Princeton University Press.

Caron, François, and Barbara Bray. 2011. *An Economic History of Modern France*. Abingdon, UK: Routledge.

Carpenter, Daniel P. 2001. *The Forging of Bureaucratic Autonomy: Reputations, Networks, and Policy Innovation in Executive Agencies, 1862–1928*. Princeton, NJ: Princeton University Press.

Carter, James G. 1824. *Letters to William Prescott L.L.D.* Boston: Cummings, Hilliard and Co.

———. 1826. *Essays upon Popular Education, Containing a Particular Examination of the Schools of Massachusetts, and an Outline of an Institution for the Education of Teachers*. Boston: Bowles and Dearborn.

Carter, Susan B., and Richard Sutch. 1995. "Fixing the Facts: Editing of the 1880 U.S. Census of Occupations with Implications for Long-Term Trends and the Sociology of Official Statistics." National Bureau of Economic Research Historical Paper 74.

Castles, Francis G. 1982. "The Impact of Parties on Public Expenditure." In *The Impact of Parties: Politics and Policies in Democratic Capitalist States*. London: Sage Publications.

Castles, Francis G., Stephan Leibfried, Jane Lewis, Herbert Obinger, and Christopher Pierson, eds. 2010. *The Oxford Handbook of the Welfare State*. Oxford: Oxford University Press.

Chambliss, J. J. 1968. *The Origins of American Philosophy of Education: Its Development as a Distinct Discipline, 1808–1913*. The Hague: Martinus Nijhoff.

Channing, William E. 1848. "On the Education of the People, and Especially of the Laboring Class." In *Memoir of William Ellery Channing*, 3:62–69. Boston: Wm. Crosby and H. P. Nichols.

Chicago Trade and Labor Assembly. 1891. "The New Slavery: Investigation into the Sweating System as Applied to the Manufacture of Wearing Apparel." Chicago: Detwiler Print.

Clark, Christopher M. 2006. *Iron Kingdom: The Rise and Downfall of Prussia, 1600–1947*. Cambridge, MA: Belknap Press of Harvard University Press.

Clark, Samuel. 1984. "Nobility, Bourgeoisie and the Industrial Revolution in Belgium." *Past and Present* 105 (1): 140–75.

Clemens, Elisabeth Stephanie. 1997. *The People's Lobby: Organizational Innovation and the Rise of Interest Group Politics in the United States, 1890–1925*. Chicago: University of Chicago Press.

Clemens, Elizabeth Stephanie, and James M. Cook. 1999. "Politics and Institutionalism: Explaining Durability and Change." *Annual Review of Sociology* 25:441–66.

Cole, Donald. 2002. *Immigrant City: Lawrence, Massachusetts, 1845–1921*. Chapel Hill: University of North Carolina Press.

Collier, Ruth Berins, V. B. Dubal, and Christopher L. Carter. 2018. "Disrupting Regulation, Regulating Disruption: The Politics of Uber in the United States." *Perspectives on Politics* 16:919–37.

Collingham, H. A. C. 1988. *July Monarchy: A Political History of France, 1830–1848*. London: Longman.

Commons, John R. 1901. "Immigration and Its Economic Effects: A Report Prepared under the Direction of the Industrial Commission." In *Reports of the Industrial Commision on Immigration and on Education*, 15:293–744. Washington, DC.

Commons, John R., Ulrich Bonnel Phillips, Eugene Allen Gilmore, Helen L. Summer, John B. Andrews, American Bureau of Industrial Research, and Carnegie Institution of Washington. 1910. *A Documentary History of American Industrial Society, Vol V: Labor Movement*. Cleveland: A. H. Clark Company.

Conze, Werner. 1954. "Vom 'Pöbel' zum 'Proletariat': sozialgeschichtliche Voraussetzungen für den Sozialismus in Deutschland." *Vierteljahresschrift für Sozial- und Wirtschaftsgeschichte* 41:333–64.

Cooper, Sarah B. 1893. "The Kindergarten in Its Bearings upon Crime, Pauperism and Insanity." In *History of Child Saving in the United States: At the Twentieth National Conference of Charities and Correction in Chicago, June 1893*, edited by National Conference on Social Welfare Committee on the History of Child-Saving Work, 89–98. Boston: Geo. H. Ellis.

Coornaert, Emile. 1941. *Les corporations en France avant 1789*. 5th ed. Paris: Gallimard.

Cousin, Victor. 1832. *Rapport sur l'état de l'instruction publique dans quelques pays de l'Allemagne et particulièrement en Prusse, Ie Partie, Francfort-Sur-Le-Mein, Duché de Weymar, Royaume de Saxe*. Paris: Imprimerie royale.

———. 1838. "Letter to Rev. Charles Brooks, April 20, 1837." *American Annals of Education and Instruction, and Journal of Literary Institutions* 8:278–280.

Craig, Gordon A. 1978. *Germany, 1866–1945*. New York: Oxford University Press.

Cremin, Lawrence. 1980. *American Education: The National Experience, 1783–1876*. New York: Harper and Row.

Cross, Gary. 1989. *A Quest for Time: The Reduction of Work in Britain and France, 1840–1940*. Berkeley: University of California Press.

Cunningham, Hugh. 2005. *Children and Childhood in Western Society since 1500*. Harlow, NY: Pearson Longman.

Curtis, Sarah A. 2000. *Educating the Faithful: Religion, Schooling and Society in Nineteenth-Century France*. De Kalb: Northern Illinois University Press.

Dahl, Robert Alan. 2005. *Who Governs? Democracy and Power in an American City*. 2nd ed. New Haven, CT: Yale University Press.

Dawley, Allen. (1976) 2000. *Class and Community: The Industrial Revolution in Lynn*. Cambridge, MA: Harvard University Press.

Deegan, Mary Jo. 1988. *Jane Addams and the Men of the Chicago School, 1892–1918*. New Brunswick, NJ: Transaction Books.

de Herdt, René. 2011. "Child Labour in Belgium 1800–1914." In *Child Labour's Global Past, 1650–2000*, edited by Kristoffel Lieten and Elise van Nederveen Meerkerk, 175–92. Bern: Peter Lang.

Delmas, Corinne. 2006. *Instituer des savoirs d'Etat. L'Académie ses sciences morales et politiques au XIXe siècle*. Paris: L'Harmattan.

Démier, Francis. 2009. "Charles Dupin: un libéralisme sans doctrine?" In *Charles Dupin (1784–1873): ingénieur, savant, économiste, pédagogue et parlementaire du Premier au Second Empire*, edited by Carole Christen and François Vatin, 165–76. Rennes: Presses universitaires de Rennes.

Deneckere, Gita. 1993. "The Transforming Impact of Collective Action: Belgium, 1886." *International Review of Social History* 38:345–67.

Dennison, Tracy, and James Simpson. 2010. "Agriculture." In *The Cambridge Economic History of Modern Europe*, edited by Stephen Broadberry and Kevin O'Rourke, 147–63. Cambridge: Cambridge University Press.Desama, Claude. 1985. *Population et révolution industrielle: Évolution des structures démographiques à Verviers dans la premiére moitie du 19e siècle*. Paris: Les Belles Lettres.

Deutsches Historisches Institut. n.d. "Wahlen zum Deutschen Reichstag (1871–1890): Ein statistischer Überblick." In *Deutsche Geschichte in Dokumenten und Bildern. Band 4. Reichsgründung: Bismarcks Deutschland 1866–1890*. Accessed February 1, 2021. http://germanhistorydocs.ghi -dc.org/sub_document.cfm?document_id=1850.

Dewey, John. 2002. *Human Nature and Conduct*. Mineola, NY: Dover Publications.

d'Hondt, Jan. 1960. "Besluit 1830–1850." In *Geschiedenis van de socialistische arbeidersbeweging in België*, edited by Jan d'Hondt. Vol. 6. Antwerpen: Ontwikkeling.

Dickinson, Samuel Nelson. 1838. *The Boston Almanac for the Year 1838*. Boston: S. N. Dickinson.

Diest, Gustav von. 1898. *Meine Erlebnisse im Jahre 1848 und die Stellung des Staatsministers von Bodelschwingh vor und an dem 18. März 1848*. Berlin: Ernst Siegfried Mittler und Sohn.

Diesterweg, Adolph. 1826. "Über den Gebrauch der Kinder zur Fabrik-Arbeit." *Rheinisch-westfälische Monatsschrift für Erziehung und Volksunterricht* 5 (3): 161–90.

———. 1828. *Rheinische Blätter für Erziehung und Unterricht mit Besonderer Berücksichtigung des Volksschulwesens* 3 (3): 33–38.

Digby-Junger, Richard. 1996. *The Journalist as Reformer: Henry Demarest Lloyd and Wealth against Commonwealth*. Westport, CT: Greenwood Press.

DiMaggio, Paul. 1982. "Cultural Entrepreneurship in Nineteenth-Century Boston: The Creations of an Organizational Base for High Culture in America." *Media, Culture and Society* 4:33–50.

———. 1988. "Interest and Agency in Institutional Theory." In *Institutional Patterns and Culture*, edited by Lynne G. Zucker, 3–22. Cambridge, MA: Ballinger Publishing Company.

Dolléans, Edouard. 1848. *Histoire du mouvement ouvrier, Tome I: 1830 à 1871*. Paris: Librairie Armand Collin.

Dörr, Nikolas, Lukas Grawe, and Herbert Obinger. 2020. "The Military Origins of Labor Protection Legislation in Imperial Germany." *Historical Social Research* 45 (2): 27–67.

Dowe, Dieter. 1970. *Aktion und Organisation: Arbeiterbewegung, sozialistische und kommunistische Bewegung in der preußischen Rheinprovinz 1820–1852*. Hannover: Verlag für Literatur und Zeitgeschehen.

Driver, Cecil. 1946. *Tory Radical: The Life of Richard Oastler*. Oxford: Oxford University Press.

Dubin, Michael J. 2007. *Party Affiliations in the State Legislatures: A Year by Year Summary, 1796–2006*. Jefferson, NC: McFarland.

Dublin, Thomas. 1979. *Women at Work: The Transformation of Work and Community in Lowell, Massachusetts, 1826–1860*. New York: Columbia University Press.

Dubois, E. 1902. "Child Labor in Belgium." *Annals of the American Academy of Political and Social Sciences* 20:203–20.

Ducpétiaux, Édouard. 1838. *De l'État de l'instruction primaire et populaire en Belgique, comparé avec celui de l'instruction en Allemagne, en Prusse, en Suisse, en France, en Hollande et aux États-Unis. Ouvrage dédié au Sénat et à la Chambre des représentants*. Brussels: Meline, Cans & Co.

———. 1843. *De la condition physique et morale des jeunes ouvriers et des moyens de l'améliorer, Vols. 1 and 2*. Brussels: Meline, Cans et Compagnie.

Dupin, Charles. 1840. *Du travail des enfants qu'emploient les ateliers, les usines et les manufactures: considéré dans les intérêts mutuels de la société, des familles et de l'industrie*. Paris: Bachelier.

Dupont-Bouchat, Marie-Sylvie 1988. "Ducpétiaux ou le rêve cellulaire." *Déviance et Société* 12:1–27.

———. 2004. "Les origines de la protection de l'enfance en Belgique (1830–1914)." In *Mères et nourrissons. De la bienfaisance à la protection médico-sociable (1830–1945)*, edited by Godelieve Masuy-Stroobant and Perrine C. Humblet, 13–42. Brussels: Editions Labor.

Earl, Henry Hilliard. 1877. *A Centennial History of Fall River, Mass*. New York: Atlantic Publishing and Engraving Co.

Ebbinghaus, Bernhard. 2001. "Reforming the Welfare State through 'Old' or 'New' Social Partnerships?" In *From Collective Bargaining to Social Partnerships: New Roles of the Social Partners in Europe*, edited by Carsten Kjaergaard and Åge Westphalen. Copenhagen: Copenhagen Centre.

———. 2010. "Reforming Bismarckian Corporatism: The Changing Role of Social Partnership in Continental Europe." In *A Long Goodbye to Bismarck?: The Politics of Welfare Reforms in Continental Europe*, edited by Bruno Palier, 255–78. Amsterdam: Amsterdam University Press.

Emerson, George Barrell. 1869. *Education in Massachusetts: Early Legislation and History*. Boston: John Wilson and Son.

Emirbayer, Mustafa, and Douglas W. Maynard. 2010. "Pragmatism and Ethnomethodology." *Qualitative Sociology* 34:221–61.

Emirbayer, Mustafa, and Ann Mische. 1998. "What Is Agency?" *American Journal of Sociology* 103 (4): 962–1023.

English, Beth Anne. 2006. *A Common Thread: Labor, Politics, and Capital Mobility in the Textile Industry*. Athens: University of Georgia Press.

Ensign, Forest Chester. 1921. *Compulsory School Attendance and Child Labor*. Iowa City: Athens Press.

Epstein, S. R. 1998. "Craft Guilds, Apprenticeship, and Technological Change in Preindustrial Europe." *Journal of Economic History* 58 (3): 684–713.

Ermakoff, Ivan. 2008. *Ruling Oneself Out: A Theory of Collective Abdications*. Politics, History, and Culture. Durham, NC: Duke University Press.

———. 2019. "Causality and History: Modes of Causal Investigation in Historical Social Sciences." *Annual Review of Sociology* 45 (29): 1–26.

Esping-Andersen, Gøsta. 1990. *The Three Worlds of Welfare Capitalism*. Princeton, NJ: Princeton University Press.

———. 1996. *Welfare States in Transition: National Adaptations in Global Economies*. Thousand Oaks, CA: Sage.

Evans, Peter B., Dietrich Rueschemeyer, and Theda Skocpol, eds. 1985. *Bringing the State Back In*. New York: Cambridge University Press.

Evans, Rhonda, and Tamara Kay. 2008. "How Environmentalists 'Greened' Trade Policy: Strategic Action and the Architecture of Field Overlap." *American Sociological Review* 73:970–91.

Eyal, Gil. 2013. "Spaces between Fields." In *Bourdieu and Historical Analysis*, edited by Philip S. Gorski, 158–82. Durham, NC: Duke University Press.

Feffer, Andrew. 1993. *The Chicago Pragmatists and American Progressivism.* Ithaca, NY: Cornell University Press.

Feldenkirchen, Wilfried. 1981. "Kinderarbeit im 19. Jahrhundert: ihre wirtschaftlichen und sozialen Auswirkungen." *Zeitschrift für Unternehmensgeschichte* 26:1–41.

Ferree, Myra Marx. 2003. "Resonance and Radicalism: Feminist Framing in the Abortion Debates of the United States and Germany." *American Journal of Sociology* 109:304–44.

Fichte, Johann Gottlieb, Reginald Foy Jones, and George Henry Turnbull. 1922. *Addresses to the German Nation.* Chicago: Open Court Publishing Company.

Field, Alexander James. 1976. "Educational Reform and Manufacturing Development in Mid-Nineteenth Century Massachusetts." *Journal of Economic History* 36:263–66.

Fine, Gary Alan. 2001. *Difficult Reputations: Collective Memories of the Evil, Inept, and Controversial.* Chicago: University of Chicago Press.

Fink, Leon. 1983. *Workingmen's Democracy: The Knights of Labor and American Politics.* Urbana: University of Illinois Press.

First Congregational Society of Providence, RI. 1867. *Memorial of Rev. Edward B. Hall, D.D.* Providence: Sidney S. Rider and Brothers.

Fishlow, Albert. 1966. "The Common School Revival: Fact or Fancy?" In *Industrialization in Two Systems: Essays in Honor of Alexander Gerschenkron by a Group of His Students,* edited by Henry Rosovsky, 40–67. New York: Wiley.

Flanagan, Maureen. 2002. *Seeing with Their Hearts: Chicago Women and the Vision of the Good City, 1871–1933.* Princeton, NJ: Princeton University Press.

Fligstein, Neil. 2001. "Social Skill and the Theory of Fields." *Sociological Theory* 19 (2): 105–25.

Fligstein, Neil, and Doug McAdam. 2012. *A Theory of Fields.* Oxford: Oxford University Press.

Fliter, John A. 2018. *Child Labor in America: The Epic Legal Struggle to Protect Children.* Lawrence: University Press of Kansas.

Flora, Peter. 1972. "Die Bildungsentwickelung im Prozess der Staaten- und Nazionalbildung: eine vergleichende Analyse." In *Soziologie und Sozialgeschichte: Aspekte und Probleme,* edited by Peter Christian Ludz, 294–319. Opladen: Westdeutscher Verlag.

Fones-Wolf, Ken. 2009. "Child Labor in the American Glass Industry." In *The World of Child Labor: An Historical and Regional Survey,* edited by Hugh D. Hindman, 468–71. Armonk, NY: M. E. Sharpe.

Formisano, Ronald P. 1983. *The Transformation of Political Culture: Massachusetts Parties, 1790s–1840s.* New York: Oxford University Press.

Fowler, Orin. 1862. *History of Fall River: With Notices of Freetown and Tiverton.* Fall River: Almy and Milne, Daily News Steam Press.

Fraser, James W. 2016. *Between Church and State: Religion and Public Education in a Multicultural America.* 2nd ed. Baltimore: Johns Hopkins University Press.

Fremdling, Rainer, and Peter Solar. 2010. "Industry." In *The Cambridge Economic History of Modern Europe,* edited by Stephen Broadberry and Kevin O'Rourke, 147–63. Cambridge: Cambridge University Press.

Furner, Mary O. 1975. *Advocacy and Objectivity: A Crisis in the Professionalization of American Social Science, 1865–1905.* Lexington: University Press of Kentucky.

Gattone, Charles F. 2006. *The Social Scientist as Public Intellectual: Critical Reflections in a Changing World.* Lanham, MD: Rowman and Littlefield.

Gerhardt, Martin. 1948. *Ein Jahrhundert Innere Mission: Die Geschichte des Central-Ausschusses für die Innere Mission der Deutschen Evangelischen Kirche. Vol 2, Hüter und Mehrer des Erbes.* Gütersloh, Germany: Bertelsmann.

———. 1950. *Friedrich von Bodelschwingh: ein Lebensbild aus der Deutschen Kirchengeschichte. Vol. 1.* Bielefeld: Verlag der Anstalt Bethel.

Germany, Reichskanzler-Amt. 1877. *Ergebnisse der über Die Frauen- und Kinder-Arbeit in den Fabriken auf Beschluß des Bundesraths angestellten Erhebungen.* Berlin: Carl Heymanns Verlag.

Germany, Reichstag. 1877. *Verhandlungen des Reichstags: Stenographische Berichte.* Accessed October 1, 2020. https://www.reichstagsprotokolle.de/rtbiauf.html.

Gerry, Elbridge. 1883. "Cruelty to Children." *North American Review* 137:68–75.

Gewerbeordnung für den Norddeutschen Bund. 1869. Accessed October 1, 2020. https://de .wikisource.org/wiki/Gewerbeordnung_f%C3%BCr_den_Norddeutschen_Bund.

Gladen, Albin. 1974. "Geschichte der Sozialpolitik." In *Deutschland: eine Analyse ihrer Bedingungen, Formen, Zielsetzungen und Auswirkungen.* Wiesbaden: F. Steiner.

Goldin, Claudia, and Kenneth Sokoloff. 1982. "Women, Children, and Industrialization in the Early Republic: Evidence from the Manufacturing Censuses." *Journal of Economic History* 42:741–74.

Goldschmidt, Paul. 1893. "Stein zum Altenstein, Karl Freiherr von." In *Allgemeine Deutsche Biographie (ADB)*, 645–60. Leipzig: Duncker und Humblot.

Goldstein, Judith, and Robert O. Keohane. 1993. *Ideas and Foreign Policy: Beliefs, Institutions, and Political Change.* Ithaca, NY: Cornell University Press.

Goldthorpe, John H. 1997. "Current Issues in Comparative Macrosociology: A Debate on Methodological Issues." *Comparative Social Research* 16:1–26.

Gontard, Maurice. 1980. "Libéralisme et instruction primaire : 1842–1879. Introduction à l'étude de la lutte scolaire en Belgique." In *Histoire de l'éducation*, edited by Jacques Lory, 6:57–61. Leuven, Belgium: Nauwelaerts.

Gooch, Brison D. 1963. *Belgium and the February Revolution.* The Hague: M. Nijhoff.

Gordon, Linda. 1985. "Single Mothers and Child Neglect: 1880–1920." *American Quarterly* 37:173–92.

Gordon, Lynn. 1977. "Women and the Anti-Child Labor Movement in Illinois, 1890–1920." *Social Service Review* 51:228–48.

Gorski, Philip S. 1993. "The Protestant Ethic Revisited: Disciplinary Revolution and State Formation in Holland and Prussia." *The American Journal of Sociology* 99 (2): 265–316.

———. 2003. *The Disciplinary Revolution: Calvinism and the Rise of the State in Early Modern Europe.* Chicago: University of Chicago Press.

———. 2013. "Bourdieusian Theory and Historical Analysis: Maps, Mechanisms and Methods." In *Bourdieu and Historical Analysis*, edited by Philip S. Gorski, 327–66. Durham, NC: Duke University Press.

Gould, Andrew C. 1999. *Origins of Liberal Dominance: State, Church, and Party in Nineteenth-Century Europe.* Ann Arbor: University of Michigan Press.

Government Accountability Office. 2008. "Fair Labor Standards Act: Better Use of Available Resources and Consistent Reporting Could Improve Compliance." GAO-08-962T.

Gräff, H., C. F. Koch, L. V. Rönne, H. Simon, and A. Wenzel. 1839. "Dienstinstruktion für die Oberpräsidenten vom 31. December 1825." In *Ergänzungen und Erläuterungen des allgemeinen Landrechts für die preußischen Staaten durch Gesetzgebung und Wissenschaft, dritte Abtheilung, Ergänzungen des 2. Theils, Titel 9–12*, edited by H. Gräff, C. F. Koch, L. V. Rönne, H. Simon, and A. Wenzel, 345–49. Breslau: Georg Philipp Aderholz.

Grattan-Guinness, I. 1984. "Work for the Workers: Advances in Engineering Mechanics and Instruction in France, 1800–1830." *Annals of Science* 41 (1): 1–33.

Gray, Marion. 1986. "Prussia in Transition: Society and Politics under the Stein Reform Ministry of 1808." *Transactions of the American Philosophical Society* 76:1–175.

Groen, Mark. 2008. "The Whig Party and the Rise of the Common Schools, 1837–1854." *American Educational History Journal* 35 (2): 251–60.

Gross, Neil. 2009. "A Pragmatist Theory of Social Mechanisms." *American Sociological Review* 74 (3): 358–79.

Grossmann, Matthew. 2014. *Artists of the Possible: Governing Networks and American Policy Change since 1945*. New York: Oxford University Press.

Gubin, Élaine. 2011. "Elites, Employers, Child Labour and Compulsory Education in Belgium before 1914." In *Child Labour's Global Past, 1650–2000*, edited by Kristoffel Lieten and Elise van Nederveen Meerkerk, 193–208. Bern: Peter Lang.

Gubin, Élaine, and Patrick Lefèvre. 1985. "Obligation scolaire et société en Belgique au XIXe siècle: réflexions à propos du premier projet de loi sur l'enseignement obligatoire (1883)." *Revue Belge de Philologie et d'histoire* 63 (2): 324–76.

Guizot, François. 1816. *Essai sur l'histoire et sur l'état actuel de l'instruction publique en France*. Paris: Chez Maradan.

———. 1889. "Exposé des motifs présentés à la Chambre des députés par M. le ministre secretaire d'État de l'Instruction publique. Séance du 2 janvier 1833." In *Instruction publique, éducation. Extraits, précédés d'une introd. par Félix Cadet*. Paris: Librairie Eugène Belin.

Haase, Annemarie. 2000. "Das 'Unruhige Dreieck': Aachen-Stolberg, Verviers und Eupen im Vormärz." In *Aachen, die westlichen Rheinlände und die Revolution 1848/49*, edited by Guido Müller and Jürgen Herres, 55–70. Aachen: Shaker Verlag.

Haber, Hanan. 2017. "Rise of the Regulatory Welfare State? Social Regulation in Utilities in Israel." *Social Policy and Administration* 51 (3): 442–63.

Hacker, Jacob S. 2002. *The Divided Welfare State: The Battle over Public and Private Social Benefits in the United States*. New York: Cambridge University Press.

———. 2005. "Policy Drift: The Hidden Politics of U.S. Welfare State Retrenchment." In *Beyond Continuity: Institutional Change in Advanced Political Economies*, edited by Wolfgang Streeck and Kathleen Thelen, 40–82. Oxford: Oxford University Press.

———. 2011. "The Institutional Foundations of Middle-Class Democracy." *Policy Network* 6:33–37.

———. 2013. "How to Reinvigorate the Centre-Left? Predistribution." *Guardian*, June 12. Accessed August 9, 2020. https://www.theguardian.com/commentisfree/2013/jun/12/reinvigorate-centre-left-predistribution.

Hacker, Jacob S., and Paul Pierson. 2002. "Business Power and Social Policy: Employers and the Formation of the American Welfare State." *Politics and Society* 30 (2): 277–325.

Hacking, Ian. 1990. *The Taming of Chance*. Cambridge: Cambridge University Press.

Hall, Peter. 1993. "Policy Paradigms, Social Learning, and the State: The Case of Economic Policymaking in Britain." *Comparative Politics* 25:275–96.

Hall, Peter, and David Soskice. 2001. "An Introduction to the Varieties of Capitalism." In *Varieties of Capitalism: The Institutional Foundations of Comparative Advantage*, 1–70. Oxford: Oxford University Press.

Hargreaves, A. S. 2009. "Artificers, Statute Of." In *The Oxford Companion to British History (1 Rev. Ed.)*. Accessed October 1, 2020. *https://www.oxfordreference.com/view/10.1093/acref/9780199567638.001.0001/acref-9780199567638-e-233*.

Harmon, Sandra D. 1981. "Florence Kelley in Illinois." *Journal of the Illinois State Historical Society* 74:162–78.

Harmond, Richard. 1968. "The 'Beast' in Boston: Benjamin F. Butler as Governor of Massachusetts." *Journal of American History* 55 (2): 266–80.

Hay, Douglas. 2004. "England, 1562–1875: The Law and Its Uses." In *Masters, Servants and Magistrates in Britain and the Empire, 1562–1955*, edited by Douglas Hay and Paul Craven, 59–116. Chapel Hill: University of North Carolina Press.

Hayes, Carlton Joseph Huntley. 1916. *A Political and Social History of Modern Europe*. New York: Macmillan.

Heclo, Hugh. 2010. *Modern Social Politics in Britain and Sweden: From Relief to Income Mainte-nance*. Colchester, UK: ECPR Press.

Heitzer, Horstwalter, ed. 1991. *Deutscher Katholizismus und Sozialpolitik bis zum Beginn der Wei-marer Republik*. Vol. 6. Paderborn, Germany: F. Schöningh.

Henderson, W. O. 1982. "Friedrich List and the French Protectionists." *Journal of Institutional and Theoretical Economics* 138 (2): 262–75.

Hennock, E. P. 2007. *The Origin of the Welfare State in England and Germany, 1850–1914*. Cambridge: Cambridge University Press.

Herbst, Jurgen. 2002. "Nineteenth-Century Schools between Community and State: The Cases of Prussia and the United States." *History of Education Quarterly* 42 (3): 317–41.

Hermann, Ingo. 2003. *Hardenberg: Der Reformkanzler*. Berlin: Siedler.

Herzig, Arno. 1983. "Kinderarbeit in Deutschland in Manufaktur und Protofabrik." *Archiv Für Sozialgeschichte* 23:311–75.

Heywood, Colin. 1988. *Childhood in Nineteenth-Century France: Work, Health, and Education among the "Classes Populaires."* Cambridge: Cambridge University Press.

———. 1992. *The Development of the French Economy, 1750—1914: Prepared for the Economic History Society*. Studies in Economic and Social History. Basingstoke, UK: Macmillan.

Hicks, Alexander. 1999. *Social Democracy and Welfare Capitalism*. Ithaca, NY: Cornell University Press.

Hicks, Alexander, and Joya Misra. 1993. "Political Resources and the Growth of Welfare in Affluent Capitalist Democracies, 1960–1982." *American Journal of Sociology* 99 (3): 668–710.

Hilden, Patricia. 1993. *Women, Work, and Politics: Belgium, 1830–1914*. New York: Clarendon Press.

Hindman, Hugh D. 2009. *The World of Child Labor: An Historical and Regional Survey*. Armonk, NY: M. E. Sharpe.

Hobson, Barbara, and Marika Lindholm. 1997. "Collective Identities, Women's Power Resources, and the Making of Welfare States." *Theory and Society* 26 (4): 475–508.

Hogan, David John. 1985. *Class and Reform: School and Society in Chicago, 1880–1930*. Philadelphia: University of Pennsylvania Press.

Hömig, Herbert. 2015. *Altenstein: der erste preussische Kultusminister: Eine Biographie*. Münster: Aschendorff Verlag.

Hoppe, Ruth, ed. 1958. *Geschichte der Kinderarbeit in Deutschland 1750–1939. Band II: Dokumente*. Berlin: Verlag Neues Leben.

Hoppe, Ruth, Jürgen Kuczynski, and Heinrich Waldmann. 1960. *Hardenbergs Umfrage über die Lage der Kinder in den Fabriken und andere Dokumente aus der Frühgeschichte der Lage der Arbeiter*. Berlin: Akademie-Verlag.

Horner, Leonard. 1840. *On the Employment of Children in Factories and Other Works in the United Kingdom and in Some Foreign Countries*. London: Longman, Orme, Brown, Green and Longmans.

Hornung, Klaus. 1995. "Preußischer Konservatismus und Soziale Frage—Hermann Wagener (1815–1889)." In *Konservative Politiker in Deutschland: Eine Auswahl Biographischer Porträts aus Zwei Jahrhunderten*, edited by Hans-Christof Kraus, 157–83. Berlin: Duncker und Humblot.

Huber, Ernst Rudolf. 1963. *Deutsche Verfassungsgeschichte seit 1789*. Vol. 3. Stuttgart: W. Kohlhammer.

Huber, Evelyne, Charles Ragin, and John D. Stephens. 1993. "Social Democracy, Christian Democracy, Constitutional Structure, and the Welfare State." *American Journal of Sociology* 99 (3): 711–49.

Huber, Evelyne, and John D. Stephens. 2001. *Development and Crisis of the Welfare State: Parties and Policies in Global Markets*. Chicago: University of Chicago Press.

Hubert, Michel. 1998. *Deutschland im Wandel: Geschichte der deutschen Bevölkerung seit 1815*. Stuttgart: Franz Steiner Verlag.

Humphrey, Herman. 1840. *Domestic Education*. Amherst: J., S. and C. Adams.

Hunt, E. K., and Mark Lautzenheiser. 2011. *History of Economic Thought: A Critical Perspective*. 3rd ed. Armonk, NY: M. E. Sharpe.

Hutchinson, K. B. 1943. "James Gordon Carter, Education Reformer." *New England Quarterly* 16:376–96.

Illinois, Bureau of Labor Statistics. 1893. *Seventh Biennial Report of the Bureau of Labor Statistics of Illinois for the Year 1892*. Springfield, IL: H. W. Rokker.

Illinois, Joint Committee to Investigate the "Sweat Shop" System. 1893. *Report and Findings of the Joint Committee to Investigate the "Sweat Shop" System, Together with a Transcript of the Testimony Taken by the Committee*. Springfield, IL: H. W. Rokker.

Illinois, Office of Inspectors of Factories and Workshops. 1893–98. *Annual Report of the Factory Inspectors of Illinois*. Springfield: Ed F. Hartman, State Printer.

Immergut, Ellen M. 1992. *Health Politics: Interests and Institutions in Western Europe*. Cambridge: Cambridge University Press.

Institut Royal de France. 1840. *Calendrier pour l'année 1840*. Paris: Imprimerie de Firmin Didot Freres.

Iversen, Torben, and David Soskice. 2006. "Electoral Institutions and the Politics of Coalitions: Why Some Democracies Redistribute More Than Others." *American Political Science Review* 100 (2): 165–81.

Iversen, Torben, and John D. Stephens. 2008. "Partisan Politics, the Welfare State, and Three Worlds of Human Capital Formation." *Comparative Political Studies* 41:600–637.

Jansen, Robert S. 2017. *Revolutionizing Repertoires: The Rise of Populist Mobilization in Peru*. Chicago: University of Chicago Press.

Jensen, Richard. 1971. *The Winning of the Midwest: Social and Political Conflict, 1888–1896*. Chicago: University of Chicago Press.

Joas, Hans. 1996. *The Creativity of Action*. Chicago: University of Chicago Press.

Jones, Jesse H. 1871. *The Kingdom of Heaven: What It Is; Where It Is; and the Duty of American Christians concerning It*. Boston: Jesse H. Jones.

Kaestle, Carl. 1976. "'Between the Scylla of Brutal Ignorance and the Charybdis of a Literary Education': Elite Attitudes toward Mass Schooling in Early Industrial England and America." In *Schooling and Society: Studies in the History of Education*, edited by Lawrence Stone, 177–91. Baltimore: Johns Hopkins University Press.

———. 1983. *Pillars of the Republic: Common Schools and American Society, 1780–1860*. New York: Hill and Wang.

Kaestle, Carl, and Maris Vinovskis. 1980. *Education and Social Change in Nineteenth-Century Massachusetts*. Cambridge: Cambridge University Press.

Kahl, Sigrun. 2005. "The Religious Roots of Modern Poverty Policy: Catholic, Lutheran, and Reformed Protestant Traditions Compared." *European Journal of Sociology* 46 (1): 91–126.

Kaplan, Steven. 1979. "Réflexions sur la police du monde de travail, 1700–1815." *Revue historique* 261 (1): 17–77.

Karl, Michael. 1993. *Fabrikinspektoren in Preussen: das Personal der Gewerbeaufsicht 1854–1945: Professionalisierung, Bürokratisierung und Gruppenprofil*. Opladen, Germany: Westdeutscher Verlag.

Kastner, Dieter. 2004. *Kinderarbeit im Rheinland: Entstehung und Wirkung des ersten preussischen Gesetzes gegen die Arbeit von Kindern in Fabriken von 1839*. Cologne: SH-Verlag.

Kästner, Karl-Hermann. 1981. "From the Social Question to the Social State." *Economy and Society* 10 (1): 7–26.

Kastner, Lisa. 2017. "Tracing Policy Influence of Diffuse Interests: The Post-Crisis Consumer Finance Protection Politics in the US." *Journal of Civil Society* 13 (2): 130–48.

Katz, Michael B. (1968) 2001. *The Irony of Early School Reform: Educational Innovation in Mid-Nineteenth Century Massachusetts*. New York: Teachers College Press.

Katznelson, Ira. 1986. "Constructing Cases and Comparisons." In *Working-Class Formation: Nineteenth-Century Patterns in Western Europe and the United States*, edited by Ira Katznelson and Aristide R. Zolberg, 3–41. Princeton, NJ: Princeton University Press.

———. 2003. "Periodization and Preferences: Reflections of Purposive Action in Comparative Historical Social Science." In *Comparative Historical Analysis in the Social Sciences*, edited by James Mahoney and Dietrich Rueschemeyer, 270–304. Cambridge: Cambridge University Press.

Keller, Eduard. 1873. *Geschichte des preußischen Volksschulwesens*. Berlin: Robert Oppenheim Verlag.

Kelley, Florence. 1887. "The Need of Theoretical Preparation for Philanthropic Work." *Christian Union* 35:12.

———. 1889. *Our Toiling Children*. Chicago: Woman's Temperance Publication Association.

———. 1898. "Die weibliche Fabrikinspektion in den Vereinigten Staaten." In *Archiv für Soziale Gesetzgebung und Statistik. Sonderabdruck*. Berlin: Carl Heymanns Verlag.

———. 1905. *Some Ethical Gains through Legislation*. New York: Macmillan. Accessed October 1, 2020. https://archive.org/details/someethicalgain01kellgoog/page/n8/mode/2up.

———. 1907. "Obstacles to the Enforcement of Child Labor Legislation." *Child Labor and the Republic: Proceedings of the Third Annual Meeting of the National Child Labor Committee*, 50–56.

———. 1923. "Should Women Be Treated Identically with Men by the Law?" *American Review Magazine* 1:276–84.

Kelley, Florence, and Kathryn Kish Sklar. 1986. *Notes of Sixty Years: The Autobiography of Florence Kelley; with an Early Essay by the Author on the Need of Theoretical Preparation for Philanthropic Work*. Chicago: C. H. Kerr Publishing Company.

Kelley, Florence, Kathryn Kish Sklar, and Beverly Wilson Palmer. 2009. *The Selected Letters of Florence Kelley, 1869–1931*. Urbana: University of Illinois Press.

Kerr, Clark, John Dunlop, Frederick Harbinson, and Charles Myers. 1960. *Industrialism and Industrial Man: The Problems of Labor and Management in Economic Growth*. Cambridge, MA: Harvard University Press.

Kersbergen, Kees van. 1995. *Social Capitalism: A Study of Christian Democracy and the Welfare State*. London: Routledge.

Kersbergen, Kees van, and Philip Manow. 2010. *Religion, Class Coalitions, and Welfare States*. Cambridge: Cambridge University Press.

Ketteler, Wilhelm Emmanuel von. 1873. *Die Katholiken im Deutschen Reiche: Entwurf zu einem politischen Programm*. Mainz, Germany: Franz Kirchheim.

Kingdon, John W. 1984. *Agendas, Alternatives, and Public Policies*. Boston: Little, Brown.

Kirby, Peter. 2003. *Child Labour in Britain, 1750–1870*. New York: Palgrave Macmillan.

Kiser, Edgar, and Joachin Schneider. 1994. "Bureaucracy and Efficiency: An Analysis of Taxation in Early Modern Prussia." *American Sociological Review* 59 (2): 187–204.

Kitchen, Martin. 2006. *A History of Modern Germany, 1800–2000*. Malden, MA: Blackwell.

Knight, Louise W. 2005. *Citizen: Jane Addams and the Struggle for Democracy*. Chicago: University of Chicago Press.

Kocka, Jürgen. 1986. "Problems of Working-Class Formation in Germany: The Early Years, 1800–1875." In *Working-Class Formation: Nineteenth-Century Patterns in Western Europe and the United States*, edited by Ira Katznelson and Aristide R. Zolberg, 279–351. Princeton, NJ: Princeton University Press.

———. 1990. *Arbeitsverhältnisse und Arbeiterexistenzen: Grundlagen der Klassenbildung im 19. Jahrhundert*. Bonn: J. H. W Dietz.

Koepke, Robert Louis. 1992. "Educating Child Labourers in France: The Parliamentary Debates of 1840." *Canadian Journal of History* 27 (3): 501–19.

Köllmann, Wolfgang. 1966. "Die Anfänge der staatlichen Sozialpolitik in Preussen bis 1869." *Vierteljahrschrift für Sozial- und Wirtschaftsgeschichte* 53:28–52.

Koopmans, Ruud. 2004. "Movements and Media: Selection Processes and Evolutionary Dynamics in the Public Sphere." *Theory and Society* 33 (3–4): 367–91.

Koopmans, Ruud, and Paul Statham. 1999a. "Ethnic and Civic Conceptions of Nationhood and the Differential Success of the Extreme Right in Germany and Italy." In *How Social Movements Matter*, edited by Marco Giugni, Doug McAdam, and Charles Tilly, 225–52. Minneapolis: University of Minnesota Press.

———. 1999b. "Political Claims Analysis: Integrating Protest Event and Political Discourse Approach." *Mobilization* 4:40–51.

Korpi, Walter. 1978. *The Working Class in Welfare Capitalism: Work, Unions, and Politics in Sweden.* Boston: Routledge and Kegan Paul.

———. 1983. *The Democratic Class Struggle.* Boston: Routledge and Kegan Paul.

Korpi, Walter, and Joakim Palme. 1998. "The Paradox of Redistribution and Strategies of Equality: Welfare State Institutions, Inequality, and Poverty in the Western Countries." *American Sociological Review* 63 (5): 661–87.

Koselleck, Reinhart. 1967. *Preußen zwischen Reform und Revolution: Allgemeines Landrecht, Verwaltung und Soziale Bewegung von 1791 bis 1848.* Stuttgart: Ernst Klett Verlag.

Koven, Seth, and Sonya Michel. 1990. "Womanly Duties: Maternalist Politics and the Origins of Welfare States in France, Germany, Great Britain, and the United States, 1880–1920." *American Historical Review* 95:1076–108.

———. 1993. *Mothers of a New World: Maternalist Politics and the Origins of Welfare States.* New York: Routledge.

Krasner, Stephen. 1988. "Sovereignty: An Institutional Perspective." *Comparative Political Studies* 21:66–94.

Kraus, Hans-Christof. 2002. "Hermann Wagener (1815–1889)." In *Politische Theorien des 19. Jahrhunderts: Konservatismus—Liberalismus—Sozialismus*, edited by Bernd Heidenreich, 537–86. Berlin: Akademie Verlag.

Kreuzer, Marcus. 2003. "Parliamentarization and the Question of German Exceptionalism: 1867–1918." *Central European History* 36 (3): 327–57.

Kuczynski, Jürgen. 1968. *Studien zur Geschichte der Lage des arbeitenden Kindes in Deutschland von 1700 bis zur Gegenwart.* Berlin: Akademie-Verlag.

Kuczynski, Jürgen, and Ruth Hoppe. 1958. *Geschichte der Kinderarbeit in Deutschland, 1750–1939.* Berlin: Verlag Neues Leben.

Kuhlemann, Frank-Michael. 1992. *Modernisierung und Disziplinierung: Sozialgeschichte des preussischen Volksschulwesens 1794–1872.* Göttingen: Vandenhoeck and Ruprecht.

Kuhn, Anne Louise. 1947. *The Mother's Role in Childhood Education: New England Concepts, 1830–1860.* New Haven, CT: Yale University Press.

Kuypers, Julian. 1960. *Les Egalitaires en Belgique: Buonarroti et ses sociétés secrètes d'après des documents inédits (1824–1836).* Brussels: Librairie Encyclopedique.

Lachmann, Richard. 2003. "Elite Self-Interest and Economic Decline in Early Modern Europe." *American Sociological Review* 68 (3): 346–72.

Lademacher, Horst. 2000. "The Netherlands and Belgium: Notes on the Causes of Abstinence from Revolution." In *Europe in 1848: Revolution and Reform*, edited by Dieter Dowe, Heinz-Gerhard Haupt, Dieter Langewiesche, and Jonathan Sperber, 259–86. New York: Berghahn Books.

Lafer, Gordon. 2013. "The Legislative Attack on American Wages and Labor Standards, 2011–2012." Briefing Paper #364. Washington, DC: Economic Policy Institute.

La Mennais, François. 1828. *Des progrès de la révolution et de la guerre contre l'église.* Paris : Belin.

Langewiesche, Dieter. 2000. *Liberalism in Germany.* Princeton, NJ: Princeton University Press.

Latour, Bruno. 1987. *Science in Action: How to Follow Scientists and Engineers through Society.* Cambridge, MA: Harvard University Press.

———. 1988. *The Pasteurization of France.* Cambridge, MA: Harvard University Press.

La Vopa, Anthony J. 1980. *Prussian Schoolteachers: Profession and Office, 1763–1848.* Chapel Hill: University of North Carolina Press.

Lefèvre, Claude. 1977. *Les Chambres de commerce et d'industrie en France.* Paris: Editions Sirey.

Legrand, Daniel. 1838. *Lettre d'un Industriel des Montagnes des Vosges à MM. Gros, Odier, Roman & Comp.: À Wesserling, distribuée aux membres des deux Chambres et du Ministère.* Strasbourg: F. G. Levrault.

Leiby, James. 1960. *Carroll Wright and Labor Reform: The Origin of Labor Statistics.* Cambridge, MA: Harvard University Press.

Lemercier, Claire. 2003. *Un si discret pouvoir: aux origines de la chambre de commerce de Paris. 1803–1853.* Paris: La Découverte.

Leon, Cedric de. 2015. *The Origins of Right to Work: Antilabor Democracy in Nineteenth-Century Chicago.* Ithaca, NY: ILR Press, an imprint of Cornell University Press.

Leonards, Chris, and Nico Randeraad. 2014. "Building a Transnational Network of Social Reform in the Nineteenth Century." In *Shaping the Transnational Sphere: Experts, Networks and Issues from the 1840s to the 1930s,* edited by Davide Rodogno, Bernhard Struck, and Jakob Vogel, 111–30. New York: Berghahn Books.

Lerman, Katherine Ann. 2004. *Bismarck.* Upper Saddle River, NJ: Pearson.

Levi-Faur, David. 2014. "The Welfare State: A Regulatory Perspective." *Public Administration* 92 (3): 599–614.

Levinger, Matthew. 1998. "Kant and the Origins of Prussian Constitutionalism." *History of Political Thought* 19 (2): 241–63.

Lieberman, Robert C. 2002. "Ideas, Institutions, and Political Order: Explaining Political Change." *American Political Science Review* 96 (4): 697–71.

Liége Chamber of Commerce. 1860. "Avis des la Chambre de Commerce de Liége sur de projet de loi relatif à la condition des classes ouvrières at au travail des enfants" (1849). In *Avis de la Chambre de Commerce de Liége sur l'avant-projet de loi relatif au travail des enfants dans les établissements industriels,* 8–31. Liége: Imprimerie de L. de Thier et F. Lovinfosse.

Lindert, Peter H. 2004. *Growing Public: Social Spending and Economic Growth since the Eighteenth Century.* Cambridge: Cambridge University Press.

Lis, Catharina, and Hugo Soly. 1994. "'An Irresistible Phalanx': Journeymen Associations in Western Europe, 1300–1800." In *Before the Unions: Wage Earners and Collective Action in Europe, 1300–1850,* edited by Catharina Lis, Jan Lucassen, and Hugo Soly, 11–52. Cambridge: Cambridge University Press.

Lohmann, Theodor, and Lothar Machtan. 1995. *Mut zur Moral: aus der privaten Korrespondenz des Gesellschaftsreformers Theodor Lohmann.* Bremen: Edition Temmen.

Loriaux, Florence. 2000. *Enfants-machines: histoire du travail des enfants en Belgique au XIXe et XXe siècles.* Brussels: CARHOP-EVO.

Lubelski-Bernard, Nadine. 1985. "Auguste Visschers." In *Biographie nationale de Belgique,* vol. 44, 746–68. Brussels: Académie royale des sciences, des lettres et des beaux-arts de Belgique.

Lüdtke, Alf. 1989. *Police and State in Prussia, 1815–1850.* Cambridge: Cambridge University Press.

Ludwig, Karl-Heinz. 1965. "Die Fabrikarbeit von Kindern im 19. Jahrhundert: ein Problem der Technikgeschichte." *Vierteljahrschrift für Sozial- und Wirtschaftsgeschichte* 52:63–85.

Luther, Seth. 1832. *An Address to the Workingmen of New-England, on the State of Education, and on the Condition of the Producing Classes in Europe and America. With Particular Reference to the Effect of Manufacturing (as Now Conducted) on the Health and Happiness of the Poor, and on the Safety of Our Republic.* Boston: S. Luther.

Luxem, Birgit. 1983. *"Die Kinder- und Jugendarbeit im 19. Jahrhundert im Regierungsbezirk Düsseldorf."* PhD diss., Heinrich Heine University of Düsseldorf.

Lynch, Katherine A. 1988. *Family, Class, and Ideology in Early Industrial France: Social Policy and the Working-Class Family, 1825–1848.* Madison: University of Wisconsin Press.

Machtan, Lothar. 1995. "Der Gesellschaftsreformer Theodor Lohmann: Grundanschauung und Programm." In *Soziale Demokratie und Sozialistische Theorie: Festschrift für Hans-Josef Steinberg,* edited by Inge Marssolek and Till Schelz-Brandenburg, 30–38. Bremen: Edition Temmen.

Mahoney, James. 2000. "Path Dependence in Historical Sociology." *Theory and Society* 29 (4): 507–48.

Mahoney, James, and Gary Goertz. 2004. "The Possibility Principle: Choosing Negative Cases in Comparative Research." *American Political Science Review* 98 (4): 653–69.

Mahoney, James, and Kathleen Thelen. 2010. "A Theory of Gradual Institutional Change." In *Explaining Institutional Change: Ambiguity, Agency, and Power,* edited by James Mahoney and Kathleen Thelen, 1–37. Cambridge: Cambridge University Press.

Majone, Giandomenico. 1994. "The Rise of the Regulatory State in Europe." *West European Politics* 17 (3): 77–101.

———. 1997. "From the Positive to the Regulatory State." *Journal of Public Policy* 17 (2): 139–67.

Mann, Horace. 1849. *The Massachusetts System of Common Schools; Being an Enlarged and Revised Edition of the Tenth Annual Report of the First Secretary of the Massachusetts Board of Education.* Boston: Dutton and Wentworth.

———. 1868. *Life and Works of Horace Mann, Vol. III: Annual Reports on Education.* Edited by Mary Tyler Peabody Mann. Boston: Lee and Shepard.

———. 1872. *Lectures and Annual Reports on Education.* Edited by Mary Tyler Peabody Mann. Boston: Lee and Shepard.

———. 1891. *Life and Works of Horace Mann, Vol. II: Annual Reports on Education.* Edited by Mary Tyler Peabody Mann. Boston: Lee and Shepard.

Mann, Mary. 1865. *Life of Horace Mann.* Boston: Walker, Fuller and Co.

Mares, Isabella. 2003. *The Politics of Social Risk: Business and Welfare State Development.* Cambridge: Cambridge University Press.

Mareska, Daniel Joseph Benoit, and J. Heyman. 1845. *Enquête sur le travail et la condition physique et morale des ouvriers employés dans les manufactures de coton, à Gand.* Ghent: E. Gyselynck.

Marshall, T. H. 1964. *Class, Citizenship, and Social Development.* New York: Doubleday and Co.

Martin, George Henry. 1894. *The Evolution of the Massachusetts Public School System.* New York: D. Appleton and Co.

Martin, John Levy. 2003. "What Is Field Theory?" *American Journal of Sociology* 109 (1): 1–49.

Marx, Karl. 2019. *The Political Writings.* Edited by David Fernbach. London: Verso.

———. 2011. *Capital Volume 1: A Critique of Political Economy.* Mineola, NY: Dover Publications.

Massachusetts, Board of Education. 1838–39. *Abstract of the Massachusetts School Returns.* Boston: Dutton and Wentworth.

Massachusetts, Bureau of Statistics of Labor. 1870–77, 1886. *Annual Report of the Bureau of Statistics of Labor.* Boston: Wright and Potter.

Massachusetts, Constable of the Commonwealth. 1868. *Report of Henry K. Oliver, Deputy State Constable.* Massachusetts Senate Document No. 21.

———. 1869. *Report of Henry K. Oliver, Deputy State Constable.* Massachusetts Senate Document No. 44.

_____. 1870. *Report of the Deputy State Constable on the Subject of the Employment of Children in Manufacturing Establishments*. Senate Document No. 13.

_____. 1871. *Fifth Annual Report of the Constable of the Commonwealth*. Senate Document No. 8.

Massachusetts District Police. 1880–1904. *Annual Report of the Chief of the Massachusetts District Police*. Boston: Wright and Potter.

Massachusetts. General Court. Acts and Resolves.

Massachusetts. General Court. House of Representatives. House Documents.

Massachusetts. General Court. House of Representatives. House Journal.

Massachusetts. General Court. Senate. Senate Documents.

Massachusetts. General Court. Senate. Senate Journal.

Massachusetts, Special Commission on the Hours of Labor. 1866. *Report of the Special Commission on the Hours of Labor and the Condition and Prospects of the Industrial Classes*. Massachusetts House Document No. 98.

———. 1867. *Report of Commissioners on the Hours of Labor*. Massachusetts House Document No. 44.

Massachusetts, State Detective Force. 1877. *Report of the Chief Detective of the Commonwealth of Massachusetts for the Year Ending December 31, 1876*. Senate Document No. 11.

Massachusetts State Police. 1874. *Annual Report of the State Police for the Year Ending December 28, 1873*. Senate Document 48.

Maynes, Mary Jo. 1985. *Schooling for the People: Comparative Local Studies of Schooling History in France and Germany, 1750–1850*. New York: Holmes and Meier.

McCammon, Holly J., Courtney Sanders Muse, Harmony D. Newman, and Teresa M. Terrell. 2007. "Movement Framing and Discursive Opportunity Structures: The Political Successes of the US Women's Jury Movements." *American Sociological Review* 72 (5): 725–49.

McCarthy, Michael A. 2017. *Dismantling Solidarity: Capitalist Politics and American Pensions since the New Deal*. Ithaca, NY: Cornell University Press.

McNeill, George E. 1875. *Report upon the Schooling and Hours of Labor of Children Employed in the Manufacturing and Mechanical Establishments of Massachusetts*. Boston: Wright and Potter.

Mehta, Jal. 2011. "The Varied Roles of Ideas in Politics: From 'Whether' to 'How.'" In *Ideas and Politics in Social Science Research*, edited by Daniel Béland and Robert Henry Cox, 23–46. New York: Oxford University Press.

Melton, James Van Horn. 1988. *Absolutism and the Eighteenth-Century Origins of Compulsory Schooling in Prussia and Austria*. Cambridge: Cambridge University Press.

Mengelberg, Kaethe. 1961. "Lorenz von Stein and His Contribution to Historical Sociology." *Journal of the History of Ideas* 22 (2): 267–74.

Messerli, Jonathan C. 1965. "James G. Carter's Liabilities as a Common School Reformer." *History of Education Quarterly* 5 (1): 14–25.

Meyer, Adolf Heinrich Georg. 1971. *Schule und Kinderarbeit: das Verhältnis von Schul- und Sozialpolitik in der Entwicklung der Preussischen Volksschule zu Beginn des 19. Jahrhunderts*. Hamburg: University of Hamburg.

Meyer, Hermann Julius. 1894. "Fabrikgesetzgebung." In *Meyers Konversations-lexicon*, 120–25. Leipzig: Bibliographisches Institut.

Meyer, Jacob, and Robert Greenleaf. 2011. "Enforcement of State Wage and Hour Laws: A Survey of State Regulators." Columbia Law School National State Attorneys General Program.

Meyers, Peter V. 1985. "Primary Schoolteachers in Nineteenth-Century France: A Study of Professionalization through Conflict." *History of Education Quarterly* 25 (1–2): 21–40.

Miller, Donald L. 1996. *City of the Century: The Epic of Chicago and the Making of America*. New York: Simon and Schuster.

Miller, Edward H. 2009. "They Vote Only for the Spoils: Massachusetts Reformers, Suffrage Restriction, and the 1884 Civil Service Law." *Journal of the Gilded Age and Progressive Era* 8 (3): 341–63.

Milward, Alan S., and S. B. Saul. 2012. *The Development of the Economies of Continental Europe, 1850–1914*. London: Routledge.

Mintrom, Michael. 1997. "Policy Entrepreneurs and the Diffusion of Innovation." *American Journal of Political Science* 41 (3): 738–70.

———. 2000. *Policy Entrepreneurs and School Choice*. Washington, DC: Georgetown University Press.

Mintrom, Michael, and Phillipa Norman. 2009. "Policy Entrepreneurship and Policy Change." *Policy Studies Journal* 37 (4): 649–67.

Mintz, Steven. 2004. *Huck's Raft: A History of American Childhood*. Cambridge, MA: Belknap Press of Harvard University Press.

Misner, Paul. 1991. *Social Catholicism in Europe: From the Onset of Industrialization to the First World War*. New York: Crossroad.

Moehling, Carolyn. 1999. "State Child Labor Laws and the Decline of Child Labor." *Explorations in Economic History* 36 (1): 72–106.

Mohl, Robert von. 1835. "Ueber die Nachtheile, welche sowohl den Arbeitern selbst, als dem Wohlstande und der Sicherheit der gesammten bürgerlichen Gesellschaft von dem fabrikmäßigen Betriebe der Industrie zugehen, und über die Nothwendigkeit gründlicher Vorbeugungsmittel." *Archiv der politischen Oekonomie und Polizeiwissenschaft* 2:141–203.

Mokyr, Joel. 1976. *Industrialization in the Low Countries, 1795–1850*. Yale Series in Economic History. New Haven, CT: Yale University Press.

Montgomery, David. 1967. *Beyond Equality: Labor and the Radical Republicans, 1862–1872*. New York: A. A. Knopf.

———. 1987. *The Fall of the House of Labor*. Cambridge: Cambridge University Press.

Moody, Joseph N. 1953. *Church and Society: Catholic Social and Political Thought and Movements, 1789–1950*. New York: Arts, Inc.

Morgan, Kimberly J. 2006. *Working Mothers and the Welfare State: Religion and the Politics of Work-Family Policies in Western Europe and the United States*. Stanford, CA: Stanford University Press.

Morgan, Kimberly J., and Ann Shola Orloff. 2017. "Introduction: The Many Hands of the State." In *The Many Hands of the State: Theorizing Political Authority and Social Control*, edited by Kimberly J. Morgan and Ann Shola Orloff, 1–34. Cambridge: Cambridge University Press.

Moss, Bernard H. 1976. *The Origins of the French Labor Movement, 1830–1914: The Socialism of Skilled Workers*. Berkeley: University of California Press.

Mudge, Stephanie L. 2018. *Leftism Reinvented: Western Parties from Socialism to Neoliberalism*. Cambridge, MA: Harvard University Press.

Mudge, Stephanie Lee, and Antoine Vauchez. 2012. "Building Europe on a Weak Field: Law, Economics, and Scholarly Avatars in Transnational Politics." *American Journal of Sociology* 118 (2): 449–92.

Müller, Hans-Eberhard. 1984. *Bureaucracy, Education, and Monopoly: Civil Service Reforms in Prussia and England*. Berkeley: University of California Press.

Müsebeck, Ernst. 1918. *Das preussische Kultusministerium vor hundert Jahren*. Berlin: J. G. Cotta'sche Buchhandlung Nachfolger.

Myles, John, and Jill Quadagno. 2002. "Political Theories of the Welfare State." *Social Service Review* 76 (1): 24.

Nardinelli, Clark. 1980. "Child Labor and the Factory Acts." *Journal of Economic History* 40:739–55.

Nassen, Ulrich. 1988. "Geschäftige, Professionisten und Industriöse. Arbeit und Arbeitswelt in Kinder- und Jugendbüchern 1750–1815." In *Märchen und Mühsal: Arbeit und Arbeitswelt in Kinder- und Jugendbüchern aus drei Jahrhunderten*, edited by Norbert Hopster and Ulrich Nassen, 31–45. Bielefeld: Antiquitariat Granier GmbH.

National Employment Law Project. 2000. "Worker Safety in Crisis: The Cost of a Weakened OSHA." Accessed February 10, 2021. https://s27147.pcdn.co/wp-content/uploads/Worker-Safety-Crisis-Cost-Weakened-OSHA.pdf.

Neugebauer, Wolfgang. 1985. *Absolutistischer Staat und Schulwirklichkeit in Brandenburg-Preußen.* Berlin: De Gruyter.

Nicholas, David. 1995. "Child and Adolescent Labour in the Late Medieval City: A Flemish Model in Regional Perspective." *English Historical Review* 110 (439): 1103–31.

Nipperdey, Thomas. 1977. "Mass Education and Modernization: The Case of Germany, 1780–1850." *Transactions of the Royal Historical Society* 27:155–72.

———. 1983. *Deutsche Geschichte 1800–1866: Bürgerwelt und starker Staat.* Munich: C. H. Beck.

———. 1990. *Deutsche Geschichte 1866–1918, vol. 1: Arbeitswelt und Bürgergeist.* Munich: C. H. Beck.

———. 1996. *Germany from Napoleon to Bismarck, 1800–1866.* Princeton, NJ: Princeton University Press.

Nique, Christian. 1990. *Comment l'école devint une affaire d'État.* Paris: Nathan.

Nolan, Mary. 1986. "Economic Crisis, State Policy, and Working-Class Formation in Germany, 1870–1900." In *Working-Class Formation: Nineteenth-Century Patterns in Western Europe and the United States,* edited by Ira Katznelson and Aristide R. Zolberg, 352–93. Princeton, NJ: Princeton University Press.

North, Douglass C. 1990. *Institutions, Institutional Change, and Economic Performance.* Political Economy of Institutions and Decisions. Cambridge: Cambridge University Press.

Novak, William J. 1996. *The People's Welfare: Law and Regulation in Nineteenth-Century America.* Studies in Legal History. Chapel Hill: University of North Carolina Press.

O'Connor, Alice. 2001. *Poverty Knowledge: Social Science, Social Policy, and the Poor in Twentieth-Century U.S. History.* Princeton, NJ: Princeton University Press.

O'Connor, Julia S., Ann Shola Orloff, and Sheila Shaver. 1999. *States, Markets, Families: Gender, Liberalism, and Social Policy in Australia, Canada, Great Britain, and the United States.* Cambridge: Cambridge University Press.

Offiong, Julia E. 2009. "History of Children in U.S. Coal Mining." In *The World of Child Labor: An Historical and Regional Survey,* edited by Hugh D. Hindman. Armonk, NY: M. E. Sharpe.

Orloff, Ann Shola. 1993. *The Politics of Pensions: A Comparative Analysis of Britain, Canada, and the United States, 1880–1940.* Madison: University of Wisconsin Press.

Orloff, Ann Shola, and Theda Skocpol. 1984. "Why Not Equal Protection? Explaining the Politics of Public Social Spending in Britain, 1900–1911, and the United States, 1880s–1920." *American Sociological Review* 49 (6): 726–50.

Otey, Elizabeth Lewis. 1910. *Report on Condition of Women and Child Wage-Earners in the United States. Vol. VI: The Beginnings of Child Labor Legislation in Certain States; a Comparative Study.* Senate Document 645. Washington, DC: Government Printing Office.

Padgett, John F., and Christopher Ansell. 1993. "Robust Action and the Rise of the Medici, 1400–1434." *American Journal of Sociology* 98 (6): 1259–319.

Palier, Bruno. 2010. "Continental Western Europe." In *The Oxford Handbook of the Welfare State,* edited by Francis G. Castles, Stephen Leibfried, Jane Lewis, Herbert Obinger, and Christopher Pierson, 601–15. Oxford: Oxford University Press.

Palmer, R. R., Joel Colton, and Lloyd Kramer. 1984. *A History of the Modern World.* New York: McGraw-Hill.

Pearson, Susan J. 2011. *The Rights of the Defenseless: Protecting Animals and Children in Gilded Age America.* Chicago: University of Chicago Press.

Pech, Klaus-Ulrich. 1988. "Aus eigener Kraft. Arbeit und Arbeitswelt in Kinder- und Jugendbüchern 1815–1880." In *Märchen und Mühsal: Arbeit und Arbeitswelt in Kinder- und Jugendbüchern aus drei Jahrhunderten*, edited by Norbert Hopster and Ulrich Nassen, 47–66. Bielefeld: Antiquitariat Granier GmbH.

Peirce, Charles Sanders. 1877. "The Fixation of Belief." *Popular Science Monthly* 12:1–15.

Persons, Charles E. 1971. "The Early History of Factory Legislation in Massachusetts: From 1825 to the Passage of the Ten-Hour Law in 1974." In *Labor Laws and Their Enforcement: With Special Reference to Massachusetts*, edited by Susan M. Kingsbury, 1–129. New York: Arno Press.

Pettinicchio, David. 2013. "Strategic Action Fields and the Context of Political Entrepreneurship: How Disability Rights Became Part of the Policy Agenda." *Research in Social Movements, Conflicts and Change* 36:79–106.

Pierce, Bessie Louise. 1957. *A History of Chicago*. New York: A. A. Knopf.

Pierson, Christopher. 2007. *Beyond the Welfare State: The New Political Economy of Welfare*. University Park, PA: The Pennsylvania State University Press.

Pierson, Paul. 1993. "When Effect Becomes Cause: Policy Feedback and Political Change." *World Politics* 45 (4): 595–628.

———. 2000. "Increasing Returns, Path Dependence, and the Study of Politics." *American Political Science Review* 94:251–67.

Piore, Michael J., and Andrew Schrank. 2018. *Root-Cause Regulation: Protecting Work and Workers in the Twenty-First Century*. Cambridge, MA: Harvard University Press.

Piven, Frances Fox, and Richard A. Cloward. 1971. *Regulating the Poor: The Functions of Public Welfare*. New York: Pantheon Books.

Polanyi, Karl. 2001. *The Great Transformation: The Political and Economic Origins of Our Time*. Boston: Beacon Press.

Pole, J. R. 1957. "Suffrage and Representation in Massachusetts: A Statistical Note." *William and Mary Quarterly* 14 (4): 560–92.

Porter, Theodore M. 1996. *Trust in Numbers: The Pursuit of Objectivity in Science and Public Life*. Princeton, NJ: Princeton University Press.

Prasad, Monica. 2012. *The Land of Too Much: American Abundance and the Paradox of Poverty*. Cambridge, MA: Harvard University Press.

Preller, Ludwig. 1954. "Von den tragenden Ideen der ersten deutschen Sozialpolitik." In *Aus Geschichte und Politik: Festschrift zum 70. Geburtstag von Ludwig Bergstraesser*, edited by Alfred Julius Moritz Herrmann, 301–11. Düsseldorf: Droste Verlag.

Price, George M. 1914. *The Modern Factory: Safety, Sanitation and Welfare*. New York: John Wiley and Sons.

Proces-verbaux des seances de la chambre des deputes. 1841. November–December, 1:331–484. Paris: Imprimerie de A. Henry.

Prude, Jonathan. 1983. *The Coming of the Industrial Order: Town and Factory Life in Rural Massachusetts, 1810–1860*. Amherst: University of Massachusetts Press.

Pryor, Frederic. 1968. *Public Expenditures in Communist and Capitalist Nations*. Homewood, IL: Irwin.

Quadagno, Jill S. 1996. *The Color of Welfare: How Racism Undermined the War on Poverty*. New York: Oxford University Press.

Quandt, Siegfried. 1978. *Kinderarbeit und Kinderschutz in Deutschland, 1783–1976*. Paderborn, Germany: Ferdinand Schöningh.

Ragin, Charles C. 2014. *The Comparative Method: Moving beyond Qualitative and Quantitative Strategies*. Berkeley: University of California Press.

Rahikainen, Marjatta. 2004. *Centuries of Child Labor: European Experiences from the Seventeenth to the Twentieth Century*. Hampshire, U.K.: Ashgate Publishing.

Ramirez, Francisco O., and John Boli. 1987. "The Political Construction of Mass Schooling: European Origins and Worldwide Institutionalization." *Sociology of Education* 60 (1): 2–17.

Ray, Raka. 1999. *Fields of Protest: Women's Movements in India*. Minneapolis: University of Minnesota Press.

Reeves, Edith, and Caroline Manning. 1971. "The Standing of Massachusetts in the Administration of Labor Legislation." In *Labor Laws and Their Enforcement*, edited by Susan M. Kingsbury, 223–71. New York: Arno Press.

Reidegeld, Eckart. 2006. *Staatliche Sozialpolitik in Deutschland, Vol. 1: Von den Ursprüngen bis zum Untergang des Kaiserreiches 1918*. Wiesbaden: Verlag für Sozialwissenschaft.

Rezneck, Samuel. 1935. "The Social History of an American Depression, 1837–1843." *American Historical Review* 40:662–87.

Riis, Jacob A. 1902. *The Children of the Poor*. New York: C. Scribner's Sons.

Rimlinger, Gaston V. 1971. *Welfare Policy and Industrialization in Europe, America, and Russia*. New York: Wiley.

Ritter, Ellen M. 1971. "Elizabeth Morgan: Pioneer Female Labor Agitator." *Central States Speech Journal* 22:242–51.

Ritter, Gerhard Albert. 1973. *Deutsche Parteien vor 1918*. Cologne: Kiepenheuer und Witsch.

Robert, Vincent. 2014. "Mutation de l'espace du travail et naissance du mouvement ouvrier." In *Histoire des mouvements sociaux en France*, edited by Michel Pigenet and Danielle Tartakowsky, 160–68. Paris: La Découverte.

Roberts, Alasdair. 2012. *America's First Great Depression: Economic Crisis and Political Disorder after the Panic of 1837*. Ithaca, NY: Cornell University Press.

Robinson, Frederick. 1834. *An Oration Delivered Before the Trades Union of Boston and Vicinity, of Fort Hill, Boston, on the Fifty-Eighth Anniversary of American Independence*. Boston: Charles Douglas.

Robinson, Harriet Jane Hanson. 1898. *Loom and Spindle: Or, Life among the Early Mill Girls. With a Sketch of "The Lowell Offering" and Some of Its Contributors*. Boston: T. Y. Crowell and Company.

Rodgers, Daniel T. 1998. *Atlantic Crossings: Social Politics in a Progressive Age*. Cambridge, MA: Belknap Press of Harvard University Press.

Rogers, Donald W. 2009. *Making Capitalism Safe: Work Safety and Health Regulation in America, 1880–1940*. Urbana: University of Illinois Press.

Rosenberg, Chaim M. 2013. *Child Labor in America: A History*. Jefferson, NC: McFarland and Co.

Rosenberg, Hans. 1966. *Bureaucracy, Aristocracy, and Autocracy: The Prussian Experience, 1660–1815*. Boston: Beacon Press.

Rosenzweig, Roy. 1983. *Eight Hours for What We Will: Workers and Leisure in an Industrial City, 1870–1920*. New York: Cambridge University Press.

Rothstein, Bo. 1992. "Labor-Market Institutions and Working-Class Strength." In *Structuring Politics: Historical Institutionalism in Comparative Analysis*, edited by Sven Steinmo, Kathleen Thelen, and Frank Longstreth, 33–56. Cambridge: Cambridge University Press.

Rowe, Michael. 2003. *From Reich to State: The Rhineland in the Revolutionary Age, 1780–1830*. Cambridge: Cambridge University Press.

Rubinson, Richard. 1986. "Class Formation, Politics, and Institutions: Schooling in the United States." *American Journal of Sociology* 92:519–48.

Rueschemeyer, Dietrich, and Theda Skocpol. 1996. *States, Social Knowledge, and the Origins of Modern Social Policies*. Princeton, NJ: Princeton University Press.

Rury, John L. 2002. *Education and Social Change: Themes in the History of American Schooling*. Mahwah, NJ: Erlbaum Associates.

Scharnau, Ralph William. 1973a. "Elizabeth Morgan: Crusader for Labor Reform." *Labor History* 14:340–51.

———. 1973b. "Thomas J. Morgan and the United Labor Party of Chicago." *Journal of the Illinois State Historical Society* 66:41–61.

Schleunes, Karl A. 1989. *Schooling and Society: The Politics of Education in Prussia and Bavaria, 1750–1900*. New York: Berg Publishers.

Schmidt, James D. 2010. *Industrial Violence and the Legal Origins of Child Labor*. New York: Cambridge University Press.

Schneiderhan, Erik. 2011. "Pragmatism and Empirical Sociology: Jane Addams and Hull-House, 1889–1895." *Theory and Society* 40 (6): 589–617.

Schneirov, Richard. 1994. "Rethinking the Relation of Labor to the Politics of Urban Social Reform in Late Nineteenth-Century America: The Case of Chicago." *International Labor and Working-Class History* 46:93–108.

———. 1998. *Labor and Urban Politics: Class Conflict and the Origins of Modern Liberalism in Chicago, 1864–97*. Urbana: University of Illinois Press.

———. 2004. "Voting as a Class: Haymarket and the Rise of a Democrat-Labor Alliance in Late 19th Century Chicago." *Labor's Heritage: Quarterly of the George Meany Memorial Archives* 12 (2): 6–21.

Schneirov, Richard, Shelton Stromquist, and Nick Salvatore, eds. 1999. *The Pullman Strike and the Crisis of the 1890s: Essays on Labor and Politics*. Urbana: University of Illinois Press.

Scholliers, Peter. 1995. "Grown-ups, Boys and Girls in the Ghent Cotton Industry: The Voortman Mills, 1835–1914." *Social History* 20:201–18.

———. 1996. *Wages, Manufacturers and Workers in the Nineteenth-Century Factory: The Voortman Cotton Mill in Ghent*. Oxford: Berg Publishers.

———. 2009. "Child Labor in Belgium." In *The World of Child Labor: An Historical and Regional Survey*, edited by Hugh D. Hindman, 602–6. Armonk, NY: M. E. Sharpe.

Schulz, Gerhard. 1961. "Über Entstehung und Formen von Interessengruppen in Deutschland seit Beginn der Industrialisierung." *Politische Vierteljahrresschrift* 2:124–54.

Schulz, Günther. 1996. "Schulpflicht, Kinderschutz, technischer Fortschritt und öffentliche Meinung: die Beschäftigung von Kindern in Fabriken und die Ursachen ihres Rückgangs (1817–1860)." In *Von der Landwirtschaft zur Industrie: Festschrift für Friedrich-Wilhelm Henning*, edited by Günther Schulz, 61–76. Paderborn, Germany: F. Schöningh.

Schumpeter, Joseph A., and Richard Swedberg. 1991. *The Economics and Sociology of Capitalism*. Princeton, NJ: Princeton University Press.

Schuurmans, Frank. 1998. "Economic Liberalization, Honour, and Perfectibility: Karl Sigmund Altenstein and the Spiritualization of Liberalism." *German History* 16:165–84.

Scott, Jonathan French. 1913. "The Decline of the English Apprenticeship System." *Elementary School Teacher* 13 (9): 445–54.

Sewell, William H. 1980. *Work and Revolution in France: The Language of Labor from the Old Regime to 1848*. Cambridge: Cambridge University Press.

———. 1992. "A Theory of Structure: Duality, Agency, and Transformation." *American Journal of Sociology* 98 (1): 1–29.

Shanahan, William Oswald. 1954. *German Protestants Face the Social Question*. Notre Dame, IN: University of Notre Dame Press.

Sheehan, James J. 1978. *German Liberalism in the Nineteenth Century*. Chicago: University of Chicago Press.

Sheingate, Adam. 2003. "Political Entrepreneurship, Institutional Change, and American Political Development." *Studies in American Political Development* 17:185–203.

———. 2007. "The Terrain of the Political Entrepreneur." In *Formative Acts: American Politics in the Making*, edited by Stephen Skowronek and Matthew Glassman, 13–31. Philadelphia: University of Pennsylvania Press.

Shelley, Thomas J. 1990. "Mutual Independence: Church and State in Belgium, 1825–1846." *Journal of Church and State* 32 (1): 49–63.

Shorter, Edward, and Charles Tilly. 1974. *Strikes in France, 1830–1968*. Cambridge, MA: Harvard University Press.

Simons, Rolf. 1984. *Staatliche Gewerbeaufsicht und gewerbliche Berufsgenossenschaften: Entstehung und Entwicklung des dualen Aufsichtssystems im Arbeitsschutz in Deutschland von den Anfängen bis zum Ende der Weimarer Republik*. Frankfurt am Main: Haag + Herchen.

Singelmann, Joachim, and Peter Singelmann. 1986. "Lorenz von Stein and the Paradigmatic Bifurcation of Social Theory in the Nineteenth Century." *British Journal of Sociology* 37 (3): 431–52.

Siracusa, Carl. 1979. *A Mechanical People: Perceptions of the Industrial Order in Massachusetts, 1815–1880*. Middletown, CT: Wesleyan University Press.

Sklar, Kathryn Kish. 1995. *Florence Kelley and the Nation's Work*. New Haven, CT: Yale University Press.

Sklar, Kathryn Kish, Anja Schüler, and Susan Strasser. 1998. *Social Justice Feminists in the United States and Germany: A Dialogue in Documents, 1885–1933*. Ithaca, NY: Cornell University Press.

Skocpol, Theda. 1985. "Bringing the State Back In: Strategies of Analysis in Current Research." In *Bringing the State Back In*, edited by Peter B. Evans, Theda Skocpol, and Dietrich Reuschmeyer, 3–43. New York: Cambridge University Press.

———. 1992. *Protecting Soldiers and Mothers: The Political Origins of Social Policy in the United States*. Cambridge, MA: Belknap Press of Harvard University Press.

Skowronek, Stephen. 1982. *Building a New American State: The Expansion of National Administrative Capacities, 1877–1920*. Cambridge: Cambridge University Press.

Smelser, Neil. 1959. *Social Change in the Industrial Revolution: An Application of Theory to the Lancashire Cotton Industry, 1770–1840*. Chicago: University of Chicago Press.

Smith, Adam. 1976. *An Inquiry into the Nature and Causes of the Wealth of Nations*. Chicago: University of Chicago Press.

Smith, Frank. (1890) 2013. *Biographical Sketches of the Residents of Dover, Massachusetts*. Lenox, MA: HardPress Publishing.

Snow, David A. 2008. "Elaborating the Discursive Contexts of Framing: Discursive Fields and Spaces." In *Studies in Symbolic Interaction*, edited by Norman K. Denzin, 30:3–28. Bingley, UK: Emerald.

Snow, David A., and Robert D. Benford. 1988. "Ideology, Frame Resonance, and Participant Mobilization." *International Social Movement Research* 1:197–217.

Snow, David A., E. Burke Rochford Jr., S. K. Worken, and Robert D. Benford. 1986. "Frame Alignment Processes, Micromobilization, and Movement Participation." *American Sociological Review* 51:464–81.

Société Industrielle de Mulhouse. 1837. "Copie de la petition addressée aux deux chambres et aux ministers de l'intérieur, du commerce et de l'instruction publique." *Bulletin de la Société industrielle de Mulhousen* 10:499–501.

Solari, Stefano. 2009. "Catholic Perspectives on Poverty and Misery: From Nineteenth Century French Catholic Social Economists to the Contribution of Jesuits." *Papers in Political Economy* 59:185–203.

———. 2010. "The Corporative Third Way in Social Catholicism (1830 to 1918)." *European Journal of the History of Economic Thought* 17:87–113.

Somers, Margaret, and Fred Block. 2005. "From Poverty to Perversity: Ideas, Markets, and Institutions over 200 Years of Welfare Debate." *American Sociological Review* 70 (2): 260–87.

Sperber, Jonathan. 1991. *Rhineland Radicals: The Democratic Movement and the Revolution of 1848–1849*. Princeton, NJ: Princeton University Press.

Steensland, Brian. 2006. "Cultural Categories and the American Welfare State: The Case of Guaranteed Income Policy." *American Journal of Sociology* 111 (5): 1273–326.

Steensland, Brian. 2008. *The Failed Welfare Revolution: America's Struggle over Guaranteed Income Policy*. Princeton, NJ: Princeton University Press.

Stein, Freiherr von und zum. 1960. "Rundschreiben an die Mitglieder des General-Departements, 'Politisches Testament' Steins." In *Freiherr vom Stein: Briefe und aemtliche Schrifte*, edited by Erich Botzenhart and Walther Hubatsch, 988–92. Stuttgart: W. Kohlhammer.

Stein, Lorenz von. 1842. *Der Socialismus und Communismus des Heutigen Frankreichs: Ein Beitrag zur Zeitgeschichte*. Leipzig: Otto Wigand.

Steinmetz, George. 1993. *Regulating the Social: The Welfare State and Local Politics in Imperial Germany*. Princeton, NJ: Princeton University Press.

———. 1999. "Culture and the State." In *State/Culture: State-Formation after the Cultural Turn*. Ithaca, NY: Cornell University Press.

Steinmo, Sven. 1994. "American Exceptionalism Reconsidered: Culture or Institutions?" In *The Dynamics of American Politics: Approaches and Interpretations*, edited by Larry C. Dodd and Calvin Jillson, 106–31. New York: Routledge.

———. 2008. "Historical Institutionalism." In *Approaches and Methodologies in the Social Sciences: A Pluralist Perspective*, edited by Donatella della Porta and Michael Keating, 118–38. New York: Cambridge University Press.

Storment, Frank Edward. 1978. "The Evolution of Child Labor Legislation in Illinois: 1818–1917." MA thesis, Eastern Illinois University.

Streeck, Wolfgang, and Kathleen Thelen. 2005. "Introduction: Institutional Change in Advanced Political Economies." In *Beyond Continuity: Institutional Change in Advanced Political Economies*, edited by Wolfgang Streeck and Kathleen Thelen, 1–39. Oxford: Oxford University Press.

Strikwerda, Carl. 1997. *A House Divided: Catholics, Socialists, and Flemish Nationalists in Nineteenth-Century Belgium*. Lanham, MD: Rowman and Littlefield.

Stryker, Robin. 1990. "A Tale of Two Agencies: Class, Political-Institutional, and Organizational Factors Affecting State Reliance on Social Science." *Politics and Society* 18:101–40.

Süle, Tibor. 1988. *Preussische Bürokratietradition: zur Entwickelung von Verwaltung und Beamtenschaft in Deutschland 1871–1918*. Göttingen: Vandenhoeck und Ruprecht.

Swartz, David L. 2013. *Symbolic Power, Politics, and Intellectuals: The Political Sociology of Pierre Bourdieu*. Chicago: University of Chicago Press.

———. 2014. "Theorizing Fields." *Theory and Society* 43:675–82.

Swedberg, Richard. 2000. "The Social Science View of Entrepreneurship: Introduction and Political Applications." In *Entrepreneurship: The Social Science View*, edited by Richard Swedberg, 7–44. Oxford: Oxford University Press.

Swenson, Peter A. 2002. *Capitalists against Markets: The Making of Labor Markets and Welfare States in the United States and Sweden*. Oxford: Oxford University Press.

Tager, Jack. 2001. *Boston Riots: Three Centuries of Social Violence*. Boston: Northeastern University Press.

Tampke, Jürgen. 1981. "Bismarck's Social Legislation: A Genuine Breakthrough?" In *The Emergence of the Welfare State in Britain and Germany, 1850–1950*, edited by W. J. Mommsen, 71–83. London: Croom Helm.

Tavory, Iddo, and Stefan Timmermans. 2014. *Abductive Analysis: Theorizing Qualitative Research*. Chicago: University of Chicago Press.

Tax, Meredith. 1980. *The Rising of the Women: Feminist Solidarity and Class Conflict, 1880–1917*. New York: Monthly Review Press.

Tenfelde, Klaus. 1987. "Die Entstehung der deutschen Gewerkschaftsbewegung vom Vormärz bis zum Ende des Sozialistengesetzes." In *Geschichte der Deutschen Gewerkschaften: Von den Anfängen bis 1945*, edited by Klaus Tenfelde, Klaus Schönhoven, Michael Schneider, and Detlev J. K. Peukert. Cologne: Bund-Verlag.

Tennstedt, Florian. 1994. "Sozialreform als Mission—Anmerkungen zum politischen Handeln Theodor Lohmanns." In *Von der Arbeiterbewegung zum modernen Sozialstaat. Festschrift für Gerhard A. Ritter zum 65. Geburtstag*, edited by Jürgen Kocka, Hans-Jürgen Puhle, and Klaus Tenfelde, 538–59. Munich: New Providence.

———. 1997. "Politikfähige Anstöße zu Sozialreform und Sozialstaat: Der Irvingianer Hermann Wagener und der Lutheraner Theodor Lohmann als Ratgeber und Gegenspieler Bismarcks." In *Soziale Reform im Kaiserreich: Protestantismus, Katholizismus und Sozialpolitik*, edited by Jochen-Christoph Kaiser and Wilfried Loth, 19–31. Stuttgart: W. Kohlhammer.

Thelen, Kathleen. 2003. "How Institutions Evolve: Insights from Comparative-Historical Analysis." In *Comparative Historical Analysis in the Social Sciences*, edited by James Mahoney and Dietrich Rueschemeyer, 208–40. Cambridge: Cambridge University Press.

———. 2004. *How Institutions Evolve: The Political Economy of Skills in Germany, Britain, the United States, and Japan*. Cambridge: Cambridge University Press.

Thelen, Kathleen, and Sven Steinmo. 1992. "Historical Institutionalism in Comparative Politics." In *Structuring Politics: Historical Institutionalism in Comparative Analysis*, edited by Sven Steinmo, Kathleen Thelen, and Frank Longstreth, 1–32. New York: Cambridge University Press.

Thies, Dirk. 1988. "Kinderarbeit und Kinderschutz unter dem Diktat von Wirtschaft, Militär, und Technik." In *Märchen und Mühsal: Arbeit und Arbeitswelt in Kinder- und Jugendbüchern aus drei Jahrhunderten*, edited by Norbert Hopster and Ulrich Nassen, 11–29. Bielefeld: Antiquitariat Granier GmbH.

Thomas, Maurice Walton. 1948. *The Early Factory Legislation; a Study in Legislative and Administrative Evolution*. Leigh-on-Sea, UK: Thames Bank Publishing Company.

Thornton, Patricia H. 1999. "The Sociology of Entrepreneurship." *Annual Review of Sociology* 25:19–46.

Tilly, Charles. 1975. "Food Supply and Public Order in Modern Europe." In *The Formation of National States in Western Europe*, edited by Charles Tilly and Gabriel Ardant, 380–455. Princeton, NJ: Princeton University Press

———. 1984. *Big Structures, Large Processes, Huge Comparisons*. 75th Anniversary Series. New York: Russell Sage Foundation.

———. 1990. *Coercion, Capital, and European States, AD 990–1990*. Cambridge, MA: B. Blackwell.

———. 1997. "Parliamentarization of Popular Contention in Great Britain, 1758–1834." *Theory and Society* 26 (2–3): 245–73.

Tilly, Charles, Louise W. Tilly, and Richard H. Tilly. 1975. *The Rebellious Century, 1830–1930*. Cambridge, MA: Harvard University Press.

Tilly, Richard H. 1980. *Kapital, Staat und sozialer Protest in der deutschen Industrialisierung*. Göttingen: Vandenhoeck und Ruprecht.

———. 1990. *Vom Zollverein zum Industriestaat: Die wirtschaftlich-soziale Entwicklung Deutschlands 1834 bis 1914*. Munich: Deutscher Taschenbuch Verlag.

Timmermans, Stefan, and Iddo Tavory. 2012. "Theory Construction in Qualitative Research: From Grounded Theory to Abductive Analysis." *Sociological Theory* 30 (3): 167–86.

Torstendahl, Rolf. 1991. *Bureaucratisation in Northwestern Europe, 1880–1985: Domination and Governance*. London: Routledge.

Trattner, Walter I. 1970. *Crusade for the Children: A History of the National Child Labor Committee and Child Labor Reform in America*. Chicago: Quadrangle Books.

Tsebelis, George. 2002. *Veto Players: How Political Institutions Work*. Princeton, NJ: Princeton University Press.

Tucker, Barbara M. 1984. *Samuel Slater and the Origins of the American Textile Industry, 1790–1860*. Ithaca, NY: Cornell University Press.

Tuckerman, Joseph. 1827. *Mr. Tuckerman's Quarterly Report Addressed to the American Unitarian Association*. Boston: Bowles and Dearborn.

Tuckerman, Joseph. 1974. *On the Elevation of the Poor; a Selection from His Reports as Minister at Large in Boston*. New York: Arno Press.

Tyack, David B. 1974. *The One Best System: A History of American Urban Education*. Cambridge, MA: Harvard University Press.

Unruh, Georg-Christoph von. 1985. "Der preußische Oberpräsident: Entstehung, Stellung und Wandel eines Staatsamtes." In *Die preußischen Oberpräsidenten 1815–1945*, edited by Klaus Schwabe, 17–31. Boppard am Rhein: Harald Boldt Verlag.

US Census. 1998. "Population of the 100 Largest Cities and Other Urban Places in the United States: 1790 to 1990." Accessed October 1, 2020. https://www.census.gov/library/working -papers/1998/demo/POP-twps0027.html.

US Census Bureau. 1895. *Report on Manufacturing Industries in the United States at the Eleventh Census: 1890. Part I: Totals for States and Industries*. Washington, DC: Government Printing Office. Accessed October 1, 2020. https://usa.ipums.org/usa/resources/voliii/pubdocs/1890 /1890a_v6p1-01.pdf.

US Congress, House of Representatives, Committee on Manufactures. 1893. "The Sweating System." House Reports, 52nd Congress, 2nd Session, No. 2309.

Van Bommel, Corneille. 1840. *Exposé des vrais principes sur l'instruction publique, primaire et secondaire, considérée dans ses rapports avec la religion*. Liège: P. Kersten.

Vanhaute, Eric. 2007. "'So Worthy an Example to Ireland': The Subsistence and Industrial Crisis of 1845–1850 in Flanders." In *When the Potato Failed: Causes and Effects of the 'Last' European Subsistence Crisis, 1845–1850,* edited by Cormac Ó Gráda, Richard Paping, and Eric Vanhaute, 123–48. Turnhout, Belgium: Brepols.

Vanhulle, Bert. 2010. "Dreaming about the Prison: Édouard Ducpétiaux and Prison Reform in Belgium (1830–1848)." *Crime, Histoire & Sociétés* 14 (2): 107–30.

Vanthemsche, Guy. 2004. "Intérêts patronaux entre sphère publique et sphère privée: la suppression des chambres de commerce officielles en Belgique (1875)." *Belgisch Tijdschrift voor Nieuwste Geschiedenis* 1:5–47.

Vedres, Balázs, and David Stark. 2010. "Structural Folds: Generative Disruption in Overlapping Groups." *American Journal of Sociology* 115 (4): 1150–90.

Verein für Socialpolitik. 2010. "Zur Geschichte des Vereins für Socialpolitik." Accessed February 2, 2021. https://www.socialpolitik.de/De/geschichte-des-vereins-f%C3%BCr-socialpolitik.

Villermé, Louis. 1837. "Discours sur la durée trop longue du travail des enfants dans beaucoup de manufactures." Paris: Institut de France.

———. 1840. *Tableau de l'état physique et moral des ouvriers employés dans les manufactures de coton, de laine et de soie*. Paris: Imprimé Chez Paul Renouard.

Vinovskis, Maris. 1970. "Horace Mann on the Economic Productivity of Education." *New England Quarterly* 43:550–71.

———. 1972. "Trends in Massachusetts Education, 1826–1860." *History of Education Quarterly* 12 (4): 501–29.

Visschers, August. 1838. *Discours sur les lacunes et les besoins de l'instruction primaire en Belgique, lu à l'assemblée générale de la Société pour l'instruction élémentaire, du 9 Août 1838*. Liège: Imprimerie de M. Dessain.

Vleugels, An. 2016. *Narratives of Drunkenness: Belgium, 1830–1914*. New York: Routledge.

Voss, Kim. 1993. *The Making of American Exceptionalism: The Knights of Labor and Class Formation in the Nineteenth Century*. Ithaca, NY: Cornell University Press.

Ware, Caroline F. 1931. *The Early New England Cotton Manufacture: A Study in Industrial Beginnings*. Boston: Houghton Mifflin.

Webb, Patrick. 2002. "Emergency Relief during Europe's Famine of 1817 Anticipated Crisis-Response Mechanisms of Today." *Journal of Nutrition* 132 (7): 2092S–5S.

Weber, Eugen. (1976) 2007. *Peasants into Frenchmen: The Modernization of Rural France: 1870–1914*. Stanford, CA: Stanford University Press.

Weber, Max. 1978. *Economy and Society: An Outline of Interpretive Sociology*. Edited by Günther Roth and Claus Wittich. Berkeley: University of California Press.

Wehler, Hans-Ulrich. (1985) 2005. *Von der Reformära bis zur industriellen und politischen "Deutschen Doppelrevolution": 1815–1845/49*. Vol. 2. Munich: Beck.

———. 1987. *The German Empire: 1871–1918*. Leamington Spa, UK: Berg Publishers.

Weir, Margaret. 1992. *Politics and Jobs: The Boundaries of Employment Policy in the United States*. Princeton, NJ: Princeton University Press.

Weir, Margaret, and Theda Skocpol. 1985. "State Structures and the Possibilities for 'Keynesian' Responses to the Great Depression in Sweden, Britain, and the United States." In *Bringing the State Back In*, edited by Peter B. Evans, Dietrich Rueschemeyer, and Theda Skocpol, 107–63. New York: Cambridge University Press.

Weissbach, Lee Shai. 1989. *Child Labor Reform in Nineteenth-Century France: Assuring the Future Harvest*. Baton Rouge: Louisiana State University Press.

White, George Savage. (1836) 2010. *Memoir of Samuel Slater: The Father of American Manufactures, Connected with a History of the Rise and Progress of the Cotton Manufacture*. Whitefish, MT: Kessinger Publishing.

White, Harrison. 1992. *Identity and Control: A Structural Theory of Social Action*. Princeton, NJ: Princeton University Press.

Whitford, Josh. 2002. "Pragmatism and the Untenable Dualism of Means and Ends: Why Rational Choice Theory Does Not Deserve Paradigmatic Privilege." *Theory and Society* 31 (3): 325–63.

Whittelsey, Sarah Scovill. 1901. "Massachusetts Labor Legislation: An Historical and Critical Study." *Annals of the American Academy of Political and Social Science* 17, Supplement 15:1–157.

Wilensky, Harold L. 1975. *The Welfare State and Equality: Structural and Ideological Roots of Public Expenditures*. Berkeley: University of California Press.

Williamson, Chilton. 1960. *American Suffrage; from Property to Democracy, 1760–1860*. Princeton, NJ: Princeton University Press.

Willoughby, William F. 1890. "Child Labor." *Publications of the American Economic Association* 5:5–70.

Wipperman, Karl. 1893. "Rochow, Gustav Adolf Von." In *Allgemeine Deutsche Biographie (ADB)*, 734. Leipzig: Duncker und Humblot.

Wishy, Bernard W. 1968. *The Child and the Republic: The Dawn of Modern American Child Nurture*. Philadelphia: University of Pennsylvania Press.

Witte, Els. 2020. *Belgische republikeinen: radicalen tussen twee revolutes (1830–1850)*. Kalmthout, Belgium: Uitgeverij Polis.

Witte, Els, Jan Craeybeckx, and Alain Meynen. 2009. *Political History of Belgium from 1830 Onwards*. Brussels: Academic and Scientific Publishers.

Wolfe, Alan. 1998. "What Is Altruism?" In *Private Action and the Public Good*, edited by Walter W. Powell and Elisabeth Stephanie Clemens, 36–46. New Haven, CT: Yale University Press.

Woodward, Donald. 1980. "The Background to the Statute of Artificers: The Genesis of Labour Policy, 1558–63." *Economic History Review* 33 (1): 32–44.

Wunder, Bernd. 1986. *Geschichte der Bürokratie in Deutschland*. Frankfurt am Main: Suhrkamp.

Zeise, Roland. 1976. "Zur Genesis und Funktion der Deutschen Handelskammern und des Deutschen Handelstages bis zur Reichsgründung 1871." *Jahrbuch für Wirtschaftsgeschichte* 17 (4): 63–81.

Zelizer, Viviana. 1985. *Pricing the Priceless Child: The Changing Social Value of Children*. Princeton, NJ: Princeton University Press.

Zilch, Reinhold. 2014. "Einleitung." In *Acta Borussica. 2. Reihe, Abteilung II: Neue Folge. Preußen als Kulturstaat. Der preußische Kulturstaat in der politischen und sozialen Wirklichkeit*, edited by Wolfgang Neugebauer, Andreas Meinecke, Bärbel Holtz, Gaby Huch, Christina Rathgeber, Hartwin Spenkuch, Reinhold Zilch, and Berlin-Brandenburgische Akademie der Wissenschaften, 1–192. Berlin: Akademie Verlag.

Zitt, Renate. 1997. *Zwischen Innerer Mission und staatlicher Sozialpolitik: Der protestantische Sozialreformer Theodor Lohmann (1831–1905). Eine Studie zum sozialen Protestantismus im 19. Jahrhundert*. Heidelberg: HVA.

Zonderman, David A. 2011. *Uneasy Allies: Working for Labor Reform in Nineteenth-Century Boston*. Boston: University of Massachusetts Press.

Zycha, Adolf. 1937. *Deutsche Rechtsgeschichte der Neuzeit*. Weimar: H. Bohlaus Nachfolger.

A NOTE ON THE TYPE

This book has been composed in Adobe Text and Gotham.
Adobe Text, designed by Robert Slimbach for Adobe,
bridges the gap between fifteenth- and sixteenth-century
calligraphic and eighteenth-century Modern styles.
Gotham, inspired by New York street signs, was designed
by Tobias Frere-Jones for Hoefler & Co.

GPSR Authorized Representative: Easy Access System Europe - Mustamäe tee 50, 10621 Tallinn, Estonia, gpsr.requests@easproject.com

www.ingramcontent.com/pod-product-compliance
Lightning Source LLC
Chambersburg PA
CBHW020452270326
41926CB00008B/580